CAPE COD *AND* PLYMOUTH COLONY *IN THE* SEVENTEENTH CENTURY

H. Roger King
Eastern Michigan University

UNIVERSITY
PRESS OF
AMERICA

Lanham • New York • London

Copyright © 1994 by
University Press of America®, Inc.
4720 Boston Way
Lanham, Maryland 20706

3 Henrietta Street
London WC2E 8LU England

All rights reserved
Printed in the United States of America
British Cataloging in Publication Information Available

Library of Congress Cataloging-in-Publication Data
King, H. Roger,
Cape Cod and Plymouth Colony in the seventeenth century /
H. Roger King.
p.   cm.
Includes bibliographical references and index.
1. Cape Cod (Mass.)—History.   2. Massachusetts—History—New
Plymouth, 1620–1691.   3. Pilgrims (New Plymouth Colony)
I. Title.
F72.C3K58   1993   974.4'92—dc20   93–13880 CIP

ISBN 0–8191–9185–X (cloth : alk. paper)
ISBN 0–8191–9186–8 (pbk. : alk. paper)

For

Barbara

CONTENTS

LIST OF MAPS   vii

PREFACE   ix

I   "healthful, secure, and defensible"   1

II   "to good effect and turned to their profit"   23

III   "resolved upon removal"   43

IV   "causes and controversies amongst the inhabitants"   65

V   "An accursed and pernicious sect"   89

VI   "to maintain the liberties of the churches"   109

VII   "For the preventing of Idleness and other evils"   127

VIII   "to maintain their Just Rights"   145

IX   "to call men to labor thereat"   161

X   "to them we may go, their land is empty"   177

XI   "in respect of the land and fish"   199

XII   "Serviceable by their Labor & Friendly to the *English*"   225

XIII   "the afflicted state of the countrey"   255

BIBLIOGRAPHICAL ESSAY   283

INDEX   289

MAPS

Pilgrim explorations of Cape Cod, 1620   10

Cape Cod, 1650   42

Cape Cod, 1680   180

PREFACE

THE history of Plymouth is more than the school book record of the *Mayflower's* passengers stepping out of a shallop onto a rock, more than learning how to use alewives to fertilize native corn, and more than inviting Indians to share in the bounty of a first harvest. It is the history of a colony, its people and its institutions, and covers a period of nearly three-quarters of a century. As such, it goes far beyond the popular depictions of the Pilgrims at Plymouth, however interesting and important they might be, and however emblazoned in the popular historical mind. As the history of a colony, the history of Plymouth is one which encompasses a geographic area far larger than that generally associated with the home of the Pilgrims and includes Plymouth, Bristol, and Barnstable counties in present-day Massachusetts. Central to this particular study is Barnstable County, more popularly known as Cape Cod, or "the Cape." The Cape is where the *Mayflower* Pilgrims first saw North America, and where they first considered establishing their settlement. It was an area into which successive generations of Massachusetts and Plymouth settlers migrated, and where at one point they considered moving entirely, abandoning their community at Plymouth. In short, Cape Cod played an important role in the history of Plymouth Colony, and it played that role throughout its entire history, from before settlement until the absorption of the colony into a reorganized and expanded Massachusetts in 1691. This study is, in general, an attempt to look at the history of Cape Cod during the period of Plymouth Colony's independence. More especially it will examine the mutual involvement and contributions of the mother settlement at Plymouth and her descendant communities on Cape Cod.

The project began at the suggestion of the Pilgrim Society of Plymouth, Massachusetts, and the Cape Cod Memorial Association of Provincetown. While the Cape Codders' interest quickly flagged, and that of the Pilgrim Society eventually followed suit, I must express my appreciation to Laurence R. Pizer, the former Director of the Pilgrim Society, for his enthusiasm, encouragement, and assistance concerning the project.

As is always the case with projects such as this one, completion has been hastened along by the aid and encouragement of people too numerous to be itemized individually. But some of them cannot be omitted; their efforts on my behalf were too important to be ignored. Three of them are teachers, Miss Anne Grant, who encouraged my historical interests at an early age, and Albert E. Van Dusen, who was instrumental in expanding my scholarly horizons. Most importantly, my appreciation goes to Douglas E. Leach, who as both a friend and mentor, developed and refined my historical skills, and whose thoughtful suggestions have significantly improved the final essay. Others of them are colleagues, JoEllen Vinyard, whose enthusiasm for the project has been greatly appreciated, to James and Judy Magee, Lester Sherer, and Lee Boyer whose perceptive readings of particular chapters I found most helpful, and David Allen, whose maps speak for themselves. If I have not heeded all their suggestions, at least they know they were appreciated.

Other assistance came in the early stages of the project, and greatly facilitated my research efforts. A one-semester Faculty Research Fellowship at Eastern Michigan University made initial bibliographic and research work easier, and I am most appreciative. My Department Heads, Ira M. Wheatley and James C. Waltz, also deserve thanks for their willingness to be creative with teaching schedules so as to make it easier to continue my work.

Outside the University, I have been met with encouragement and assistance at whatever archive or library I have visited. At the head of the list of archivists and librarians is Charlotte S. Price, archivist of the William Brewster Nickerson Memorial Room at Cape Cod Community College. Her collection of Cape Cod historical material is matched only by her enthusiasm for Cape Cod and exceeded only by her willingness to help. Similarly helpful librarians and archivists aided me at the Massachusetts Archives, the Massachusetts Historical Society, the Rare Book and Manuscript Division of the Boston Public Library, and the Beinecke Rare Book and Manuscript Library at Yale University. My particular thanks to these institutions for their permission to cite material in their possession. Closer to home, the open guest privileges of the Harlan Hatcher Graduate Library at the University of Michigan eased my way far more than its staff will ever realize. John Dann and his staff at the William L. Clements Library, especially Richard Ryan, David Bosse, and Joyce Bonk, were always encouraging and helpful in my requests for obscure material, as well as a delight to visit. For their willingness to help in the ordering and reading of the microfilmed copies of local records from Cape Cod, the Ann Arbor Family History Library of the Church of Christ of Latter Day Saints deserves a special thank you. My passages through other libraries were quicker, but no less pleasant. My thanks to those unnamed folks at the John Carter Brown Library and the Rhode Island Historical Society in Providence, as well as those at the State Library of Connecticut in Hartford.

Finally, there are those friends and colleagues who have helped merely by being interested in what I was doing and encouraging me to continue. They and I know who they are, and they need not be listed. My final thanks go to those closest not only to me but to the effort which went into the following work. My appreciation to my children, Sarah and Christopher, for occasionally reminding me that there is more to life than the seventeenth century, and to she who gets her own page of appreciation for reminding me that there is more to life than history and children.

One last note regarding the mechanical aspects of names and chronology in the writing of seventeenth-century history. For the sake of clarity, I have left specific dates as I have found them, and have identified years both by the seventeenth-century label and by the twentieth. Thus William Bradford's 11 January 1631, will be written 11 January 1631/32. In the spelling of names, I have used that spelling which was most often found in the sources or used by the individual involved.

H. Roger King

Ann Arbor, Michigan
April 1993

I

"healthful, secure, and defensible"

IN the early morning of 9 November 1620, the bark-rigged *Mayflower* "after long beating at sea . . . fell with that land which is called Cape Cod." Sixty-five days out from Plymouth, England, it had been a long and difficult passage. Hampered by fierce wind storms and high seas, the crew had lowered the sails, and the ship had drifted for several days. It is little wonder that the passengers, known to us as the Pilgrims, expressed great joy at their arrival in the waters off Cape Cod.[1]

It had been their original intention to establish a "particular plantation" within the jurisdiction of the Virginia Company, whose authority extended north to include Manhattan Island. Thus, after deliberating among themselves and with the master of the ship, Christopher Jones, they tacked about, and with fair wind and weather, decided to sail southward to find some place near the Hudson River for their settlement. But the seas turned against them. After a half day of sailing toward the south, they encountered dangerous shoals and roaring breakers, and became so entangled in them that they became frightened. Having run into the treacherous waters of The Broken Part of Pollock Rip off Monomy Point, they wisely decided to return to safer waters. During the night of 9 November the *Mayflower* remained in safe waters off Pollock Rip, but with southerly breezes on the next day made good progress up along the

1

back side of the Cape. Master Jones worked the ship slowly along the coast throughout the night, and in the early morning hours of 11 November rounded Long Point, and sailed into Provincetown Harbor, where the ship, its crew, and its passengers rode in safety.[2] With this anchorage, rests the justifiable claim of Cape Cod as the first home of the Pilgrims in America.

The *Mayflower* was not the first ship to sail in Cape Cod Bay waters, and its crew and passengers were not the first people to view the scenery of its shores. Claims that the Irish had visited the Cape, and that the Vikings under Leif Ericsson had spent the winter of 1003 at Follins Pond in present-day Dennis are at best conjectural, and more likely spurious.[3] But European fishermen had visited the area for many years, and French and English explorers had examined it for two decades before the Pilgrims arrived. The man who deserves the real credit for being the first European to discover Cape Cod is Bartholomew Gosnold, and is the man who christened the Cape with its distinctive and descriptive name. Born into a prominent Suffolk County English family, Gosnold had certainly acquired the dreams of empire fostered by the voyages of Sir Humphrey Gilbert and Edward Hayes, and had received the encouragements of Richard Hakluyt, Sir Walter Ralegh, and others at the end of the sixteenth century. It is quite probable Gosnold had personal connections with Hakluyt, and his biographer asserts that it was the famous geographer who encouraged the voyage.[4] Gosnold, with a group of thirty-two, had set sail on the *Concord* from Falmouth, England, on 26 March 1602, and arrived off the coast of southern Maine eight weeks later. The party made contact with some Indians, but left that afternoon, sailing directly south on its primary mission, the location of Verrazzano's "Refugio." The next day the *Concord* sailed into Cape Cod Bay, and anchored. While there, its crew caught so many codfish, that it commemorated the fish by calling the land Cape Cod.[5] John Smith would later try to change the name to Cape James, but the descriptiveness of Gosnold's label could not be bettered, and it has been Cape Cod ever since.

The next day Gosnold and his followers rounded the tip of the Cape, sailed southerly, and came up off Monomy Point.[6] Because of the islands and the breaches between them, the ship remained at anchor while members of the party explored the land. After three days they sailed off around the dangerous shoals of Monomy Point, which they named Point Care, and entered Nantucket Sound. For two days they cruised the islands off Cape Cod, one of which they named

Martha's Vineyard, perhaps after a daughter of Gosnold, and came to anchor off one of the Elizabeth Islands between Buzzard's Bay and Vineyard Sound on May 25.[7] Gosnold put some of his men to work building a fort on the island, while he explored Buzzard's Bay. In addition to exploring and fort-building, they devoted most of their time to harvesting sassafras.[8] The Indians visited them a number of times, and in early June fifty strong and aggressive Indians, armed with bows and arrows, menacingly appeared.[9] The English indicated they would not be cowed, and after an exchange of gifts, and the establishment of peaceful intentions, the English spent the rest of the day trading with the Indians for furs.[10] By the middle of June, with supplies running short, it was time to leave. After they had loaded the ship with as much sassafras, cedar, furs, skins, and other commodities, as was thought convenient, some of the English who had promised Captain Gosnold they would remain at the trading post changed their minds. Seeing that there were only twelve men willing to remain, and those only meagerly provided for, Gosnold missed establishing the first English settlement in New England when he weighed anchor with as much sorrow at leaving as there had previously been anticipation at arriving.[11] Five weeks later the expedition anchored off Exmouth, England.[12] The Gosnold expedition was an important one. It was the first significant English exposure to the Cape Cod region, and indicated the potential of the area for the mother country. The reports of it by Archer and Brereton, as well as Gosnold's letter to his father, are extremely flattering regarding the Cape, and the cargo of furs, cedar, and sassafras indicated that the northern portion of Virginia could be profitable. Any direct impact on the Pilgrims is impossible to gauge. Bradford understood that Gosnold had been there and named it Cape Cod, but any claim for greater influence is unfounded, if for no other reason than the Pilgrims had not originally intended to settle where Gosnold had been.

One of the most direct influences of Bartholomew Gosnold's expedition was on Martin Pring who traveled the same route for much the same purposes the following year. Pring left Bristol, England, with over forty men and boys on two ships, the *Discoverer* and the *Speedwell*, and cleared Milford Haven, Wales, on 10 April 1603.[13] The party arrived off the coast of Maine sometime in June and sailed along the coast in a southerly direction searching for trade goods. Pring probed the coast line more thoroughly than Gosnold had done, entering Boston Harbor, which Gosnold had passed by the year before.[14] Pring continued his journey, and came to anchor in a bay, which they called Whitson Bay, named after the mayor of the expedition's home port.[15] Near the mouth of the Pamet River, they built a small fort for trade and protection, and concentrated their efforts on trading with the Indians and collecting sassafras. The sassafras search was successful, and at the end of July the *Discoverer* returned to England with its cargo to pacify the Adventurers.[16] There were the usual sparrings with Indians, but Pring's men were uniquely protected by two large dogs, Foole and Gallant, of whom the natives were especially in awe. Early in the second week of August, the remaining force loaded up the second vessel and set sail for home, arriving off Kingrode 2 October 1603.[17] Pring's voyage had been neither significant nor spectacular. It had, however, confirmed Gosnold's experience of the year before, indicating that a summer trip to northern Virginia was possible and reiterating the economic potential of the region. Together with Gosnold, Pring had offset the earlier failures of Sir Humphrey Gilbert and Sir Walter Ralegh, and renewed west-country England's interest in settlement of the New World. When that interest turned to colonization in 1606 with the Popham Colony, however, those in charge chose to reject the promise of Cape Cod in preference for the mouth of the Kennebec River. There would be other explorers to Cape Cod before the Pilgrims landed, but Pring was the last one to take the area seriously.

The explorations of the English alarmed the French, who had long been interested in settlement and trade in the northern regions of North America. In 1604 Pierre du Gua, Sieur de Monts, received a fur trade monopoly, with the understanding that he would establish a settlement in North America. Accompanying him, as geographer and map maker, was Samuel de Champlain, already known for his history of the French expedition to the St. Lawrence the previous year. Champlain's reports of the explorations contain some of the best descriptions of coastal New England written in the seventeenth century, and his maps and charts are some of the best representations we have of coastal phenomena. The party set sail on 7 April 1604, and reached its destination, the North American coast, the next month. Champlain explored the Bay of Fundy, and in early June de Monts established his trading fort on an island in the St. Croix River. From there, Champlain made his first of three voyages along the New England coast, getting as far as the Kennebec River before turning back to spend a difficult winter at the St. Croix fort.[18] He later complained there were six months of winter in North America, and the experience nearly ended the expedition.[19]

Having survived the winter, Champlain, with de Monts this time, set out again the following June for a second attempt to find a suitable site for the colony.[20] They proceeded to the Kennebec River, coasted to Casco Bay, explored Boston Harbor, and on 17 July came around the Gurnet, and ran aground entering Plymouth Harbor, which Champlain named St. Louis Harbor. Champlain went ashore to survey the territory, and drew a map of the region which Bradford would have found useful fifteen years later.[21] They weighed anchor on 19 July, discovered they had unknowingly entered a bay, and were required to reverse their direction in order to sail around the land they named White Cape.[22] On 20 July they entered Nauset Harbor, named Mallebarre because of its numerous breakers, and the next day went ashore to inspect the land and meet the Indians.[23] It was at Nauset that the French ran into their first trouble with the native Americans. Four or five men took kettles to the mainland to get water, and the Indians tried to steal one of the kettles. In the fracas which followed, the Indians killed one of the French sailors, and the French opened fire on the Indians. De Monts managed to take a captive from some Indians who had come onto the ship, but let him go when other Indians came to apologize for the mishap.[24] Two days later, running low on supplies and fearing the weather, the party weighed anchor and headed back to St. Croix.

The winter of 1605-06 was not as disagreeable as the one of the previous year, and the hardy band of settlers survived in better condition. Partly, the season was not as long and cold, and partly de Monts abandoned St. Croix and moved the settlement to Port Royal, across the Bay of Fundy. As soon as the settlement was complete, de Monts returned to France. Finally in late August, Champlain began his third and last voyage in search of a settlement site on the New England coast.[25]   Jean de Biencourt de Poutrincourt, the newly arrived commander of the settlement, accompanied him, and insisted on viewing much of the Maine coast already investigated. Poutrincourt's demands unfortunately prevented Champlain from sailing directly to Cape Cod as he had wished. At last the ship reached Cape Cod Bay. It went almost to Plymouth Harbor, turned east across the bay, and came to anchor in Wellfleet Harbor before dawn on 1 October. In honor of the harbor's oysters they named it "port aux Huistres."[26] The next day they rounded the tip of the Cape and came to Nauset Harbor, but the seas prevented their entering. A group of Indians canoed out to meet them, and told them of a safe harbor to the south. At that point Champlain entered new seas, his object from the very beginning of the expedition. At the shoals and rocks of Pollock's Rip, the wind was against them, and they encountered rough seas.[27] They broke their rudder, and finally made their way into Stage Harbor at modern Chatham. The group remained at Stage Harbor for two weeks, repairing the ship and exploring the area. At one point Poutrincourt ordered all men to the ship, as he feared an Indian attack. Four or five men baking bread on the mainland refused to return. That night four hundred Indians surrounded them, and all were killed. An attempt to pursue the Indians failed, and the bodies of the dead were buried, only to be later exhumed by the Indians. The French fired ineffectually at the returning Indians from their ship, and went after them a second time, but to no avail. Naming the area Misfortune Harbor, they left on 16 October. They sailed Nantucket Sound as far as the beginnings of Vineyard Sound, but decided to return to Port Royal. They stopped at Nauset Harbor for another shot at revenge against the Nauset Indians, killed a few, and were back at their home port on 14 November. The last effort of the French to settle on the New England coast came to an end. In three voyages, no significant fur trade had appeared, and no major mineral wealth had been discovered. While the Indians had been generally friendly, the incidents at Nauset and Stage Harbor had indicated potential hostility. The late start of the 1606 voyage, and Poutrincourt's desire to retrace earlier explorations had taken valuable time away from the goal of investigating the coast as far as possible. Who knows what would have happened had Champlain and the other French been as satisfied with Cape Cod as Gosnold and Pring, or if they had passed into Narraganset Bay or Long Island Sound in 1606. Instead French interest turned to northern North America, and with the rebirth of Quebec in 1608, the French effectively left the New England coast to the English and Cape Cod to the Pilgrims.

    With the departure of Champlain from Stage Harbor, serious exploration of Cape Cod and its surrounding islands came to an end. It would be renewed only with the arrival of the *Mayflower* and its passengers in 1620. From 1606 until 1620 the Cape and its treacherous waters became primarily a topographical sighting on a master's log or a description in a sailor's journal. One of these passersby was George Waymouth, sent out in 1605 as part of the English Catholic effort to colonize North America. He may have been attempting to take up Gosnold's abandoned search for the

"Refugio," for he headed directly for Cape Cod. His ship, the *Archangel*, sighted Nantucket, but ran afoul of the Cape's shoals and rocks, and headed north to explore the St. George River.[28] Another, and more famous, explorer also passed by Cape Cod in search of a different goal. On his third voyage to the New World and in search of the Northwest Passage, Henry Hudson encountered ice earlier than expected, and decided to turn south and explore the North American coast instead. His ship, the *Half Moon*, sailed into Cape Cod Bay on 2 August 1610, and landed a small party the next day who were impressed with the wild grapes and roses of the Cape. They made contact with the Indians the fourth day, and sailed off to the Chesapeake on the fifth.[29] Blown off course sailing from Jamestown to Bermuda, Samuel Argall passed by the Cape in 1610,[30] and Edward Harlow, on an Indian kidnapping spree in 1611, penetrated to Martha's Vineyard and Buzzard's Bay, the first European to have done so since Bartholomew Gosnold.[31]

Two other adventurous explorers also visited the Cape Cod area in the years before the Pilgrims arrived. One of those was the man who did as much as anyone to publicize the area, John Smith. The other was Thomas Dermer, a lesser known traveler in Cape waters. Smith is best remembered for his exploits in the Virginia colony, but on 3 March 1614 he set sail in command of two ships to take whales and search for gold and copper in Northern Virginia.[32] When the search proved fruitless, and the whales could not be snared, the practical-minded Smith turned the venture to the catching of fish. In addition to paying some return to the expedition's investors, fishing allowed Smith time to explore the coast. He left his base at Monhegan Island and headed south, following the coastline more closely than Gosnold had done. When he reached Plymouth he began to retrace the route his countryman had traveled some years before. He cruised along the shore of Cape Cod Bay, rounded the tip of the Cape and sailed down the ocean side of it as far as Nauset Beach. At that point he ended his exploration and returned to Monhegan Island, and from there to England.[33] Unfortunately, Smith had left a scoundrel, the commander of the second ship Thomas Hunt, with orders to complete the drying of the fish, and to sell them in Spain. Hunt did as he was ordered, but before he left New England, he traveled to Cape Cod. There he captured twenty-four Indians and sold them into slavery when he arrived in Spain. It was a treachery Cape Indians would long remember, and one which would haunt the Pilgrims for many years.[34] The only semi-silver lining to this dark

cloud of English perfidiousness was Squanto.   One of Hunt's
captives, Squanto, eventually found his way to England and even to
Newfoundland.   In 1619 he sailed with Thomas Dermer, the last
Englishman to visit Cape Cod before the arrival of the Pilgrims.
When Dermer's ship left New England waters, Squanto was not on
board, presumably having been captured by some Indians, released by
Dermer, or having jumped ship on his own.   Squanto later appeared
in Plymouth, where he played an important role in aiding the success
of the struggling colony.   In the beginning, he was viewed by the
Pilgrims as "a special instrument sent of God."[35]

The importance of John Smith's brief journey to Cape Cod lies
less in his exploration of New England, and far more in his writing of
it. His *A Description of New England*, published in 1616, did much
to publicize the area, and in fact it was Smith whose "New England"
label turned out to be as permanent as Gosnold's "Cape Cod."   A
champion of settlement over speculation, Smith strongly advocated
New England as a promising location for colonies, and his influence
in the beginnings of New England has long been underrated and
unappreciated.   Certainly the leaders of the English Separatists in
Leyden were familiar with Smith's writing even though they did not
openly propose to settle in the region he had named.

Thomas Dermer had left the waters of Cape Cod Bay in late June
of 1620, only a little over four months before the *Mayflower*
arrived.[36]   But those four months witnessed a most significant change
in the role Cape Cod would play in the expansion of England into
North America.   From being a place to explore, harvest sassafras, and
capture Indians, it became a potential site for permanent settlement.
Rather than a place to visit, it would be a home for colonists.   That
change was the direct result of the decision of the *Mayflower* Pilgrims
not to gamble on rounding Pollock's Rip and sailing to the Hudson,
but to remain where they were and establish their colony in New
England.

Once having decided to settle in New England, the Pilgrims then
turned to some of the practical problems of establishing a colony.   As
their patent from the Virginia Company was of no use in New
England, and as some of the *Mayflower's* passengers were not given
to cooperation with the Pilgrim leadership and made mutterings about
independence, their first problem was that of political organization
and the imposition of community discipline.[37]   The answer was the
fabled Mayflower Compact.   In it, forty-one men, including all the
free adult males, agreed to form themselves into a political body and

to enact whatever laws and other ordinances would be necessary for the good of the colony, to which they pledged their loyalty.[38] While there were those who were unhappy, the majority of settlers supported both the leaders of the group and the order and discipline which the Compact represented. As a result, little came of the discontent.[39]

With the establishment of authority and general support for the expedition as it had developed, the Pilgrims then faced the task of finding a permanent site for their settlement. The same day as the signing of the Mayflower Compact, fifteen or sixteen well-armed men went ashore to explore the immediate territory. They liked what they saw, finding the land well-wooded and with excellent black earth.[40] After a Sabbath day of rest, on Monday, 11 November, the Pilgrims became serious about their future in New England. They unloaded their battered shallop, which had been brought from England, and took it ashore for repairs. In addition, the passengers went on shore to "refresh" themselves and the women to wash, "as they had great need," as well they might after two months on the open sea.[41] The carpenter required seventeen days to repair the shallop, and while he worked, some of the Pilgrims became impatient with the delay, and desired to go ashore and explore the Cape without the shallop. With much instruction, and repeated cautions, a company of sixteen men under the command of Myles Standish went ashore on Wednesday. They had marched off along the beach for about a mile when five or six Indians, accompanied by a dog, came towards them. The natives fled into the woods, with the explorers following as best they could, but the Indians evaded them. Tired and thirsty, the pursuers halted for the night, and when they finally found water declared it as pleasant to their taste as wine or beer had been before.[42] A continued search the next morning failed to discover any Indians, but did find more fresh water, as good as that of the previous evening. They then marched to the shore to light a signal fire identifying their location, and returned to explore the interior. As the group tramped back and forth through the Cape Cod wilderness, it came upon various tracts of land where the Indians had cultivated and harvested corn.   At what is still known as Corn Hill, the men discovered a large kettle, a cache of about three dozen good ears of corn, as well as a basket containing three or four bushels of dried corn, most of it yellow, red, and blue, certainly a most welcome find. Promising themselves to reimburse the Indians, the explorers decided to take the kettle with them, and also as much of the corn as they could carry.[43] While the confiscation of the corn can be seen as little

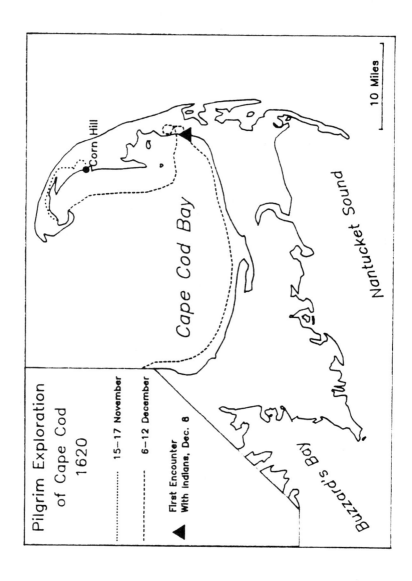

Pilgrim Exploration
of Cape Cod
1620

.... 15–17 November

— — — — 6–12 December

▲ First Encounter
   With Indians, Dec. 8

Corn Hill

Cape Cod Bay

Nantucket Sound

Buzzard's Bay

10 Miles

better than larceny, the Pilgrims viewed it as a special gift of God, who had provided seed to plant the following year, and most likely had prevented starvation.[44]   On the whole, they were probably correct.

Before the little band of explorers left the Corn Hill area, it discovered the remains of an old fort, identified as having been built by Europeans, and quite possibly the ruins of Pring's trading house built in 1603.[45] Having been ordered to be gone only two days, the wanderers headed back, returning to the shores of the fresh water pond of the night before. There, against a driving rain, they erected a barricade to protect them from the wind, and maintained a protective watch of three sentinels. The next morning they sank the kettle from Corn Hill in the pond, and started for the shore of Cape Cod Bay and a return to the *Mayflower*. Along the way they came upon a deer snare, but it was William Bradford who was caught in the noose rather than a deer. They eventually reached the shore near their ship, fired a signal from their muskets, and the long boat came to ferry them to the *Mayflower*. Thus they returned, weary but welcome home, from the first of their explorations.[46] The journey had not been especially productive. While it had found some seed corn for the following year, it had not discovered a suitable site for settlement, and despite seeing game in abundance, the explorers had not been able to shoot or capture anything with which to expand or vary their limited food supply.

Some days later a second expedition, consisting of thirty-four passengers and crewmen, set off in the shallop and long boat to explore the Pamet River.[47] Rough seas and strong winds forced the men to row the boats to the nearest shore, where they left the shallop, and continued their exploration. The group spent a cold wet night on the beach. About eleven the next morning the shallop sailed up, and the entire party boarded her to return to the previously discovered Pamet River, which they named Cold Harbor. They followed one of the creeks for a few miles until enough of the party was tired enough to call a halt for the night. At least they ate well that evening, for they shot three fat geese and six ducks for their supper, which they ate with "soldiers' stomachs."[48] The next morning, their third day away from the *Mayflower*, they abandoned their trek along the creek, crossed it, and returned to Corn Hill, where they successfully expanded their search for more corn, finding about ten bushels in all. The weather turned bad once again, and the group divided, with some of the weaker men and those who had become ill returning to the

Mayflower.[49] After another night on shore, the expedition continued.
The quest turned up two of the more interesting things as yet
unearthed by the explorers. One of these was an Indian grave,
containing the bodies of an adult and a child, and the other was the
discovery by two of the sailors of some abandoned Indian dwellings.
As usual, they brought some of the prettier things away with them
from the gravesite, and a few of the best items from the dwellings. In
both instances, the explorers promised themselves to pay the Indians
for the goods as soon as they met them. Evening darkness began to
set in, and the men hurried to the shallop with their booty, and
returned to the ship.[50]

With the completion of two sorties onto the mainland, they
debated the question of whether to settle in the area they had
explored. It was a controversial question, with those advocating a
settlement at the tip of the Cape pointing to its good harbor, the
existence of planting fields ready for use, the potential for good
fishing, and the prospect that the tip of the Cape would be "healthful,
secure, and defensible."[51]   Finally, it was winter, and they
recognized that they could not continue to explore without risking the
loss of both men and boat, and the eventual failure of the whole
enterprise.[52] But others disagreed. Some of them proposed going
northward to "Anguum, or Anguom."[53]   Some believed that
somewhere on the New England coast a better site must exist and
should be found so that they would not have to move a second time.
And critics of the tip of the Cape noted that the water was in ponds,
and therefore not a sure thing in summer, and that it would have to be
carried up a steep hill. Finally, one Robert Coppin, or Coffin, a
crewman who had been in Cape Cod waters previously, told the
passengers of a large navigable river and good harbor on the other
side of the bay. So the company agreed that one last expedition
would be sent out, but with instructions to go no further than
Coppin's "Thievish Harbor."[54]

Sometime in the afternoon of Wednesday, 6 December, the party
set out in very cold and difficult weather. The group comprised ten
of the Pilgrims' most important leaders, two hired hands, and six
members of the *Mayflower* crew, including the instigator of the effort,
Coppin.[55] The shallop had difficulty getting over a sandy bar, but
eventually made it clear, and within two hours came under the
protection of the weather shore, and found smoother water and better
sailing. The cold made the water freeze to their clothes, making them
like "coats of iron," but they persevered and in the evening came

around the point and entered Wellfleet Harbor. They camped that night on its shores.[56] In the morning the group divided, part of it taking to the sea in the shallop, the other exploring the land. Those on the land went searching for some Indians they had seen the day before, along the way finding a grampus, or small whale, on the beach. Following a path into the woods, they found corn fields and buried corn, four or five abandoned Indian dwellings, and gravesites which were more elaborate than those at Corn Hill. This time they left the graves alone. Late in the day they came out of the woods and joined up with those in the shallop.[57] The group made camp that evening on the beach, where early next morning came their long sought contact with the Indians. As they prepared breakfast and for another day of exploration, one of the men came running, crying "'They are men! Indians! Indians!'" and arrows went flying among the explorers. Those with ready weapons responded with musket fire, and the attackers fled, with some of the Pilgrims in pursuit. In all there were no casualties. The Englishmen managed to avoid the Indians' arrows, and the musket fire was either insufficient or inaccurate enough not to have wounded any Indians. The only damage was to some coats hanging on the barricade which were shot through with holes. Calling the spot "The First Encounter," the men boarded the shallop and continued their search for Coppin's harbor.[58]

They sailed all that day along the Bay shore, and the weather turned nasty. It began to snow and rain late in the morning, and by the middle of the afternoon the wind had increased and the seas began to roughen. The hinges on the rudder broke, but Coppin spurred them on with the assertion that through the mist and rain he could see the harbor. One last catastrophe hit them, for as they raised more sail to get themselves into the harbor, the mast broke into three pieces. With a sturdy seaman steering and encouraging the men to row through the surf to the beach, the shallop made it through the breakers and rocks and came to rest upon the sandy beach.[59] They had landed on Clark's Island, which they explored thoroughly the next day. The following day was the Sabbath, and so it was Monday, 11 December before they could investigate the mainland. They took soundings of the harbor, and found it well suited for shipping. They landed on the beach and explored the area, where they found running brooks and corn fields. In sum, it was a site considered excellent for settlement, and so they returned to the *Mayflower* with the good news.[60]

On 15 December, the *Mayflower* and its passengers weighed anchor and sailed toward the newly discovered harbor. Contrary winds prevented their entering that day, but they shifted, and the Pilgrims sailed into the harbor the next day, a Saturday.[61] After the Sabbath, various members of the group went ashore to search for a place for their settlement. Some preferred an interior site, but that was rejected because of the distance to the sea and the difficulties of fishing, as well as being too wooded. Others suggested Clark's Island, but upon investigation it was discovered to have no dependable supply of water. Finally, a majority agreed to settle on the mainland, and so they prepared to disembark.[62] A two-day storm prevented any significant number of settlers from going ashore, but on Saturday, 23 December, the weather cleared and the Pilgrims began the process of building a community in the New England wilderness.[63]

With the decision to settle at Plymouth, the Pilgrims abandoned their interest in Cape Cod, and Cape Cod lost the honor of providing the site for their first permanent settlement in New England. But it was not an overwhelming loss, for the Cape would come to play an important role in the history of Plymouth Colony. It would provide many of its leaders, such as governors Prence and Hinckley; much of its economic strength, from fish, hay, and land; much of its expansion, in the form of new towns; as well as a good portion of its diversity, such as the Quakers and the Indians. As the history of Cape Cod in the seventeenth-century cannot be separated from the history of Plymouth Colony, so the history of Plymouth Colony cannot be separated from Cape Cod. It is the purpose of the following pages to explore that inter-relationship.

Notes

1. William Bradford, *Of Plymouth Plantation*, ed. Samuel E. Morison (New York, 1959), pp. 59-60 (Hereinafter cited as *Plymouth Plantation*). References to the more scholarly edition by Worthington C. Ford, 2 vols. (Boston, 1912), will be specifically identified in the footnotes. Othewise all references to Bradford's famous history are to the Morison edition. Regarding the Cape Cod landfall, see Samuel E. Morison, "Plymouth Colony Beachhead," *U.S. Naval Institute Proceedings* 80(1954):1344-1357, where the Pilgrim activities on Cape Cod are discussed in terms of a naval amphibious maneuver (Hereinafter cited as "Beachhead"). The landfall of the Pilgrims in the *Mayflower* is most exhaustively discussed in W. Sears

Nickerson, *Land Ho!--1620: A Seaman's Story of the Mayflower, Her Construction, Her Navigation and Her First Landfall* (Boston, 1931) (Hereinafter cited as *Land Ho!*).

2. Bradford, *Plymouth Plantation*, p. 60; Morison, "Beachhead," pp. 1348-1349; Nickerson, *Land Ho!* pp., 100, 121-141. For a forceful presentation of the reasons the Pilgrims really did intend to settle within the northern regions of the Virginia Company's sphere of authority and not outside it, see Samuel E. Morison, "The *Mayflower's* Destination, and the Pilgrim Fathers' Patents," Public., Col. Soc. Mass., *Transactions*, 38(1951):387-413 (Hereinafter cited as "Destination"). In his discussion, Morison also absolves the master, Jones, of any duplicity in conniving with the Dutch to keep the *Mayflower* passengers out of Dutch territory.

3. On St. Brendan specifically and the Irish generally, see Samuel E. Morison, *The European Discovery of America: The Northern Voyages, A. D. 500-1600* (New York, 1971), chap. 2. Frederick J. Pohl gives them a more sympathetic hearing in his *Atlantic Crossings before Columbus* (New York, c. 1961), chap. 3. Pohl is the major proponent of the assertion that the Vikings explored extensively on the North American continent, and that Lief Ericsson encamped at Follins Pond. See especially his *The Vikings on Cape Cod* (Pictou, Nova Scotia, 1957), and for a shorter version of the argument "Leif Ericsson's Visit to America: Discoveries of 1947," *American-Scandinavian Review* 36(1948):17-29. After an investigation, the Massachusetts Archaeological Society remained unconvinced. See Benjamin L. Smith, "A Report on the Follins Pond Investigation," *Bulletin*, Massachusetts Archaeological Society 14(1953):82-88 (Hereinafter cited as *Bulletin*, Mass. Arch. Soc.). Pohl defended his views, primarily in ibid., 14(1953):105-109; 16(1955):53-60; 17(1956):49-50; 20(1958):15; and 21(1960):48-49.

4. Warner F. Gookin, *Bartholomew Gosnold: Discoverer and Planter, New England--1602, Virginia--1607*, with footnotes and a concluding part by Philip L. Barbour, (Hamden, CT, 1963), chaps. 1-7 (Hereinafter cited as *Gosnold*). For Gosnold's genealogy and a shorter assessment of the colonizer, see Gookin's "Who Was Bartholomew Gosnold?" *William and Mary Quarterly*, 3d Ser., 6(1949):398-415; for a brief account of Gosnold's voyage, see Gookin's *A Voyage of Discovery to the Southern Parts of Norumbega, . . .* , (Edgartown, MA, 1950). See also David. B. Quinn, *North America From Earliest Discovery to First Settlements: The Norse Voyages to 1612* (New York, c. 1977), pp. 391-393 (Hereinafter cited as *North America from Earliest Discovery*); and David B. Quinn and Alison M. Quinn (eds.), *The English New England Voyages, 1602-1608*, (London, 1983), pp. 31-53 (Hereinafter cited as *New England Voyages*). For a

discussion of sixteenth and seventeenth-century maps and charts of Cape Cod
and the New England coast, see William P. Cumming, "The Colonial
Charting of the Massachusetts Coast," in Philip C. F. Smith (ed.), *Seafaring
in Colonial Massachusetts*, Public., Col. Soc. Mass., *Collec.* 52(1980):68-
92.

     5. Gabriel Archer, *The Relation of Captaine Gosnolds Voyage to the
North part of Virginia . . .1602 . . . .* (Hereinafter cited as *Relation*) in Quinn
and Quinn, *New England Voyages,* p. 118. Archer, whose *Relation* was
published in Samuel Purchase, *Hakluytus Posthumus or Purchase his
Pilgrims,* 4 vols., (London, 1625), 4:1647-1651, was one of two members of
the party who wrote a narrative of the voyage (Hereinafter cited as *Pilgrims*).
The other member was John Brereton, whose *A Briefe and True Relation of
the Discoverie of the North Part of Virginia,* was originally published the
year of the voyage (Hereinafter cited as *Relation*). Both reports, in heavily
annotated editions, are published in Quinn and Quinn, *New England
Voyages,* pp. 112-203, and are the ones used here. The reports are printed
side by side for easy comparison in Lincoln A. Dexter (comp. and ed.), *The
Gosnold Discoveries . . .in the North Part of Virginia, 1602* (Brookfield,
MA, 1982) (Hereinafter cited as *Gosnold Discoveries*). Archer's account is
also available as *Old South Leaflet* No. 120 (Boston, 1902), which contains
Gosnold's letter to his father written at the completion of his voyage. The
Quinns and Dexter also include the letter.   Brereton's version of the
expedition can also be found in Henry S. Burrage (ed.) *Early English and
French Voyages, 1534-1608* (New York, 1906), pp. 329-340 (Hereinafter
cited as *Early Voyages*). Both accounts and Gosnold's letter can be found in
Charles H. Levermore (ed.), *Forerunners and Competitors of the Pilgrims
and Puritans,* 2 vols. (Brooklyn, NY, 1912), 1:30-56 (Hereinafter cited as
Forerunners); as well as in *Collec.*, Mass. Hist. Soc., 3d Ser., 8(1843):70-
123, which includes a number of tracts originally appended to Brereton's
report.

     6. Archer, *Relation*, pp. 120-121. I have followed Gosnold's routing
as mapped out by Quinn and Quinn, *New England Voyages* p. 1l9. Gookin,
Gosnold, frontispiece, gives a different route, one which has Gosnold
rounding Nantucket to enter Nantucket Sound rather than entering the Sound
between the island and Monomy Point. See also Quinn and Quinn, *New
England Voyages*, pp. 498-500, where they argue the evidence regarding
Gosnold's route.

     7. Quinn and Quinn, *New England Voyages*, pp. 122-126. Quinn and
Quinn, along with Gookin, *Gosnold, passim,* and Dexter, *Gosnold
Discoveries,* p. 26, assume Cuttyhunk Island, the island farthest out into the
ocean, was Gosnold's landing. Harold C. Wilson and William C. Carr,

"Gosnold's Elizabeth Isle: Cuttyhunk or Nuashon?" *American Neptune* 33(1973):131-145 make the case for the island of Nuashon, the largest island and the one closest to the mainland, although Quinn and Quinn, *New England Voyages*, pp. 503-504 are not convinced.

8. Archer, *Relation*, pp. 130, 133. Sassafras was widely used as a medication, primarily for the treatment of the "French Poxe," or syphilis. Charles Manning and Merrill Moore, "Sassafras and Syphilis," *New England Quarterly* 9(1936):473-475.

9. Archer, *Relation*, p. 133.

10. Brereton, *Relation*, p. 155.

11. Brereton, *Relation*, p. 159.

12. Brereton, *Relation*, p. 159.

13. Martin Pring, *A Voyage set out from the Citie of Bristoll . . . .* (Hereinafter cited as *Voyage*) in Quinn and Quinn, *New England Voyages*, pp. 214-216. This edition is the same heavily annotated style of the Archer and Brereton reports, and is found on pp. 214-228. The account was published in Purchase, *Pilgrims*, 4:1654-1656. It is reprinted in Levermore, *Forerunners*, 1:60-68; and in Burrage, *Early Voyages*, pp. 345-352. David B. Quinn, *England and the Discovery of America, 1481-1620*, (New York, 1974), pp. 423-427 (Hereinafter cited as *Discovery of America*); Quinn and Quinn, *New England Voyages*, pp. 53-55

14. Pring, *Voyage*, p. 219.

15. Pring, *Voyage*, p. 219.   Pring's harbor has been variously identified as at Martha's Vineyard, Plymouth, and Provincetown. The issue is best summarized and Provincetown established as the site in David B. Quinn, "Martin Pring at Provincetown in 1603?" *New England Quarterly* 40(1967):79-91. See also Quinn and Quinn, *New England Voyages*, p.219, n.1; and Quinn, *Discovery of America*, pp. 423-427.

16. Pring, *Voyage*, pp. 226-227.

17. Pring, *Voyage*, p. 228.

18. Samuel de Champlain, *The Works of Samuel de Champlain*, ed. H. P. Biggar, 6 vols., (Toronto, 1922-1936), 1:280-300 (Hereinafter cited as *Works*) . This chapter covers the 1604 voyage. The New England and Cape Cod explorations are also published in Levermore, *Forerunners*, 2:76-170 and in W. L. Grant (ed.), *Voyages of Samuel de Champlain*, in "Original Narratives of Early American History" (New York, 1907), pp. 21-118. See also David B. Quinn, *North America from Earliest Discovery*, pp. 396-398; Samuel E. Morison, *Samuel de Champlain: Father of New France* (Boston, 1972), pp. 45-53 (Hereinafter cited as *Champlain*).

19. Champlain, *Works*, 1:307.

20. Champlain, *Works*, 1:311-366 covers the 1605 expedition. Quinn, *North America from Earliest Discovery*, pp. 398-399; Morison, *Champlain*, pp. 55-70.

21. Champlain, *Works*, 1:plate LXXIV.

22. Champlain, *Works*, 1:347.

23. Champlain, *Works*, 1:349-351.

24. Champlain, *Works*, 1:353-355.

25. Champlain, *Works*, 1:392-437 deals with the 1606 expedition. Quinn, *North America from Earliest Discovery*, pp. 404-405; Morison, *Champlain*, pp. 71-88.

26. Champlain, *Works*, 1:403-404.

27. Champlain, *Works*, 1:407.

28. James Rosier, *A True Relation of the most prosperous voyage made this present yeere 1605, by Captaine George Waymouth*, in Quinn and Quinn, *New England Voyages*, pp. 251-311. Extracts of Rosier's account of the journey were published by Purchase, *Pilgrims*, 4:1659-1667. It has been reprinted in Levermore, *Forerunners*, 1:313-351; in Burrage, *Early Voyages*, pp. 357-394; and in *Collec.*, Mass. Hist. Soc., 3d Ser., 8(1843);125-157. See also Quinn, *North America from Earliest Discovery*, p. 400; Quinn, *Discovery of America*, pp. 388-390; and Quinn and Quinn, *New England Voyages*, pp. 55-70.

29. Robert Juet, *The Voyage of the "Half Moon" from 4 April to 7 November 1609*, ed. Robert M. Lunny (New York, 1959), pp. 17-19. Juet's account was published in Purchase, *Pilgrims*, 3:581-595. Levermore, *Forerunners*, 1:391-422 contains the Cape Cod incident, but J. Franklin Jameson (ed.), *Narratives of New Netherland, 1609-1664*, in "Original Narratives of Early American History" (New York, 1909) pp. 16-28 does not (Hereinafter cited as *New Netherlands*). See also Quinn, *North America from Earliest Discovery*, p. 410.

30. Samuel Argall, *The Voyage of Samuel Argall*, in Levermore, *Forerunners*, 2:428-437. It had originally been published in Purchase, *Pilgrims*, 4:1758-1762.

31. Quinn, *North America from Earliest Discovery*, pp. 412-413; Levermore, *Forerunners*, 2:438-440.

32. Philip L. Barbour, *The Three Worlds of Captain John Smith* (Boston, 1964), p. 306 (Hereinafter cited as *John Smith*); John Smith, *A Description of New England* (Hereinafter cited as *New England)*, in Philip L. Barbour (ed.), *The Complete Works of Captain John Smith*, 3 vols. (Chapel Hill, NC, 1986), 1:323.

33. Smith, *New England*, 1:340-341; Barbour, *John Smith*, p. 312.

34. Barbour, *John Smith*, p. 313; Bradford, *Plymouth Plantation*, p. 81, n. 2.

35. Thomas Dermer to Samuel Purchase, December 27, 1619, in Levermore, *Forerunners*, 2:579-584; Henry S. Burrage, *The Beginnings of Colonial Maine, 1602-1658* (Portland, ME, 1914), p. 140; Bradford, *Plymouth Plantation*, pp. 81-84. Squanto's complexity has fascinated historians for decades. As did the Pilgrims, historians have recognized his importance to the success of the Plymouth colony as its agricultural agent and guide, as well as emissary and interpreter to the Indians. But both have also understood that Squanto later sought his own ends and played his own game. His efforts to exploit his special relationship to the Pilgrim colonists by plotting and intriguing to challenge the Wampanoag chief Massasoit and become an independent Indian leader are well documented. Bradford, *Plymouth Plantation*, p. 99. For a biography and balanced evaluation of Squanto, see Charles Francis Adams, *Three Episodes of Massachusetts History*, 2 vols., (Boston, 1892):1:23-44 (Hereinafter cited as *Three Episodes*); Alden T. Vaughan, *New England Frontier: Puritans and Indians, 1620-1675* (Boston, 1965), pp. 82-87 (Hereinafter cited as *New England Frontier*); and Neal Salisbury, "Squanto: Last of the Patuxets," in David B. Sweet and Gary B. Nash (eds.), *Struggle and Survival in Colonial America* (Berkeley, CA, c. 1981), pp. 228-246. On the competition between Squanto and Massasoit especially, see John H. Humins, "Squanto and Massasoit: A Struggle for Power," *New England Quarterly* 60(1987):54-70. For a pamphlet-sized biography which claims eight trans-Atlantic crossings for the Indian, see Matthew R. Thompson, *Tasquantum, 1589-1622: The Pilgrims' Interpreter--A Biography* (Salem, OR, 1980). See also Leonard A. Adolf, "Squanto's Role in Pilgrim Diplomacy," *Ethnohistory*, 11(1964):247-261; and Frank Shuffleton, "Indian Devils and Pilgrim Fathers: Squanto, Hobomock, and the English Conception of Indian Religion," *New England Quarterly*, 49(1979):108-116.

36. Bradford, *Plymouth Plantation*, p. 81.

37. *A Journal of the Pilgrims at Plymouth: Mourt's Relation.* ed. Dwight B. Heath (New York, c. 1963), p. 17 (Hereinafter cited as *Mourt's Relation).* I have used the title first assigned to the book in 1736 by Thomas Prince in his *A Chronological History of New England* . . . (Boston, 1736), 1(pt. 2):71, n. 38 (Hereinafter cited as *Chronological History*).

38. *Mourt's Relation*, pp. 17-18. The compact is also contained in Bradford, *Plymouth Plantation*, p. 76. The original has long since been lost. A list of the signers first appeared in Nathaniel Morton, *New England's Memoriall*, originally published in 1669. See same, ed. Howard J. Hall (New York, 1937), p. 15. The list is reprinted in Heath's edition of the

Mourt's Relation, p. 18, fn. 6, and its signers are identified in Morison's edition of Bradford's history, pp. 441-443.

39. Bradford, *Plymouth Plantation*, pp. 76-77.

40. *Mourt's Relation*, p. 18.

41. Bradford, *Plymouth Plantation*, p. 64; *Mourt's Relation*, p. 19.

42. *Mourt's Relation*, pp. 19-21; Bradford, *Plymouth Plantation*, p. 65. *Mourt's Relation*, identifies the finding of water with the next morning.

43. *Mourt's Relation*, pp. 22-23; Bradford, *Plymouth Plantation*, pp. 65-66.

44. Bradford, *Plymouth Plantation*, p. 66.

45. *Mourt's Relation*, p.22; Quinn and Quinn, *New England Voyages*, p. 219, n.2.

46. *Mourt's Relation*, pp. 23-24; Bradford, *Plymouth Plantation*, p. 66.

47. *Mourt's Relation*, pp. 24-25.

48. *Mourt's Relation*, p. 25.

49. *Mourt's Relation*, pp. 26-27.

50. *Mourt's Relation*, pp. 27-29. The adult body found in the grave was no doubt that of an elderly Indian, either a chief or some other individual of importance. Its yellow hair and European clothing were the cause of a variety of opinions among the explorers as to its origins, but Warner F. Gookin, "The Pilgrims as Archaeologists," *Bulletin*, Mass. Arch. Soc. 11(1950):19-21, explains both phenomena. The yellow hair was the result of the chemical reaction of the red ochre embalming powder on the Indian's white hair, and the European clothing came from some French sailors shipwrecked on the Cape a few years earlier. As Gookin notes, the Pilgrim episode began the archaeological exploration of pre-European Cape Cod. It has continued ever since, and can best be traced through articles in the *Bulletin*, Mass. Arch. Soc., published since 1940.

51. *Mourt's Relation*, p. 30.

52. *Mourt's Relation*, pp. 29-30.

53. Agawam, or Ipswich, Massachusetts. See *Mourt's Relation*, p. 30, n. 27.

54. *Mourt's Relation*, pp. 30-31. It had received that name as the result of the theft of a harpoon by an Indian during Coppin's previous visit to the place. For a discussion, not always accurate, of explorers who had specifically been to Plymouth Harbor before the Pilgrims, see Henry F. Howe, *Early Explorers of Plymouth Harbor, 1525-1619* (Plymouth, MA, 1953).

55. Bradford, *Plymouth Plantation*, p. 68; *Mourt's Relation*, pp. 31-32. *Mourt's Relation*, p. 32, gives the names of all of the party except three of the sailors. The ten "principals" were "Captain Standish, Master Carver,

William Bradford, Edward Winslow, John Tilley, Edward Tilley, John Howland, and three of London, Richard Warren, Stephen Hopkins, and Edward Dotte." John Allerton, a sailor hired by the Pilgrims, and Thomas English, similarly hired by them to manage the shallop, were also members of the expedition. It was completed by the inclusion of two mates, Clarke and Coppin, the master gunner, and three unnamed crewmen of the *Mayflower*. See Eugene A. Stratton, *Plymouth Colony: Its History & People, 1620-1691* (Salt Lake City, c. 1986), pp. 234-274 *passim*, for biographical information on the participants (Hereinafter cited as *Plymouth Colony*).

56. *Mourt's Relation*, pp. 32-33.

57. *Mourt's Relation*, pp. 33-35; Bradford, *Plymouth Plantation*, pp. 68-69.

58. *Mourt's Relation*, pp. 35-37; Bradford, *Plymouth Plantation*, pp. 69-70.

59. *Mourt's Relation*, pp. 37-38; Bradford, *Plymouth Plantation*, pp. 71-72. *Mourt's Relation* incorrectly gives the date of 10 December for the Saturday the men spent on Clark's Island. Saturday was actually 9 December, as Monday, the day of the landing, was most assuredly the 11.

60. *Mourt's Relation*, p. 38; Bradford, *Plymouth Plantation*, p. 72.

61. *Mourt's Relation*, p. 38.

62. *Mourt's Relation*, pp. 39-41.

63. *Mourt's Relation*, pp. 41-42.

II

"to good effect and
turned to their profit"

WHEN the *Mayflower* sailed across Cape Cod Bay from
Provincetown harbor in December of 1620, the Pilgrims may have
turned their backs on Cape Cod as a site for habitation, but they
certainly had not rejected its advantages or ignored its potential.
Even though the 1620's saw the Plymouth settlers expand their
explorations into the interior surrounding their colony and northward
up the coast of New England, the Cape remained important for the
colonists throughout their first decade of settlement. The inhabitants
of the small plantation continued to journey to its sandy shores on a
variety of expeditions, although two decades would elapse before
Plymouth residents would once again give serious thought to
establishing a settlement on its beaches. Through it all, Cape Cod, its
lands, its crops, its waters, and its Indians would be a constant theme
in the development of the struggling isolated colony.

It did not take long. Less than four months after the departure
of the *Mayflower* from Plymouth in early April 1621, Plymouth
settlers were back on the Cape. In late July, six-year old John
Billington wandered off into the woods and disappeared.[1] Despite the
troublesomeness for which the family was noted, the colony sent ten
of its seventeen available men off in search of the boy when it was

learned from the Indians that he had appeared on the Cape.[2] Why it was decided to leave the colony virtually defenseless to search for the boy is not explained. Perhaps the leaders of the colony took the parable of the lost sheep to heart, or perhaps their first encounter with the Nauset Indians on the Cape indicated that a show of force would be desirable. Maybe some were just looking for a bit of excitement. But for whatever reason, the men set out in the shallop, accompanied by Squanto as their interpreter and one Tokamahamon, a friendly Indian. A storm came up late in the day, and the expedition put into harbor that night at Cummaquid, or modern Barnstable.[3] In the morning the Indian interpreters were sent to tell a group of Indians gathering shellfish the purpose of the expedition. They told the interpreters that the boy was well, but was at Nauset, much further out along the Cape. In a gesture of hospitality, the Indians invited the men ashore to eat with them, and six did so, leaving four of their number to protect the boat. On shore, the men met Iyanough, the sachem of the tribe, a young man in his early twenties, noted for his personable and gentle demeanor.[4] While with Iyanough, the Englishmen had one of their more unpleasant reminders of earlier visitors to the Cape. An elderly Indian woman came to see the strangers and broke into a fit of passion, weeping excessively. When asked the reason for the display of emotion, she answered that she had lost three sons to the kidnapper Thomas Hunt, and had therefore been deprived of the comfort of her children in her old age. The Pilgrims condemned Hunt, promising that they would never do such a thing themselves, and made an effort to appease the woman with a gift of some small trinkets.[5]

After eating, the Plymouth men, joined by Iyanough and two of his men, set sail for Nauset and arrived in the evening. The Nausets urged them to come ashore, but as they were the Indians who had greeted the Pilgrims with arrows at First Encounter Beach, it was judged prudent to remain on guard and a little off shore. But Iyanough and his men did go ashore, as did Squanto, who was sent to inform the Nausets of the purpose of the visit. After sundown, Aspinet, the Nauset chief, appeared with young Billington and an entourage of at least one hundred men. Half the Indians came with the boy to the side of the shallop, and with the gift of a knife to both Aspinet and the Indian who had first cared for Billington, an exchange was made.[6] At Nauset the Pilgrims picked up the information that the Cape Indians had experienced trouble with the Narragansetts, and began to fear for the safety of Plymouth. Recognizing the settlement was not well guarded, they hastened home, but opposing winds and a lack of drinking water forced them to put in again at Cummaquid. Iyanough, ever wishing to be helpful, provided them with fresh water, and the women of the tribe sang and danced for the visitors. They started out again, but did not get far, and the next morning Iyanough assisted them once again. They departed for Plymouth a third time, and arrived safely at the settlement that night.[7] In all, the journey had been a good one. The lost boy had been found and brought back. The Plymouth settlers had discovered a most friendly Indian chief, and one who would be invaluable in the months ahead as an ally in the search for food. Even the Nausets had indicated their willingness to deal peacefully with their new neighbors to the north. Such generally good relations would be important as the contacts between Plymouth and the tribes of the Cape area increased.

Later contacts with Cape Indians turned out to be vital to the very survival of the colony. While the harvest of 1621 was sufficient for the original settlers and a Thanksgiving had been held, new arrivals and visitors strained the food resources of the colony almost to the breaking point.[8] Of greatest significance was the arrival of the first contingent of reinforcements for the colony. In early November of 1621 the *Fortune*, which like the *Mayflower* made its landfall at Cape Cod, sailed into Plymouth harbor with thirty-six passengers and a new patent aboard. Although the patent did not establish boundaries for the colony, it at least confirmed the colony's right to settle in New England and sanctioned the Mayflower Compact.[9] While Plymouth Colony was pleased to have its location confirmed and glad of the additional manpower, there was also a plaintive wish that many of the new arrivals had landed better equipped, and that all of them had been better supplied with provisions.[10] In response to the heavy burden of caring for the new arrivals, the colony's leaders took stock of their food supply, and put the entire community on half rations, expecting they could survive six months. It was no doubt a difficult winter for everyone, but in the perseverance for which they are known, they bore the hardships patiently, and hoped supplies would arrive early the next year.[11]

By the time spring arrived, their food was virtually exhausted, and still more people arrived in the colony. Included were seven people off a fishing vessel sent by their English agent, Thomas Weston, and sixty or so "lusty men" sent over by Weston to be the founders of a new settlement in New England. Weston's men stayed two months in the colony, their sick even longer, and proved a sore trial to Plymouth's residents, being an unruly and undisciplined group. The colony accommodated the undesirables as a favor to Weston, but when their conduct is coupled with the strain they must have put on the food supply, one can well imagine the collective sigh of relief which occurred when they departed in the fall to establish the Wessagusset settlement.[12]

The only aid during these trying months came from a passing fishing vessel, whose captain notified the Pilgrims that he was willing to assist them to the best of his ability. The colony dispatched Edward Winslow with a boat to accompany the captain to Monhegan Island and purchase supplies from the fishing vessels there. Received sympathetically, Winslow returned with a good quantity of supplies, but by the time they were divided among the colony's residents, no one received very much.[13]

The most important of the efforts to relieve the starvation of the struggling colony was an expedition to the Cape to purchase corn from the Indians. By the late fall of 1622, Weston's band of roughnecks at Wessagusset had exhausted their provisions, and proposed to the Pilgrims that the two colonies join forces to look for food on Cape Cod. They were to use a small vessel, the *Swan*, which had remained in New England for the use of the Wessagusset men.[14] The Plymouth people, desperate themselves, agreed to the proposal, but the venture ran into more bad luck than even Weston's men deserved. The Wessagusset governor, Richard Greene, died in Plymouth before the expedition started; strong opposing winds twice turned the men back; and Myles Standish, who replaced Greene as leader, became ill and could not continue. Finally, in November, William Bradford took command, and with Squanto as interpreter and pilot, the ship set sail for the southern regions of the Cape. Under Squanto's guidance, the goal had been to round the shoals of Monomy Point, but the expedition failed of that, and put in at Manamoycke, now Chatham Harbor. That evening Bradford, Squanto, and some others went ashore, where after a bit of initial reluctance, the Indians came to them, bringing venison and other food. With the encouragement of Squanto, the Cape Indians abandoned their hesitancy and agreed to sell the English traders eight hogsheads of corn and beans.[15] It was at Manamoycke, that Squanto, the Pilgrim Colony's Indian ally and interpreter, caught a fever, died, and was buried. He had been an important resident of the Plymouth settlement, acting as a guide and interpreter in the colonists' doings with the Indians. Although he had been less than wholeheartedly their own, and had been careful to mind his own main chance, nonetheless Bradford noted the English had suffered a significant loss at his death.[16]

Squanto's death meant that the English would not attempt the passage through the Monomy shoals to Nantucket Sound. Instead they sailed back around the tip of the Cape and northward to the Massachusetts Indians. They found the Massachusetts ill with a plague-like sickness, but at least well enough to renew their complaints against the Wessagusset settlement for its stealing of the Indians' corn. As a result, they purchased nothing, and the searchers doubled back across the harbor to the Bay side of the Cape.[17] They stopped at Nauset, where they purchased eight or ten hogsheads of corn and beans, and at Mattachiest, where they bought corn.[18] While at Mattachiest, violent winter storms came up, and the shallop, which they had been using to ferry themselves between the *Swan* and the land, was blown ashore and nearly buried in the sand some distance away. Bradford directed that the corn be gathered into a round pile and covered with mats and grass to protect it from the elements, and he ordered the Indians to leave it alone. Meanwhile the Indians had found the shallop, and Bradford gave similar instructions regarding the preservation of what was left of it. In both cases, he informed the Indians that the English would be back for both the corn and beans as well as the shallop. One has the sense that he lectured them sternly about the preservation of the all important food and the vessel, and left no doubt in the minds of the Indians that they would indeed be in serious trouble if the shallop and provisions were not as they had been left. Having made himself clear, Bradford decided to leave the *Swan*, and accompanied by the men from Plymouth, walked the fifty miles back to Plymouth.[19] Three days after the weary and footsore hikers arrived, the *Swan* sailed in and the nearly thirty hogsheads of corn and beans they had on board were divided. The Wessagusset men returned to their own settlement, with orders to send their carpenter so that the shallop could be repaired and the remaining corn brought back from the Cape.[20]

The entire trip had been quite successful. The Indians of the Cape at least had proven cooperative, and as Bradford observed, had sold the English more provisions than they could easily spare.[21] It is interesting to note that those Cape Cod Indians who had dealt previously with the Plymouth Colony were the ones who were willing to extend aid, and that those to the north who had become the victims of the Wessagusset settlement's treachery were not. As relations with the Indians would go, it was indicative of the future that the Indians of the Cape would be friendly, and those to the north would not.

By the time of their return, Myles Standish had recovered, and with a second shallop went with some of the men who had returned from the Cape to collect the corn and repair the stranded vessel. They found the corn as it had been left, mended the broken shallop, and returned to Plymouth. While the men were at Nauset repairing the other shallop, an Indian stole some beads, scissors, and other goods from one of the boats. Standish responded with the kind of forcefulness for which he was well known. He and some of the men went to the sachem of the tribe and demanded the return of the goods and promised revenge if they were not brought back. The Indians returned the goods the next morning with much apology, presenting themselves as very sorry for the theft, and glad of reconciliation.[22]

As the first of the various expeditions to the Cape for provisions, the one in 1622 received the most attention from the chroniclers of Plymouth, Bradford and Winslow. But it was not the only such journey. In the spring of 1623 Bradford was once again on the Cape in search of provisions at Manomet, the site of Plymouth's future trading post. He purchased corn which was left in the custody of the local sachem, and Standish went to retrieve it the following March.[23] In the meantime, Standish had also made another trip to Mattachiest, where he experienced a second example of Indian pilfering and treated it as he had the one at Nauset. Despite the problem, the Indians were willing to trade, and sold the men a good supply of corn.[24]

At both Manomet and Mattachiest, the Indians had been willing to trade for corn, but at both places, Standish had heard rumors and witnessed indications that trouble was at hand at Weston's Wessagusset settlement. As seen by Plymouth, Wessagusset was inhabited by undesirables and their conduct toward the natives had so antagonized the Indians that they threatened to attack both settlements. This belief received confirmation during Winslow's journey to Massasoit's village to cure the chief of costiveness. Friendly Indians at the settlement informed Hobbamock, the colonists' interpreter, of the impending attack.[25] Plymouth's response was to devote more of its energies to improving its defenses and to send Myles Standish and a small contingent to Wessagusset. Standish's solution to the problem was to kill a number of the Indians, while that of the Wessagusset men was the agreement to abandon the settlement, a decision with which the Plymouth Colony was no doubt quite pleased, and probably encouraged.[26]

Standish's preemptive maneuver had prevented a possible coordinated Indian assault on Plymouth and Wessagusset. But while it may have saved Plymouth and prevented an attack on the Indians of the Cape, the incident did have its repercussions among both Cape Cod Indians and Plymouth settlers. The suddenness of the assault on the Massachusetts Indians, and the fear that Standish would move against them next caused the Indians of the Cape to become so terrified that they abandoned their homes for the swamps and deserted areas of the Cape. As a result they became susceptible to contagious disease. A large number of them became ill, and many of them died. Included among the dead were the three chiefs of the Cape tribes, Canacum of Manomet, Aspinet of Nauset, and the helpful Iyanough of Mattachiest.[27] The Plymouth settlers apparently made no attempt to calm the Indians of the Cape, as no mention is made of such an effort. But it seems strange that they did not. Cape Indians had been most cooperative in returning John Billington and in supplying corn, and a policy of reconciliation would have seemed a good idea if that cooperation were to continue. The failure to reassure the Indians of the Cape is especially interesting when one considers that as a result of their fright, the Indians stopped planting corn. Certainly, the Plymouth settlers, seemingly dependent on Indian corn to survive, would want to see the supply continued. Why they did not act to do so remains a puzzle.

After the Wessagusset venture, Plymouth's contact with the Cape diminished. Certainly a reduction in corn production as the result of the death of some of its Indians explains part of the decline. Probably more important was the general feeling among those Cape Indians still alive that after Wessagussset, the Plymouth settlement was not quite to be trusted.[28] But there were other considerations as well. Increasingly during the 1620's Plymouth Colony's major concern was its effort to organize its finances so that it could reimburse its London investors, known as the Adventurers. In an attempt to raise the large sums of money necessary, the colony turned both to new geographic areas and to new economic activities. Rather than the search for Cape Cod corn and beans on which to survive, the Pilgrim leaders instead looked for goods to sell in England, and turned their interests first to fishing off Cape Ann and the Maine coast, and later to the fur trade in the Kennebec and Connecticut River Valleys.[29]

From the mid-1620's until the first settlements on the Cape in the late 1630's, Plymouth's contact with Cape Cod was sporadic, lacking the sense of urgency that had marked the earlier voyages in search of provisions. There was one trading expedition that traveled in the area, and there were two rescue missions to shipwrecks, but only the building of a trading post at Manomet represented any serious consideration by Plymouth of the opportunities of the Cape.

In the summer of 1623 two ships had arrived in Plymouth, the *Anne* and *Little James*. The *Anne* returned to England with a load of clapboard and furs, but the *Little James* was to stay in New England, having been directed by the Adventurers to remain for the use of the colonists. She was a excellent vessel, but her arrival had not been without problems. The ship's unruly crew were men who thought they had been hired for a privateering venture and would be paid in shares. When ordered to catch fish instead of foreign vessels, they refused unless they were paid wages. Bradford intervened, and it was agreed to pay the wages demanded, and the ship was sent around Cape Cod to trade with the Narragansetts. Regrettably that is all that is said about the expedition. No mention is made of whether any stop was made along the Cape, or whether the *Little James* just sailed around it on its way to Narragansett Bay. But whether the ship stopped at the Cape or not, the voyage was not successful. Dutch traders offered better quality goods, and although the *Little James* came back with a few beaver pelts and some corn, in all the expedition was a disappointment. The disappointment was compounded by the near wreck of the vessel in a storm on its return to Plymouth.[30]

Those same coastal storms of New England, and especially the perils of them near Cape Cod, were responsible for a major rescue expedition to the Cape in the early winter of 1627. The ship *Sparrowhawk*, headed for Virginia with a good number of passengers and a quantity of goods, found itself in Cape Cod waters. It had either lost its way or its captain, fearing a passenger mutiny, had sailed a course most likely to find land. The passengers had nearly exhausted their food, water, and fuel, so when the ship ran aground on a sandbar off Chatham Harbor, one can safely presume that the passengers regarded any land as better than none at all.[31] The vessel was not damaged, but when the winds increased, the anchor cable parted, and the gusts drove the ship over the sandbar into the harbor, breaking some of its planking and loosening its calking. The passengers and their goods, however, were safe, but wet. At low tide, they removed all their goods to dry land and aired out those that were wet. At first thought, the accident appeared to its participants not to have been as bad as it could have been. There were no casualties, other than some damp cargo.[32]

But upon more sober consideration, and after having revived themselves with something to eat, the group began to worry. They did not know where they were, did not seem to know what to do, and became seriously concerned about their condition. They were first approached by the Indians who spoke to them in English. The Indians asked if the group was associated with Plymouth, and offered to take the stranded passengers to the colony or deliver their letters. In appreciation, the passengers fed the Indians and gave them gifts. They also sent two men and a letter with the Indians to Plymouth to ask for assistance, both in repairing their vessel and in bringing supplies so that they might continue their voyage to Virginia.[33]

Governor Bradford and the colony responded quickly and generously. They prepared and collected the requested supplies. As others were away on various missions, Bradford himself went with the boat, and took along some trade goods so as to buy the castaways Indian corn. Winter weather made a voyage around the tip of the Cape unsafe, and so the relief expedition sailed across Cape Cod Bay to Namskaket Creek in modern Orleans, and then hiked across the Cape to the stranded vessel and its passengers. The party was very pleased to see Bradford, especially as he supplemented the group's supplies and forced some of the crew who had moved in with the Indians to return to the ship. Bradford left the passengers well supplied and comfortable, stopped in at some other harbors to purchase corn for Plymouth, and returned home.[34]

Unfortunately, that was not the end of it. Before the *Sparrowhawk* could be repaired and the passengers sail away, a second storm occurred which so battered the vessel that it was no longer sailable. This time the passengers requested sanctuary in Plymouth until they could find transportation to Virginia. Considering their distress, Plymouth agreed. The people and goods made their way to Plymouth and remained in the colony some nine or ten months, leaving the end of the following summer. The visitors were apparently not a burden on the colony. No mention is made of short rations, and except for one Mr. Fells, who was suspected of keeping one of his female servants as his mistress, their actions were no more criticized than would be expected from a society which viewed all private behavior as public acts. In fact, Plymouth gained from its visitors. Plymouth residents were able to purchase clothing and other goods they needed, and when the visitors left, they sold the corn they had planted to Plymouth citizens.[35]

A similar rescue mission to Cape Cod was made in the winter of 1630/31, when Richard Garrett, a shoemaker from Boston, sailed to Plymouth from Boston with his daughter and four men. Before it was over, four of the six in the party would die of exposure. Kept out of Plymouth Harbor by strong winds, their small vessel lost its makeshift anchor and drifted southward along the Cape. Despite a wind and cold so severe that ice formed around the legs of the passengers, those on board managed to get themselves to land. After a cold wet night on the open beach, two of the men started for Plymouth, but one died on the way and the other died in Plymouth. Meanwhile an Indian had assisted the remainder of the party as best he could, but was unable to prevent the death of Garrett. A relief party eventually arrived, and returned to Plymouth with the three survivors, one of whom died there. Only one Henry Harwood, a reputable member of the Boston congregation, and Garrett's daughter survived what must have been a most frightening ordeal. Samuel Fuller, the colony's doctor, treated Harwood, and he and the Garrett girl eventually returned to Boston.[36] While it is important to note that the Indians had perhaps grown somewhat fearful of English settlers after Standish's assault at Wessagusset, in both the case of the *Sparrowhawk* and the Garrett wreck, without the assistance of the natives, neither group would likely have survived. The Indians of the Cape were apparently, at least, not overly hostile to the colony.

Plymouth's most important involvement with Cape Cod in the years before the establishment of settlements on its lands resulted from the colony's financial reorganization in 1626 and 1627. The principle of a communal property system to repay the debt to the London Adventurers had not worked well in the colony. As early as 1624 Bradford had urged upon the London investors a reorganization of their arrangement. In November 1626, the London Adventurers finally agreed to liquidate the joint stock company, and drew up a new contract with the colonists. In this new agreement the financial interests of the Adventurers were separated from the colonists, with the colonists assuming ownership of their property and the Adventurers expecting repayment of their investment. Thus, in exchange for assuming a debt of 1800 pounds to the Adventurers and one of 600 pounds remaining from 1624, the English investors allowed the colonists to take control of their own financial future. Although the debt was large, and would eventually grow much larger, the new agreement was approved of and supported by the settlers, even though they were decidedly unsure as to how to raise the payment.[37]

Within Plymouth Colony itself, the new arrangement resulted in important changes. As to the assets held by the colony, it was agreed to distribute the livestock and land on a share basis to fifty-six Purchasers or Old Comers. It was also determined that furs were a more profitable commodity than fish, and so the colony significantly shifted its efforts away from fishing and toward the Indian fur trade. But fifty-six individuals was far too large a group to be involved in the fur trade, or even to be held responsible for paying off the debt to the investors. Therefore a bargain was struck. A group of eight of the colony's leaders, known as the Undertakers, assumed responsibility for the debt, and in exchange received a monopoly of the Indian trade for six years.[38] With a clear goal in mind and the authority to govern and conduct the Indian trade, the Undertakers began to exploit that trade in earnest. It was, therefore, out of the reorganization of the colony's financial relations with its English associates that Plymouth established its trading posts on the Kennebec River to the north, the Connecticut River to the west, and expanded its interests at Manomet to the south on Cape Cod.

Generally referred to by its Indian name, Aptucxet, the Indians had used the Manomet site for years, and the Pilgrims had become familiar with it on their corn-buying expedition in 1623. Its proximity to Plymouth and its obvious trade potential had apparently resulted in some trade at Manomet, for a "boat" is mentioned as being there even before the Undertakers made their trade agreement with the colonists.[39] But the newly created trading system required the Undertakers to enlarge the colony's involvement at Aptucxet. First off they decided to construct a small pinnace for use at the post, probably to replace the earlier boat, and followed this action by an agreement to erect a house at the site.[40] The Undertakers were obviously serious, and they had chosen well. The trading post was located about twenty miles south of Plymouth on the south side of the Manomet River, fairly near its mouth. It was easily approached from Buzzard's Bay, and opened up the possibility of extending trade westward into Narragansett Bay and perhaps even to the Dutch in New Netherland. From Plymouth, the journey was a little more tedious. It required sailing down the coast to Scusset Creek, up the creek four or five miles, and then overland to the trading post.[41] The route described closely follows the route of the modern canal, and offered the same advantages then as now: to avoid going around Cape Cod and its dangerous shoals, making any voyage to the southward shorter and less dangerous.[42] To solidify Plymouth's claim to the post and to be always ready to go out in the pinnace when necessary, the colony manned the trading post with a few men who also planted corn and raised swine. The post remained in operation for some years and "took good effect and turned to their profit," no doubt contributing significantly to the repayment of the colony's debt to the London investors.[43]

One of the most important outgrowths of the Aptucxet post was an increased exposure to the Dutch who had been trading in the area for some years and had settled at New Netherland in 1626. It was Dutch competition that had been one of the reasons for the lack of success of the *Little James* expedition of 1623, and certainly one of the goals of the Aptucxet post was to compete more successfully with the Dutch in the regions south and west of Plymouth. The Dutch, in turn, recognized both a potential rivalry and a possible market, and investigated the Aptucxet fort. The chief trading officer of the Dutch colony, Issack de Rasieres, exchanged letters with Plymouth in the winter of 1626/27, and visited the colony in the autumn of 1627, coming by way of the Aptucxet trading post. He liked what he saw and recognized the trading opportunities which Plymouth presented. As a result, Plymouth continued to trade with the Dutch through the post for a number of years, a practice which brought much benefit to the colony.[44]

In addition to the advantages of trade, contact with the Dutch greatly increased the Pilgrims' understanding of the benefits of trading in "wampumpeag," or wampum. Although they were familiar with wampum, as the Undertakers had assumed ownership of the colony's supply as part of the agreement, it was apparently the Dutch who taught the Pilgrims its use as a trading commodity. Certainly Bradford recognized the role of the Dutch in this instance, pointing out that over time it was wampum which brought in most of Plymouth's profit. Much in demand among the Indians, wampum's steady value tended to stabilize the Indian trade by serving as a medium of exchange in the fur trade. In fact it even passed for legal tender in New England for small debts during the seventeenth century. Its obvious role and value in the fur trade was an important aspect of the Undertakers' shift from fish to furs in the attempt to repay the London creditors.[45]

The operation of the Aptucxet trading post was Plymouth's only regular and ongoing contact with the Cape in the 1620s. Its establishment indicated permanent settlement was possible, and represents a watershed in Plymouth's relations with the Cape. It brought to a close the second phase of Plymouth's contact with the Cape, temporary exploitation, and began the third, permanent settlement.

Although the Pilgrims' exploration of Cape Cod in the late months of 1620 and their visits to it during the ensuing decade had not resulted in permanent settlement, Plymouth was certainly well aware of the Cape's advantages and potential. In the first struggling years of the colony, the Cape had been an invaluable supplier of provisions, and it is possible the colony would have collapsed without the corn and beans sold to it by the Indians. And the Indians themselves had proven uncommonly helpful, not only selling food to starving settlers, but also finding lost boys and rescuing shipwrecked sailors and stranded passengers. In all of these activities, the Plymouth Colony settlers were becoming increasingly familiar with the Cape. With the establishment of the Aptucxet post, they also indicated that the area was in the future to be more than an occasional place to visit for a specific purpose. Plymouth Colony was growing. In addition to the trading expansion necessitated by the agreement to pay the English debt, there was similarly a population growth which made movement northward across Plymouth Harbor to Duxbury desirable. To the lament of Governor Bradford, it was becoming increasingly impossible to confine Plymouth Colony to the bounds of Plymouth Town. In that general expansion of the second decade of Plymouth Colony's history, Cape Cod would come into its own as a place for permanent settlement.

Notes

1. *Mourt's Relation*, p. 69 sets the date as June 11, but Bradford's *Plymouth Plantation*, p. 87 indicates that the expedition actually occurred later the next month. Prince, *Chronological History*, 1:107 and n. argues for the later date, and subsequent historians have agreed. See Ford edition of Bradford's history, 1:224, n. 1. The Billingtons were a sorry trial for the infant colony. John's older brother, Francis, had nearly set fire to the *Mayflower* while playing with the ship's supply of ammunition. The father,

John Billington, Sr. was involved in the Lyford--Oldham affair, and in 1630 was the first person to be hanged in Plymouth, found guilty of murder. It is little wonder Bradford described them as one of the "profanest families" and wondered how they had been mingled into the group leaving England. Bradford, *Plymouth Plantation*, pp. 156-157, 234; *Mourt's Relation*, p. 31.

2. Bradford, *Plymouth Plantation*, pp. 87-88; Young (ed.), *Chronicles*, pp. 217-218, n. 4, points out that there were only nineteen adult males in the colony, and that two of them, Hopkins and Winslow, were already absent when the ten men left for the Cape.

3. *Mourt's Relation*, p. 69.

4. *Mourt's Relation*, pp. 69-70.

5. *Mourt's Relation*, p. 70.

6. *Mourt's Relation*, p. 71.

7. *Mourt's Relation*, pp. 71-72.

8. *Mourt's Relation*, p. 82.   Winslow's description of the first Thanksgiving is found in a letter to an anonymous recipient, dated 11 December 1621 and written in Plymouth Colony. *Mourt's Relation*, pp. 81-87. See also Bradford, *Plymouth Plantation*, p. 90.

9. Bradford, *Plymouth Plantation*, pp. 90-93; *Mourt's Relation*, pp. 84-85. The Pilgrims' first patent had been for a site within the jurisdiction of the Virginia Company, and had not been valid for their New England location. The new patent is known as the second Peirce Patent, dated 1 June 1621. It is on display at the Pilgrim Hall Museum, Plymouth Massachusetts, and is reprinted, along with a facsimile of the original, in the Ford edition of Bradford's history, 1:246-251. See also George D. Langdon, Jr., *Pilgrim Colony: A History of New Plymouth, 1620-1691* (New Haven, 1966), p. 17 (Hereinafter cited as *Pilgrim Colony*); and Stratton, *Plymouth Colony*, pp. 21, 141-142, and 393-397 where the patent is printed.

10. Bradford, *Plymouth Plantation*, pp. 90-92; *Mourt's Relation*, p. 84.

11. Bradford, *Plymouth Plantation*, p. 96.

12. Bradford, *Plymouth Plantation*, pp. 99-100, 102-110; E[dward] W[inslow], *Good Newes from New England: Or A true Relation of things very remarkable at the Plantation of PLIMOUTH in New England*, ed. George E. Bowman, in *The Mayflower Descendant*, 26(1924):12, 14-16 (Hereinafter cited as *Good Newes*).   The version used here was published serially in *The Mayflower Descendant* 25(1923):151-163; 26(1924):11-23, 68-80, 128-138, 150-161.   The work is also included in Young (ed.), *Chronicles*, pp. 269-375.

13. Bradford, *Plymouth Plantation*, p. 111. The letter from Capt. John Huddleston is in ibid., p. 110. See also Winslow, *Good Newes*, 26(1924):12-13, where he notes that he was hampered in his mission by a lack of

sufficient goods on the part of the fishermen and their unwillingness to take "Bils" for what goods they did have. The Pilgrims were beginning to learn the hard lessons they would need to know in order to trade in New England.

14. Bradford, *Plymouth Plantation*, pp. 103-110, 113-114; Winslow, *Good Newes*, 26(1924):14-15.

15. Bradford, *Plymouth Plantation*, pp. 113-114; Winslow, *Good Newes*, 26(1924):16-17.

16. Bradford, *Plymouth Plantation*, p. 114; Winslow, *Good Newes*, 26(1924):17.

17. Winslow, Good Newes, 26(1924):17-18.

18. Winslow, *Good Newes*, 26(1924):18.

19. Winslow, *Good Newes*, 26(1924):18-19.

20. Bradford, *Plymouth Plantation*, p. 114; Winslow, *Good Newes*, 26(1924):19.

21. Bradford, *Plymouth Plantation*, p. 114.

22. Winslow, *Good Newes*, 26(1924):19.

23. Winslow, *Good Newes*, 26(1924):19-20, 22. Winslow departs from his discussion of the search for food to comment quite favorably on the potential for a water route between the Cape Cod and Narragansett Bays in the Manomet area. By implication he suggests both the trade which would eventually develop there and the much later Cape Cod Canal.

24. Winslow, *Good Newes*, 26(1924):21-22.

25. Bradford, *Plymouth Plantation*, p. 117; Winslow, *Good Newes*, 26(1924):70-73.

26. Bradford, *Plymouth Plantation*, pp. 116-119; Winslow, *Good Newes*, 26(1924):75-80, 128-133. The Wessagusset settlement plays an important part in the contemporary accounts of Plymouth Colony at the time, and has engaged historians ever since. Some have stressed the sins of the Wessagusset men and the actuality of a possible Indian attack. They have defended or sympathized with Plymouth. In addition to the sources cited above, Bradford concisely explains Plymouth's view of the Wessagusset affair in his letter, written with Isaac Allerton, to the London Adventurers, dated 8 September 1623, from Plymouth. It is published in *Amer. Hist. Rev.* 8(1902/03):297-299. Phineas Pratt, a Wessagusset settler opposed to the Indians, escaped to Plymouth seeking aid, and his arrival caused Plymouth "to make the more haste" in sending Standish and his contingent to Wessagusset. Bradford, *Plymouth Plantation*, p. 118. See also Pratt's narrative, *A Decliration of the Afaires of the Einglish People [That First] Inhabited New England*, ed. R[ichard] F[rothingham], Jr., in *Collec.*, Mass. Hist. Soc., 4 Ser., 4(1858):474-487. The Pilgrim view is reflected in Nathaniel Morton, *New England's Memoriall*, ed. Howard J. Hall (New

York, 1937), pp. 41-43. Morton's history was originally published in 1669. See also Charles Francis Adams, *Three Episodes*, 1:65-83; and Vaughan, *New England Frontier*, pp. 82-87. Thomas Morton, one of early Plymouth's major thorns, was more critical of the colony's actions. See his *The New English Canaan*, ed. Charles Francis Adams, Publications of the Prince Society, vol. 14 (Boston, 1883), pp. 245-255. Morton's book was originally published in 1637. That he was not related to any of the Mortons in Plymouth should be clear from the tone of his discussion. For an historian's viewpoint which reflects Thomas Morton and sees the issue at Wessagusset as a pretext for a wanton attack on the Massachusetts Indians and an opportunity for Plymouth to rid New England of a group who did not live by the rules of English Puritanism, see Neal Salisbury, *Manitou and Providence: Indians, Europeans, and the Making of New England, 1500-1643* (New York, 1982), pp. 125-133 (Hereinafter cited as *Manitou and Providence*). For a similar view, more stridently expressed, see Francis Jennings, *The Invasion of America: Indians, Colonialism and the Cant of Conquest* (New York, c. 1975), pp. 186-187 (Hereinafter cited as *Invasion of America*). Thomas B. Adams argues that Plymouth's decision to attack was influenced by knowledge of the March 1622 assault on Jamestown. See his "Bad News from Virginia," *Virginia Magazine of History and Biography*, 74(1966):131-140.

27. Winslow, *Good Newes*, 26(1924):133. For a discussion of Iyanough's supposed grave site, see Ripley P. Bullen and Edward Brooks, "Shell Heaps on Sandy Neck, Barnstable, Massachusetts," *Bulletin*, Mass. Arch. Soc. 10(1948/49):12-13.

28. Even John Robinson, living in Holland, recognized that the Pilgrims had been a little overly ambitious in their actions at Weston's settlement and recommended restraint. See his letter to Bradford, Leyden, 19 December 1623, in Bradford, *Plymouth Plantation*, pp. 374-375.

29. Bradford, *Plymouth Plantation*, pp. 99n. 140, 145-147, 201-202, 219-222, 257-260. The fullest discussion of the all important task of satisfying Plymouth's self-seeking, and not always worthy, creditors is Ruth A. McIntyre, *Debts Hopeful and Desperate: Financing the Plymouth Colony* ([Plymouth, MA], c. 1963) (Hereinafter cited as *Debts Hopeful*).

30. Bradford, *Plymouth Plantation*, pp. 127, 132, 139. Winslow, *Good Newes*, pp. 136-137. Edward Winslow returned to England on the *Anne* as an emissary of the colony, and thus his narrative of Plymouth events does not extend beyond her departure. The *Little James* had an extensive history during its brief stay in New England. After its Cape Cod and Narragansett Bay venture, it sailed to the Maine coast to fish, where it sank in a storm. Plymouth men salvaged the vessel, but Turkish pirates captured

her on the return to England, where members of her crew eventually sued for back pay. Bradford, *Plymouth Plantation*, pp. 140, 163, 176-177. For the litigation papers regarding the vessel, which add much to our understanding of the ship and her troubles, see Bradford and Allerton to [Adventurers], in *Amer. Hist. Rev.* 8(1902/03):294-301; and John Bridge to James Sherley, Plymouth, 9 September 1623, as well as Emanuell Altham to Sherley, New England, May [?], 1624, in *Proc.*, Mass. Hist. Soc. 44(1910):178-181, 182-189, respectively. The Altham letter is also in Sydney V. James, Jr. (ed.), *Three Visitors to Early Plymouth: Letters about the Pilgrim Settlement in New England During its First Seven Years* ([Plymouth, MA], c. 1963), pp. 42-52 (Hereinafter cited as *Three Visitors*). John Bridge was the master of the *Little James*, responsible for its sailing; Altham was its captain, responsible for its military and mercantile ventures; and Sherley was Treasurer of the London Adventurers.

31. The ship had run aground on the southern portion of Nauset Beach, near where at one time Chatham Harbor opened to the sea. The place was called Old Ship Harbor long after the remains of the vessel had disappeared and the name had lost its meaning. Amos Otis, "An Account of the Discovery of an Ancient Ship on the Eastern Shore of Cape Cod," *New Eng. Hist. & Geneal. Reg.* 43(1864):37-44 (Hereinafter cited as "Ancient Ship"). Otis makes the geological and archeological arguments to prove that the vessel was indeed the *Sparrowhawk*.

32. Bradford, *Plymouth Plantation*, pp. 189-190.

33. Bradford, *Plymouth Plantation*, p. 190.

34. Bradford, *Plymouth Plantation*, pp. 190-191.

35. Bradford, *Plymouth Plantation*, pp. 191-192. Like the *Little James*, the *Sparrowhawk* has a history beyond Cape Cod and Plymouth, although it is a history that extends chronologically rather than geographically. Shifting sands soon covered the abandoned ship, and eventually a salt marsh meadow grew up over the sunken hull. In May of 1863, the sea reclaimed the marsh, and the remains of the ship appeared near Nauset Beach, where they became quite a local attraction. The wreck was briefly reclaimed by the sand before the summer was over, but when it reappeared, steps were taken to preserve what was left of the ship's framework. Before the *Sparrowhawk* came to its final dockage at the Pilgrim Hall Museum in Plymouth, it had been reconstructed by two ship carpenters, exhibited on Boston Common, and then stored by its owner in Providence, Rhode Island. The owner, C. W. Levermore, who had been a member of the Boston City Council when the ship was exhibited in that city, wrote the Massachusetts Historical Society in 1889 asking what should be done with it. Charles Deane, a vice president of the society responded that it should go to

the Pilgrim Society, and Mr. Levermore subsequently agreed. The society accepted the offer, and the relic is currently on display at the Pilgrim Hall Museum, Plymouth, Massachusetts. Otis, "Ancient Ship," 43(1864): 37-44; Charles W. Levermore and Leander Crosby, *The Ancient Wreck: Loss of the Sparrow-Hawk in 1626*, (Boston, 1865). The most recent, and fullest, discussion of both the construction and history of the Sparrowhawk is Hobart H. Holly, "Sparrow-Hawk, a Seventeenth-Century Vessel in Twentieth-Century America," *American Neptune* 13(1953):51-64. For the correspondence concerning the acquisition of the *Sparrowhawk* by the Pilgrim Society, see Pilgrim Society Meetings, 15 December 1888, vol. 1, box 3, The Pilgrim Society, Pilgrim Hall, Plymouth, Massachusetts. See also [Charles Deane] "Report of Correspondence Regarding the SparrowHawk, "*Proc.*, Mass. Hist. Soc., 2 Ser., 4(1889):217-219; Lucy E. Treat, "Early Wrecks on Cape Cod," *Cape Cod and all the Pilgrim Land* 5(1921):12-14; and Josiah Paine, *A History of Harwich* (Rutland, VT, 1937), pp. 20-24.

36. John Winthrop, *Journal, 1630-1649*, ed. James K. Hosmer, in Original Narratives of Early American History, 2 vols. (New York, c. 1908), 1:55-56 (Hereinafter cited as *Journal*).

37. Bradford, *Plymouth Plantation*, pp. 184-186, which includes the text of the Agreement; McIntyre, *Debts Hopeful*, p. 32; Langdon, *Pilgrim Colony*, pp. 26-29; Stratton, *Plymouth Colony*, pp. 27-28.

38. Bradford, *Plymouth Plantation*, pp. 186-189, 194-196. The agreement between the Undertakers and the Plymouth colonists is on pp. 195-196. See also McIntyre, *Debts Hopeful*, pp. 47-48; Langdon, *Pilgrim Colony*, pp. 29-32; Stratton, *Plymouth Colony*, pp. 28-29.

39. Bradford, *Plymouth Plantation*, p. 195; Winslow, *Good Newes*, pp. 19-20.

40. Bradford, *Plymouth Plantation*, pp. 192-193.

41. Bradford, *Plymouth Plantation*, pp. 192-193; Percival H. Lombard, "The First Trading Post of the Plymouth Colony," *Old-Time New England* 18(1927):70-86 (Hereinafter cited as "First Trading Post); George F. Lombard, "Aptucxet, A Trading Place of the Pilgrims," *Bulletin*, Business History Society, 8(1934):108-111. See also Percival H. Lombard, "The Old Trading Post," *Cape Cod and All the Pilgrim Land* 5(1921):7-9. Lombard's various essays on the Aptucxet fort are reorganized into a single presentation in his *The Aptucxet Trading Post: The First Trading Post of the Plymouth Colony* (Wareham, MA, 1934; repr. Bourne, MA, 1968).

42. Bradford, *Plymouth Plantation*, p. 193.

43. Bradford, *Plymouth Plantation*, p. 193. For a description of the post, see Isaack de Rasieres to Samuel Blommaert, [New Amsterdam], ca.

1628, in James, (ed.), *Three Visitors*, p. 74. The letter is also published in *Collections*, New York Historical Society, 2 Ser., 2(1849):343-354, and in Jameson (ed.), *New Netherland*, pp. 102-115. The post was apparently abandoned after the great hurricane of 1635 blew the roof off the building. Bradford, *Plymouth Plantation*, p. 279. The land must have fallen into private hands by the summer of 1652, as the property is referred to as "formerly" belonging to the company. Nathaniel B. Shurtleff and David Pulsifer (eds.), *Records of the Colony of New Plymouth in New England*, 12 vols., (Boston, 1855-1861; reprint edition., New York, 1968), 3:84 (Hereinafter cited as *Ply. Col. Recs.*). After the hurricane of 1635 the building was allowed to deteriorate and its location forgotten until an interested local historian, John Bachelder, discovered the site in 1850 and excavated part of it in 1852. He submitted a report of his work to the Massachusetts Historical Society in 1857. The site was left only partially excavated until 1926, when the Bourne Historical Society commenced a complete exploration and reconstruction. It has since been completely restored, and is one of the spots where the modern observer may get a glimpse of life in the seventeenth century. See John Bachelder to Massachusetts Historical Society, Monumet, [MA], 27 October 1857, *Proc.*, Mass. Hist. Soc. 3(1857):252-256; William S. Russell, *Pilgrim Memorials, and Guide to Plymouth* (Boston, 1855), pp. 148-150; Lombard, "First Trading Post." For a discussion of the archeological and architectural evidence used to reconstruct the fort, see Percival H. Lombard, "The Aptucxet Trading Post: Its Restoration on the Original Foundations," *Old-Time New England* 23(1933):159-174.

44. Bradford, *Plymouth Plantation*, pp. 202-203; de Rasiere's first letter and Bradford's reply are in ibid., pp. 378-380. There is more correspondence between Plymouth and the Dutch, as well as between Plymouth and England about the Dutch, in "Governor Bradford's Letterbook," *Collec.*, Mass. Hist. Soc., [1 Ser.,] 3(1794):51-57. The letters are also printed in *Collections*, New York Historical Society, 2 Ser., 1(1841):360-367. For de Rasiere's description of Plymouth, see his letter to Blommaert in James (ed.), *Three Visitors*, pp. 75-78. See also Salisbury, *Manitou and Providence*, pp. 150-151.

45. Bradford, *Plymouth Plantation*, p. 203; James (ed.), *Three Visitors*, p. 63.

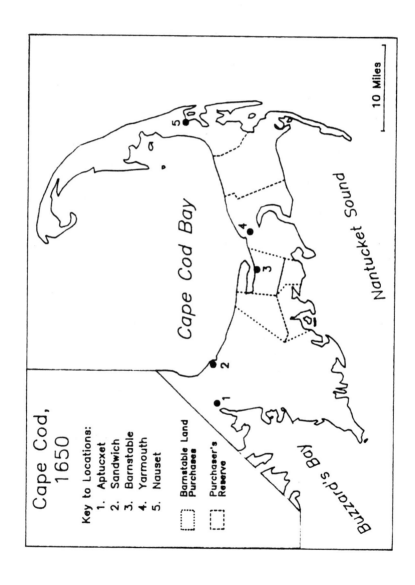

Cape Cod, 1650

Key to Locations:
1. Aptucxet
2. Sandwich
3. Barnstable
4. Yarmouth
5. Nauset

▢ Barnstable Land Purchases

▢ Purchaser's Reserve

Cape Cod Bay

Buzzard's Bay

Nantucket Sound

10 Miles

III

"resolved upon removal"

BY 1635 Plymouth Colony was a distinctly different plantation from what the original passengers of the *Mayflower* had established. No longer a small starving colony, uncertain of its future, it had grown markedly, both by the natural increase of its first settlers and the subsequent arrival of new colonists. As the end of its second decade approached, Plymouth was about to embark on the period of its most significant growth. Certainly, the revision of the contract with the London Adventurers had improved the economic outlook of the colony. While the debt assumed by the Undertakers was extremely large, its payment had been carefully arranged, and would eventually be paid. The accompanying abandonment of the communal property arrangement had created a system of private land ownership which meant that men now worked for their own survival and prosperity rather than the colony's or its investors'. This internal combination of population growth and private property would assuredly have resulted in the expansion of Plymouth Colony by itself, as evidenced in the establishment of Duxbury across the harbor in the late 1620's. But the expansion was further encouraged by the founding of the Massachusetts Bay Colony to the north of Plymouth in 1630. Not only did Plymouth people need more land to produce the grain and cattle they so profitably sold to an expanding Massachusetts, but settlers who originally had come to Massachusetts perceived both

economic opportunity and a more tolerant religious policy in
Plymouth Colony and began moving to it soon after their arrival.

By 1636, with the addition of Duxbury and Scituate, Plymouth
had come to recognize its change in status from a plantation to a
colony. It acted upon that realization when it codified its laws to
create a consistent and stable legal system for its three communities.[1]
Three years later, when the explosion of expansion demanded that the
legislature be made representative, Plymouth Colony had grown to
include seven towns. Three of them were on Cape Cod: Sandwich,
Barnstable, and Yarmouth, and people from the Bay Colony
dominated the founding of each. The other towns of the colony were
Plymouth, Duxbury, Taunton, and Scituate, of which both Taunton
and Scituate had Massachusetts origins.[2] In sum, Plymouth Colony
no longer embraced only those with a Plymouth connection. Five of
its seven communities, including all three on the Cape, were
predominately composed of people from the Bay. Plymouth would
become a far more heterogeneous colony by 1640 than it had been in
1630, and the inherent variety which accompanied the growth, one
might even say progress, would present interesting problems for the
original settlers in their efforts to maintain control over growth and
diversification.

In the final years of the 1630's, Cape Cod became the major area
of Plymouth Colony's expanison.   The colony had secured
jurisdiction over the Cape with the granting of the Warwick Patent by
the Council for New England. Dated 13 January 1629/30, the patent
replaced the earlier Peirce Patent of 1621, and established boundaries
for the colony which included the Cape.[3] With authority over the
peninsula acquired, the colony expanded upon its commercial
involvement at the Aptuxcet trading post, and began to encourage the
creation of permanent settlements on Cape Cod. By the end of the
decade, Sandwich, Barnstable, and Yarmouth were part of the colony,
and five years later Eastham made it a quartet.

The first of the towns to be settled on Cape Cod, Sandwich, is
most closely associated with ten men from Saugus, who on 3 April
1637 received permission to search for a settlement site to
accommodate sixty families.[4] But the real leader of both the Saugus
men and the town of Sandwich was Edmund Freeman, who had
arrived in Massachusetts with his family in October 1635. In addition
to his association with Saugus and Massachusetts, he also had
connections with Plymouth Colony, for he was the brother-in-law of

John Beauchamp, one of Plymouth's English creditors. It is possible Freeman went to Plymouth in search of a place to settle, but he almost certainly went there to inquire as to his kinsman's business interests.[5]

At some point during his time in Plymouth Colony, Freeman met the Reverend William Leveridge, perhaps at Duxbury. Freeman persuaded Mr. Leveridge, along with some of his followers from Plymouth Colony, to join with Freeman and his Saugus associates in establishing a new settlement.[6] They discussed the issue with Governor Bradford and Edward Winslow, who drew up the provisions of settlement. Later, at its 3 April 1637 meeting, the Court of Assistants allowed the Saugus men to search for a site. During the summer, they selected the Sandwich location, and by the winter of 1637 had begun to take up residence, probably to be there when spring planting time arrived. Subsequent developments indicate that by the time the Massachusetts people appeared, the Reverend Leveridge and some of his Plymouth followers were already there.[7] Certainly by the spring of 1638 Sandwich was an established community with a significant population.

Plymouth Colony's acceptance of an outlying settlement was acknowledged in different ways. It was done geographically by establishing boundaries and transferring land rights to the town, or politically by allowing the town to send delegates to the General Court. Indeed, the whole concept of a representative General Court, which replaced the earlier direct participation of all freemen, was the result of the Colony's geographic expansion. It was an acknowledgement by the Colony of the numerous inconveniences and significant expense which resulted when all freemen were required to vote personally in the General Court.[8] In this, Sandwich and the other Cape Cod towns cannot be overlooked in their contribution to this major alteration in the governance of Plymouth Colony.

Politically, Sandwich came of age when it elected Richard Bourne and John Vincent as its Deputies to the June 1639 General Court, the first one under the new representative political system.[9] Sandwich's control over its land was somewhat less direct. While the boundaries of the town were quickly taken care of by appointing Myles Standish and John Alden to accomplish the task, with orders to do it speedily, actual ownership took a good deal longer.[10] William Bradford, acting in association with the Old Comers or Purchasers, bought the land for Sandwich from the Indians in 1637 for sixteen pounds, nineteen shillings in goods. In return for its purchase price, Bradford surrendered the property to Edward Freeman in 1647. In all cases, Freeman and Bradford were acting on behalf of their respective governments, Sandwich and Plymouth.[11]   The delay was in reality only a formality, necessitated by Sandwich's efforts to raise the necessary money.[12]   Saugus grantees in Sandwich behaved as though they owned the land long before Bradford made the transfer.

Within a year or two of Sandwich's settlement, two more towns were established on Cape Cod, Barnstable and Yarmouth.   Their earliest beginnings were somewhat intertwined, but like Sandwich, each had its roots in Massachusetts people interested in moving to Cape Cod. Involvement in the lands which would become Barnstable seems to have occurred first, but there were settlers in both communities before the General Court officially recognized either one.   The beginnings of Barnstable were more similar to Sandwich than were the beginnings of Yarmouth.   Like Sandwich, Barnstable's early settlers were composed of two groups, neither of which had traditional ties with the colony of the *Mayflower* passengers.   The larger of the Barnstable groups, under the leadership of the Reverend John Lothrop, was from Scituate.   On Plymouth's northern border with Massachusetts, Scituate itself was a town originally settled by people from the Bay Colony. The smaller party, under the leadership of Thomas Dimmock and Joseph Hull, came directly from Massachusetts. Yarmouth, on the other hand, was settled by people from a number of Massachusetts towns, as well as some from Plymouth. No controversy seems to have caused their migration to Yarmouth, as it had to Barnstable, and Yarmouth's beginnings were more eclectic, peaceful, and general than the other towns.

The first person apparently interested in the Mattacheese, or Barnstable area, was Richard Collicut of Dorchester, Massachusetts.   Collicut recognized the economic potential which would later draw others to Barnstable and Yarmouth and secured the option of establishing a settlement there, probably as early as 1638. Although he never resided in Barnstable himself, and lost his claim to land in Barnstable, some of those associated with his original request did move to the town.[13] Most notable of them were Joseph Hull, living in the Weymouth section of Dorchester, and Thomas Dimmock, who began his New England career in Hingham, and lived briefly in Dorchester before moving on to Scituate and Barnstable.   Dimmock is generally regarded as Collicut's agent in the settlement of Barnstable, and Hull as the leader of its first settlers.   Dimmock was one of Yarmouth's earliest settlers, and his appointment on 5 March 1638/39 to train the militia at Barnstable is the first official mention of the town by that name.[14] In the midst of the economic pressures and religious squabbles which so wracked Scituate in the middle 1630's, Dimmock may well have moved to Barnstable to avoid the trouble and get on with establishing the settlement, possibly in preparation for the arrival of Joseph Hull and others from Massachusetts.

By the time Dimmock had moved to the Barnstable site, Scituate had become so divided religiously and so straitened for land that emigration was seen as the only alternative. At the heart of the religious furor was a difference over the nature of baptism, with many of the congregation advocating the anabaptist principles of adult baptism by total immersion, a position completely unacceptable to the rest of the congregation, including John Lothrop, the minister. The baptism issue was further complicated by the agitation for religious toleration advocated by William Vassall, a position designed to protect the baptist position in Scituate.[15] The clergyman caught up in the crossfire of these controversies was the Reverend John Lothrop. Accompanied by some thirty of his parishioners, he had come directly to Scituate upon his arrival in Boston in 1634. He had previously served an English congregation in Kent, and quite possibly moved to Scituate to join some of his former Kent parishioners who had preceded him to Plymouth and Scituate.[16]

Unfortunately, a significant lack of sufficient arable land aggravated Scituate's religious problems, and agitation for more land had begun early. On 3 Janaury 1636/37, upon petition of Scituate residents who noted their land was stony and inconvenient for planting, the General Court allowed them to search for a convenient settlement site within the Colony.[17] It was no doubt under this opportunity that people in Scituate became familiar with the lands on Cape Cod. The Cape's appeal was not immediately overpowering, however, and the townspeople were still searching for new land two years later. On 22 January 1638/39 the Court granted eight Scituate men land for a township at Sippican, on the northern shore of Buzzards Bay.[18] But Sippican appeared little better than Scituate, lacking open fields and salt marsh, and was not acceptable to many residents. The problem of where to settle continued to be a concern, and the town held a day of humiliation to discuss the question. By the end of June of the same year, they had decided to go to the Cape. The decision had been hastened by a fear on the part of those who wanted to go, Lothrop among them, that if they did not move to Barnstable soon, they would lose the opportunity. Thomas Dimmock and probably Joseph Hull with others from Massachusetts were already in Barnstable, representing Collicut's interests.[19] If Scituate people were to settle there, they understood the necessity for both prompt action and the support of the Plymouth authorities. Lothrop believed there was collusion between those in Barnstable and some in Scituate to thwart the move to the Cape. In his letter to Governor Prence and William Bradford seeking the assitance of the Plymouth leadership, he made note of "privie undermineing and secret plotting" which he believed were designed to prevent their migration to Barnstable.[20]   Prence and Bradford, desirous of encouraging settlement on the Cape, answered positively. The eradication of Collicut's claim in the spring of 1639 was the Plymouth Court's official response to Lothrop's entreaty. In the process the Court hoped to bring some degree of religious peace to Scituate.

Although the Court was willing to encourage the Scituate people's move to Barnstable, it chose not to grant the land directly to them.   To acknowledge the earlier claims of Collicut and his associates, the Court instead made Joseph Hull and Thomas Dimmock the grantees of Barnstable lands.[21]   The Court was opposed to absentee speculators, but was unwilling to ignore the claims of those with an original interest in the Barnstable territory.

With the decision made, and with the support of the Plymouth Court of Assistants, the Scituate people moved to Barnstable. They were there by 11 October 1639, and held a day of humiliation to give thanks at the end of the month.[22] Shortly after the Lothrop group settled at Barnstable, the town elected its two leaders, Joseph Hull and Thomas Dimmock, as its Deputies to the General Court. They had not been elected in time to sit at the first meeting of the Court as a representative body, but took their places in December of 1639.[23]

Thus by the autumn of 1639 a second community existed on Cape Cod.   Like Sandwich before it, Barnstable had secured its citizens   primarily   from   those   who   had   originally   come   to Massachusetts and moved southward into the seemingly more inviting atmosphere of Plymouth.   That the Cape offered abundant economic advantages in the reaping of salt marsh hay to feed cattle, the availability of cleared planting ground left by the Indians, and the pursuit of fish only made migration the more sensible.

While Scituate's congregation debated its move to Mattacheese, others were moving into the territory just east of its harbor. But the founding of Yarmouth, as the settlement eventually would be called, lacked the kind of individual leader and steward associated with the establishment of either Sandwich or Barnstable. Regrettably, perhaps, Yarmouth lacked its Edmund Freeman or its John Lothrop. Rather, a number of men from various Massachusetts communities, as well as Plymouth, took an interest in the region in the late 1630's, and created a settlement of some sort by the winter of 1638/39. Because the founding of Yarmouth missed the kind of protracted wrangling associated with Barnstable, it occurred more quickly than the latter community. Settlement started later, and recognition happened sooner.

The Reverend Stephen Bachelor has traditionally been viewed as the first settler in Yarmouth, but his stay was brief and the settlement site was later included within Barnstable's boundaries. He had journeyed on foot to the Cape in the winter of 1637/38, but remained there only a year or so, and never received official recognition from Plymouth Colony.[24] Bachelor was succeeded at Yarmouth by a far less homogeneous group of settlers than had settled either Sandwich or Barnstable. Just as the town lacked a central leader, there was a similar want of geographic consistency and group migration in the backgrounds of its first settlers. Those who had an interest in Yarmouth before actual permanent settlement occurred were from Plymouth, the first of whom was Stephen Hopkins. On 7 August 1638 the General Court permitted him to build a house at Mattacheese and to cut silage there for his cattle. The house may have been designed for servants or tenants, as Hopkins received his grant with the provision that his interests in Yarmouth should not cause him to leave Plymouth.[25] Hopkins's representatives most likely were Gregory Armstrong and Gabriel Wheldon. The next month the Court allowed the two men to reside at "Mattacheese" and to take up land there so long as they had the consent of those who controlled it.[26] Apparently some kind of settlement was under way at Yarmouth, and Plymouth was either allowing people to move there or acknowledging and legitimizing the settlement of some few people who were already residents.

Whoever had settled in Yarmouth had migrated there from a variety of New England towns. Twenty-two men can be identified as early settlers of the town, having been grantees of the land, having taken the oath of allegiance, coming to the notice of the General Court, or otherwise being placed in Yarmouth. Of these, four cannot be identified as to their previous place of residence. The remaining eighteen divide into two groups, the slimmest majority from

Plymouth Colony and the rest from Massachusetts. The Plymouth group contained six men from the town of Plymouth and four from Scituate. The Massachusetts band comprised eight men from six different towns. The only consistency, outside of those from Plymouth, was that three of the Massachusetts men, including two grantees of Yarmouth, had migrated there from Cape Ann, perhaps drawn by the separatist tradition of Plymouth at a time soon after the expulsion of Roger Williams from the Bay Colony. The grantees from Cape Ann were Anthony Thacher from Marblehead and Thomas Howes from Salem. The third man was Hugh Tilley, also from Salem. Other than the geographic proximities of the three men from Cape Ann and the group from Plymouth, no outside connection can be made among Yarmouth's first settlers. One comes away from looking at the founding of Yarmouth with the conclusion that while the religious difficulties of Massachusetts may have encouraged some to leave the Bay, Yarmouth's establishment was far more a classic example of the lure of the frontier. Yarmouth offered the same attractions for prospective settlers as the Connecticut River Valley, the western regions of Plymouth Colony, or the other Cape Cod towns. It was simply a question of going where the opportunities were to be found, and no pre-set criteria were needed in order to take advantage of them.[27]

From what then must be regarded as the unrecorded hopes of a rather diverse group of settlers, came the third of the Cape Cod towns. Whatever the actual situation, it is apparent there were people living at Yarmouth by the winter of 1638/39, as four men took the oath of allegiance and fidelity. John Crow and Thomas Howes took it in December, Anthony Thacher in January, and the Reverend Marmaduke Matthews in February.[28] The Court of Assistants fully acknowledged Yarmouth as a settlement when on 7 January 1638/39 it identified Thacher, Howes, Crow, and one John Coite as the grantees of "Mattacheeset," which had come to be called Yarmouth.[29] In addition, Yarmouth proposed thirteen other men for freemanship, but the Court deemed four of them undesirable, and expressed opposition to them.[30] Two months later the names of five additional men are listed as being of Yarmouth when the General Court made orders relative to town affairs.[31] Obviously, by the early spring of 1639, Yarmouth had become a settled community, large enough to be accepted as a town. As with Sandwich, its elected delegates, Thomas

Payne and Philip Tabor, attended the first session of the Colony's new representative assembly.[32]

The settlement of the Cape Cod towns before 1640 had been largely accomplished by people with little or no close association with Plymouth. People from Massachusetts Bay had dominated the leadership of each community, and even those who had migrated to the Cape from within the colony had not come from the village established by the *Mayflower* passengers. In Sandwich Edmund Freeman and his Saugus associates had dominated the settlement; Leveridge and his party were from Duxbury but had not been part of the original Pilgrim founders of the town. In Barnstable the leaders were Hull and Dimmock from Dorchester; Lothrop and his followers moved there from Scituate. The leadership of Yarmouth's settlement was less precisely identified, but the men who were granted control of land distribution were from Massachusetts. Of the six men from Plymouth, only Giles Hopkins, son of the *Mayflower* passenger Stephen, had any identifiable connection with Plymouth's original settlers.[33] Indeed, in each of the three Cape Cod towns, the land grant had been made to men from outside Plymouth Colony. The goal of this procedure was no doubt to encourage the growth of the colony, but not at the expense of dispersing the original Plymouth settlers and their descendants. Certainly the early Pilgrim leaders wished to keep the founding group together, and Bradford openly lamented the development of Duxbury in the late 1620's.[34] By granting land to outsiders, and thus giving them the controlling power, the Plymouth authorities may have hoped to discourage the scattering of their own people by deliberately limiting their opportunities. More likely, the establishment of Duxbury in the late 1620's and Marshfield in the early 1630's had satisfied whatever expansionist urges existed within Plymouth during the first two decades.[35] By the time the pressure rebuilt in the third decade, the town even considered transplanting itself in its entirety to Cape Cod. Out of this interest, and the investigation which followed, came the founding of Eastham. It was the final of the four major settlements on Cape Cod in the seventeenth century, and the only one on the Cape directly involving the people of Plymouth town.

The successes of the first three towns no doubt spurred Plymouth's interest in migration to Cape Cod. But there were concerns within the community itself which also made a move to the Cape desirable. The passengers of the *Mayflower* had not selected especially well in their original choice of Plymouth. The barren and inhospitable soil had forced others to leave earlier, and the establishment of Boston had virtually eliminated Plymouth's role as a port. In the early 1640's much serious thought was given to the idea of abandoning the Plymouth site and reestablishing the community, or at least its congregation, elsewhere. There was much discussion and consultation, and a variety of opinions were expressed. Some were still for remaining in Plymouth, and maintained those interested in moving were more concerned with worldly advancement. Willing to accept the limitations of Plymouth, those disposed to remaining there asserted people could survive in the town if they would be satisfied with their worldly condition. The group favoring migration, however, were determined to migrate and not convinced. They refused to continue in Plymouth, and announced they would move even if the rest of the town did not. Putting the virtue of congregational unity above personal desire, those opposed to abandoning Plymouth condescended to leave it if a satisfactory location could be found that would accommodate the entire group.[36]

Much of the colony's better and closer land to Plymouth had already been granted to others, but the congregation finally agreed to move to Nauset. The site was some fifty miles away and further out along the Cape than the other towns, but was not unfamiliar. It had been the scene of their first encounter with the Indians in 1620, had been visited at the retrieval of young Billington, and most importantly had proven its potential agricultural value during the starvation times of the early 1620's. Part of the territory to be acquired was one of the three parcels reserved for the Purchasers or Old Comers in March 1640/41, when the colony had assumed the land-granting powers of the Warwick Patent. Through the cooperation of those Purchasers, many of whom were Plymouth residents and at least sympathetic to the Nauset project, the leaders of the proposed settlement obtained title to that portion of the future town.[37] The rest of the land they received as an "addition" from the General Court in March 1644/45.[38] To solidify and complete their ownership of the territory, Bradford and the leaders of the settlement purchased the Indian claim to the land, and the Indians confirmed their sale by a deed in 1666.[39]

As the move to the outer Cape became more serious, some in Plymouth began to have second thoughts. Nauset was beyond the outer fringes of the colony's settlements, too remote from the center of Pilgrim society. Plymouth, on the other hand, was in the middle of that society. And while the promise of fertile planting fields was strong, there was a fear that the amount was small and there would not be enough for all current prospective settlers, much less any for future inhabitants. Uncertainty about the future made some believe that a move to the Cape would eventually make them worse off than they then were in Plymouth, and it was decided to dissolve the earlier agreement to migrate as a group. But those "resolved upon removal," who had no doubt pressured the others into the original agreement as well as its subsequent surrender, would not give up their plans.[40] Sometime in the spring or summer of 1645, the emigrants left Plymouth for the Cape.[41]

The leader of those who moved to Nauset was one of Plymouth's most important citizens, Thomas Prence. He had been regularly elected an Assistant and had previously served two terms as governor of the colony.[42] A variety of other prominent Plymouth people joined him, most notably John Doane, Nicholas Snow, Josias Cook, Richard Higgins, John Smalley, and Edward Bangs.[43] Formal acknowledgment of the Cape's fourth town came over the next two years. At its 2 June 1646 meeting, the General Court appointed Samuel Hicks as town Constable, and more importantly granted Nauset the status of township, granting it all the appropriate privileges of such communities.[44] A year later, John Smalley became town Constable, and Nicholas Snow and Edward Bangs surveyors of highways. The election of Josias Cook and Richard Higginson as the town's Deputies to the June 1647 meeting of the General Court indicated Eastham's full membership within the colony.[45] And perhaps the final test of acceptability and participation in colonial affairs was reached the following October. When the General Court taxed the towns for officers' pay, it added Nauset to the list and ordered it to pay forty shillings.[46] The town acquired its current name on 7 June 1651 when the Court declared that Nauset would henceforth be known as Eastham.[47]

Although Bradford had regretted the dispersion of the Plymouth congregation to yet another settlement, the establishment of Eastham on the outer Cape certainly made its positive contributions. It extended the settlement of Englishmen further out along the Cape, and Eastham was the forerunner of those subsequent communities from Pleasant Bay to Race Point. The presence of white settlers in the area must also have given a calming message to the native Indians. The Nausets, from their attack on Champlain to their encounter with the *Mayflower* exploring party, had been one of southern New England's more aggressive tribes. Their later support for Plymouth Colony may in part have been due to the creation of an English town within their domain.

With the establishment of Eastham, the third major phase of Plymouth's relations with Cape Cod came to an end. In the earliest days of the *Mayflower*'s arrival, the colony had explored the Cape and even considered making its permanent settlement on its shores. While it had chosen to settle permanently at Plymouth instead, it had not erased the Cape from its mind. During its first decade, Plymouth continued its contact with the Cape. The colony discovered the productivity of its soil when it went searching for food, and utilized its potential for trade when it established its trading post at Aptuxcet. In the second and third decades of the colony, Plymouth finally exploited the Cape's potential for settlement. While the people of Plymouth satisfied their expansionist yearnings by moving to Duxbury and Marshfield rather than the Cape, new arrivals from Massachusetts siezed upon the hospitality and encouragement of Plymouth to create three communities along its shores, Sandwich, Barnstable, and Yarmouth. Plymouth ultimately joined in this settlement of the Cape by sending a portion of its own people to the Nauset area of the outer Cape. Eastham turned out to be a fourth community in two respects. It was the fourth offshoot of the original Leyden congregation, and it was the fourth town created on Cape Cod during the period of Plymouth Colony's independence. While the expansion onto the Cape can certainly be seen from Plymouth's view as a desirable move in its efforts to become a large and well-established colony likely to survive, the creation of new towns was not without problems for the mother colony. These problems showed themselves early, and should have raised questions about the wisdom of too rapid an expansion and the inclusion of too many unknown people from outside Plymouth.

Notes

1. *Ply. Col. Recs.*, 11:6-24. See also Charles F. Swift, *Cape Cod: The Right Arm of Massachusetts, An Historical Narrative* (Yarmouth, MA, 1897), p. 38 (Hereinafter cited as *Right Arm*).

2. *Ply. Col. Recs.*, 11:31. See also Langdon, *Pilgrim Colony*, pp. 85-86; Stratton, *Plymouth Colony*, p. 68.

3. Bradford, *History of Plymouth* (ed. Ford), 2:69, n. 2. gives the boundaries as set forth by the patent. For a discussion of the various patents issued for the colony, see Samuel E. Morison, "Destination," pp. 396-398, Morison lists all the applicable patents, and prints the texts of those that are extant in ibid., pp. 398-413. The Warwick Patent is on display at the Pilgrim Hall Museum, Plymouth, Massachusetts.

4. *Ply. Col. Recs.*, 1:57.

5. R. A. Lovell, Jr., *Sandwich: A Cape Cod Town* (Sandwich, MA, 1984), pp. 3-5, 7, 28 (Hereinafter cited as *Sandwich*); McIntyre, *Debts Hopeful*, p. 63. Freeman represented Beauchamp in the final settlement of the colony's accounts with its creditors, receiving land from the Undertakers to pay the debt, and in turn selling the land to others in order to send the money to Beauchamp. *Ply. Col. Recs.*, 12:127-133 contain the various legal documents illustrative of Freeman's agency. It is interesting to note that Freeman, who served as an Assistant from 1640 to 1646, was not reelected after he completed his activities on behalf of Beauchamp. While Edward Winslow maintained it was "his professed Anabaptistry and separation from the Churches" which caused his rejection, one cannot help but think that his role in representing one of Plymouth Colony's less than popular creditors may have turned many against him. *Ply. Col. Recs.*, 1:140, 2:8, 33, 52, 71, 83, 115; Edward Winslow to John Winthrop, Plymouth, 4 June 1646, in Allyn B. Forbes (ed.), *Winthrop Papers, 1498-1649*, 5 vols. (Boston, 1929-1947), 5:80 (Hereinafter cited as *Winthrop Papers*). See also Lovell, *Sandwich*, pp. 16, 29-30; Stratton, *Plymouth Colony*, p. 294; Frederick Freeman, *The History of Cape Cod: The Annals of Barnstable County and of Its Several Towns, Including the District of Mashpee*, 2 vols. (Boston, 1860), 2:48-49 (Hereinafter cited as *Cape Cod*).

6. Langdon, *Pilgrim Colony*, p. 50; Stratton, *Plymouth Colony*, pp. 64-65; Lovell, *Sandwich*, pp. 3-5, 7. Educated and ordained in England, William Leveridge had arrived in Salem in 1633. He at first settled in Dover, New Hampshire, moved to Boston in 1635, and then to Duxbury in 1637. He was minister in Sandwich from 1639 to 1653, when he left for Long Island. Frederick Lewis Weis, *The Colonial Clergy and the Colonial Churches of New England* (Lancaster, MA, 1936; repr., Baltimore, 1977), pp. 126-127 (Hereinafter cited as *Colonial Clergy*); Winthrop, *Journal*, 1:111.

7. *Ply. Col. Recs.*, 1:57. It is impossible to state with certainty just who arrived when in early Sandwich. The first Plymouth mention of Sandwich is in reference to a suit brought by Michael Turner against John Davis "for not delivering his goods . . . from Weymouth to Sandwich." The court decision is dated 2 January 1637/38, which connotes that Turner was

living in Sandwich in 1637. *Ply. Col. Recs.*, 8:9. Edmund Freeman became a   freeman on that same date, indicating his residency in the colony. *Ply. Col. Recs.*, 1:74. The earliest Massachusetts reference to the settlement of Sandwich is a 16 January 1637/38 comment on the movement of "many families" from Saugus to Sandwich in Winthrop, *Journal*, 1:259.

8. *Ply. Col. Recs.*, 11:31; Langdon, *Pilgrim Colony*, pp. 85-86; Stratton, *Plymouth Colony*, p. 68.

9. *Ply. Col. Recs.*, 1:126. Apparently Thomas Armitage had been first elected but did not serve. His name is crossed out in the records, and Vincent's substituted.

10. *Ply. Col. Recs.*, 1:80.

11. *Ply. Col. Recs.*, 12:210-212.

12. At its meeting on 7 July 1646, the General Court noted Sandwich had not yet paid "the old company" for the land. *Ply. Col. Recs.*, 2:106.

13. On 1 April 1639 the Plymouth Colony Court of Assistants acknowledged that the people to whom the Mattacheese lands had been first granted, presumably Collicut and others, were not likely to migrate there. *Ply. Col. Recs.*, 1:120. The next month the Court mentioned specifically that if Collicut did not appear personally at Barnstable, then the grant would be voided. *Ply. Col. Recs.*, 1:121. Finally, in March 1644/45, the General Court of the colony ordered that any land of Collicut's in Barnstable was to be seized by the Constable for the use of the colony. *Ply. Col. Recs.*, 2:81. Collicut was active in Massachusetts affairs during this period, serving four terms as a Deputy; supply officer, for the Massachusetts participants in the Pequot War; one of three surveyors of the Dedham-Dorchester town line; licensed for the Indian trade; and one of four men appointed to bring cattle from Providence. *Mass. Col. Recs.*, 1:178, 191, 194, 195, 205, 209, 231, 322, 2:48, 54. See also Richard Cobb, "The Beginnings of Barnstable," (Hereinafter cited as "Beginnings of Barnstable") in Donald G. Trayser (ed.), *Barnstable: Three Centuries of a Cape Cod Town* (Hyannis, MA, 1939; repr., Yarmouthport and Taunton, MA, 1971), pp. 7-8 (Hereinafter cited as *Barnstable*); and O. Herbert McKenney, "The Beginnings" in Barnstable National Bicentennial Commission (comp.), *The Seven Villages of Barnstable* (Barnstable, MA, 1976), pp. 4-8 (Hereinafter cited as *Seven Villages*). Stratton, *Plymouth Colony*, pp. 62-64 has a short survey of Barntable's beginnings. Despite the withdrawal of his grant, Collicut never abandoned his assertion of right to land in Plymough colony. In 1666 there was an agreement to arbitrate his claim, and in February 1667/68 Thomas Danforth of Massachusetts requested Governor Prence to intercede on Collicut's behalf. In 1673 the Plymouth government allowed him 150 acres. Thomas

Danforth to Thomas Prence, Cambridge, 18 February 1667/68, Winslow Papers, 1638-1759, Box 1, #32, used with permission of the Massachusetts Historical Society, Boston, MA; Plymouth Colony Deeds, vol. 3, pt. 1:75; pt. 2:276. The colony's deeds for the period before 1685 are on file at the County Commissiners' Office, Plymouth, MA.

14. Samuel Deane, *History of Scituate, Massachusetts* (Boston, 1831), p. 263 (Hereinafter cited as *Scituate*); Cobb, "Beginnings of Barnstable," pp. 7-8; *Ply. Col. Recs.*, 11:31.

15. Edward Winslow to John Winthrop, Careswell, 10 October 1640, in *Winthrop Papers*, 4:291-292; Bradford, *Plymouth Plantation*, pp. 313-314; Deane, *Scituate*, p. 8; Cobb, "Beginnings of Barnstable," pp. 6-7; John J. Waters, Jr., *The Otis Family in Provinicial and Revolutionary Massachusetts* (Chapel Hill, NC, c. 1968), p. 32. Anabaptism and toleration caused enough concern to prompt a day of humiliation for the Scituate church on 11 November 1636, and Vassall was specifically mentioned as an object of controversy on 28 December 1638. See Ezra Stiles [ed.], "Records of the Beginning of the Churches of Scituate and Barnstable," in "Miscellaneous Papers," no. 501, Stiles Papers, The Beinecke Rare Book and Manuscript Library, Yale University, New Haven, CT, pp. 24, 39. This item is Stiles's copy of Lothrop's autograph record of his pastorates in Scituate and Barnstable. That baptism was an important issue in Scituate, and the cause of Lothrop's departure from it, is indicated by the selection of Charles Chauncy, a believer in immersion, to replace Lothrop. Charles Chauncey, "Life of the Rev. President Chauncy, Written at the Request of Dr. Stiles," *Collec.*, Mass. Hist. Soc. [l Ser.], 10(1809):174. See also Winthrop, *Journal*, 1:332. On Vassall, see Edward Winslow to John Winthrop, [Plymouth,] 24 November 1645, in *Winthrop Papers*, 5:55-56; and Robert Emmett Wall, Jr., *Massachusetts Bay: The Crucial Decade, 1640-1650* (New Haven, CT, 1972), pp. 157-224.

16. Educated and ordained in England, Lothrop left his first pastorate in Kent to assume the leadership of Henry Jacob's church in London when Jacob migrated to Virginia in 1624. As a prominent London dissenter, Lothrop was imprisoned with many of his congregation in 1632. Released two years later, probably to care for his motherless children, Lothrop sailed on the *Griffin*, and arrived in Boston on 18 September 1634 and in Scituate ten days later. Amos Otis, *Genealogical Notes of Barnstable Families*, revised by C. F. Swift, 2 vols. (Barnstable, MA, 1888; repr., Baltimore, 1979, 1991), 2:170-211 (Hereinafter cited as *Genealogical Notes*); John Lathrop, "Biographical Memoir of Rev. John Lothrop," *Collec.*, Mass. Hist. Soc., 2 Ser., 1(1814):163-178 (Hereinafter cited as "Memoir"); Winthrop, *Journal*, 1:134, 136; Lothrop, "Diary," p. 3. See also Weis, *Colonial*

Clergy, p. 129; Swift, *Right Arm, pp. 48-49;* William B. Sprague, *Trinitarian Congregational*, vol. 1, *Annals of the American Pulpit*, advisory ed. Edwin Gaustad (New York, 1866; repr., New York, 1969), pp. 49-51. Given Lothrop's trouble with Baptists in Scituate, it is interesting to note that Lothrop's former London church became Baptist in 1638. William G. McLoughlin, *New England Dissent, 1630 to 1833: The Baptists and the Separation of Church and State*, 2 vols. (Cambridge, 1977), 1:5. For a brief summary of Lothrop's early career, see Walter R. Goehring, *Being an Account of the Gathering of the Church Body . . . And particularly of the West Parish Meetinghouse* (West Barnstable, MA, 1959).

17. *Ply. Col. Recs.*, 11:25.

18. *Ply. Col. Recs.*, 1:108. Less than two years later, more land was granted, but adjacent to the town along the North River. *Ply. Col. Recs.*, 1:168. By then, of course, there were far fewer Scituate residents, as Lothrop and his followers had left for Barnstable.

19. The position of Hull is difficult to determine. That he was from Massachusetts and one of the founders of Barnstable is certain. What is less sure is the nature of his contribution. He was indeed a clergyman, having been educated at Oxford and having served as a rector in Devon. He may have ministered to a congregation in Weymouth, but there is little specific evidence that he moved to Barnstable as the clerical leader of a band of religious dissidents. Certainly he did not serve for Barnstable the role Leveridge did for Sandwich or Lothrop would for Barnstable. It is possible no congregation was formed in Barnstable while Hull was its only trained clergyman, and that he functioned only as a lay leader. There is no evidence of his being ordained in Barnstable. Most telling of all, he was elected as one of the town's first Deputies to the Plymouth General Court, an office clergymen did not hold. Weis, *Colonial Clergy*, p. 113; *Ply,. Col. Recs.*, 1:126.

20. John Lothrop to Thomas Prence, Scituate, 18 February 1638/39, in Lathrop, "Memoir," pp. 171-173. See also a similar letter to Prence, dated the previous September in ibid. pp. 173-175, in which Lothrop asserts that he and his people in Scituate "stand stedfast in our resolution to remove our tents and pitch elsewhere." The letters are also reprinted in Otis, *Genealogical Notes*, 2:198-201. By the time Lothrop wrote, Thomas Dimmock had already been appointed militia leader at Barnstable. Others as well had been interested in the area, and had probably moved there, although it is impossible to tell whether they went to Barnstable or Yarmouth. The cause of the confusion comes primarily from the failure of the official records to be precise. Mattacheese (Barnstable) in it various spellings, and

Mattacheeset (Yarmouth) in its, are used interchangeably in the Plymouth Records to refer to settlement in the Barnstable Bay region. The modern historian is forced to rely on the writings of nineteenth century historians and antiquarians to identify certain individuals with specific places. See especially the histories of Cape Cod written in the nineteenth century: Freeman, *Cape Cod*; Simeon Deyo (ed.), *History of Barnstable County Massachusetts* (New York, 1890) (Hereinafter cited as *Barnstable County*); and Swift, *Right Arm*. After the creation of counties in Plymouth Colony in 1685, Barnstable County and Cape Cod became virtually synonymous terms.

21. The assignment of lands at Barnstable to Hull and Dimmock is not noted in the published records of Plymouth Colony. It appears only as a confirmatory deed prepared by Thomas Hinckley and Barnabas Lothrop in response to a concern in Barnstable about the Dominion of New England's challenge to land titles. It is dated 14 July 1685. Plymouth Colony Deeds, vol. 5, pt. 2:37. Trayser (ed.), *Barnstable*, pp. 23-26 contains a discussion and transcript of the confirmatory deed. See also ibid., pp. 172-173; and Cobb, "Beginnings of Barnstable," in Trayser (ed.), *Barnstable*, pp. 24-26. The text of the deed is also in Barnstable (comp.), *Seven Villages*, pp. 495-497. For a discussion of Plymouth's dismissal of Collicut's claims to Barnstable land, see fn. 13, this chapter. For Hinckley and Lothrop's charge from the town to search the Plymouth records for Barnstable's original grant and to determine if there was any defect in it, see Barnstable Town Records, 1640-1753, p. 126. Local records from the seventeenth century are generally in deplorable condition, being fragile, faded, and difficult to read. Transcriptions were made in the nineteenth century, and the Church of Christ of Latter-day Saints microfilmed both the originals and the transcripts in the 1970's. For all local records of the Cape Cod towns consulted in this study, I have used the microfilm copies of the nineteenth-century transcripts available through the church's genealogical services.

22. Lothrop, "Diary," pp. 9, 25. See also Cobb, "Beginnings of Barnstable," pp. 9-11. On 11 December 1639 the town held a day of thanksgiving "for Gods exceeding mercye in bringing us hither Safely keeping us healthy & well in our weake beginnings." Lothrop, "Diary," p. 31. John Winthrop noted Barnstable as one of the a number of new settlements begun in the summer of 1639. *Journal*, 1:308.

23. *Ply. Col. Recs.*, 1:126.

24. Winthrop, *Journal*, 1:266; Charles F. Swift, *History of Old Yarmouth, Comprising The Present Towns of Yarmouth and Dennis: From The Settlement To The Division in 1794, With The History of Both Towns To 1876*, ed. Charles A. Holbrook, Jr. (Yarmouth Port, MA, 1975), p. 21 (Hereinafter cited as *Old Yarmouth*); *Ply. Col. Recs.* 2:21-22. Though brief,

Bachelor's New England career was a fascinating one. He was no stranger to controversy, having been brought before the Star Chamber Court in 1613 for libel, the result of a suit brought by one Reverend George Widley, of whom Bachelor had written some humorous verses of a less than complementary nature. Bachelor had originally migrated to Massachusetts and settled as pastor in Lynn. His troublesomeness, which in New England seems to have centered on his pursuit of handsome women, soon became evident. In 1632 the Massachusetts Court restricted his freedom to preach because of his "contempt of authority, and till some scandles be removed," although it reversed the sentence six months later. He was in trouble again in Lynn in 1636 and probably left for Yarmouth to escape the Bay Colony's jurisdiction. After leaving the Cape, he settled in Hampton, where personal and religious controversy continued to surround him, and he eventually returned to England. During Bachelor's second sojourn in Massachusetts, his church excommunicated him. *Mass. Col. Recs.*, 1:100, 103, 236; Winthrop, *Journal*, 1:80-81, 169, 266, 2:45-46, 179, 221; John Cotton to Stephen Bachelor, Boston, 9 April 1641, Cotton Papers, pt. 3, #2, The Prince Library, Rare Books and Manuscripts, by courtesy of The Trustees of the Boston Public Library, Boston, MA. Weis, *Colonial Clergy*, p. 23; Trayser (ed.), *Barnstable*, pp. 178-180; Charles E. Banks, "Early New Englanders in Chancery," *Proc.*, Mass. Hist. Soc. 60(1926/27):131-144. See also Swift, *Right Arm*, pp. 42-43; Swift, *Old Yarmouth*, chap. 3; and Stratton, *Plymouth Colony*, pp. 65-67 for accounts of Yarmouth's founding.

  25. *Ply. Col. Recs.*, 1:93.

  26. *Ply. Col. Recs.* 1:95.

  27. The Plymouth men were Gregory Armstrong, Joshua Barnes, Andrew Hallett, Sr., Giles Hopkins, Gabriel Wheldon, and Peter Worden, Sr. Exception was taken to Worden for unspecified reasons, but he moved there anyway. He died in Yarmouth shortly after his arrival. James Savage, *A Genealogical Dictionary of the First Settlers of New England*, 4 vols. (Boston, 1860), 4:504 identifies Whelden with Malden (Hereinafter cited as *Genealogical Dictionary*). The Scituate representatives were William Chase, Thomas Hatch, William Palmer, and Thomas Starr. The Massachusetts immigrants were John Crow, Charlestown; Thomas Howes, Salem; the Reverend Marmaduke Mathews, a new arrival in Massachusets at the time of Yarmouth's settlement; William Nickerson, Watertown; Nicholas Simpkins, Boston; Philip Tabor, Watertown; Anthony Thacher, Marblehead; and Hugh Tilley, Salem. The four of whom nothing is known as to their background were Robert Dennis, William Lumpkin, Thomas Payne, and Samuel Rider. *Ply. Col. Recs.*, 1:93, 95, 107, l08-109, 116, 117; *Mass. Col. Recs.*, 1:99,

114, 115, 154, 157, 165, 174, 181, 183, 191, 273, 401; Winthrop, *Journal*, 1:277; Savage, *Genealogical Dictionary*, 1:64, 121, 365, 479, 2:38, 340, 375, 461, 478, 3:130, 176-177, 284, 336, 343, 540, 4:101, 171, 247, 270-271, 302, 504, 651; Swift, *Old Yarmouth*, pp. 22, 69; Swift, *Right Arm*, p. 44; Stratton, *Plymouth Colony*, pp. 245, 307-308; Weis, *Colonial Clergy*, p. 137. For brief biographies of the three grantees and the minister, see Swift, *Old Yarmouth*, pp. 46-48 (Thacher), 48-49 (Crow), 49-50 (Howes), and 54-55 (Mathews).

28. *Ply. Col. Recs.*, 1:107.

29. *Ply. Col. Recs.*, 1:108. Coite's interest in Yarmouth raised questions, as the Court noted he was "to be enquired of," and he apparently never migrated. Coite may have been part of the Cape Ann group, as there was one by that name living in Marblehead. Stratton, *Plymouth Colony*, p. 65.

30. *Ply. Col. Recs.*, 1:108-109. One of the four "excepted against," was "Old Worden" (Peter, Sr.), mentioned previously.

31. *Ply. Col. Recs.*, 1:116-117.

32. *Ply. Col. Recs.*, 1:126.

33. Bradford, *Plymouth Plantation*, pp. 441-443; Stratton, *Plymouth Colony*, pp. 307-308; Swift, *Old Yarmouth*, 50-51, 74. Yarmouth lost its direct *Mayflower* connection when Hopkins moved to Eastham.

34. Bradford, *Plymouth Plantation*, pp. 252-253.

35. Langdon, *Pilgrim Colony*, pp. 38-39; Stratton, *Plymouth Colony*, pp. 48, 58-60.

36. Bradford, *Plymouth Plantation*, p. 333. The same narrative can be found in *Plymouth Church Records, 1620-1859*, 2 vols. in *Collections* series, *Publications* of the Colonial Society of Massachusetts 22, 23(1920, 1923):1:84 (Hereinafter cited as *Ply. Church Recs.*). That it was a congregational concern is evidenced by the failure of the debate over Eastham to appear in the Plymouth town records. W. T. Davis, (ed.), *Records of the Town of Plymouth*, 3 vols. (Plymouth, MA, 1889-1903), 1:11-20. See also a letter of Edward Winslow to John Winthrop, Plymouth, 28 March 1645, in *Winthrop Papers*, 5:17, where he refers to those desiring to leave as "unsettled br[ethre]n." It is doubtful Winslow intended the pun.

37. *Ply. Col. Recs.*, 2:10-11 contains the text of the Purchasers' agreement. It is reprinted in Bradford, *Plymouth Plantation*, pp. 428-430. There were fifty-eight names listed, fifty-three colonists and five English investors. They are identified in *Ply. Col. Recs.*, 2:177. A comparison of that list with a roster of Plymouth men eligible for military service dated 1643, about the time of the migration to Nauset, indicates at least twenty Purchasers were still living in Plymouth. And three of the Purchasers,

Prence, Bangs, and Snow would be among Nauset's first settlers. Obviously those concerned with the planned migration to the Cape coincided significantly with those who controlled a large portion of the potential settlement site. *Ply. Col. Recs.*, 8:187-189. For a discussion of Bradford's surrender of the patent and its significance in the development of representative government and land policy, see Langdon, *Pilgrim Colony*, pp. 40-41; and Stratton, *Plymouth Colony*, pp. 75-76.

38. Bradford, *Plymouth Plantation*, p. 333; *Ply. Col. Recs.*, 2:81. The tract reserved for the Purchasers was down the Cape from Yarmouth's eastern border, three miles east of Maemskeckett Creek, and from sea to sea. *Ply. Col. Recs.*, 2:10. The land granted by the Court went from the Purchasers' outer boundary to Herring Brook at Billingsgate, also from sea to sea. *Ply. Col. Recs,,* 2:81. The territory was the largest of the Cape Cod grants, inlcuding everything from modern Brewster and Harwich at one end to Wellfleet at the other.

39. Plymouth Colony Deeds, vol. 3, pt. 2:278. See also Mass. Archives, 33:12-17. The 1666 deed is reprinted in *Proc.*, Mass. Hist. Soc. 44(1910/11):257-260.

40. Bradford, *Plymouth Plantation*, p. 334.

41. The arrival of the first settlers at Nauset is usually given as 1644, after the Julian calendar which used March as the first month of the new year. The grant from the General Court is more accurately dated 3 March 1644/45, rather than simply 1644. Groups of settlers did not usually occupy new towns without the sanction of a land grant from the General Court, and certainly people from Plymouth would be the least likely to do so. Similarly, the wording of the grant makes it unlikely settlement had occurred before land was granted *Ply. Col. Recs.*, 2:81. Also, Edward Winslow's letter to John Winthrop about the founding of Eastham bears the date 28 March 1645. See footnote 36 this chapter. For the 1644 date, see Enoch Pratt, *A Comprehensive History, Ecclesiastical and Civil, of Eastham, Wellfleet and Orleans, County of Barnstable, Mass. from 1644 to 1844* (Yarmouth, MA, 1844), pp. 11-12 (Hereinafter cited as *Eastham*); and Alice A. Lowe (comp.), *Nauset on Cape Cod: A History of Eastham*, 2d ed. (Eastham Historical Society, c. 1968), pp. 11-13. Josiah Paine recognized but did not explain the error in "Eastham and Orleans Historical Papers," *Library of Cape Cod History and Genealogy*, no. 55 (Yarmouthport, MA, 1914), p. 1. Bradford touchingly compared the departure of the Nauset settlers to "an ancient mother grown old and forsaken of her children . . . like a widow left only to trust in God." Nauset was the third church to be created from the

original Plymouth congregation. Duxbury and Marshfield were the first and second. Bradford, *Plymouth Plantation*, p. 334 and n. 2.

42. *Ply. Church Recs.*, 1:85; *Ply. Col. Recs.*, 1:21, 32, 36, 48, 79, 116, 140.

43. Morton, *New England's Memoriall*, p. 121; Pratt, *Eastham*, p. 12. Biographies of these seven men can be found in ibid., pp. 13-21. Doane was a Deacon in the Plymouth Church and had been twice elected an Assistant, but released from serving the second time because of his church responsibilities. He was also selected as one of Plymouth's first Deputies, but did not serve for the same reason. *Ply. Col. Recs.*, 1:15, 23, 121, 126. The other five men had similarly served in positions of public responsibility, although not at the level of Prence or Doane. See *Ply. Col. Recs,,* 1:*passim.* The Richard Higgins of the *Plymouth Church Records* and the Richard Higginson of the *Plymouth Colony Records* are probably the same individual.

44. *Ply. Col. Recs.*, 2:102.

45. *Ply. Col. Recs.*, 2:117.

46. *Ply. Col. Recs.*, 2:119.

47. *Ply. Col. Recs.*, 11:59.

IV

"causes and controversies amongst the inhabitants"

MEMBERS of the English Puritan movement, in any of their various interpretations of it, were firm believers in their faith, and willing to act decisively in support of their convictions. The Scrooby migration to Holland and the Winthrop fleet's arrival in New England are only two of the better known examples of that resolve. In its own way, the same devotion to one's beliefs is evident in the migration to Cape Cod. Lothrop's antagonism towards the anabaptist position and his leadership of the migration to Barnstable is the most obvious example of such dedication relative to Cape Cod. Although Leveridge's religious authority in the move to Sandwich is less obvious, it certainly illustrates the leadership role performed by Puritan clergymen. The debate in Plymouth over transplanting to Nauset delineates yet another Puritan ideal; the unity of the congregation. At some level or another, then, the establishment of towns on Cape Cod depicts some basic Puritan idea about the implementation of religious concepts.

But Puritans were also practical people, not immune to the worldly benefits which might result or accompany their religious principles and actions. Both Bradford and Winthrop recognized the practical aspects of their ventures, and dealt openly with both the attractions and obstacles which were part of any migration to the New World in the seventeenth century.[1] Much the same can be said for those interested in moving to Cape Cod. Lothrop led a company of followers who needed land, and Leveridge surely recognized the economic opportunities of Sandwich. For Dimmock and Hull in Yarmouth, those opportunities were primary. Although the supply was not abundant, improved planting fields were a major goal of the move to Eastham.

Thus, in the establishment of the first three towns on Cape Cod, religious controversy and economic opportunism had played complementary roles. But migration to the Cape did not solve or cure the problems which had generated it. Religious dispute and a concern for protecting one's economic interests continued to be a part of those settlements in their early years. While personal and community problems in established towns may have been at least partially resolved by the movement of a group of dissidents out of town, migration did not in any way eliminate controversy as a basic thread in the fabric of society. Economic opportunity had been a strong attraction of the Cape, and in an agrarian economy, it was only natural that squabbles over land should be a major source of conflict. Similarly, religious wrangling had been behind a good deal of the migration to the Cape, but did not disappear because dissidents moved. In each of the first three towns a major controversy developed over either or both issues. In each case it was a clash between groups of settlers who had migrated to the Cape from different places. And in each situation the colonial government in Plymouth intervened to wrestle with the problem. Plymouth Colony was expanding, but the government created by the *Mayflower* passengers certainly intended to see that growth was at least as peaceful and orderly as possible.

Land distribution developed into a major controversy in both Sandwich and Yarmouth, and in each community it was not long in coming. The problem resulted from the method used to distribute land in Plymouth Colony before 1640. In the granting of land for the first three Cape Cod towns, Plymouth Colony followed the pattern established under the Warwick Patent of 1629/30. That patent conferred title to Plymouth's land upon William Bradford and a group of undefined "associates." They were most likely those who had bought out the London investors in 1627 and thereafter referred to as "Purchasers" or "Old Comers." While it was the Court of Assistants which actually granted land on Cape Cod prior to 1640, it no doubt did so in the name of the associates. Indeed, a majority of those elected as Assistants during the period had been among the 1627 Purchasers.[2] But no matter in whose name the Assistants granted land, for all practical purposes land distribution was under the control of a relatively small group of individuals. When the Assistants distributed the colony's lands to other groups of individuals in order to establish new settlements, it duplicated the colony's system. Just as the Assistants controlled land distribution for the colony, "grantees," sometimes called "committees," were responsible for its distribution at the local level. And just as those who received land from the Assistants took what was given them, "townsmen," or inhabitants, in the various new settlements received what the grantees wanted to distribute. The prospect for conflict between a small band of givers and a large group of recipients should be so obvious as to be expected.

Nowhere is the problem more clearly illustrated than in Sandwich. Not only were the settlers divided between grantees and townsmen, but each group had its roots in different towns. The Plymouth group, under the Reverend Leveridge's leadership, was the first to settle in Sandwich. They were the townsmen, and had arrived in the early winter of 1637. Freeman and the Saugus, Massachusetts, troop, who were the grantees, soon followed. Almost immediately, controversy over land holdings arose, and within months the Plymouth-connected townsmen petitioned the General Court about land grants in Sandwich.

At its June 1638 meeting, the General Court took up a set of questions regarding land at Sandwich submitted by the Reverend Leveridge and a group of Sandwich residents, representative of the concerns of settlers from Plymouth. The thrust of the issue was the power of the Saugus grantees in relation to the settlers from Plymouth. The Plymouth people were fearful that the Massachusetts grantees had been given unlimited control over the land, and thereby the economic future of Sandwich. Freeman and the Massachusetts people had possibly asserted their position as grantees more aggressively than necessary, creating fear among the Plymouth men and a desire on their part to be sure of their right to the land. Certainly the settlers from Plymouth did not want to become the victims of speculators from Massachusetts.

In general the Court attempted to strike a balance between the legitimate interests of the Saugus grantees and the anxieties of the Plymouth petitioners. The Court had previously adopted the position that Plymouth people were to be protected in matters of land distribution, and its intervention in the Sandwich controversy would be an effort to reconcile two contrasting land programs within the colony. On the one hand, the colony desired to encourage expansion, and therefore had granted land to the Saugus men. On the other, it wanted to insure that Plymouth people were protected in their participation as part of that expansion.[3] The Court acknowledged the ownership position of the Saugus grantees, but attempted to alleviate the petitioners' qualms by stressing the conditional nature of the April 1637 grant and emphasizing that absentee speculators had not been part of the plan.[4]

Sandwich divided its concerns into six "Propositions," and the General Court provided an answer to each of them. To the question whether the undertakers had received full title to the lands at Sandwich, the Court tellingly responded that it preferred the word "committies" to "undertakers," probably because undertaker implied an independence, permanence, and power the Court did not intend. Undertakers was what the holders of the fur trade monopoly had been called ten years before, and was not a label the Court wished to attach to non-Plymouth land grantees. The Court then stated the grant at Sandwich had been conditional rather than absolute, and had been given for the mutual benefit of both the Saugus settlers and the Plymouth government in order to encourage settlement. The next three questions dealt with the role of those living in Saugus, their rights to own lands in Sandwich, and questions regarding replacement settlers. The Court's answer was favorable to the Plymouth interest in all three issues, stressing that only inhabitants could own land, and that substitutes were acceptable, provided those chosen were acceptable to the town. To the problem of the potential for the abuse of power by the grantees, the Court replied that those with power to distribute land were expected to do so justly. The last question, and in many ways the most immediately important one, was whether it was an abuse of power by the grantees if they monopolized the best land for themselves to the disadvantage of the town in general, and the specific detriment of those from Plymouth. To this direct, precise, and practical inquiry, the petitioners got a rather vague and political answer, designed to calm the fears of the Plymouth petitioners, but not threaten the interests of the Saugus party. The Court acknowledged that such a situation might happen, but pointed out that the land interests of the grantees had to be provided for. Hoping for the best, the Court indicated it trusted the grantees to be responsible and just, and that it expected all residents of Sandwich to recognize the committee's efforts would require more than an ordinary amount of good will.

The Plymouth General Court had responded to the whole problem in a most evenhanded manner. It had indicated that settlement, not speculation, was the purpose of the Sandwich grant, and that the Court expected all settlers, regardless of origin, to be treated without excessive prejudice. While the Court no doubt hoped that Sandwich settlers would make the necessary accommodations so as to settle the town's land problems, it would soon find it had failed. Feelings were strong in Sandwich, and apparently not to be easily moderated. Even as early as this first petition, there had been an inquiry whether two communities might be created. To this proposal, the Court responded negatively. The residents of Sandwich were required to settle their dispute as one body.

Compelled, then, to divide their land among both groups of residents, the Sandwich grantees did just that, and by the late winter of 1638/39 had accomplished the task. But it was not done to the satisfaction of all residents, and at its March 1638/39 meeting, the General Court took up the issue a second time. It attempted to answer the concerns of the townsmen recipients by ordering that Sandwich's meadow land be redivided, and that some of those from Plymouth be added to the Saugus grantees to do it.[5] Even this joint venture by the contending parties met with dissatisfaction. At its September 1639 session, the General Court took up a complaint regarding this second attempt at a division. The charge in the complaint had less to do with inequality of grants, and more to do with the nature of the recipients, who were described as "divers persons unfitt for church societie." But land remained an issue. The complaints also indicated that it was these undesirable individuals who had received the largest portion of the land. Not only was land being distributed inequitably, but the beneficiaries were the wrong kind of people. In response, the Court required members of the distribution committee to answer the complaint at the next General Court and ordered them not to distribute any more land in Sandwich until after they had been answered the summons.[6]

The Court also attempted to increase its influence in Sandwich, by sending its own representatives to Sandwich. The Court appointed Myles Standish and Thomas Prence, two Assistants probably chosen at the September meeting, to investigate the problem and settle the controversy between the grantees and the inhabitants of Sandwich.

Acting as moderators and arbitrators between the contentious factions, the two men held a meeting in Sandwich on 3 October 1639 and began making adjustments in Sandwich land holdings. They reserved three sections for public use as common land, including Moonuscaulton and Shame Necks, as well as acreage of Joseph Winsor, for which he was compensated. To prevent the influx of any more undesirable settlers, it was agreed that in the future no new settlers would be allowed in Sandwich without the prior consent of Mr. Leveridge and the church. And finally, in order to maintain an official finger in the Sandwich land pie, Standish and Prence ordered that town leaders would in the future select one of the Assistants, with whom they could consult and receive advice regarding town problems. For the immediate future the responsibility fell to Thomas Prence.[7]

Although they had solved the problem of undesirable settlers by making Leveridge, one of the townsmen, responsible for the admission of new settlers, Prence and Standish had not dealt with the core of the Sandwich controversy, the land holdings of individuals. On 16 April of the following year, Prence, now joined by John Alden, was back in Sandwich to make a final determination of the question. A new group was formed, composed of five of the Saugus grantees, five of the Plymouth townsmen, and Thomas Prence. The Court directed these eleven men to examine the meadow land, to balance the wealth and social position of the individual with the quality and condition of the land, and finally to assign to each man a proportion of land deemed equitable and suitable to his needs and abilities.[8] The Court also made a number of stipulations, designed to state the rules publicly so as to avoid controversy, and also to insure that each man's portion would be properly surveyed and protected.[9] With a committee formed and a set of regulations to guide it, the problem of dividing Sandwich's meadow land proceeded to a solution.

Part of the committee's obligation was to insure that what was agreed upon would be committed to the public record, implying permanence and protection for the individual.[10] As a result, each man's specific grant became part of the Court's official minutes. Two things are clear. The general nature of the division was such that the townsmen, most of them residents originally from Plymouth, received only small grants of land, while large tracts were reserved for the ten men from Saugus, the grantees. The committee distributed a total of 339.5 acres in fifty-seven grants to fifty-six men. Eight of them received over half of all the land, 179 acres. In contrast, thirty-one men, well over half the total, divided up seventy and one-half acres, each receiving a parcel of four acres or less. It was the Saugus men, rather, who were the major recipients of the larger grants. The ten men identified as grantees by the Court in April 1637 received 172 acres, over half the land. The five of their number who served on the distribution committee received 113 acres, one-third of the total, for an average grant of over 22 acres each. In contrast, the five townsmen representing the Plymouth residents received a total of forty and one-half acres, slightly over 8 acres each.[11] Clearly, the Saugus grantees represented the economic elite in Sandwich. They had been entrusted with dividing up the land, and even when forced to share responsibility with men from Plymouth and under the supervision of Thomas Prence, they had managed to dominate the distribution. On their behalf, it must be admitted they had been granted the land, and it was theirs to distribute. But given the final outcome, the complaints that brought agents from the Plymouth government to Sandwich and the earlier petition of William Leveridge seem to have had great validity. There indeed had been a problem, and the colonial government had been required to send its agents to solve it. They had been generally successful. While it is impossible to know how personally well-satisfied each Sandwich landowner actually was, the issue passes from the records of the colony, indicating that at the very least dissatisfaction had been significantly reduced.

The Sandwich land controversy had also had an impact on the colony. At a February 1638/39 meeting, even before the Sandwich problem had been settled, and in a desire to prevent a duplication elsewhere, the Court of Assistants laid down some general rules for the grantees of new settlements. The instructions clearly reflect the problems presented by Sandwich. The Court directed the future grantees to allow the settlement of only those people who were faithful and peaceful, and to distribute land fairly, according to the rank, estate, and quality of the recipient.[12]

In contrast to Sandwich, Barnstable's early problems were far more religious than economic, as befitted a community where theological issues had been a major motivation for its establishment. If there was any dissension between grantees and townsmen in Barnstable it did not develop to any noticeable degree. Hull and Dimmock were the only identifiable grantees, and either they took less land as a way to prevent a repetition of the Sandwich experience in Barnstable, or because there were only two of them the problem did not appear as significant to the townsmen. It is also possible the townsmen under Lothrop's leadership had enough power to prevent an excess of greed on the part of the grantees.

Even the religious dispute was more personal than doctrinal. The controversy resembled the land problem in Sandwich in that it turned primarily on the conflicting loyalties and interests of people who had come to Barnstable from different places. The issue revolved around the relative positions of Joseph Hull and John Lothrop. Hull had arrived in Barnstable first, and while he apparently did not perform the role of ordained clergyman, he no doubt had his followers among the Massachusetts people. With the arrival of Lothrop and the Scituate settlers, there was a population large enough to support a congregation, and Lothrop expected to be its minister. Hull may have had ambitions for the position, but the selection seems never to have been in doubt. In the beginning, the two men cooperated, with Hull participating as a member of Lothrop's congregation. The townspeople used Hull's home as a meeting house for Barnstable's first Day of Thanksgiving on 11 December 1639, and his was one of the three houses where the congregation went to feast in honor of the event.[13] Hull assisted in the investing of John Mayo as Teaching Elder in April 1640, and had two daughters baptized into the Barnstable church, one in 1639 and the other in 1641.[14]

But Hull was dissatisfied with his role in Barnstable. Despite his position as one of the town's Deputies and one of its grantees, he must have longed to reestablish himself as a minister leading a congregation. Early in 1641 Hull moved to Yarmouth to establish its second church, composed of a few followers from Barnstable and those dissatisfied with the Yarmouth minister, Marmaduke Mathews. Hull was in trouble from the beginning. A number of Barnstable men sued him for trespass or debt, and on 1 May 1641 the Barnstable congregation excommunicated him for his having left it for the pastorate at Yarmouth.[15] The issue was still a matter of concern two years later, when the Plymouth General Court entered the controversy. At its March 1642/43 meeting, the Court issued a warrant directing Yarmouth's constable to apprehend Hull if he should act as a clergyman so that Hull could be made to answer for his actions.[16] Hull apparently recognized his problem, for he returned to the Barnstable fold, and on 10 August 1643, acknowledged his error, renewed his covenant, and was welcomed back into the church.[17]

The return did not mean the end of Hull's difficulties in Barnstable nor the end of Lothrop's problems with dissatisfaction. There was still no room for Hull as a minister in Barnstable, and with the collapse of his cattle business, he finally left the town to settle elsewhere.[18] And Lothrop continued to face hostility from some of his parishioners, no doubt those who had supported Hull or believed he had been badly treated. Lothrop's diary records a number of excommunications of its members, far more than one would expect, and for reasons which hint of retribution.[19] As late as the summer of 1646, Lothrop noted the animosity and lack of religious earnestness in Barnstable, when he recorded a day of humiliation to encourage personal reformation, especially regarding the "deadnes and drousynes in publique dutyes."[20] Barnstable and its minister certainly had their problems. While Joseph Hull was obviously not responsible for all of them, his presence had given focus and leadership to the disaffected.

If the controversy in Sandwich had been largely political and economic, and the one in Barnstable more personal and religious, the problems in early Yarmouth were a combination of the two. It is difficult to determine not only which of the issues was the more important, but even whether one of them actually predominated. The two problems are so intertwined in the records, that it is nearly impossible to separate them. But one thing is certain, early Yarmouth was deeply divided on both issues of land distribution and the worthiness of its minister, the Reverend Marmaduke Mathews. While the problems in Sandwich and Barnstable can be seen as rooted in the pre-Cape Cod loyalties and interests of their inhabitants, the more eclectic background of Yarmouth settlers indicates that controversy was not limited solely to such divisions. Land ownership and religious conformity were major concerns of all communities, and it did not take pre-settlement differences to inaugurate disputes concerning them.

The land issue surfaced first, but only because Andrew Hallett had laid claim to a tract in the area before settlement occurred. The General Court, as concerned about speculators in Yarmouth as it had been in Sandwich, decided to investigate the matter. On 5 March 1638/39, the General Court ordered Joshua Pratt of Plymouth and John Vincent of Sandwich to examine the lands at Yarmouth and report to the Court. The Court especially ordered the two men to determine if the land Hallett had taken for himself would be detrimental to the town. If it were, the Court intended to intervene to prevent any problems that Hallett's holdings in Yarmouth would mean for the town.[21]   Vincent and Pratt's investigation satisfied the Court that Hallett's land would not hinder the development of Yarmouth. Two months after calling for the investigation, the Court ordered that Hallett could keep his land in Yarmouth, and when the Court ordered a survey of the Barnstable--Yarmouth boundary, it made the point that Hallett's land grant should be recognized and conveniently located.[22] On 3 September 1639, The General Court formally confirmed his claim when it identified the specific parcel and recorded its boundaries.[23]   Although Hallett had gained his land at Yarmouth, the potential of additional settlers acquiring similar large plots was a concern to the Court.   It intended that others should not follow in Hallett's path.   At the same session where it had confirmed his land, the Court declared that at least in Yarmouth, no one would be allowed to combine two or more house lots together but build a house on only one of them.   Clearly, Hallett's acreage in Yarmouth was acceptable, but similar acquisitions would not be.   Consistent with the response of the Court to the petition of Leveridge at Sandwich, the Court generally supported settlement and not speculation.

The real land problem in Yarmouth, however, had less to do with the potential for speculation than with the problems of satisfying the demands of the residents.   At the time of Yarmouth's first land division, the Court was deeply involved with the Sandwich land controversy, and had begun to learn its lesson.   At its March 1638/39 session, the General Court had ordered a redivision of Sandwich lands and added townsmen to the committees to protect the interests of both groups.   At the same session of the Court, it attempted to prevent, or at least soften, a similar controversy in Yarmouth by adopting the same approach.   The Court ordered that Nicholas Simpkins, William Palmer, Philip Tabor, and Joshua Barnes, Yarmouth townsmen, join Anthony Thacher, Thomas Howes, and John Crow, the original grantees of Yarmouth, to divide planting lands in the town according to the economic and social position of the recipients.[24]   Broadening the membership of the distribution committee before Yarmouth's situation became as bad as Sandwich's certainly must have made sense to the Court.   Unfortunately, it would have no more success in Yarmouth than it had had in Sandwich.

The problem apparently revolved around the question of the assignee's general quality.   Almost a year after expanding the committee, the General Court received complaints against Thacher,

Crowe, and Howes for having made an inequitable land division at Yarmouth. The Court considered the issue and supported the grantees over the complainants. It noted the three men had performed a very detailed division of the lands, and that the Court was well satisfied with what had been done. It is possible the discontent in Yarmouth mirrored the one in Sandwich regarding the acceptability of recipients. While making no acknowledgment of such a problem, the Court did order the committees not to admit new settlers unless they arrived from their previous congregation with letters certifying to their general honesty and religious orthodoxy.[25] With the acceptance of the Yarmouth division and restrictions on new residents, the Court considered the Yarmouth land problem settled.

Even if the Court had reconciled land differences, dispute had not been eliminated from Yarmouth. Midway between the enlargement of the land committee and the complaints to the General Court, religious controversy materialized in Yarmouth. Its relationship to the town's land problems cannot be measured, but certainly individual concerns about one's economic future would not have blunted religious diversity. And just as surely, religious antagonisms would not have reduced worries about land. Each question probably fed upon the other, making each of them more difficult to resolve.

The religious issue in Yarmouth revolved around the quality of the Reverend Marmaduke Mathews's leadership. As early as April 1639, a group in Yarmouth had complained about the unacceptability of Mathews's religious views, and in the fall, Mathews and William Chase appeared at the Court in Plymouth for an unspecified purpose. One can assume it concerned the minister, as Chase reported after they had returned home, that Mr. Mathews had not defended himself. Chase also expressed his surprise that anyone would participate in Mathews's communion service. The report further noted that at one point, and in the presence of some Magistrates, a group of people taunted Mathews, crying "Fye fye! for shame!"[26] What was specifically at issue has never been discovered. Born in Wales and educated at Oxford, Mathews had arrived at Boston in September 1638. He joined the Yarmouth project almost immediately and migrated to Yarmouth without a ready-made congregation. Without his own following, it is probable that he just never won the support and loyalty he so sorely needed if he was to be an effective minister in Yarmouth.[27] But Mathews was not without some defenders, and they took the issue back to the Court. On 1 September 1640 the General

Court censured Chase for his criticisms of Mr. Mathews, and for disturbing the peace of the church, the Court, and the colony. The Court fined Chase and gave him six months to leave the colony.[28] He no doubt had been a member of at least a small group of Yarmouth people opposed to Mr. Mathews, but no connection to those involved in the land dispute is clear.

The land dispute continued; and the General Court remained involved. The situation had reached such a degree of concern by June of 1641 that the General Court appointed four Assistants to hold a special court session at Yarmouth to hear and settle legal disputes and general controversies among the residents of Yarmouth, Barnstable, and Sandwich.[29] After deciding a few law suits, the three Assistants concentrated their energies on the problems in Yarmouth. They ordered the town to levy a rate to pay its public charges, indicating it had not done so, and then attacked the land issue. First off, the Court accepted the distribution as it had been laid out, and ordered the lots assigned to people as they had been granted. The Assistants also hoped to forestall future problems, and adopted another of the devices used at Sandwich two years before, the appointment of an Assistant to investigate. Selecting Standish, the Court required him to be joined to the committee at Yarmouth for the distribution of land and that no land be given out in the future without his consent. To quell arguments about individual selections, the Court also required that future grants in the town be assigned by lot.[30] After formally recognizing the boundary line between Yarmouth and Barnstable, and noting a purchase of Indian land by Barnstable, the Court adjourned. It certainly had made an honest attempt. The problems of Mr. Mathews had not been considered, but the Court had settled the land problem. The grants that had been made would for the most part remain, and the Court, through Myles Standish, would retain an influence on future divisions.

But land issues were not religious ones, and the controversy over Mr. Mathews wore on. At its meeting on 1 March 1641/42, the General Court ordered Thomas Starr, Hugh Tilley, Joshua Barnes, and William Nickerson to appear at its next meeting. Criticism had been leveled against the four men for being antagonistic toward the church, and for causing trouble at the town meeting.[31] A grand jury on 7 June 1642, indicted the four, plus Thomas Howes and Robert Dennis, all of whom posted a bond of forty pounds to insure their good behavior.[32] It was almost certainly these men who were the leaders of the Yarmouth supporters of Joseph Hull and had encouraged him to leave Barnstable to try his luck in Yarmouth. And it was these men who lost when the Court prohibited Hull from preaching there.

By the late 1640's the troubles in Yarmouth began to wind down. After a decade of personal and religious sniping about the worth of Marmaduke Mathews and extensive disagreement about the value of one's land grants, the issues lost their appeal. Life on the Cape in the seventeenth century was not easy. The work was strenuous and the days were lengthy. As the people of Yarmouth turned their attentions to the more practical problems of survival in the wilderness, their proximity to each other and the commonness of their difficulties forced them to moderate their differences, even if they did not resolve them.

The people of Yarmouth may also have tempered their dissension because the controversy in the town was itself more varied than in either Barnstable or Sandwich. For one thing, there were not the sharp divisions which pitted one fairly united group against another of comparable size or power. Yarmouth's residents came from varied backgrounds, which negated the importance of past loyalties, and there are no discernible geographic affiliations associated with the participants in the controversies.[33] For another, they argued over two issues, which diffused the hostility. Like Sandwich, the land controversy set grantees against townsmen. But unlike Sandwich, the General Court accepted the grantees' first division, and when agents of the Court came eventually to make specific land allocations, only a minority of land holders were involved.[34] The land situation in Yarmouth lacked the clear cut division which had been indicated in Sandwich both by Leveridge's petition and the assignment of land grants under the direction of the three Assistants. On the religious front, like Barnstable, Yarmouth's question involved loyalty to the minister. But unlike Barnstable, Marmaduke Mathews had not arrived with his own congregation, and the problem was less a rivalry between two clergymen than it was a dissatisfaction with the one who was there. It needs to be noted that Plymouth gave Marmaduke Mathews far more support than it gave Joseph Hull, and despite the continuation of disagreement, Mathews's replacement would be able to live with it for a decade.

Religious tension eased somewhat in Yarmouth with the departure of the Reverend Mr. Mathews about 1645.[35] The Reverend John Miller replaced him in 1647, but discovered that some of the former differences remained.[36] Under Miller's leadership, and with the support of some of the colony's Elders, Plymouth invited three of Massachusetts's most respected clergymen, Thomas Shepard, John Wilson, and John Eliot to investigate the situation in Yarmouth. They went, according to Shepard, to listen and perhaps to heal the difference and difficulties which had wracked Yarmouth for nearly a decade. The trio left well satisfied with their work. It had gone swiftly, and they departed believing they had instituted for both the Church and the community, a hopeful beginning of a period of peace and harmony.[37]

Unfortunately, the Massachusetts clergymen were more optimistic than they should have been. At a meeting of the General Court in March 1650/51, the grand jury presented Emanuel White and Robert Allen for the attacking the Reverend Mr. Miller. The Court fined each five shillings for the offense.[38] Miller's opponents got their turn the next year. The General Court, upon learning of very serious charges made against the colony by Miller, recommended that the grand jury take the charges under consideration so as to prove the colony's innocence.[39] The nature of Miller's charges is not revealed, and the findings of the grand jury are not given. All that is evident is that some degree of religious dissension was still alive in Yarmouth as late as the early 1650's. Miller remained in Yarmouth for another ten years, and the controversy hung on at some level throughout the period, until Miller finally left for Groton in 1661.[40] Less is heard of the religious differences of Yarmouth after 1652. Perhaps like both Mathews and Miller, the town just got worn down by the controversy and moved on to something else.

As the religious disagreements of Yarmouth declined in the late 1640's, so also did the problem over land distribution. Back in 1641 the Court had assigned Myles Standish the task of supervising the distribution of Yarmouth lands, and he wrestled with his responsibilities for a number of years. The length of time it took him to reach a solution should indicate something of the depth of feeling on the issue in Yarmouth. Finally in the spring of 1648, matters began to conclude. The General Court at its 7 March 1647/48 meeting ordered Standish to hold a hearing and bring an end to all differences remaining in Yarmouth.[41] Two months later, Standish was in Yarmouth for two days to review the problem and promulgate his decisions. His verdict went into the records of the colony for the same reason the Sandwich distribution had. There needed to be a public record to settle the problem permanently. In addition to reserving Sauset Neck for the town, Standish made nineteen decisions concerning the holdings of fifteen men. Included among them were the three grantees of the town, Thacher, Howes, and Crow. He did not deal with the holdings of everyone in Yarmouth, and in only seven cases did anyone either lose or gain land. By 1648 most of the land dispute had seemingly been settled, and Standish was merely finishing off the loose ends. Those who lost land were Thomas Payne, who lost eight acres, and the three grantees, each of whom had twenty acres taken from quite sizable holdings. The three additions of acreage were six acres to John Darby, eighteen to William Nickerson, and eight to Edmund Hawes. There were eleven decisions in which acreage remained the same. In these, Standish either confirmed land already held or transferred acreage from one field to another. The remaining decision was the order to accommodate the minister, John Miller.[42]   If the decisions registered in the colony's records are indicative, the Yarmouth land problem was not as severe as that of Sandwich ten years before. But the Yarmouth decisions had been far longer in coming, and most likely much of the antagonism which had brought on the problem in Yarmouth had been diffused, settled or accommodated to by the time Standish issued his final report.

There are, however, two aspects of his report which are similar to the earlier situation in Sandwich. For one thing, the grantees of Yarmouth, like the grantees of Sandwich, assumed for themselves extremely large tracts of land. Even though Thacher, Howes, and Crow each lost twenty acres, those losses came from holdings of 156, 120, and 120 acres respectively. Standish's other decisions ranged from a high of twenty-two acres confirmed to Robert Dennis to a low of three confirmed to one Clarke.[43]   The advantages to being a grantee in Plymouth Colony were as obvious in Yarmouth as they had been in Sandwich. Finally, as in Sandwich, an attempt was made to broaden participation in the land distribution system by including non-grantees in the group which made the decisions. Standish and the grantees agreed to add three townsmen, Thomas Starr, William Nickerson, and Robert Dennis, to the group to distribute land. In the future, no land would be divided without the participation of at least two of these men, or similar men selected by the town. If differences arose which these men could not solve, they were to consult with Standish for his direction.[44]   The Plymouth authorities could not have been too disappointed in Standish efforts, for it rewarded him for his labors by a grant of land in Yarmouth. It was a parcel of forty or fifty acres, based not only on the value of his past services on behalf of the town, but also on the prospect that he would have more

of it in the future.[45]   In contrast to the Massachusetts divines, the
Court, anyway, was not too optimistic that the problems of Yarmouth
could be solved, even by Myles Standish. But the Court's pessimism,
while certainly well placed, given the record of disagreement in
Yarmouth, was unfounded. As in Sandwich, it is impossible to know
how well individual landowners were satisfied with their holdings,
but at least dissatisfaction passes from the public record.

The extensive controversy so evident in early Sandwich,
Barnstable, and Yarmouth did not develop during the beginning years
of Eastham, and community relations in the town contrasted vividly
with those of the three earlier Cape Cod settlements. While the
prolonged disputation of the other towns is partially explained by
conflict between a faction of Massachusetts dominated committees and
a party of Plymouth inhabitants, and partially by differences over
ministerial leadership, the comparable peacefulness of early Eastham
is attributed to the very lack within the community of any similar
divisions.

In contrast to the other Cape Cod towns, Eastham's original
population was almost entirely from the colony of Plymouth, and in
the beginning all residents apparently participated equally in decisions
regarding land distribution.   The seven men who founded the
community, Thomas Prence, John Doane, Edward Bangs, Richard
Higgins, Josiah Cook, John Smalley, and Nicholas Snow had all been
residents of the town of Plymouth itself and prominent in both the
town's and the colony's affairs.[46]   There is strong indication that
these men were simultaneously regarded as both the committees and
the inhabitants of the settlement, a meaningless distinction anyway,
given the smallness and cohesiveness of the group.   And the
homogeneity of Eastham's first residents continued into the early
years of the town.   Whether Massachusetts immigrants were
specifically excluded or not cannot be determined, but a significant
majority of those who migrated to Eastham during its first decade and
a half came from the town of Plymouth, and the rest migrated from
other towns within the colony.

From the colony records, it is possible to compile a roster of
thirty-five adult males living in Eastham at the end of the 1650's.[47]
The backgrounds of all but three of them are identified with one or
another of the colony towns. Eleven of the group arrived when the
settlement was established, the seven founders, and four male
dependents.[48]   Over the next decade or more, nine additional
emigrants from the town of Plymouth joined the original settlers,

bringing the Plymouth element in Eastham to twenty, or approximately sixty percent.[49] The other Cape Cod towns provided nearly all the rest of Eastham's residents; Yarmouth four, Sandwich three, and Barnstable two.[50] Those who moved to Eastham from colony towns off the Cape, other than the town of Plymouth itself, were two from Duxbury and one from Bridgewater.[51] The only two people from outside the colony were from Hingham, and there was one unidentifiable resident.[52] In sum, just over ninety percent of Eastham's population in 1659 had a bond with Plymouth, either the colony or the town. Eastham was a direct example of the expansion of Plymouth in a way that no other Cape Cod town could claim.

The homogeneity of background among Eastham's early settlers certainly goes far in accounting for the lack of dissension in the town. The inclusion of all those who migrated to Eastham as owners of the land reflects, as well as reinforces, that homogeneity. When the General Court sanctioned the move to the region in 1644/45, it granted the land either to the town church or to those who would actually reside at Nauset, and there is no indication that later arrivals were excluded from equal participation in the distribution of land. In contrast to the other settlements on the Cape, where a specific group within the community controlled land grants, land at Eastham was distributed in town meeting, where all potential land owners participated equally.[53] Such a combination of a traditional association with Plymouth and the lack of a unique land committee could not help but reduce the causes of friction so evident elsewhere.

Finally, it must be noted that any serious controversy, regardless of its cause, would have been noted in the colony's official documents. Sandwich's land troubles were played out in the pages of the colony's records, and the problems in Yarmouth and Barnstable received not only the notice but the intercession of the Plymouth government. While Eastham's local records do not exist for much of the earliest period and cannot be checked, the silence of those of the colony must stand as testimony to a less divisive and disputatious community than was the general experience on Cape Cod. When land distribution eventually did become an issue in Eastham, it was not a question of newly-arrived conflicting groups from different colonies, but a problem of town growth and diversity, and it did not occur until the 1690's.[54]

By the end of the 1650's, the settlement period of seventeenth-century Cape Cod was at an end. Four communities had been established, and they would remain the only recognized towns on the

Cape until after Plymouth colony's independence had ended. The composition of the colony's population had been greatly altered by those immigrants to Cape Cod who came from Massachusetts. They introduced a diversity which contrasted significantly with the relative homogeneity of the original Plymouth settlers, and where the new arrivals came into contact with those already residents of the colony, there was conflict, always important, and sometimes bitter. Except for Eastham, the only one of the Cape towns created as a descendant of the original Plymouth, the early history of the communities on Cape Cod is highlighted by the existence of differences between new arrivals from Massachusetts and people associated with Plymouth. In each instance, circumstances forced the Plymouth government to intervene in order to hasten the settlement of the problem and reduce the discord. Before it was over, Plymouth may well have wondered whether its encouragement of settlement had been worth the effort. But the towns were there, and must be dealt with. Cape Cod was an important part of the whole colony and would remain so for the rest of the century. The centrality of that importance would soon be evident with the emergence of Quakerism in Sandwich and Plymouth's extraordinary efforts to eradicate it.

Notes

1. Bradford, *Plymouth Plantation*, pp. 23-27; Edmund S. Morgan, *The Puritan Dilemma: The Story of John Winthrop* (Boston, c. 1958), pp. 38-39.

2. Langdon, *Pilgrim Colony*, pp. 30-31, 40.

3. In 1636 the General Court had decreed that children born in Plymouth, and after them, children raised in Plymouth should receive land in the colony before anyone from England or another colony. *Ply. Col. Recs.*, 11:16. See Langdon, *Pilgrim Colony*, p. 46; Stratton, *Plymouth Colony*, pp. 173-174. Stratton misstates the date as 1633.

4. *Ply. Col. Recs.*, 1:88-89. See Langdon, *Pilgrim Colony*, pp. 50-51; and Lovell, *Sandwich*, pp. 20-25 for discussions of the Sandwich land issue. For a look at the process as experienced in Taunton, but without the controversy, see Langdon, *Pilgrim Colony*, pp. 48-50.

5. *Ply. Col. Recs.*, 1:117. The number of townsmen to be joined with the grantees is not given.

6. *Ply. Col. Recs.*, 1:131.

7. *Ply. Col. Recs.*, 1:133-134.

8. *Ply. Col. Recs.*, 1:147.

9. *Ply. Col. Recs.*, 1:148.

10. *Ply. Col. Recs.*, 1:147.

11. *Ply. Col. Recs.*, 1:149-150. The five committee members from the grantees, and their acreages, were: Edmund Freeman, 42; John Carman, 28; Henry Feake, 20; Richard Chadwell, 15; and Edward Dillingham, 8. The five townsmen with their acreages were: Joseph Halloway, 15; Richard Bourne and John Vincent, 7 each; George Allen, 6-1/2; and Robert Botfish, 5. Of nine grants of ten acres or more, five had gone to members of the distribution committee. The others went to Mr. Potter, 10; Mr. Edge, 14; Mr. Thomas Dexter, a miller, 32; and Mr. Wolleston, 13. Wolleston and Dexter's grants were contingent upon their moving to Sandwich. For some perspective, the Reverend Leveridge received 5 acres. See also Lovell, *Sandwich*, pp. 21-25, especially for a different look at the statistical information.

12. *Ply. Col. Recs.*, 1:113-114.

13. Lothrop, *Diary*, p. 31. See Cobb, "Beginnings of Barnstable," in Trayser (ed.), *Barnstable*, pp. 16-17; and McKenney, "The Beginnings," in Barnstable (comp.), *Seven Villages*, pp. 5-6 for reviews of the Hull issue.

14. Lothrop, *Diary*, pp. 9, 26.

15. *Ply. Col. Recs.*, 7:16, 30, 31, 33, 34; Lothrop, *Diary*, p. 36.

16. *Ply. Col. Recs.*, 2:53.

17. Lothrop, *Diary*, p. 36. The personal nature of the difficulty is best seen in Thomas Dimmock's support for John Lothrop rather than his Massachusetts associate Hull.

18. Trayser (ed.), *Barnstable*, p. 173; Weis, *Colonial Clergy*, p. 113.

19. Lothrop, *Diary*, pp. 35-39. See especially the case of "Goodye Shelley," cast out for making her dissatisfaction with Lothrop more public than the clergyman could tolerate.

20. Lothrop, *Diary*, p. 27.

21. *Ply. Col. Recs.*, 1:117. Six months after the 5 March order, the Court identified Hallett's land as being two hundred acres at Yarmouth. *Ply. Col. Recs.*, 1:130. For Hallett's land claim, see Swift, *Old Yarmouth*, pp. 22-23, and for a biography of him, see ibid., pp. 50-53.

22. *Ply. Col. Recs.*, 1:121.

23. *Ply. Col. Recs.*, 1:130-131. Hallett must not have antagonized the Yarmouth settlers or the Court too extensively with his land claim. He received seventeen acres of meadow in the town on 7 October 1639, and the Court reconfirmed his land holdings when the Court of Assistants formally adopted the boundary line between Yarmouth and Barnstable at its special session at Yarmouth on 17 June 1641. *Ply. Col. Recs.*, 2:21.

24. *Ply. Col. Recs.*, 1:117.

25. *Ply. Col. Recs.*, 1:142. The Court's order did not mention the four men appointed to join the three grantees. It is possible they had assisted in the acceptable division, but were omitted from the record as unnecessary. It is also possible the grantees had ignored them and excluded them from the decision, which had thus brought on the complaint, but that situation would surely have been mentioned by the Court. One thing is clear, the Court did not add Simpkins, Palmer, Tabor, and Barnes to the group after the complaint, but a year before. Swift, *Old Yarmouth*, pp. 42-43 and *Right Arm*, p. 45 confuses his chronology, and has the four additions being made in response to the 1639/40 complaint.

26. Philip Tabor *et al.* to Thomas Prence, Yarmouth, 12 April 1639, Winslow Papers, 1638-1759, Box 1, #2, Mass. Hist. Soc.; *Ply. Col. Recs.*, 1:135. The Court learned of this report from the deposition of one Edward Morrell. Morrell may not have been the most trustworthy of witnesses. On 1 June 1641 he was indicted for stealing corn in Yarmouth, but had run away. *Ply. Col. Recs.*, 2:18. Chase was still in Yarmouth in June 1641 when he won one lawsuit and had another referred to arbitration. *Ply. Col. Recs.*, 2:20.

27. Proposed as a settler of Yarmouth on 7 January 1638/39, Mathews took the Plymouth oath of allegiance one month later. Winthrop, *Journal*, 1:277; *Ply. Col. Recs.*, 1:107, 108. See also Weis, *Colonial Clergy*, p. 137; Swift, *Old Yarmouth*, pp. 54-55.

28. *Ply. Col. Recs.*, 1:162.

29. *Ply. Col. Recs.*, 2:19. Edward Winslow, Myles Standish, Edmund Freeman, and John Brown were the four Assistants assigned to the task, although only two or three of them were required to attend. Brown was the only one who did not.

30. *Ply. Col. Recs.*, 2:21.

31. *Ply. Col. Recs.*, 2:36.

32. *Ply. Col. Recs.*, 2:41. A marginal note indicates the Court eventually released the men.

33. While it is true the three grantees were Massachusetts men, Crow, Howes, and Thacher, the townsmen added to the land committee represented both Massachusetts and Plymouth; Simpkins and Tabor from the former, and Barnes and Palmer from the latter. The anti-Mathews group was similarly divided, with Barnes and Chase from Plymouth and Howes and Tilley from Massachusetts. For biographical information, see chapter 3, n. 27.

34. *Ply. Col. Recs.*, 1:142; 2:128-130.

35. Swift, *Old Yarmouth*, pp. 39, 55; Weis, *Colonial Clergy*, p. 137. Poor Mr. Mathews went to Massachusetts where his troubles must have

made those in Yarmouth appear as next to nothing. He was briefly in Hull in 1649, but was refused allowance to return because of unspecified erroneous statements and other doctrinal errors. He seems to have considered a call to New London in 1649, but did not go. Malden called him to be their minister in 1650, but the General Court would not allow his ordination. He remained under investigation, was fined, and partially recanted before returning to his native Wales. He died there in 1683. For a look at the troubles of Mathews in the Bay Colony, see Marmaduke Mathews to Jonathan Brewster and others of New London, Boston, 7 October 1649, in *Winthrop Papers*, 5:380-382; *Mass. Col. Recs.*, 2:276; 3:153, 158-159, 203, 236-237, 250, 257, 294.

36. Miller was a Cambridge University graduate, ordained in England, who arrived in New England in 1634. He seems to have tried his hand in a number of towns, having served either as elder or ministerial assistant in Roxbury, Rowley, Watertown, and Braintree before arriving in Yarmouth. His daughter was born there on 2 May 1647, and twelve days later Myles Standish, in his efforts to settle the land divisions of the town, ordered Miller be "sufficiently accommodated." The grantees may have been waiting to see how they liked him before granting him land. *Ply. Col. Recs.*, 8:3; 2:130; Freeman, *Cape Cod*, 1:249-250, n. 1. See also Swift, *Old Yarmouth*, pp. 76-77.

37. Thomas Shepard, "The Cleare Sunshine of the Gospell, Breaking forth upon the Indians of New-England," in *Collec.*, Mass. Hist. Soc., 3d Ser., 4(1834):42-43. It was during this sojourn on the Cape, that Eliot received his first exposure to its Indians.

38. *Ply. Col. Recs.*, 2:165.

39. *Ply. Col. Recs.*, 3:10.

40. Swift, *Old Yarmouth*, p. 76.

41. *Ply. Col. Recs.*, 2:121.

42. *Ply. Col. Recs.*, 2:128-130.

43. *Ply. Col. Recs.*, 2:128-130.

44. *Ply. Col. Recs.*, 2:130.

45. *Ply. Col. Recs.*, 2:164-165.

46. Pratt, *Eastham*, p. 12. Eastham's association with the original Plymouth church and community was so strong, that the town should be viewed as a direct descendant of both the colony's original settlement and the earlier Scrooby congregation.

47. The list was assembled from three sets of Eastham birth registrations recorded by the colony in 1652, 1660, and 1656, *Ply. Col. Recs.*, 8:15, 26-28, 30; a 1657 enumeration of men who took the oath of fidelity that year, ibid., p. 184; a 1658 registration of Eastham's freemen, ibid., pp. 201-202; and two acknowledgments of Eastham men being elected

to political office in the town, ibid., 2:156, 3:116. In his *Cape Cod*, 2:358-359, Freeman gives a list of twenty-nine "voters" in 1655. It includes one man who does not appear in the official records, and omits seven who do. Freeman does not give the source of his 1655 voter list.

48. There were three sons: John Bangs, son of Edward; Jonathan Higgins, son of Richard; Mark Snow, son of Nicholas; and one ward, Joseph Harding, the charge of John Doane. Savage, *Genealogical Dictionary*, 1:111, 2:354, 412, 4:138.

49. The nine later arrivals were Henry Atkins, George Crisp, Richard Knowles, Richard Sparrow and his son Jonathan, Robert Wicksen, Thomas Williams, Stephen Wood, and John Young. Freeman, *Cape Cod*, 2:359, n. 1, 371, n. 2; Savage, *Genealogical Dictionary*, 1:73, 473, 3:42, 4:144, 375, 570-571, 629, 669-670. Freeman's Stephen Atwood is probably Stephen Wood, *Cape Cod*, 2:359. Robert Wicksen's name appeared in any one of five different spellings, ranging from Wexam to Vixen.

50. The four from Yarmouth were Daniel Cole, Giles Hopkins, Thomas Paine, and William Twining. Freeman, *Cape Cod*, 2:373, n. 2, 359, n. 3; Savage, *Genealogical Dictionary*, 1:425, 2:461, 3:336, 4:353. The three from Sandwich were John and Samuel Freeman, both related to Thomas Prence by marriage, and Joseph Rogers. Freeman, *Cape Cod*, 2:361, n. 3; Savage, *Genealogical Dictionary*, 2:204, 3:477, 563-564. Barnstable provided the Rev. John Mayo and his son Nathaniel. Freeman, *Cape Cod*, 2:358, n. 1, 362, n. 1; Savage, *Genealogical Dictionary*, 3:187-188.

51. Job Cole, who had previously been in Yarmouth, and Thomas Roberts came from Duxbury. Freeman, *Cape Cod*, 2:373, n. 2; Savage, *Genealogical Dictionary*, 1:427, 3:548. William Merrick, who had been in Duxbury at one time, came from Bridgewater. Savage, *Genealogical Dictionary*, 3:198. Freeman, *Cape Cod*, 2:365, n. 2, apparently has him confused with his son, William, born 15 September 1643.

52. William Walker and Ralph Smith came from Hingham, while John Mantah was the only one of the thirty-five about whom nothing could be learned. Freeman, *Cape Cod*, 2:367, n. 1, 372, n. 1; Savage, *Genealogical Dictionary*, 4:129, 397. The Ralph Smith in Eastham is almost certainly not the Reverend Ralph Smith, Plymouth's first ordained clergyman, who resigned his pastorate in 1636, left the colony about 1645, and died in Boston in 1661. Savage, *Genealogical Dictionary*, 4:128-129. See also Langdon, *Pilgrim Colony*, pp. 117-118; and Stratton, *Plymouth Colony*, pp. 41-42, 353. For additional information about at least some of the early settlers of Eastham, see Pratt, *Eastham*, pp. 12-31; and Stratton, *Plymouth Colony*, pp. 238-239, 267-268, 282-283, 307-308, 340-341, 353, 354, 356-357.

53. *Ply. Col. Recs.*, 2:81; Eastham Record of Town Meetings, 1654-1745; Eastham Record of Land and Meadow Grants, 1654-1743. Both sets of local records indicate that land was granted by the town rather than by a land "committee."

54. Eastham Record of Land and Meadow Grants, 1654-1743, pp. 114-115, 122-123, 147-158. "A case of differences" developed in Eastham between the "inhabitants," or residents, and the "purchasers," the earliest settlers or those descended from them. Both groups agreed to the formation of a town committee with a "negative vote" over future land distributions. No colonial government intervened in the issue, and Eastham settled the problem without the rancor associated with the early years of the other Cape Cod towns. Most of the problem probably resulted from changes brought about by the turmoil surrounding Andros and the Dominion of New England, as well as Plymouth's subsequent incorporation into Massachusetts under the 1691 charter.

V

"An accursed and pernicious sect"

QUAKERISM (the Society of Friends) came to New England in July 1656 when Anne Austin and Mary Fisher arrived in Boston. It spread to Plymouth a few months later. The two Boston arrivals, who had sailed from Barbados, were the first wave of an army of Quaker missionaries fanning out across England's North Atlantic empire to spread the Quaker message in the middle of the seventeenth century. Austin, Fisher, and the many who followed them had been inspired by the teachings of George Fox and others during the turmoil and experimentation of England's civil war in the seventeenth century. Stressing the doctrine of the "Inner Light," Quakers believed in the presence of God in everyone and maintained He spoke to individuals directly. They also believed God's message could be found in Scriptures, but denied an ordained ministry any particular authority and ability to interpret it. The Quaker emphasis on a personal religion placed them very broadly in the Puritan spiritist tradition as expressed in New England by Anne Hutchinson, but their extremism in other matters set them far beyond the limits of religious debate, much less accommodation. For a number of reasons, New England Puritans viewed the Quaker message as a danger which would lead ultimately to the destruction of both true religion and social order.

Traditional Puritans and their Separatist neighbors in Plymouth interpreted the "inner light," with its denial of ministerial authority, as excessive self-centeredness which could lead only to chaos and anarchy. New Englanders saw in Quaker equality, with its use of the more personal thee and thou, and the refusal to remove one's hat in "hat honor," as a denial of authority and the breakdown of civil order. And finally, the Puritans regarded the Quaker emphasis on the equality of women and children and the itinerancy of male and female missionaries as threats to male supremacy and the permanence of the family, leading eventually to sexual licentiousness. Puritans and Separatists alike found no redeeming characteristics whatsoever in the Quaker movement. Quakers were not good people gone wrong. They were agents of the devil, come to destroy not only the institutions of society, but society itself. New England was ready for them when they arrived.[1]

The Massachusetts Court responded to the Quakerism of Mary Fisher and Anne Austin by immediately imprisoning both women and banishing them from the colony a few weeks later. But within days of their departure, eight more Quakers arrived to take their place. It is from the experiences of this second group that Quakerism came to Plymouth Colony, and specifically to Sandwich. Nicholas Upsall, a Dorchester innkeeper, supplied food to the prisoners while they were in the Boston jail, having bribed the jailer for an opportunity to converse with them. He apparently liked what he heard, for when the Massachusetts General Court passed its first anti-Quaker laws, Upsall spoke publicly against them. For his efforts the Court fined him twenty pounds, confiscated his property to pay for the fine, and banished him from the colony in October 1656.[2] Upsall journeyed to Plymouth Colony, and the General Court allowed him to settle in Sandwich for the winter, where he found a group of receptive listeners for his newfound Quaker teachings. At its February 1656/57 meeting, the Court of Assistants required Upsall, along with some of Sandwich's eventual Quaker leaders, to appear at the next session of the General Court to answer the charge of holding an unauthorized Quaker meeting at William Allen's. The Court also ordered Upsall to leave the colony within a month and directed Tristram Hull, who had brought him to Sandwich in the first place, to see that he left. In March the General Court fined Allen, and directed the Barnstable and Sandwich constables to deliver Upsall to Hull for deportation.[3] Whether solely responsible for Sandwich's Quakerism or not, Upsall's winter stay in the town certainly went far in bringing together what would be Plymouth's most important Quaker meeting.

It is certainly doubtful that Upsall arrived in Sandwich accidentally or that there were not some residents predisposed to his message. Dissension had existed in the community from the beginning, and William Leveridge's departure just a few years before had left the town without a settled minister. Significantly, none of Sandwich's prominent Quakers were members of the Saugus families which had founded the town. Its Quakers came instead from within the Plymouth people who had migrated to Sandwich with Leveridge and then later opposed him. Indeed, it was those most vocal in their opposition to Leveridge who later became Quakers, although there is no way to determine what the issues were that turned them against Leveridge or later drove them to Quakerism.[4]

The relationship between opposition to Leveridge and the presence of Quakerism in Sandwich is initially obvious in the failure of some townspeople to attend church services regularly. A year and a half before Upsall arrived, the General Court had called three future Quakers before it for their attendance failures. One of them, Peter Gaunt, stated in the examination that he knew of no acceptable church then in existence in the world, and Ralph Allen, Sr., agreed with him.[5] It was a statement consistent with Quaker beliefs, and if not proof of the Quakerism of its speaker, at least indicated a potential sympathy for Quaker views. The large number of Sandwich residents who became Quakers, the extent of their sufferings, and the longevity of their Meeting are all indications that Upsall's teachings had fallen on ready and attentive ears.

But it was actually during Upsall's months in Sandwich that the town's Quakers came together and took on a unified public presence. Increasingly over the succeeding four years, they were more numerous in their challenges to the colony's authority and the colony more repressive in its dealings with them. In their actions, which they viewed as expressions of their faith, they were supported and encouraged by the presence of "foreign Quakers." One of the fundamental tenets of early English Quakers was that God called them to be missionaries, and they traveled extensively all over the English empire in North America, from the West Indies to Newfoundland. Boston's first Quaker arrivals had sailed from Barbados, and George Fox himself toured the colonies. Quakers seemed to prefer those places where the persecution was the strongest, and Massachusetts drew them like a magnet. Once the Bay Colony had enacted severe fines against ship masters who brought Quakers into the colony, itinerant Quakers landed in New Amsterdam or Rhode Island and passed through Plymouth Colony on their way to Boston. They usually stopped in Sandwich, both to bear witness to their faith and to encourage local Quakers to persevere. Like Massachusetts, Plymouth saw Quaker missionaries as a special threat to the peace and order of the colony, and passed laws to punish both those who came and those who entertained them when they did.[6] If the colony truly expected to be successful in prohibiting itinerants, it simply did not understand the nature of early Quakerism. But it probably did, and more likely, the colony was merely giving legislative authority to its punishment of them.

Two of Plymouth's earliest Quaker itinerants were John Copeland and Christopher Holder. They had been among the second group of Quakers to land in Boston in the summer of 1656, and had already been imprisoned in Boston and banished from Massachusetts. The two men were returning to the Bay Colony by way of New Amsterdam and Rhode Island, and in August of 1657 arrived on Martha's Vineyard. Expelled from the island, they went to Cape Cod, and moved on to be welcomed in Sandwich. They then journeyed to Plymouth, and although the Court did not physically punish them, it did banish them to Rhode Island. Copeland, at least, returned to Plymouth Colony by the end of the winter, and he may have been in Sandwich. On 2 February 1657/58 the Court of Assistants sentenced him to be whipped for unspecified actions he had committed earlier in conjunction with Holder. It carried the sentence out six days later when Copeland was apprehended. He was also certainly banished, but he may have reappeared during the summer of 1658. He eventually returned to Boston where the colony jailed and whipped him.[7]

Another important foreign Quaker to visit Sandwich and Plymouth was Humphrey Norton, who was there during the same summer and fall as Copeland's second trip in 1657. After examination, the General Court found Norton guilty and banished him to Rhode Island, ordering the under marshall to see that he went. True to Quaker witnessing, Norton returned to Plymouth. Accompanied by John Rouse, he was back in the colony in the summer of 1658, and was probably apprehended in Sandwich. Both men went to jail in Plymouth, and the General Court examined them twice. Norton railed against Governor Prence at the first session, calling him a liar, and demanded to read a statement against Prence at the second. When the two Quakers refused to take the oath of allegiance, the Court ordered them whipped. With the payment of their prison fees, probably by someone sympathetic to their message, the two men left the colony. Four months later the Court took another swipe at Norton. Noting his written attacks on the governor, the Court ordered Norton captured and brought in for punishment.[8] There is no record Norton returned for the honor.

Imprisonment, whipping, and banishment did not accomplish the General Court's goals in Plymouth, just as similar and even worse punishments in Massachusetts had not. Copeland, Holder, Norton, and Rouse's places at Sandwich meetings and in Plymouth's jail were taken by other foreign Quakers who continued to invade the colony. Their route was the one used earlier by the Dutch in trading at Aptucxet. Coming up Buzzard's Bay from Rhode Island, they landed in the Manomet area, and journeyed overland to Sandwich. The authorities recognized the problem. In December 1658 the Court of Assistants ordered the special marshall, with the aid of anyone he needed, to capture the invading Quakers and confiscate their boats.[9] But laws against them and efforts to stop them only made the Quakers more anxious to go to Sandwich and Plymouth. In the summer of 1659 the Court imprisoned Peter Pearson and William Leddra as foreign Quakers. Brought before the Court three times, they refused to leave the colony until called to do so by God, and spent well over six months in the Plymouth jail.[10] A year later Pearson was back, this time with William Reap, and the authorities caught up with both men at a Quaker meeting in Sandwich. This time the Court did not allow the men to wait upon a call from God to leave Plymouth. The Court ordered them out of the colony and gave the two men twenty-four hours to depart.[11] Between Pearson's two appearances in the colony, Mary Dyer had arrived in Sandwich, escorted there by one of its residents, Thomas Greenfield. They went to jail as foreign Quakers, and the Court of Assistants examined them both. After Edmond Freeman, Sr., attested to Greenfield's residency in Sandwich, the Court allowed the Quaker to return home, and directed the special marshall to confiscate Greenfield's property to cover his jail costs. The Court could only banish Mary Dyer to Rhode Island because she was a foreign Quaker, but it ordered Greenfield to pay her imprisonment charges.[12] The last of the Quaker itinerants to visit Sandwich and Plymouth was Wenlock Christoferson. Entertained in Scituate, he visited Sandwich, and went to jail in Plymouth. The Court of Assistants questioned him and sent him back to jail when he refused to leave the colony. He was back before the General Court a few weeks later. It ordered him tied "neck and heels," for his

insubordination towards the Court, whipped for his refusal to leave
the colony, and finally sent out of Plymouth.[13]

Over a five-year period, nearly a dozen itinerant Quaker
missionaries had visited Sandwich and received punishment at the
hands of the colonial authorities.   While those officials no doubt
disliked Quakers as much as their Massachusetts neighbors, their
punishments were significantly less severe.   Plymouth seemed
primarily interested in simply getting foreign Quakers out of the
colony.   Whippings were reserved for those like John Copeland or
Wenlock Christoferson who refused to stay away or like Humphrey
Norton who was especially outspoken against the colony's leaders.
Unlike Massachusetts, there were no executions.   Plymouth's more
moderate reaction to the Quakers was also because so much of the
colony's Quaker problem was with its own citizens rather than with
itinerant or foreign Quakers.   In Sandwich itself, Quakers were not
just an outside force, they were neighbors and fellow residents. The
town was sympathetic, even protective, and the Quaker problem took
on an aspect of a struggle for local independence, in addition to being
one of religious confrontation with wandering missionaries.

But while the resident nature of Plymouth's Quaker problem
may have mitigated the cruelty or severity of the punishment, it did
not mean the colony would tolerate the spread of Quakerism among
its own citizens.   In fact, the Quaker challenge proved to be a
watershed in the religious and political life of the colony.   Quakerism
in Plymouth was one of the major reasons for the colony's efforts to
restrict political participation and to institute a tax-supported clergy.[14]
Unfortunately for its goals, the colony had no more success in
squashing native Quakers than it did in ridding itself of foreign ones.

Plymouth Colony utilized both political and religious weapons in
its assault upon the Quaker problem.   One of its most often used
techniques was to take advantage of the Quaker refusal to swear an
oath by punishing them for that refusal.   In June 1657, the General
Court required all men who had not taken the oath of fidelity to the
colony to do so within four months.   Those who had not done so six
months after the deadline, would pay a five-pound fine or be
deported.[15]   At the height of the Quaker problem, the Court
repeatedly fined as many as twelve or fourteen Sandwich Quakers for
their unwillingness to take that oath.[16]   Similarly the Court used the
juryman's oath to trap Quakers.   The Court fined William Allen
twenty shillings at its March 1656 meeting for his refusal to take that
oath.   His fellow Quaker, William Newland, paid a ten-shilling fine

for the same offense in October 1657, and a month later was in the Duxbury jail. There were other cases as well.[17] A related technique was the fining of those who declined to aid the constable or special marshall in the enforcement of the laws against Quakers. The Court fined Stephen Wing three times for the offense, and even Edmund Freeman, Jr. paid a ten shilling fine for his refusal to assist the special marshall. Freeman was the husband of Governor Prence's daughter, and hardly a serious candidate for Quakerism.[18] And finally, under a 1650 law, the Court disfranchised Quakers and their sympathizers.[19] The most famous case was that of James Cudworth, who in addition to being an Assistant and commander of the militia had resided briefly in Barnstable in its early years. Cudworth had held a Quaker meeting at his home, and more significantly, had written a letter to England critical of the colony's treatment of the Quakers. For calling attention to Plymouth's actions against the Quakers, Cudworth lost his political positions and his right to vote, and also agreed to give up his captaincy of the Scituate militia. Isaac Robinson would later lose his vote for becoming a Quaker, and in the fall of 1658 the Court curtailed the political power of Quakers in Sandwich by denying nine men the right to participate in town meetings.[20]

The continual return to the colony of banished foreign Quakers and the persistent refusal of native converts to give up their religion failed to convince the Plymouth authorities to abandon persecution, quit their efforts, and seek accommodation. Rather, failure merely proved they had not been aggressive enough in their efforts to demonstrate the unacceptability of Quakerism. On that assumption, the General Court started to deal more directly with the colony's native Quakers. One of its efforts to rid itself of Quakers, adopted in the summer of 1659, was to waive the fines of those Quakers who would leave the colony within six months. To insure the success of the project, it offered to subsidize those too poor to bear the costs.[21] Future developments indicate Quakers ignored the offer. Another of its efforts was to appoint a committee to debate the Quakers to show them their errors and bring them back to orthodoxy. As three of the men appointed were from Barnstable, it is certain Sandwich Quakers were the ones to be debated. Isaac Robinson, son of the Leyden pastor, was one of the four appointed, and if he is any indication, the committee failed completely.[22] Robinson became convinced of the Quaker view of truth and wrote a letter defending them. The General Court took notice of the letter at its March 1659/60 meeting, and disfranchised him the following June.[23] On a harsher note, at its June

1660 meeting, the General Court ordered a cage erected in each town for the imprisonment of Quaker women and children who were not in a position to pay fines.   Sandwich was one of the Quaker towns especially mentioned.[24]

The Plymouth government also used laws stipulating acceptable religious practices and the punishment of non-conformists as ways to quell the Quaker surge.   Some of the laws had been enacted earlier, but most of them were passed in direct response to the new Quaker threat.   Such laws had the effect of making it possible to deal with the sect's female element, a significant issue because of the Quaker emphasis on equality of the sexes.   Female Quakers were difficult to punish, however, because the laws regarding the oath of fidelity, jury duty, or disfranchisement applied only to males.   But laws requiring regular church attendance, peaceful deportment, and prohibiting the entertaining of Quakers or attendance at their services were as applicable to women as to men.[25]   As early as February 1656/57, Sarah Kirby and her sister Jane, the wife of William Landers, were before the General Court for disturbing the Sandwich church service. The Court ordered Sarah whipped for the offense the next month, but allowed her sister to go free.[26]

Attending or hosting Quaker meetings were the most serious of the purely religious misdeeds of the Quakers.   The same Court of Assistants which ordered the Kirby sisters to appear also ordered their father Richard, William Allen, and the wife of John Newland to present themselves at Court and answer the charge of attending a Quaker meeting led by Nicholas Upsall.[27]   The General Court had William Newland before it in October 1657 for conducting a number of Quaker meetings at his house.[28]   The following March, the Court examined seven Sandwich men for attending a Quaker meeting.   It admonished them all, and fined four of them for their refusal to remove their hats when appearing before the authorities.[29]   A general sweep of Quakers must have been made sometime in the summer of 1660.   On 2 October the Court fined twenty-four people for being at Quaker meetings.   Seven of them were women and four of them were from outside Sandwich.[30]   It was equally as bad to entertain traveling Quakers in one's home.   Someone, probably the special marshall, reported William Allen, William Newland, and Peter Gaunt for doing just that.[31]

Plymouth's Quaker problem was obviously centered in Sandwich.   It was the only Plymouth community where Quakers were anything more than a small minority, and it served as a major stopover for itinerant Quakers on their way to the jails of Plymouth and Boston. Writing from the Boston jail, John Rouse asserted that along with Newport, Rhode Island, Sandwich was one of New England's two strongest Quaker outposts.[32] But Quakerism in Sandwich was more than just a problem for the colony government to deal with by punishing individual believers. It was an issue within the town itself, as well as one between the colony and the town. Although the town made note of Robert Allen's rejection of the orthodox church, for the most part the people of Sandwich saw Quakers as neighbors, friends, and even relatives, not fanatics or madmen.[33] Some who had become Quakers had been residents of the town for many years and others had held positions of responsibility. George Allen and William Newland had been Deputies to the General Court, and Peter Gaunt and Stephen Wing had been Constables. A large number of eventual Quakers had pledged subscriptions to the building of the meeting house in 1655. The religious troubles that had bothered the town for years and had forced William Leveridge to leave a few years earlier had at least not developed to such a degree that Quakerism was seized upon as an open opportunity to settle old scores. Differences there may have been, but they were dealt with generally through accommodation rather than vindictiveness. Many in Sandwich did not join with the Quakers, but neither did they participate in their persecution.

Sandwich residents expressed protectiveness of their Quaker neighbors in a number of ways. On the one hand, they refused to participate in colony government. At its Court of Election meetings in June of 1657 and 1658, the Court noted Sandwich had not sent men to serve on the Grand Jury.[34] In June 1659, the Court disapproved of James Skiffe as one of Sandwich's two Deputies, but allowed John Vincent to take his seat.[35] Similarly, Sandwich residents did not pay their colony taxes. The Court authorized William Bassett, the Constable, to confiscate the property of delinquents, and later awarded him a five-pound bonus for his troubles.[36] The residents of Sandwich also showed their opposition to colonial persecution of the Quakers at a more personal level. Thomas Burgess allowed two Quakers to get hold of a warrant ordering their appearance at Plymouth, thereby permitting them to escape punishment.[37] When Thomas Greenfield refused to testify before the Court regarding his association with Mary Dyer, Edmund Freeman, Sr., spoke on his behalf.[38] Freeman's son was also one of a number of non-Quaker men who attempted to thwart the efforts of the special marshall in confiscating Quakers' property.[39]

   Although it is clear a large number of non-Quakers in Sandwich were concerned enough about the colony's treatment of the Quaker minority to oppose it in some way, the opposition was not unanimous. It was inevitable that before it was over, Quakerism would become an issue in local affairs. Sometime in the summer of 1658, a group of Sandwich men submitted a petition to the Plymouth government against Quakers voting in town meetings. The General Court responded by sending Governor Prence and some of the Assistants to Sandwich to investigate. The Court's decision was to prohibit nine Quaker men from participating in local affairs, and to order that no one be admitted as an inhabitant of Sandwich without the sanction of the church, as well as that of Governor Prence or some group of Assistants.[40]

   By the summer of 1658, the General Court had come to recognize it did not have local support for its efforts against the Quakers of Sandwich. William Bassett's tax collection troubles had proven the inability of a local constable to accomplish much among his fellow residents, and the Court felt compelled to send its own representative into Sandwich to enforce the colony's laws. To that end it created the office of Under Marshall, with specific responsibility for the towns of Sandwich, Barnstable, and Yarmouth. It was the only instance in Plymouth's history of the colony becoming directly involved in local government for any period of time. For the post it chose George Barlow. He probably had come from Massachusetts, but his arrival in the colony and the reasons for his selection are unclear. As he was not a resident of Sandwich at the time of his appointment, his commission underscores strongly the desire of the colonial government to deal forcefully with Sandwich Quakerism. To insure Barlow's success in Sandwich, where he was to concentrate his efforts, the Court granted him extensive powers in addition to enforcing colonial law. In consultation with the head marshall, but without a representative of the victim, he was empowered to evaluate goods confiscated for fines. In practice, he no doubt did it alone. He was allowed to impress the services of other people to assist him, and the Court instituted a fine on those who would not cooperate. Later the Court ordered him to conduct general searches of Quaker homes.[41] In all the controversy over the Quaker movement in Plymouth Colony, no one, including Governor Prence and the Assistants, reveals himself as more hateful, brutal, and grasping than Barlow. One did not need to be a lover of Quakers to conclude they did not deserve his brand of treatment.

Barlow attacked his new responsibilities with more enthusiasm and greater harshness than the colony's authorities had probably expected. Along the way he managed to antagonize most of Sandwich's residents, increasing sympathy for the Quakers rather than ending it, and solidifying Sandwich's antagonism toward the colonial government. His actions are best represented by the multitude of complaints against him and his counter charges against Sandwich's residents. William Newland complained about the damages resulting from Barlow's breaking into his house at night. John Jenkins and Peter Gaunt brought charges against Barlow for his taking of a replacement cow when one of those originally confiscated died.[42] Barlow's overzealous enthusiasm for the suppression of the Quakers led him to seize property without warrant, and the Court on a number of occasions required him to return it. Barlow had to restore a pair of oxen to Francis Allen, a pair of wheels to Samuel Hicks, a barrel of whale oil to John Ellis, and a shirt to Ralph Allen. For putting Benjamin Allen in the stocks without cause, the Court ordered him to compensate Allen twenty shillings.[43] Barlow's response to many of the charges against him was to sue for defamation of character. He did so four times against five of the town's leading Quakers.[44]

Barlow's petty suits against his critics, his unwarranted seizure of property, and his role as a direct representative of the colonial government could not help but rally Sandwich residents to the defense of their town and the protection of its Quaker residents. Local hostility best expressed itself through the refusal of both Quakers and non-Quakers to assist Barlow when ordered, a direct violation of his commission as Under Marshall. At least sixteen men, half of whom were not Quakers, either publicly criticized Barlow or refused to assist him when called. The non-Quakers included Edmund Freeman, Jr., and Henry Dillingham, both sons of Sandwich founders.[45] Daniel Butler not only refused to assist Barlow, he actively attacked him. In June 1660 the General Court ordered Butler whipped for his rescue of an itinerant Quaker from Barlow's capture.[46] All in all, Barlow was as much a problem as the Quakers. His overly ambitious execution of his commission during his three-year tenure was an embarrassment to the Plymouth government, and his actions certainly antagonized the residents of Sandwich and aroused sympathy for its Quakers. Quakerism in Sandwich, and in Plymouth generally, would undoubtedly have been less confrontational had the colony chosen someone other than George Barlow for its Under Marshall.

But Barlow's appointment represented the Plymouth leadership's abhorrence of Quakers and its passion to see them and their ideas rooted out of the colony. For foreign Quakers the solution was easy. Banishment would eliminate the problem. For resident Quakers the situation was more difficult. Their ideas were no less objectionable, but the colony's own Quakers needed to be controlled within the confines of the colony. The thrust of the solution was to bankrupt them into submission. Virtually all the laws the Quakers violated, whether refusing to take the oath of fidelity, declining to aid the Constable or Under Marshall, or attending Quaker services contained fines to be levied on the transgressor. While some Quaker reporters and later historians have tried to give specific amounts to Quaker fines, it is actually impossible to determine just how much the fines actually totaled. But as there were nearly twenty Quaker families in Sandwich, the regular and frequent fines assessed against them reached astronomical amounts before the trouble ended. A few examples will demonstrate the magnitude of the question.[47]

The official records for the period of the Quaker agitation include eight specific occasions when the General Court or Court of Assistants levied fines against Sandwich Quakers for their failure to take the oath of fidelity. The usual fine was five pounds, although once it was ten. Twenty-three men are listed, twenty-two of whom paid fines which eventually totaled 413 pounds.[48] The law against attending unauthorized Quaker meetings carried a ten-shilling fine, and it was used repeatedly. At its December 1658 session, the Court fined William Newland nine pounds for eighteen such visits, and his wife ten pounds for twenty of them.[49] In October it fined a group of Sandwich Quakers, including six women, for the same offense.[50] The fines against Quakers became so numerous that they came to be a major portion of the colony budget. In the Treasurer's report submitted 13 June 1660, fines, most of them against Quakers, totaled a little over 227 pounds, and the next year almost 214. In both cases, fines amounted to approximately one-third the colony's total income.[51] By contrast, once the Quaker repression had ended, income from fines dropped to approximately 23 pounds in the June 1665 report and 31 pounds in 1666.[52]

Such fines would have been ruinous if collected. Cattle and grain were the life-blood of an agricultural community, and their confiscation could only result in the economic collapse of the victim.

It was the efforts of George Barlow to appropriate Quaker property to pay their fines that most antagonized Sandwich Quakers and prompted non-Quakers to refuse their assistance. While it is certain Plymouth collected a great deal of grain and cattle as fines from Quakers, it did not receive all it had assessed. By June of 1661, the colony Treasurer regarded a little over 288 pounds in fines as "desperate," or uncollectible.[53] Probably by 1661 some Quakers had no more property that could reasonably be taken. It must be assumed that those with food, tools, animals, and money, both Quakers and non-Quakers, came to the aid of their victimized neighbors with both loans and moral support. After five years of colonial repression as witnessed locally in the aggressiveness of George Barlow, there was probably not a soul in Sandwich who did not pray for better and more peaceful times.

Those times arrived with the restoration of Charles II to the English monarchy. Except in Rhode Island, the foreign Quakers who had visited New England as missionaries had been met with various degrees of open hostility. Unwilling to suffer in silence, early Quaker itinerants had written widely of their treatment, especially in Massachusetts. By 1661 their story, especially as told in George Bishop's *New England Judged*, had reached the hands of the newly restored king. Despite Massachusetts's attempts to justify its treatment of Quakers and the employment of an agent to present its petitions, Charles ordered the corporal punishment and execution of Quakers stopped.[54] If the King's Missive, as it is usually called, did not change the minds of Quaker antagonists, it at least ended the crueler forms of persecution.

Just as Massachusetts understood it had no alternative to the King's directive other than to cease repression, Plymouth similarly recognized it would have to change its policies. The colony repealed some of its harsher laws against the Quakers, and stopped enforcing the others. Banishments and imprisonments ceased, the Court no longer levied fines, and George Barlow became an ordinary citizen.[55] A more tolerant attitude towards religious dissent was also encouraged in the Royal Commissioners' recommendations to Plymouth in the spring of 1664/5.[56] Finally, through dedication and perseverance, the Quakers had at long last won.

In the town of Sandwich itself, Quakers began to worship as they pleased, and eventually worked themselves back into the life of the town. The Sandwich Meeting is generally regarded as the first permanent Quaker meeting in America, gathering regularly after 1658 and with records from 1672.[57]   Although town voters never selected Quakers for colony office, they did appoint them to minor town positions.   Given the burden of work and the willingness of Quakers to participate so long as religious beliefs were not violated, there was little choice.   Between 1669 and 1684 the town appointed Daniel Wing, William Allen, Edward Perry, William Newland, Peter Gaunt, and John Jenkins as surveyors of the highways.[58]   The crisis of King Philip's War necessitated a further slackening of resistance to the participation of Quakers in the town's political life.   Sandwich appointed Ralph Allen to a committee to meet in Barnstable and discuss using the Cape towns as havens for displaced English settlers.[59]   The town made William Newland a surveyor of veterans' land grants and an assessor for taxes levied in conjunction with the war.[60]   At a meeting on 23 April 1675, the town's voters recorded the names of those eligible to participate in Sandwich's political business.   The list contained sixty-six names, including George Barlow.   Twelve were Quakers, including Ralph Allen and William Newland.[61]   Politically, Quaker restrictions had come to an end.

But political rights did not include economic privileges.   In 1678, Peter Gaunt, William Newland, and John Jenkins complained to the town on behalf of its Quakers that they were being excluded from land grants.[62]   In the summer of 1681 they petitioned the General Court, which reacted favorably.   It allowed those long-term settlers who had helped in the purchase of the town's land to vote in their disposal, as well as to vote for tax assessors and serve in that post if elected.[63]   With the restoration of land and political rights to accompany their religious freedom, Sandwich's Quakers were as welcomed back to Sandwich as they were going to be.   There may have remained a residue of mistrust on the part of the non-Quaker majority, but it was no longer public policy.

The entire Quaker episode in Plymouth had served as a period of redirection in the colony's development.   Coming as it did at the death of Bradford, it inaugurated a new era in the colony's political and religious evolution.   The Quaker challenge to established authority ended any official recognition of traditional Separatist voluntarism and in turn solidified support for a tax-supported clergy and the establishment of religion.   It had a similar effect in the political life of the colony.   While Plymouth had begun to regulate political participation before the arrival of the Quakers, the problems posed by their appearance only proved to the colony the necessity for stricter political controls.

Notes

1. Seventeenth-century Quakerism has attracted enormous interest among historians for many years. They have generally tended to concentrate on Massachusetts, however, as the Bay Colony had the harshest laws against the Quakers, and it was the colony the Quakers favored for their proselytizing. Book-length studies of the Quaker movement in America which include sections on Plymouth Colony are Rufus M. Jones's sympathetic study, *The Quakers in the American Colonies* (London, 1911; repr., New York, c. 1966), pp. 57-62 (Hereinafter cited as *Quakers, Colonies*) and Arthur J. Worrall, *Quakers in the Colonial Northeast* (Hanover, NH, 1980), pp. 15-18 (Hereinafter cited as *Quakers, Northeast)*. Worrall's bibliographic essay will lead to other major works dealing with the early Quakers. The Quakers are also important parts of the histories of Plymouth and its towns on the Cape. See especially Langdon, *Pilgrim Colony*, pp. 69-78; Stratton, *Plymouth Colony*, pp. 89-95; and Lovell, *Sandwich*, pp. 79-104, 113-116. For a discussion of a predisposition of Puritans and Separatists for the Quaker message, see James F. Maclear, "'The Heart of New England Rent:' The Mystical Element in Early Puritan History," *Mississippi Valley Historical Review* 42(1956), especially pp. 646-652. For an analysis of why the New England response to the Quakers was so extreme, see Carla Gardina Pestana, "The City upon a Hill under Siege: The Puritan Perception of the Quaker Threat to Massachusetts Bay, 1656-1661," *New England Quarterly*, 56(1983):323-353. Pestana's essay deals only with Massachusetts, but is indicative that in terms of attitudes and general policies, if not specifics, Plymouth's view of Quakerism was little different from its northern neighbor's. See also Jones, *Quakers, Colonies*, introduction.

2. *Mass. Col. Recs.*, 3:415-418; Mass. Archives, 10:238. George Bishop, *New England Judged, Not by Man's but the Spirit of the Lord*, (London, 1661), pp. 9, 31-33. Bishop was one of many Quakers who wrote of his treatment at the hands of New England Puritans. Upsall had been a long-term resident of the colony. His name appears on a jury list for 1630, and he was licensed as an ordinary keeper in 1637. *Mass. Col. Recs.*, 1:77, 199.

3. *Ply. Col. Recs.*, 3:111, 113; Bishop, *New England Judged*, pp. 122-123. Upsall went to Rhode Island from Plymouth, and from there made his way back to Boston. The Court again imprisoned and fined him, and upon appeal from his wife, eventually placed Upsall under house arrest in Dorchester. Ibid., p. 94; *Mass. Col. Recs.*, 4(1):337; 4(2):21, 27, 50; Mass. Archives, 10:239, 282.

4. *Ply. Col. Recs.*, 1:57, 2:172-173, 205; 3:4, 74; Lovell, *Sandwich*, p. 104.

5. *Ply. Col. Recs.*, 3:74. George Allen, probably Ralph's brother, was the third man examined, and chose not to agree with Gaunt's assertion. The Court could not decide what to do with the men, and left the issue for further consideration.

6. *Ply. Col. Recs.*, 11:68, 100-101. The Commissioners of the United Colonies later recommended banishment for Quakers and death for those who returned. Ibid., 10:212.

7. *Ply. Col. Recs.*, 3:127; Bishop, *New England Judged*, pp. 123-124; Humphrey Norton, *New-England's Ensigne* (London, 1659), pp. [21]-24. There is an error in the pagination of the original. Both Bishop and Norton include a second major visit of Copeland and Holder to Sandwich in the summer of 1658. Both authors report that Constable William Bassett and Under Marshall George Barlow apprehended Copeland and Holder at a Quaker meeting. The Sandwich selectmen supposedly turned the two Quakers over to Thomas Hinckley, who as a Magistrate, supervised their whipping. Bishop, *New England Judged*, pp. 136-137; and Norton, *New-England's Ensigne*, pp. 39-40. Lovell, *Sandwich*, pp. 89-90, accepts the visit of Copeland and Holder to Sandwich, but disputes the occurrence of the whipping on the grounds that Hinckley would not have had the legal power to impose a whipping without a court order, and there is no outside supportive evidence. Quakers used strong words to condemn their enemies, and did so imaginatively. In this case their imagination got the best of them.

8. *Ply. Col. Recs.*, 3:123, 139-140, 149; Norton, *New-England's Ensigne*, pp. 25-26; Bishop, *New England Judged*, pp. 124-125. Another telling of the tale, principally statements by both Norton and Rouse regarding their treatment in Plymouth can be found in Francis Howgill, *The Popish Inquisition Newly Erected in New-England* (London, 1659), pp. 13-15, 17-18. The General Court preserved Norton's written attack on Governor Prence and another on John Alden, as well as a deposition by Christopher Winter and Norton's reply. They are published in *Mayflower Descendant*, 18(1916):71-77. Henry J. Cadbury has a comment on Norton and his writings in *Huntington Library Quarterly*, 15(1951/52):291-296. For a brief sketch of Norton, see Frederick B. Tolles, "A Quaker's Curse--Humphrey Norton to John Endicott, 1658," ibid., 14(1950):415-421. See also Lovell, *Sandwich*, pp. 86-87.

9. *Ply. Col. Recs.*, 3:154.

10. *Ply. Col. Recs.*, 3:176, 178, 184. Their last examination was on 7 March 1659/60. The General Court informed both of them that they would be allowed to leave the colony as soon as they received a call from God to do

so. The disappearance of their cases from the records indicates they complied. While in the Plymouth jail, Leddra addressed a lengthy defense of Quaker itinerancy to the colony's authorities. It is reprinted, along with a brief biography, in John Noble, "William Leddra the Quaker," *Publications, Colonial Society of Massachusetts, Transactions,* 10(1906):335-345. See also Lovell, *Sandwich,* pp. 93-94. Leddra later became one of the four Quakers executed by Massachusetts. Jones, *Quakers, Colonies,* pp. 87-89.

11. *Ply. Col. Recs.,* 3:203-204; Lovell, *Sandwich,* pp. 99-100.

12. *Ply. Col. Recs.,* 3:178; Lovell, *Sandwich,* pp. 95-96. The Mary Dyer who visited Sandwich is the some woman hanged by Massachusetts in 1660. Ibid., p. 98.

13. *Ply. Col. Recs.,* 3:197, 199; Lovell, *Sandwich,* p. 98.

14. See chapter six for a discussion of state support of religion and chapter eight for one pertaining to the efforts to restrict voting. The death of William Bradford and his replacement by Thomas Prence as governor should not be seen as the cause of the colony's stance against the Quakers. Bradford was certainly by nature more tolerant and forgiving than the fairly severe Prence. But his opposition to the 1645 toleration proposal, his 1655 ultimatum regarding state support of religion, and general disappointment in the colony late in life indicate, had he lived, he would have been as punitive toward the Quakers as the colony became. See Langdon, *Pilgrim Colony,* pp. 70-71; Stratton, *Plymouth Colony,* pp. 89-90; Bradford, *Plymouth Plantation,* p. 33., n. 6. Similarly, Plymouth's persecution of Quakers cannot be blamed on intimidation from Massachusetts or the Commissioners of the United Colonies. It is true Massachusetts set an example and the Commissioners recommended repression, but the longevity of Plymouth's actions and the appointment of a special marshall signify the colony's seriousness in ridding itself of Quakerism. *Ply. Col. Recs.,* 10:155-158; *Mass. Col. Recs.,* 4(1):passim. See also Swift, *Right Arm,* pp. 90-91.

15. *Ply. Col. Recs.,* 11:68, 100-101.

16. *Ply. Col. Recs.,* 3:138, 154, 168, 176, 181, 191, 201, 209.

17. *Ply. Col. Recs.,* 3:223, 224; 3:143; William Newland to Thomas Prence, Duxbury jail, 28 November 1657, Winslow Papers, 1638-1759, Box 1, #6, Mass. Hist. Soc.

18. *Ply. Col. Recs.,* 3:124, 131, 137, 173, 180-181, 213, 221; Stratton, *Plymouth Colony,* p. 294.

19. *Ply. Col. Recs.,* 3:167; 11:57-58, 68.

20. *Ply. Col. Recs.,* 3:130, 153, 162, 183, 189, 198-199. Reprints of Cudworth's letter are in Bishop, *New England Judged,* pp. 128-134 and Joseph Besse's compilation of Quaker experiences *Collection of the Sufferings of the People Called Quakers,* 3 vols. (London, 1733), 1:371-380

(Hereinafter cited as *Sufferings*). The colony later reinstated Cudworth to his political and military offices, and he was well thought of enough in 1675 to be made commander of Plymouth's troops in King Philip's War. Ibid., 5:124, 150; Langdon, *Pilgrim Colony*, pp. 74-75, 169.

21. *Ply. Col. Recs.*, 11:122.

22. *Ply. Col. Recs.*, 11:124. The other two Barnstable men were John Smith and John Chipman; the fourth member was John Cook from Plymouth.

23. *Ply. Col. Recs.*, 3:183, 189. Like Cudworth, he had his vote restored to him. Ibid., 5:126. Robinson later joined with other Quakers in the founding of Falmouth.

24. *Ply. Col. Recs.*, 11:125-126.

25. *Ply. Col. Recs.*, 11:100-101, 125.

26. *Ply. Col. Recs.*, 3:111-112.

27. *Ply. Col. Recs.*, 3:111.

28. *Ply. Col. Recs.*, 3:123.

29. *Ply. Col. Recs.*, 3:130

30. *Ply. Col. Recs.*, 3:200.

31. *Ply. Col. Recs.*, 3:213.

32. John Rouse to Margaret Fell, [Boston], 3 September 1658, cited in Frederick B. Tolles, *Quakers and the Atlantic Culture* (New York, 1960), p. 24.

33. Sandwich Town Records, 1652-1692, p. 46.

34. *Ply. Col. Recs.*, 3:118, 143.

35. *Ply. Col. Recs.*, 3:162. Skiffe had some forbearance for Quakers, but he was not one of the more active sympathizers. Also at this meeting the Court did not allow James Cudworth to assume his post as Deputy from Scituate.

36. *Ply. Col. Recs.*, 3:131, 137. On some issues, however, the town was willing to participate in colony decisions. When the Court called a meeting to discuss leasing the Kennebec trading post, Sandwich sent Thomas Tupper to the meeting. Ibid., p. 170.

37. *Ply. Col. Recs.*, 3:123-124.

38. *Ply. Col. Recs.*, 3:178.

39. *Ply. Col. Recs.*, 3:173.

40. *Ply. Col. Recs.*, 3:153. The nine men were Ralph Allen, Sr., Thomas Ewer, Thomas Greenfield, Richard Kirby, Jr., Henry Sanders, Mathew Allen, John Jenkins, Daniel Wing, and Stephen Wing.

41. *Ply. Col. Recs.*, 3:140-141, 173. Plymouth's Barlow was probably the same one made a freeman of Saco by a special court at Wells, Maine, in June 1653 and the one investigated by a special commission two months later

as a disturbance in the area. Certainly the personalities are the same. *Mass. Col. Recs.*, 3:336-337.

42. *Ply. Col. Recs.*, 3:158, 183-184, 190.

43. *Ply. Col. Recs.*, 3:165, 169, 182, 206.

44. *Ply. Col. Recs.*, 7:89-90, 92, 97. The five defendants in these cases were William Gifford, Edward Perry, William Newland, John Jenkins, and Thomas Burgess, Jr.

45. *Ply. Col. Recs.*, 3:158, 173, 180-181, 190, 191, 213, 221; 8:95. The Quakers in this group were Thomas Butler, Thomas Burgess, Jr., Edward Perry, William Gifford, Stephen Wing, Thomas Greenfield, Daniel Wing, and Richard Kirby. The non-Quakers, in addition to Freeman and Dillingham, were William Bassett, Ludovich Hawks, Joseph Chandler, Richard Smith, Nathaniel Fish, and Thomas Clark. Dillingham had married into the Quakerish Perry family. The Court fined his wife, Hannah, ten shillings for attending a Quaker meeting in 1660. Ibid., 3:200; 8:97, 103. For a discussion of the inherent right of New England towns to govern themselves, see James and Marylin Blawie, "Town vs. State; Interposition and Secession in New England," *Journal of Public Law*, 5(1956):90-109. See also Lovell, *Sandwich*, pp. 122-124.

46. *Ply. Col. Recs.*, 3:191.

47. It was standard practice for Quaker writers of the seventeenth century to recount the fines levied against members of the sect. But their totals must be read with some skepticism. The figures used by the Quakers are impossible to check, and there are numerous discrepancies in the official records. Among Quaker writers, Bishop, *New England Judged*, p. 137 claims fines against Sandwich Quakers totaled 900 pounds. Besse, *Sufferings*, 1:381 asserts the Sandwich total was just under 660 pounds. In the official records, volume 3 of *Ply. Col. Recs.* includes the imposition of many Quaker fines, and volume 8 catalogs the collection of them in the Treasurer's Accounts. The specifics of the two volumes do not agree, and are one of the major factors for the inability to state with any certainty how much was assessed, much less actually collected. It is significant that the recording of those treasury accounts commences in the summer of 1658, just as the colony's repression of the Quakers hit full stride. Lovell, *Sandwich*, p. 99 exceeds even the Bishop figure. Langdon, *Pilgrim Colony*, pp. 74-76; and Stratton, *Plymouth Colony*, pp. 92-93 acknowledge that fines against Quakers were high, but wisely forbear particulars.

48. *Ply. Col. Recs.*, 3:138, 154, 168, 176, 181, 191, 201, 209; 8:93, 96, 97, 98, 103. William Newland was the only one not fined because he had previously taken the oath of fidelity when he became a freeman. Ibid., 8:176.

49. *Ply. Col. Recs.*, 8:95.

50. *Ply. Col. Recs.*, 3:200; 8:103.

51. *Ply. Col. Recs.*, 8:101, 8:104.

52. *Ply. Col. Recs.*, 8:113-114, 116-117.

53. *Ply. Col. Recs.*, 8:105.

54. *Mass. Col. Recs.*, 4(1):386-390, 450-453; 4(2):34; Noel W. Sainsbury, *et al.* (eds.), *Calendar of State Papers, Colonial Series, 1661-1686*, #168 (Hereinafter cited as *Cal. State Papers, Col. Ser.*). This, and all subsequent *Cal. State Papers* references, are to the document number.) The King's dispatch is also found in Besse, *Sufferings*, 3:212. See also Jones, *Quakers, Colonies*, pp. 90-100; Worrall, *Quakers, Northeast*, pp. 14-15.

55. *Ply. Col. Recs.*, 4:passim; 11:101, 125. A most telling comparison is the difference between the forty-two references under the "Quaker" entry in the index to volume 3 of *Ply. Col. Recs.*, and the absence of even the entry in volume 4. It is perhaps a misnomer to refer to Barlow as a normal citizen, certainly in seventeenth-century Plymouth. Despite his record, he and his family remained in Sandwich, an interesting development in itself. Over the next thirty years most of the family seem to have carried on the same kind of belligerence with which the patriarch had persecuted the Quakers. Ibid., 4:7, 10, 17, 66, 88; 5:236, 238, 261, 264; 6:98

56. *Ply. Col. Recs.*, 4:85-86; *Cal. State Papers, Col. Ser., 1661-1668*, #1103.

57. Jones, *Quakers, Colonies*, pp. 141-142 and n.; Freeman, *Cape Cod*, 2:61, n.; Sandwich, MA, Men's Monthly Meeting Records, 1672-1818 (microfilm), Rhode Island Historical Society, Providence, RI. See also Arthur J. Worrall, "Toleration Comes to Sandwich," in J. William Frost and John M. Moore (eds.), *Seeking the Light: Essays in Quaker History in Honor of Edwin B. Bronner* (Wallingford, PA, 1986), pp. 73-78.

58. Ebenezer W. Peirce, *Peirce's Colonial Lists . . . . Plymouth and Rhode Island Colonies* (Boston, 1881; repr. Baltimore, 1968), pp. 12-14, 19 (Hereinafter cited as *Colonial Lists*).

59. Sandwich Town Records, 1652-1692, p. 123.

60. Sandwich Town Records, 1652-1692, p. 124; 134-1/2.

61. Sandwich Town Records, 1652-1692, pp. 198-199. The ten Quakers, other than Allen and Newland, were Peter Gaunt, Thomas Butler, George Allen, John Jenkins, Edward Perry, John Newland, William Allen, Francis Allen, William Gifford, and John Allen, Sr.

62. Sandwich Town Records, 1652-1692, p. 203.

63. *Ply. Col. Recs.*, 6:71.

VI

"to maintain the liberties
of the churches"

PLYMOUTH'S efforts to suppress the Quaker challenge in the
1650's forced the colony on a broader scale to reassess its attitude
concerning church--state relations. Having come out of the English
Separatist movement of the sixteenth century, Plymouth's early
leaders had been heirs to the principle of congregational autonomy,
characterized by the free association of members and the voluntary
support of clergymen. As their original congregation had survived
without government support in England and in Holland, they initially
expected the churches of their colony to do likewise. The emphasis
on local independence and a trusting expectation that individual
communities would do the right thing had resulted, during
Plymouth's early years, in an unwillingness to legislate the
establishment and support of local churches and their ministers.[1]
    The problems of dealing with Quakerism had clearly illustrated
the pitfalls of such congregational autonomy and voluntary ministerial
subsistence. Without a method of permanent support, congregations
often found it a formidable task to secure the services of a minister or
to keep one after he had been hired. Many communities went for
years without a settled clergyman. And without a cadre of secure,
permanent ministers, colonial authorities found it similarly difficult to

preserve those principles of true religion which they knew they were obligated to enforce. It was a troublesome question. The spirit of voluntarism and local autonomy was strong among Plymouth's towns, as Sandwich's protective response to the Quakers had illustrated. Despite the General Court's efforts, it would be many years before a system of tax-supported ministers was in place.[2]

The securing of a settled minister, much less a well qualified one, should have been recognized from the outset for the problem it would become. John Robinson had remained in Holland when the original Pilgrims sailed for New England, and Plymouth had no ordained clergyman until Ralph Smith's arrival from Salem in 1629. He remained for seven years, and no one was sorry to see him return to Massachusetts. His replacement, John Reyner, lasted longer, but seems not to have made much impression on the community. The congregation finally requested his resignation in 1654, even though it was unable to find a successor until it secured the services of John Cotton in 1665. Other, more eminent, clergymen passed through Plymouth briefly, but moved on elsewhere. Roger Williams and John Wilson left the colony, and Charles Chauncy moved to Scituate.[3]

The impact of Plymouth's inability to employ a first rate clergyman may have been mitigated by the leadership of William Bradford generally, and Elders William Brewster and later Thomas Cushman specifically. In the absence of an ordained minister, Brewster had led church services in the first decade of the colony, and he and Cushman had no doubt remained important figures in the religious life of the town even after Smith and Reyner arrived.[4] The other towns of the colony were not so fortunate. When a minister died or left, there was rarely a similar lay leader to take his place.

The towns on Cape Cod were particularly susceptible to interruptions in ministerial leadership and to the problems of dissension which tended to accompany them. In 1654 Sandwich's William Leveridge resigned his pastorate, having lost both the moral and financial support of the town. Sandwich quickly fell into the morass of the Quaker controversy, and two decades passed before John Smith settled in the town as its permanent minister in 1675.[5] The ministerial gap was shorter in Yarmouth, but there were similar problems of leadership. The Grand Jury investigated Yarmouth's John Miller for unspecified charges against the government in 1652. Miller had replaced the controversial Marmaduke Mathews some years before. While Miller remained in the town for nine more years, his effectiveness should at least be questioned. Thomas

Thornton replaced him in 1663.[6] True to its more homogeneous beginnings, Eastham experienced neither the long breaks in ministerial succession nor the controversy when they occurred. John Mayo assumed the pastorate of the church soon after the town's founding, and when he left in 1655 Thomas Crosby quickly replaced him. When Crosby left the ministry to go into business, Samuel Treat as quickly succeeded him.[7]

But the Eastham experience was not the usual one. The protracted troubles of Barnstable in finding a qualified minister to replace Thomas Walley provide an enlightening glimpse of both the ministerial question and the operation of local politics. Following the death of John Lothrop in 1653, two or three men had served the town intermittently, but Barnstable could not settle on a permanent pastor until the appointment of Thomas Walley in 1663. Walley served effectively for fifteen years, but even before his death, controversy over a successor emerged.[8] The town considered hiring Samuel Angier as an assistant for the aging Walley, but after a visit to Barnstable and consultation with others, Angier rejected the offer and eventually took over the Rehoboth church in April 1679.[9]

A month after Walley's death, the Barnstable church sought John Cotton's assistance in securing Isaac Foster as a temporary replacement. The town later offered him the permanent position, but Foster chose to remain at Harvard.[10] Barnstable, apparently divided into opposing factions, each with its own candidate, found itself unable to find a minister in 1678. Peter Thacher, then living in Boston, visited Barnstable in the early summer of that year, preached on two successive Sundays, but declined the pastorate when it was offered.[11] John Cotton recommended John Bowles, and indicated to Thomas Hinckley that the longer the town went without a minister the more difficult it would become to find one. Hinckley, leader of one of the factions, supported Samuel Phillips of Rowley and would hear none of it.[12] And some in Barnstable's divided church continued to hold out hope for Peter Thacher.[13]

Unable to secure Angier, Foster, or Phillips, the church eventually agreed to renew its offer to Thacher in the summer of 1679. It was not a unanimous decision. Approximately one-third of the congregation, led by Thomas Hinckley, opposed his appointment. Thacher seems to have consulted with every clergyman within a day's ride of Boston, and eventually, and with great reservation, agreed to visit Barnstable again. He was there in early September, preached once to the congregation, and at long last accepted Barnstable's offer.

He returned to Boston, and moved his family to Barnstable at the end of October.[14] It would be a long and troubling winter.

The division in the church which had preceded his appointment continued without letup. Thacher received a cool reception from the Hinckleys, and the congregation met the day after his arrival to discuss its ongoing dissension.[15] The differences remained unconcealed over the winter, and resulted in an extremely unpleasant life for Thacher and his family. In February he discovered his wife weeping uncontrollably in the cellar over the troubles that had been brought down upon them.[16] Thacher went off to Boston in the early spring to discuss his concerns and returned in April, having decided to leave Barnstable. On 11 July 1680 he preached his farewell sermon and the next day left town permanently. Thomas Hinckley, at least, was unprepared for the announcement, learning of Thacher's decision only from his sermon.[17]

With the departure of Thacher, the public discussion of Barnstable's troubles in finding a minister ceased. Personal animosity no doubt remained, but it has gone unrecorded, and does not appear to have hampered the success of Jonathan Russell, who assumed the Barnstable pastorate in 1683.[18] Perhaps like the earlier problems with Lothrop, the people of Barnstable needed to get on with more immediate and practical matters. The division over calling a minister had occurred while the colony recovered from King Philip's War and as it faced the uncertainties of increased English involvement in colonial affairs. But although these broader issues may have influenced the controversy, they did not create it. Barnstable's ministerial trials were primarily a matter of personal, local disagreement.

There are no indications that other Cape Cod towns duplicated the depth of wrangling and personal animosity of Barnstable. The more common problem was the general unavailability of qualified ministers. That situation was neither unique in Barnstable nor new in the late 1670's. It had been present from the beginning. Coupled with the perception of a general moral decline among the colonists, it had elicited a demand for reform by the 1650's. In the political sphere, the colony would limit political participation to its most trustworthy voters by instituting more restrictive voting qualifications. In the religious quarter, it moved against error and voluntarism by requiring towns to support orthodox clergymen and punishing a variety of religious actions.

From the beginning, the Plymouth government had suppressed such blatant religious falsity as the ideas of John Lyford or Samuel Gorton, the attempt to set up a Baptist church in Rehoboth, or William Vassall's proposal for toleration.[19]   But it had been a defensive action, moving to silence error only after it had become public.   At its 10 June 1650 session, however, the General Court took the offensive against religious differences, attempting to prevent their appearance in the first place.   The Court led off by disfranchising anyone who established a congregation or public meeting without its sanction and requiring the perpetrators to appear before the next General Court for punishment.   Further, it protected clergymen by instituting a ten-shilling fine for anyone who criticized a minister or church, and levied the same fine against anyone who did not treat the Sabbath as a day of rest.   A year later, the Court added absence from public worship to its list of punishable actions.   With adjustments in wording and modifications in fines, the laws remained on the books for the remainder of the century.[20]

Cape Codders occasionally fell afoul of these religious standards, some of them even before the laws had been passed. Clerical authority and religious uniformity had been significant aspects of the General Court's involvement in the early controversies in Sandwich, Yarmouth, and Barnstable.[21]   But with the passage of particular legislation, the Court's power could be more specifically and straightforwardly exercised.   Those brought before the courts for their criticism of the existing churches included the future Quakers Ralph Allen, Sr., and Richard Kirby of Sandwich.   Each of them ultimately paid a five-pound fine.[22]   In March 1666/67, the Court fined William Lumpkin and Peter Worden of Yarmouth ten shillings each for causing an unspecified disturbance at the meeting house, and six months later William Sutton of Barnstable paid a one-pound fine for stealing a Bible from the meeting house and an extra ten shillings for lying about it.[23]   Not everyone accused was found guilty.   The Court cleared Yarmouth's Thomas Baxter of a misdemeanor charge in connection with the meeting house.[24]

While some people expressed their nonconformity by attacking the institution of the church, others did so by criticizing the minister. In March 1650/51, the Grand Jury presented Emanual White and Robert Allen of Yarmouth for their accusations against John Miller, and fined each five shillings.[25]   At a General Court held 2 July 1667, Nicholas Nickerson, of the Nickerson enclave at Manomoit, acknowledged the error of his words in criticizing Thomas

Thornton.[26]   At its July 1670 meeting, the Court ordered Robert Harper of Barnstable whipped for his criticism of Thomas Walley.[27] In 1684/85, the Court fined Elizabeth Snow of Eastham ten shillings for her verbal attacks against Samuel Treat.[28]

Not resting on Sunday and not attending church services were other ways in which people indicated their disregard for acceptable religious practices.   Traveling on the Sabbath was apparently a particular problem.   In 1653/54 the Grand Jury presented Josias Hallett and Thomas Gage for sailing from Sandwich on a Sunday.[29] The General Court fined William Hedge, John Gray, and Edward Sturgess, all of Yarmouth, thirty shillings each for the same offense in March 1670/71, and six months later did the same to Samuel Mathews, also of Yarmouth.[30]   Yarmouth's Kenelm Winslow, Jr. rode his horse on a Sunday, and received a ten-shilling fine from the General Court as a result.[31]   In 1654 the Grand Jury presented William Chase, Sr., of Yarmouth for using a pair of oxen on the Sabbath.[32]

The attendance problem was somewhat less significant. As part of the troubles surrounding William Leveridge in Sandwich, the Grand Jury presented thirteen people, including four married couples, in October 1651 for failure to attend church, and added two more men to the list within months.[33]   Peter Gaunt, and George and Ralph Allen were before the Court in March 1654/55 for failure to attend worship services. There was some discussion of the problem, but no decision was made.[34]   In June 1667 the selectmen of Yarmouth indicted two of the town's residents, Teague Jones and William Nickerson, for a similar failure to abide by the attendance rules.[35]

While the various laws designed to limit criticism of acceptable religious practices and institutions caught their share of Cape Cod violators, the total number was not large. With the exception of the Quakers, who were generally punished under other laws, violations of the religious statutes involved only a small portion of Cape residents, and certainly were neither numerous nor flagrant. Once the initial controversies accompanying the settling of towns on the Cape had ceased, one is struck rather by the small number of cases from Cape Cod involving transgressions of the laws dealing with religion. In the end, it is the relative rarity of the infractions that is most important.

But laws concerning church attendance, traveling on the Sabbath, and criticism of the clergy did not deal with the decline of political leadership which Governor William Bradford viewed as the cause of the problems facing the colony. When reelected in 1655, he decided to take the initiative. Distressed at the failure of some Assistants to serve as elected and the Deputies to do anything about the collapse of the ministry and the rise of erroneous religious ideas, he threatened to resign as governor unless changes occurred. His ultimatum was successful. Those who had been elected Assistants agreed to assume their positions, and the Deputies started to deal with the issues.[36] Before the session was over, the General Court had passed laws which inflicted corporal punishment on those who denied the truth of the Scriptures. It also prohibited pastors and teachers from resigning until the Magistrates had heard both the complaints of the parishioners and the defense of the minister. If the laity were found at fault, the Court authorized the Magistrates to attempt to convince congregations to support their ministers and to punish individuals who obstinately refused.[37]

The 1655 General Court had not, however, dealt with the issue of requiring towns to support their local clergyman. Just as Plymouth viewed congregations as voluntary associations, it similarly saw ministerial salaries as contributions from the congregation.[38] But the Court believed voluntarism had not been totally successful, and at its June 1657 meeting began work on solving the problem. Noting that the lack of a settled minister was a serious detriment to any town and that all towns had been created with the understanding religion would be supported, the Court ordered both the congregation and the town to support an acceptable minister. In those communities where voluntary contributions were inadequate, the Court ordered the town to appoint four men to levy the necessary taxes.[39] In addition to the recommendations of the Commissioners of the United Colonies and the warnings of Governor Bradford, the requirement of a tax-supported clergy was certainly a reaction to the Quaker agitation. It could also have been a broader based response to the increased diversity of the colony's population. The influx of those from Massachusetts and not out of the Pilgrims' Separatist heritage had created a group not by nature sympathetic to that tradition and less willing to support it.

The possibility of a tax-supported ministry met with strong opposition from Cape Cod. Within months of its passage, Matthew Fuller, Barnstable's militia chief, called the law "wicked and devilish" and asserted Satan had been at the tiller of the ship of state when the law was passed. The Court fined him fifty shillings for his insult to the Government.[40] A group in Yarmouth expressed its opposition by noncompliance, and at its March meeting in 1658/59, the Court took notice of the situation. It ordered the Constable to call a town meeting, and instructed Yarmouth to raise fifty pounds for the support of John Miller. If the money were still not forthcoming, the Court authorized a four-man committee to charge those who would not pay and confiscate their property if they still refused.[41] With such opposition to a tax-supported ministry, it is little wonder the General Court found it necessary to refine and expand its efforts to insure the compensation of clergymen in an appropriate manner.

The very next year, 1658, the Court stipulated new towns would not be established unless there was a population large enough to support both ecclesiastical and political institutions. Those towns already settled which were not large enough to do so, and Saconesett (Falmouth) was one of two mentioned, were to make efforts to enlarge their populations. Also included in the law was the requirement that unoccupied lands in a town were to be taxed for the support of both town and church. To indicate it was serious about its proposals, the Court ended the law with an offer to assist towns having trouble in complying, and particularly mentioned Sandwich when it did so.[42] But the traditional ideal of voluntary support for ministers persisted, and not every town complied with the new law. Many towns simply ignored it and continued a system of voluntary contributions. In a different approach to the problem, the Court suggested in 1662 that a portion of each whale washed up on shore, or some of the oil from it, be used to support the minister.[43]

Over a decade after town maintenance had been required, some towns were still not adequately supporting their ministers. Barnstable's Thomas Walley addressed that issue in his election sermon in June 1669. One of his first recommendations to the Magistrates was the securing of an acceptable clergyman for every town in the colony.[44] The practical side of the problem was the difficulties in collecting the money. It is clear from later developments, that while the Court compelled the town to support the minister, it had not deemed it necessary for town officials to collect the money. Ministers were expected to do that themselves. The Court attempted to deal with the difficulties of collection in 1668. It required either magistrates or selectmen to summon anyone who did not pay his share of the minister's salary to the next session of the Court to explain his delinquency. An unsatisfactory explanation was to result in a double charge.[45] One of the few men brought before the Court under this law was Nathaniel Fitzrandall of Barnstable. The Court viewed his explanation of the failure to pay twenty-one shillings insufficient, and ordered Fitzrandall to pay forty-two shillings to the Treasurer.[46] The Court repealed the law two years later when it restructured the collection process.

The Court finally realized that local responsibility for the collection of ministerial salaries had become a burden and created antagonism among the parishioners. Under a revised law, towns were still required to pay the minister's salary, but no longer was it to be done solely under the authority of the town. Instead, it became a colony function. Each year at the June Court of Elections, the General Court was to appoint two men in each town who were to have the responsibility of collecting the minister's salary and attaching the property of those who would not cooperate. Towns without ministers, and thus not liable for the tax, were to have it collected anyway under the authority of the General Court. In those towns, the money was to be used to build a meeting house or to encourage a minister to settle. In contrast to the original 1657 law, which had provided for tax support only where voluntary contributions had failed, the 1670 revision required the money to be collected even if voluntary support had been successful.[47]

Expecting opposition from those who believed in voluntarism, including the ministers it hoped to help, the Court added a provision requiring the collection of the money despite ministerial scruples to the contrary. And the Court was correct. The new law did not work successfully. In July 1677 the General Court bemoaned the failure of some towns to have any minister at all, and the refusal of others to support properly the one they had. It proceeded to revise the system yet again. This time it took the whole process out of the hands of the town and made it a colony responsibility. No matter how the amount was determined, by agreement of the townsmen or assigned by the Court, the Constable was to collect it as part of the colony's taxes. It was then to be turned over to the Treasurer of the colony, who would in turn see to its disbursement among the ministers of the colony.[48] Even this mechanism of collection met with some opposition. At a town meeting in August 1679, Yarmouth ordered four men to collect salary still owed to Thomas Thornton, authorizing them to confiscate property if necessary.[49] But the taxpayers must have recognized resistance was no longer possible. Regular payments for Thornton's salary began the next year.[50] But in general, the 1677 law was more successful than the previous ones. Certainly the balkiness with which the earlier laws had been met and the need for constant revision demonstrate a rather strong opposition to a tax-supported ministry.

But the 1677 law is the last of the series. The increased inclusion of taxes to support the minister in the local records surely indicates that at long last the colony had found at least a moderately successful way to accomplish its goal.

The tradition of a voluntarily supported clergy and the twenty-year attempt to replace it with a successful system of tax support are well reflected among the towns on Cape Cod. Before the General Court became involved in the matter, either ministerial support was omitted from the town records because it was not official business, or was mentioned only in terms of voluntary contributions. The salaries of William Leveridge in Sandwich, John Lothrop in Barnstable, or John Mayo in Eastham are not included in the records of the towns they served.[51] Surely they received some sort of salary, but it was apparently not a town tax matter. Only in Sandwich and Eastham are ministers' salaries even mentioned as town affairs before 1677, and they are clearly voluntary subscriptions. At a May 1655 town meeting in Sandwich, thirty-seven men "freely engaged themselves" for the building of a meeting house, and two years later fourteen men pledged sums ranging from six shillings to two pounds for the yearly support of a minister.[52] Eastham was the only other Cape town to include its salary for the minister in its records before the General Court made financial support a part of colony taxes. On 12 August 1663 the town "agreed" to raise fifty pounds for the support of Thomas Crosby's ministry, and ten years later again "agreed" to offer the same salary to Samuel Treat if he would come to replace the departed Crosby.[53]

Beginning in 1677, almost immediately after the passage of the law requiring towns to pay ministers through a colony tax, those tax levies appear in the local records of the Cape Cod towns. Just a month after the Court's action, Yarmouth included Thomas Thornton's salary in its tax obligations and continued to do so fairly consistently.[54] Although Samuel Treat's salary in Eastham is mentioned earlier, it became a tax item in February 1678/79. It was included again in 1680, but while there are other references to his salary, they do not specifically refer to it as a tax.[55] John Smith's salary in Sandwich first appeared as part of the town's taxes in August 1680 and again in 1686, although as with the other towns, it is obvious Sandwich had accepted the 1677 maintenance laws.[56] Barnstable's records do not mention the minister's salary as part of its taxes, although the town conformed to the 1677 salary requirements. In 1681 the town voted Jonathan Russell a salary of either eighty pounds value in goods or seventy pounds in money, provided he assumed the Barnstable pastorate. He opted for the money, and there is a receipt for seventy pounds paid him by the constable in 1682.[57]

These actions of the towns demonstrate the Cape's general acceptance of ministers' salaries as taxes. Before the entry of the General Court into the issue, they had compensated their clergymen voluntarily, and generally continued to do so while the Court groped for a satisfactory means of regularizing that support. When the Court finally settled on a colony imposed and collected tax, the towns acknowledged the demise of voluntarism, cooperated with the new law, and included the minister's salary in their annual collections.

But ministers did not live by salaries alone. They needed homes to live in, land to farm, and wood to burn. Although the Plymouth Colony government had not required towns to supply either a house, land, or wood, Cape Cod communities clearly recognized their necessity for the survival of ministers. Towns regularly included land grants, firewood, and homes as part of their compensation for the minister. Yarmouth had reserved six acres for church usage at the beginning of settlement.[58] Barnstable granted Thomas Walley six acres of upland in 1665. When it was attempting to hire Jonathan Russell to replace him, the town offered Russell the lands it had purchased for Walley, as well as the house it had built for the former minister.[59] In 1659 Eastham set aside twenty acres at the head of the town cove for the use of the minister, and Samuel Treat was utilizing it in 1673/74.[60] In 1673 Sandwich offered John Smith ten acres if he would move there, and after he had, granted him two lots near the meeting house and one in the swamp. As an accepted resident, Smith was also entitled to rights in the town's common land.[61] Perhaps pleased Sandwich had at long last found a minister, the General Court also granted Smith land at Pinguine Hole in the Manomet area of the town.[62] Even Falmouth, despite its small size, recognized the need to have a resident clergyman and made attempts to provide for his support. In August of 1677, the town agreed to reserve twenty acres for the encouragement of a prospective minister, and in January of 1687/88 added twenty more.[63] The General Court had strongly encouraged Falmouth to take these actions.[64] The land received by ministers in the towns they served was not permanently theirs, however. Both Sandwich and Eastham specifically noted in their records that the land assigned to the minister was for his use while serving as pastor. It was not his to keep, and it was not to be sold by the town.[65]

The towns similarly recognized the necessity of housing and firewood as both inducements for prospective ministers to settle and as part of the overall compensation to which they were entitled. The reference to these added benefits are scarce, but frequent enough to indicate their significance. Eastham promised to supply Samuel Treat with firewood as part of its offer of the pastorate, and Yarmouth allowed Thomas Thornton all the wood he needed as part of its pension to him at his retirement.[66] Both Eastham and Sandwich supplied a parsonage for their minister at one time or another. In 1650 Sandwich voted five pounds to construct interior walls and finish the roof of William Leveridge's house, a responsibility the town admitted was long overdue.[67] In a general discussion of its expenses in support of a minister, Eastham recorded it had built a house for the minister's use.[68]

The final aspect of a town's support for its minister was the erection of a meeting house in which to preach. Like a home, firewood, and land, it was a part of the general support of religion that was not mandated by the colony, but which was provided anyway. When they were involved in settling the Sandwich land dispute in 1639, Thomas Prence and Myles Standish had ordered the town to acquire by purchase or exchange a centrally located lot for public use. The land later became the site for the meeting house.[69] At a town meeting in May 1655, thirty-eight Sandwich subscribers at last committed themselves to erecting a building. The town records contain references both to the collection of those pledges, and to the maintenance and repair of the building throughout the century.[70] The other towns were not as complete in their recording of the construction of a meeting house, but it is clear that each of them did so.[71] The building of a meeting house, like the supply of firewood and a house and lands, was part of the overall support for religion to be found among the towns of the Cape. Each community recognized the necessity for such support and provided it voluntarily, without pressure from the General Court.

In matters regarding the support of religion, the people of the Cape generally did what was expected of them. Other than the Quakers, only a few individuals had violated the laws designed to protect acceptable clergymen and churches, and Cape residents had compensated their ministers through voluntary payments in the early years of settlement. Cape towns seem to have preferred that method of support, and certainly had not rushed to comply with the General Court's various attempts to institute more formal procedures after

1657. But when the Court made the collection of ministers' salaries a colonial rather than a local matter, the Cape Cod towns soon conformed to the new law. Similarly, in the broader religiously related area of public morality, most residents of Cape Cod accepted the colony's general standards.

Notes

1. For discussions of church--state relations in Plymouth Colony, see Langdon, *Pilgrim Colony*, pp. 58-68; Harry M. Ward, *Statism in Plymouth Colony* (Port Washington, NY, 1973), pp. 53-54 (Hereinafter cited as *Statism*); J. M. Bumsted, "A Well-Bounded Toleration: Church and State in the Plymouth Colony," *Journal of Church and State* 10(1968):265-279 (Hereinafter cited as "Toleration"). For an analysis of the voluntary nature of Separatist congregations, see Edmund S. Morgan, *Visible Saints: The History of a Puritan Idea* (Ithaca, NY, c. 1963), pp. 24-32. The failure to create a tax-supported church did not mean the Pilgrims denied any relationship between political and religious power. As identified in both the 1672 and 1685 codifications of the colony's laws, one of Plymouth's "fundamentals" was that a major obligation of government was to protect and encourage the churches of the colony. *The Book of the General Laws of the Inhabitants of the Jurisdiction of New-Plimouth . . . 1672*, p. 3 (Hereinafter cited as *General Laws, 1672*); *The Book of the General Laws of the Inhabitants of the Jurisdiction of New-Plimouth . . . 1685*, pp. 2-3 ((Hereinafter cited as *General Laws, 1685*). Both compilations can be found in John D. Cushing (ed.), *The Laws of the Pilgrims* (New York, c. 1977).

2. For a discussion of the inherent conflict between congregational independence and the desire for religious orthodoxy, see Edmund S. Morgan, *The Puritan Dilemma: The Story of John Winthrop* (Boston, c. 1958), pp. 69-83. One of the earliest official recognitions of the problem can be seen in a memorandum included in the colony records at the end of the July 1646 meeting of the General Court. The Court noted "that something be done to maintain the liberties of the churches, without intermeddling or wronging each other, according to the statutes of England, that they may live in peace." *Ply. Col. Recs.*, 2:106.

3. *Ply. Church Recs.*, 1:63-64, 73, 107; Langdon, *Pilgrim Colony*, pp. 60-62, 117-119.

4. Langdon, *Pilgrim Colony*, pp. 116-117.

5. Lovell, *Sandwich*, p. 36; Langdon, *Pilgrim Colony*, pp. 66-67, 119. For Leveridge's own comments on his troubles in Sandwich, see William Leveridge to John Wilson, Sandwich, 22 September, 1651, in *Collec.*, Mass. Hist. Soc., 3d Ser., 4(1834):180-183. Henry Whitfield originally published Leveridge's letter in London in 1652 as part of his *Strength out of Weaknesse*, a collection of writings about New England Indians. Whitfield was a founder and the minister of Guilford in the New Haven Colony, and published his collection after his return to England in 1650. See also a long letter of Leveridge's regarding his views on sin and evil. William Leveridge to Thomas Hinckley, Sandwich, 22 February 1645/46, Misc. Bound Manuscripts, Massachusetts Historical Society, Boston, MA.

6. *Ply. Col. Recs.*, 3:10; Swift, *Old Yarmouth*, p. 76, 95.

7. Pratt, *Eastham*, p. 23; John L. Sibley, *Biographical Sketches of Graduates of Harvard University*, 3 vols. (Cambridge, 1873-1885; repr. New York, 1967), 1:382-383, 304 (Hereinafter cited as *Harvard Graduates*). Eastham had requested Plymouth's John Cotton to inquire about a suitable minister for the town when he traveled to Boston and Cambridge, and Treat may have come to Eastham as the result of his efforts. John Freeman *et al.* to John Cotton, Eastham, [31 July] 1672, Cotton Papers, pt. 6, #13, Boston Public Library.

8. *Ply. Church Recs.*, 1:72; Elizabeth C. Jenkins, "The First Church-- The Interim Years," (Hereinafter cited as "First Church") in Trayser (ed.), *Barnstable*, pp. 35-37. For a brief biography of Walley and his correspondence with Plymouth's John Cotton, see Walter Muir Whitehill (ed.), "Letters of the Reverend Thomas Walley of Barnstable to the Reverend John Cotton of Plymouth," *Proceed.*, Amer. Antiq. Society, 58(1948):247-262 (Hereinafter cited as "Walley Letters").

9. Thomas Walley to John Cotton, Barnstable, 19 November 1677, Cotton Papers, pt. 7, #36, Boston Public Library; Thomas Hinckley to John Cotton, Barnstable, 10 December 1677, ibid., #37; ; Thomas Cooper and Daniel Smith for the Rehoboth Church to the Plymouth Church, Rehoboth, 17 September 1679, ibid., pt. 8, #13; Samuel Angier to Thomas Hinckley, Cambridge, 27 January 1677/78, in "The Hinckley Papers," *Collec.*, Mass. Hist. Soc., 4th Ser., 5(1861):11-13 (Hereinafter cited as "Hinckley Papers"). For the death of Thomas Walley, see *Mather Papers*, in *Collec.*, Mass. Hist. Society, 4th Ser., 8(1868):242-243 and 242, n. (Hereinafter cited as *Mather Papers*).

10. Thomas Hinckley to John Cotton, Barnstable, 27 April 1678, Cotton Papers, pt. 8, #5, Boston Public Library; Thomas Hinckley to Isaac Foster, Barnstable, [May 1678], "Hinckley Papers", pp. 11-16, and p. 17n.; Records of the West Parish of Barnstable, Massachusetts, 1668-1807, p. 7

(Hereinafter cited as West Parish Records). The Massachusetts Historical Society made photostat copies of the original church records in 1924. Barnstable's West Parish was the successor to the original congregation when it divided in 1717. See also Sibley, *Harvard Graduates*, 2:338.

11. West Parish Records, p. 7. For a biography of Thacher, see Sibley, *Harvard Graduates*, 2:370-377.

12. John Cotton to Thomas Hinckley, Plymouth, 14 February 1678/79, in "Hinckley Papers," pp. 22-23; Samuel Phillips to Thomas Hinckley, Rowley, 18 June 1679, in ibid., pp. 26-28; Sibley, *Harvard Graduates*, 2:223-224, 392-393.

13. Thomas Hinckley to John Cotton, Barnstable, 15 July 1678, Cotton Papers, pt. 8, #7, Boston Public Library; John Cotton to Increase Mather, Plymouth, 15, 16 July 1678, *Mather Papers*, pp. 244-245. See also the notes of Thomas Prince regarding the issue in "Hinckley Papers," pp. 28-29.

14. Peter Thacher, Diary, 1678/79-1681/82, typescript, Massachusetts Historical Society, Boston, MA, pp. 34-38; West Parish Records, p. 7. See also Edward Pierce Hamilton, "The Diary of a Colonial Clergyman: Peter Thacher of Milton," *Proceed.*, Mass. Hist. Soc., 71(1953-1957):50-63.

15. Thacher, Diary, 1678/79-1681/82, pp. 43-44, 57, 71-73.

16. Thacher, Diary, 1678/79-1681/82, p. 91.

17. Thacher, Diary, 1678/79-1681/82, pp. 100-114, 155-156; Thomas Hinckley to John Cotton, Barnstable, 13 July 1680, Cotton Papers, pt. 8, #22, Boston Public Library. The Reverend Thacher found a more receptive congregation in Milton, and became its minister on 1 June 1681. Robert Tucker and William Blake for the Milton Church to Second Church of Boston, Milton, 17 May 1681, Mather Papers, vol. 4, #13, The Prince Library, Rare Books and Manuscripts, Boston Public Library, Boston, MA. This item is not part of the published *Mather Papers*.

18. West Parish Records, p. 7; Sibley, *Harvard Graduates*, 2:455-456.

19. Langdon, *Pilgrim Colony*, pp. 58-68.

20. *Ply. Col. Recs.*, 11:57-58. A marginal note indicates the General Court later repealed the 1650 law punishing the establishment of new churches without consent. The 1672 law code required a forty-shilling fine for violations of the Sabbath and the death penalty if a violation was "presumptuous." The fine was reduced to five shillings for some specific offenses in the 1685 code. *General Laws, 1672*, pp. 6-7; *General Laws, 1685*, p. 26. Attacking the Bible could bring a five-pound fine or a whipping in the 1685 code, while criticism of a minister or church brought a twenty-shilling fine for the first offense and a forty-shilling one for subsequent transgressions. *General Laws, 1672*, p. 7; *General Laws, 1685*, pp. 23-24. The 1672 code included a ten-shilling fine for failure to attend church

services, as well as the prospect of a fine, banishment, or "severe punishment" for speaking heresy and trying to convert others to it, an obvious reference to the Quakers. These restrictions were apparently not included in the 1685 codification. *General Laws, 1672*, p. 7.

21. See chapter four for details of these problems.

22. *Ply. Col. Recs.*, 2:172-173; 3:4.

23. *Ply. Col. Recs.*, 4:140; 8:118.

24. *Ply. Col. Recs.*, 5:87.

25. *Ply. Col. Recs.*, 2:165.

26. *Ply. Col. Recs.*, 4:158. The Nickerson family was notorious for its verbal and legal combativeness. Its concerns had less to do with religion, however, than with land claims and the right to live an independent life.

27. *Ply. Col. Recs.*, 5:43.

28. *Ply. Col. Recs.*, 6:152-153.

29. *Ply. Col. Recs.*, 3:47.

30. *Ply. Col. Recs.*, 5:53; 8:135.

31. *Ply. Col. Recs.*, 4:29.

32. *Ply. Col. Recs.*, 3:52

33. *Ply. Col. Recs.*, 2:173, 205.

34. *Ply. Col. Recs.*, 3:74.

35. *Ply. Col. Recs.*, 4:153.

36. *Ply. Col. Recs.*, 3:80-81. Bradford was responding to two different events, both calling for formal support of ministers. One was just such a recommendation from the Commissioners of the United Colonies, who had been prompted to action by a letter from Massachusetts calling attention to the problem. *Ply. Col. Recs.*, 10:155-158. The second event was Rehoboth's appeal to the General Court for assistance in forcing some of its inhabitants to support the minister. Ibid., p. 81. See also Bumsted, "Toleration," pp. 269-270; Stratton, *Plymouth Colony*, p. 95.

37. *Ply. Col. Recs.*, 11:64, 98.

38. John Winthrop, visiting Plymouth in the fall of 1632, describes the contribution process in his *Journal*, 1:93-94. For a discussion of voluntary maintenance, see Samuel S. Green, ["The Voluntary System in the Maintenance of Ministers,"] *Proceed.*, American Antiquarian Society, New Ser. 4(1886):85-126. Pp. 103-105 deal specifically with Plymouth.

39. *Ply. Col. Recs.*, 11:67, 98-99, 175-176. If the town refused to obey the law, a trio of Magistrates would levy the tax.

40. *Ply. Col. Recs.*, 3:150.

41. *Ply. Col. Recs.*, 3:155.

42. *Ply. Col. Recs.*, 11:140-141, 210.

43. *Ply. Col. Recs.*, 11:135, 207-208.

44. Thomas Walley, *A Balm in Gilead to heal Sions Wounds* (Cambridge, MA, 1670), pp. 13-14.

45. *Ply. Col. Recs.*, 11:224.

46. *Ply. Col. Recs.*, 5:31.

47. *Ply. Col. Recs.*, 11:226-227. In the early 1670's the General Court included its selections for collectors of the minister's salary in the official records. Thomas Huchens and Thomas Hinckley were collectors in Barnstable in 1670 and 1671. The Court selected John Freeman and Jonathan Sparrow for Eastham in 1670. Reflective of Sandwich's lack of a minister until 1675, none were selected for the town until then, when Thomas Tupper and Thomas Dexter were chosen. Yarmouth's collectors were Thomas Howes and John Thacher in 1670 and Samuel Rider and John Miller in 1671. Ibid., 5:37, 58-59, 172.

48. *Ply. Col. Recs.*, 5:241-242.

49. Yarmouth Town Records, 1677-1726, p. 14.

50. Yarmouth Town Records, 1677-1726, p. 18.

51. Yarmouth's records do not exist for the period of Marmaduke Mathews's tenure in the town.

52. Sandwich Town Records, 1652-1692, pp. 29-30. The total pledge to support the minister was fifteen pounds, six shillings. For the meeting house, the pledges ranged from five shillings to two pounds and totaled twenty-six pounds, three shillings. Many of those who pledged to build the meeting house but not to support the minister had joined the Quaker meeting by 1657. Three men, George Buit, Richard Chadwell, and Richard Smith, contributed to the proposed minister's support but not the meeting house, while twenty-six men contributed to the meeting house but not the minister. Such a small degree of similarity between the two lists represents the central role of voluntarism in the support of religion in Sandwich. William Leveridge had recently left Sandwich, and these efforts to build a meeting house and support a minister were measures taken to aid in securing a replacement. Nineteen men signed a letter to one Mr. Lovering in 1655 encouraging him to accept the pastorate at Sandwich. He declined the offer. Ibid. p. 7.

53. Eastham Record of Town Meetings, 1654-1745, pp. 12, 17-18. The records for 12 May 1675 also mention Treat's salary. Ibid., p. 20.

54. Yarmouth Town Records, 1677-1726, p. 2. For other town actions which include the minister's salary as part of the tax, see ibid., pp. 3, 8, 13, 29, 34, 46.

55. Eastham Record of Town Meetings, 1654-1745, pp. 26, 27, 30, 41, 42-43.

56. Sandwich Town Records, 1652-1692, pp. 158, 172, 182, 216, 222, 242.

57. Barnstable Town Records, 1640-1753, p. 122.

58. *Ply. Col. Recs.*, 2:62. Yarmouth's action came to light when someone tried to sell the land illegally.

59. Barnstable Town Records, 1640-1753, pp. 112-113, 118-119.

60. Eastham Record of Land and Meadow Grants, 1654-1743, p. 17. The land had been included in the town's offer to Treat in 1673. Eastham Record of Town Meetings, 1654-1745, pp. 17-18. The town granted him more land in 1676. Eastham Record of Land and Meadow Grants, 1654-1743, p. 18.

61. Sandwich Town Records, 1652-1692, pp. 108, 109, 147. Similar grants were made to Rowland Cotton when he assumed the ministry in 1690. Ibid., pp. 235-237.

62. *Ply. Col. Recs.*, 5:171. The Court allowed John Holmes, teacher at the Duxbury church, to succeed to his father's Duxbury land rights at the same time.

63. Falmouth Proprietors' Records, 1661-1804, pp. 10, 20. The January 1687/88 allotment was composed of two twenty-acre parcels. One had been left vacant by the original purchasers for the purpose of ministerial support, and the other was to be purchased by exchanging town-owned land for twenty acres held by Jonathan Dunham. Ibid. p. 10.

64. *Ply. Col. Recs.*, 6:72.

65. Sandwich Town Records, 1652-1692, pp. 108, 109, 235, 236-237; Eastham Record of Land and Meadow Grants, 1654-1743, pp. 18-19. Eastham Record of Town Meetings, 1654-1745, pp. 17-18.

66. Eastham Record of Land and Meadow Grants, 1654-1743, pp. 18-19; Yarmouth Town Records, 1677-1726, p. 57.

67. Sandwich Town Records, 1652-1692, p. 10.

68. Eastham Record of Land and Meadow Grants, 1654-1743 pp. 18-19.

69. *Ply. Col. Recs.*, 1:133; Lovell, *Sandwich*, p. 38. The lot contained somewhat over one-half acre.

70. Sandwich Town Records, 1652-1692, pp. 29, 52, 72, 137, 152.

71. Yarmouth Town Records, 1677-1726, pp. 25, 30; Barnstable Town Records, 1640-1753, 116-117; Eastham Record of Town Meetings, 1654-1745, p. 25.

VII

"For the preventing of
Idleness and other evils"

JUST as Plymouth Colony's leaders believed state and church existed to support each other and had acted to insure the relationship, they also viewed governmental regulation of personal behavior as part of that alliance. Heirs to the broader Puritan principle that the virtue of society was to be played out by the actions of its members, Plymouth's leadership believed individual behavior represented the moral worth of the community. Personal error needed to be prevented so as not to corrupt society. Within this system, the Plymouth leaders hoped to educate the younger generation both in the broader goals of the colony, and the personal costs of wandering from them. The result of such an intertwining of political, religious, and social purposes was a colony where individual rights and personal beliefs were distinctly secondary to broader communal purposes.

Two aspects of human behavior in which the authorities took a special interest were the consumption of tobacco and alcohol. Except for prohibiting the sale of intoxicants to the native Indians, their emphasis was on the regulation of excess rather than abstinence. The General Court assessed fines for drunkenness, and increased them for subsequent offenses. The standard fine was five shillings for the first infraction, rising to twenty for the third and subsequent ones.

Ultimately, a freeman who was habitually drunk would lose the right to vote.[1] Despite the implication of the colony's laws that liquor was an issue requiring extensive control, Cape Codders do not seem to have found it a significant problem. Only a handful of its residents were prosecuted for violations of the laws against drunkenness. The General Court fined Teague Jones of Yarmouth six pounds at its October 1660 meeting for being drunk several times, and fifty shillings two years later for being drunk again. The Court assessed Thomas Starr of Yarmouth and John Hathaway of Barnstable five shillings each at the June 1668 Court. Christopher Blake of Yarmouth received two hours in the stocks for getting drunk on a military training day and acting suggestively toward an Indian woman at the time.[2] But these are infrequent cases in the colony records, and they are not supplemented with any from the local ones. It is possible the government took notice only of habitual offenders, but for the men of Cape Cod, drunkenness was not such a problem that any large number of them were in trouble for it. Either the fear of paying the fines kept men from over-indulgence, or the colony's other efforts to restrict access to liquor were effective enough to prevent a problem from appearing.

Based, perhaps, on the assumption that it was easier to prevent immoral behavior than punish it, Plymouth Colony made serious attempts to restrict the availability of liquor. Its most important effort was to permit the sale of liquor only at inns and ordinaries and to license those who managed them. Those found selling liquor without a license paid a prohibitive five-pound fine. The Court also severely restricted the general operation of inns and ordinaries. Among the Court imposed regulations were ones relating to the quality of beer and the prices charged, a time limit on tippling, and prohibitions on selling on Sundays and lecture days, after dark, and to children and servants. To enforce its restrictions, the Court in 1671 appointed a two-or three-man committee in each town to inspect ordinaries and report breaches of regulations to the Court.[3]

Cape Cod towns appear to have been as responsible and accountable to the aims of the legislation as could be expected. Primarily, the General Court was careful in its selection of licensees. Those men allowed to operate ordinaries were almost always freemen of the colony and men who served as Deputies and selectmen. They included such individuals as Anthony Thacher, a grantee and freeman of Yarmouth; Henry Cobb, an early settler and freeman of Barnstable; and, before he became a Quaker, William Newland, one of

Sandwich's few freemen.   The Court licensed all three to operate ordinaries in their respective towns at its June 1644 meeting.   Thomas Huchens and Joseph Lothrop, two of Barnstable's leading citizens, served as ordinary keepers in the 1650's and 1660's.   Edward Sturgess was a frequent licensee in Yarmouth.[4]   Obviously, the leaders of the colony in the General Court intended that the retailing of intoxicating liquor should be under the rather strict control of its most responsible citizens.

The General Court did, however, recognize the special needs of travelers.   To provide for their refreshment, the Court issued special licenses which allowed the recipient to sell only to transients.   In order to control local consumption, these licenses specifically prohibited local residents from participating.   The Court granted such a license to Isaac Robinson at Saconesett, or Falmouth, in 1664/65, in order to serve those going to Martha's Vineyard and Nantucket. William Bassett and his successor John Ellis received the same type of license in Sandwich in 1659.[5]

Occasionally, the colonial government found it necessary to institute restrictions or administer discipline regarding the sale of alcohol.   In 1671, the Court fined John Otis of Barnstable forty shillings for selling hard cider without a license.   It fined Ann, the widow of Barnstable's Anthony Annable, twenty shillings for illegally selling liquor to both English and Indians and required her to post a twenty-pound bond for future good behavior.   It similarly charged Francis Baker of Yarmouth but later cleared him.[6]   At other times, the problem was not illegal sales, but the conduct of the tipplers. George Crispe of Eastham received a twenty-shilling fine for the disorderliness of his ordinary in 1662.   At the June 1670 session of the General Court, Yarmouth's license changed hands.   The Court revoked John Miller's license, while issuing Edward Sturgess, Sr., one of his numerous ones.   Sturgess received his license with the specific stipulation that he operate a respectable ordinary, and one can only assume Miller had lost his license for his failure to do just that.[7] But like drunkenness, illegal sales and turbulent drinkers were not the normal experience of Cape Cod.   Considering the amount of liquor which entered the towns of the Cape, one would expect far more references to violations of both the colony's laws and society's standards.

In addition to significant fines for drunkenness and the licensing of retail sales, Plymouth Colony also attempted to control liquor by a system of excise taxes and the appointment of local collectors.   While the colony had instituted such taxes and appointed collectors as early as the 1640's, it was not until the early 1660's that the Court specifically assigned them the task of keeping invoices of imports brought into the town and laid down elaborate stipulations concerning their recording.[8] For a few years following the passage of the law, the colony included the returns of its excise collectors in its records. Nearly all the reports are from Cape Cod towns, and are a strong indication of the Cape's commercial importance to the colony of Plymouth in the seventeenth century. Liquor was, without question, the major item mentioned in the accounts. Anthony Thacher listed sixty-nine gallons and one barrel brought into Yarmouth in his 1662 report.[9] The next year, he and Robert Dennis reported that from May of 1663 to March of 1663/64, the town imported over 123 gallons of liquor. For the same period in Barnstable, Joseph Lothrop listed 177 gallons and seven "cases." The reports from other collectors indicate a similar level of importation, although much of it was done for others and was not solely for local consumption.[10] Certainly, there would have been far more punishment of drunkenness and violations of the laws regarding ordinaries on the Cape, if those who imported liquor there had sold it only to their friends and neighbors. But if the few reports to be found in the official records are any indication, the people of Plymouth consumed a goodly amount of liquor. They give some substance to the General Court's demand that eight Cape Codders appear at the next session of the Court to explain why they imported such great quantities of intoxicants.[11] It may also explain why the church at Plymouth found it necessary to petition the colonial government to reduce the number of ordinaries in the town, on the assumption that one was enough.[12] But while such concerns may represent a fear that alcoholic consumption in the colony might get out of hand, evidence from Cape Cod intimates that in actual practice, it did not.

Plymouth viewed the smoking, or "drinking," of tobacco in much the same way it did the consumption of alcohol. The General Court attempted to limit usage by prohibiting it where it was regarded as dangerous or inappropriate. Among the occasions when smoking was not allowed were while on jury duty until the verdict had been submitted, on public streets or in barns and haystacks, and on Sunday while traveling to or from church services.[13] As with violations of the laws against alcohol, the small number of cases from the Cape do not indicate the existence of a serious problem. In March 1640/41 the Grand Jury presented John Bryant and Daniel Pryor of Barnstable for smoking on the public highway.[14] In 1663 the Court fined Nehemiah Besse of Sandwich five shillings for smoking at church on Sunday, and five years later Richard Berry, Sr., James Maker, and Jedediah and Benjamin Lombard received the same fine for the same offense in Yarmouth.[15] Certainly the Cape Cod towns had more smokers than these cases indicate, and it is probable only those who flagrantly flaunted the restrictive laws appeared before the courts for punishment.

But Plymouth Colony was not concerned only with the consumption of alcohol and tobacco. There were other areas of personal behavior which the governmental authorities intended to regulate so as to insure the general godliness of the colony. Of primary concern for the colony's leaders was the problem of controlling what they believed to be deviant sexual practices. Just as the excessive consumption of alcohol and the inappropriate use of tobacco were deemed blots on the colony, so also was any sexual activity outside of heterosexual marriage. While the laws may seem severe and the punishments extreme, they actually were more representative of the fear of evil than any general occurrence of it. And they were not always enforced with the rigidity their harshness implied. Although there are examples from Cape Cod towns of the violation of each of the laws against unacceptable sexual behavior, to assume that the Cape was awash with licentiousness and the guilty pitilessly punished is an error.

Throughout the century, sodomy and bestiality were punishable by death, but the 1642 case of Thomas Granger is the only example of any one being executed for either crime.[16] The Cape apparently had no bestiality cases, or at least none appear in the records. It did, however, witness two convictions for male homosexuality and one for female. All three instances occurred in the first decade of Cape settlement. Because John Lothrop recorded the particulars in his "Diary," the case of William Carsley is the fullest. A freeman and Constable of Barnstable, as well as a member of Lothrop's congregation, Carsley apparently had made advances towards Giles Hopkins on three occasions. Hopkins brought charges against him, which Carsley denied, although he admitted to having engaged in those practices with others. Before it was over, Carsley was excommunicated from the congregation, replaced as Constable, and required to post a twenty-pound bond to appear before the General Court to answer the charges. With a hint of sadness and pastoral empathy, Lothrop noted Carsley bore his punishment, especially

excommunication, with great patience.[17]   Three months later, the
Court ordered Edward Mitchell and Edward Preston, possibly
servants in Barnstable, whipped at both Plymouth and Barnstable for
sodomy.[18]   The only case of lesbianism involving Cape residents
came before the General Court at its March 1648/49 session.   At it,
the Grand Jury presented Sarah, wife of Hugh Norman, and Mary
Hammon for lewd behavior with each other.   Mrs. Norman, who had
apparently victimized Mary Hammon, did not appear in Plymouth to
answer the charges until October 1650.   At that session, the Court
required her to make a public acknowledgment of her transgressions
and warned her to be careful in the future, lest she be punished more
severely.   A second offense would seemingly bring a double
whipping.[19]

It is difficult to know how to evaluate these instances.   There is
no indication there were false charges or the defendants were treated
unjustly.   But they occurred within a few years of each other, at a
time when Plymouth was adjusting to its new role as a colony instead
of a plantation.   The kind of problems which led to the land and
religious squabbles of Sandwich, Yarmouth, and Barnstable may well
have heightened the criticism of neighbors by Cape Cod residents.   It
seems unlikely there were not similar scattered instances of sexual
deviance in the years after 1650, but they do not appear in the
records.   Perhaps it was less necessary to make an issue of them once
Plymouth had made peace with its early expansion.   Or perhaps the
colony turned its concerns to what it saw as more important problems.
Certainly, however, the disregard for the legally mandated death
penalty in the cases from the Cape indicates at the least a sense of
compassion   and   charitableness   not   usually   associated   with
seventeenth-century New England.

While the colony reserved its harshest punishments for what it
viewed as unnatural sexual practices, it also passed laws intended to
regulate more normal sexual activity not within the bonds of
matrimony.   Plymouth recognized rape, fornication, and adultery as
the three areas of sexual conduct needing governmental punishment.
Like the more unnatural activities, incidents of occurrence in the
towns of the Cape were not numerous, and indicate less a serious
problem with violations than that Cape Codders lived relatively
normal sex lives.

Rape was the only one of the heterosexual activities calling
consistently for the death penalty, although the only case of a Cape
resident being found guilty of the crime resulted in a whipping.[20]

The laws against fornication were more complicated, with the level of punishment declining the closer the occurrence was to marriage. Outright fornication was punishable by a ten-pound fine. If the couple married, the charge was lowered to pre-marital sex, and the fine reduced by half. It was cut in half again if the sexual activity had occurred during the espousal period and was discovered by the birth of a child too soon after marriage. Whippings were an alternative to fines, and the couple could also be jailed for up to three days.[21] That all three levels of fornication occurred should not be surprising. A straightforward case involved David Linnett and Hannah Shelley, whom the Court ordered whipped in Barnstable. The local congregation also punished the couple by rescinding their church privileges.[22] Ruhamah Turner of Sandwich found herself in trouble with the Court twice for fornication. The Court fined her five pounds on 4 October 1664 and again on 7 March 1664/65, but she may have been the victim of malicious gossip or unsubstantiated charges. A group of her neighbors agreed to pay the first fine, and the Court reduced her second one to one-half the five pounds originally levied.[23] The third fornication case involving a Cape Codder is both the saddest and most revealing of the ones chronicled in the records. At the 4 October 1655 session of the General Court, the Grand Jury presented Jane Powell, a servant of William Swift of Sandwich, for fornication. Her partner was David Ogillior, an Irishman and servant of Edward Sturgess. Upon examination, Powell admitted to the charge, but asserted that she hoped to marry Ogillior in an effort to escape her servitude, which she went on to describe as hard, sad, miserable, and without proper clothing. Her description of servitude in the household of Sturgess and her expressions of regret for her actions must have struck a responsive strain in the Court. It temporarily cleared her of the charges and ordered her to return home.[24] The authorities apparently understood something of the hard life of servants in seventeenth-century New England, as well as a good deal about human nature.

The cases of premarital sex, involving couples engaged to marry, were more numerous than outright fornication between individuals who were not. They involved charges against a married couple, and were usually proven by the birth of a child significantly sooner than nine months after marriage. For example, the Court fined Thomas Launders of Sandwich and his wife for premarital fornication because she gave birth thirty weeks after their marriage. Similarly, the Grand Jury indicted Nicholas Davis of Barnstable and his wife for the birth of a child five weeks and four days earlier than expected after marriage.[25]   There were similar cases distributed across the records.   Fines and punishments differed, determined by the special considerations and circumstances of the particular case at hand.   John Carsley of Barnstable and John Ellis of Sandwich were whipped, while their wives watched.   Others, like Jabez Snow and his wife, were fined.[26]

As sexual activity before marriage was discouraged, it was similarly disapproved of when it occurred outside the marriage contract.   Although originally a capital crime, the more usual punishment was to be whipped twice, once in Plymouth and again in the town where the offense occurred.   Both parties were also required to wear the letters A and D sewn to the clothing when in public.   It must be noted that the crime was defined in terms of a married woman's adultery with either a single or married man, and not a married man's involvement with a single woman.[27]

Like the other unacceptable sexual activities which appear in the records, adultery had its small number of practitioners on the Cape. In a December 1641 decision the General Court gave Thomas Bray and Anne, wife of Francis Linceford, exactly the prescribed sentence.[28]   At its July 1670 session, the Court fined Abisha Marchant of Yarmouth forty shillings for adultery with Mary, wife of Morgan Jones.[29]   Other adultery cases were adjuncts of divorce proceedings.   Adultery was one of the few acceptable grounds for the dissolution of a marriage.   The Court convicted Sandwich's Thomas Burgess, Jr., of adultery with Lydia Gaunt in June 1661, and ordered him whipped in Plymouth and Sandwich.   His wife Elizabeth sued for divorce over the matter, which the Court granted, along with an award of one-third of Burgess's estate and some bedding.[30]   In June 1686, the Court of Assistants granted John Glover of Barnstable a divorce after he petitioned and then appeared personally to plead his case.   Not only had his wife committed adultery, but she had spread venereal disease to him as a result.[31]

More broadly than the regulation of sexual activity, the government of Plymouth also attempted to control marriage in general.   Seen as a civil matter, the General Court passed laws requiring the public announcement and recording of marriages, gave parents all reasonable control over the marriages of their children, and stipulated that marriage ceremonies were to be performed by either a Magistrate or an individual specially commissioned to do so.[32]   Those selected for the responsibility of conducting marriages were usually the more prominent members of the community, noted for their respectability and no doubt generally selected for their ability to add a certain solemnity to the occasion. Typical were the June 1650 appointments of Thomas Tupper for Sandwich and Thomas Hinckley for Barnstable and Yarmouth.[33]

Occasionally the Court became embroiled in controversial marriage proceedings as well. On 2 March 1646/47 Francis Crocker of Barnstable petitioned the Court about his prospective marriage to Mary Gaunt, a match opposed by her kinsman, Henry Coggin. The Court settled the dispute by permitting the marriage to occur if Crocker could produce medical evidence that his illness was not the "falling sickness."[34] The Court was a little less sympathetic to Thomas Dunham in 1648. It prohibited him from visiting or communicating with Martha Knott of Sandwich until the Court could determine the validity of his marriage proposal to her.[35] The 1653 marriage of Edward Perry, who would become a prominent Quaker, and Mary Freeman, somehow related to Edmund Freeman, is the most complicated of the marriages whose circumstances brought its participants to the attention of the General Court. The Court, at its March 1653/54 session, ordered Perry to pay a five-pound fine for marrying Miss Freeman in violation of the Court's order that marriages be performed by those licensed to do so. It also took away Thomas Tupper's authorization to conduct marriages in Sandwich because of his negligence in this affair. To resolve the matter, the Court commissioned Thomas Prence to intervene and perform the marriage properly while on his journey home to Eastham. Prence failed in his assignment, and at its next session the Court again fined Perry five pounds for his refusal to cooperate with the Governor. The Court also stated the same fine would be levied at every future session of the General Court until the marriage was correctly executed.[36] There is no evidence an acceptable wedding service ever occurred or that the fines were ever paid. It was a most interesting case, and one can only wish there were more details to clarify both the relationships of the individuals involved and the events which actually happened.

While the General Court seems to have concerned itself primarily with the legitimacy of particular marriages and the confinement of sexual activity to them, local churches became more intimately involved with married couples. The most extraordinary example concerned John Hinckley and his wife Bethia. John was the brother of Governor Thomas Hinckley, and Bethia, the granddaughter of John Lothrop. Independent and certainly less than servile, Mrs.

Hinckley presented serious problems for the Barnstable church and its newly ordained minister Jonathan Russell. Russell, assisted by Elder John Chipman, included in the church records in 1684 a lengthy litany of her sins. The church accused her of violating four of the ten commandments, although defining its terms rather loosely. The commandment against murder was expanded to include her refusal to help her husband, and the one requiring the honoring of parents was similarly interpreted to include him. Apparently her independence, her refusal to assist and revere her husband, and her willingness to laugh at those who tried to correct her marked Mrs. Hinckley as a less than proper wife. She left the church no alternative but to excommunicate her.[37] In the end, the case says as much about the expected standards of wifely behavior as it does the sins of Bethia Hinckley.

The violations of Plymouth Colony's sexual and marriage standards by its residents on Cape Cod combine to give a fairly clear message of both the transgressions themselves and the nature of the punishment. The variety of instances indicates on the one hand that nearly all the specific types of unacceptable practice occurred at some time or other on the Cape. On the other hand, the number of them which appear in the records denotes that their presence was not a general or usual event. Considering all the people who lived on the Cape during the over half century it was part of Plymouth Colony, sexual misdeeds involved an extremely small number of its inhabitants. And when misconduct did occur, the variability of the punishments given out by the Courts represents an unexpected sympathy for transgressors.

From the severity of the punishments and the number of cases from the Cape before the colony's courts, excessive drinking and unnatural sexual activity appear to have been the aspects of human behavior of most concern to the leaders of the colony. But there were other elements of personal conduct about which the authorities worried.

Lying and swearing were both activities the Court hoped to control in order to keep the colony on course and were treated by the General Court much the same as unacceptable sexual activity and excessive drinking. Each action generally carried a ten-shilling fine or a sojourn in the stocks if the guilty party could not pay.[38] Scattered examples of the Court punishing both crimes are recorded, and their small number indicates the authorities probably punished only the more serious or blatant liars and swearers. Certainly more people lied or cursed in Plymouth Colony than are recorded in the records. At the March 1641/42 session of the General Court, the Grand Jury indicted John Gray of Yarmouth for swearing, and at its May 1665 meeting, the Court of Assistants fined Ralph Smith of Eastham ten shillings for telling a lie.[39]

Local congregations took action against liars and swearers as well. The Barnstable church disciplined one "brother Henricke" for lying, and excommunicated Samuel Jackson for lying and the suspicion of stealing.[40] In 1649 it cast out Mrs. Shelly in absentia for her verbal attacks on John Lothrop, regarded as lies, and for similar false attacks on two women of the church.[41]

The overseers of the public good were also concerned with two other related behavioral issues, the question of people living alone and the problem of unknown newcomers. Both matters were concerns which have a more specific seventeenth-century flavor to them than the issues of alcohol, tobacco, or sexual deviance. Unfamiliar and single persons challenged the strong communal spirit of both the colony and its individual towns. People living alone were too independent and difficult to control. "Strangers" were by definition unknown individuals, who by their very nature instilled the fear of unforeseen problems and the threat of unacceptable ideas. In addition, both groups were mistrusted as potential public charges. The colony and its towns each made serious efforts to control the presence of unmarried adults and new inhabitants, hoping thereby to limit the prospect of mischief which they represented. Originally, the colony had demanded new settlers receive the consent of both the Governor and two Assistants. By 1658 it had adopted the more realistically enforceable policy of requiring new inhabitants to have either the sanction of the Governor, a Magistrate, or the selectmen of the town where they settled. The Court also presumed new residents would take the oath of fidelity, and allowed towns to "warn" undesirable people out of town.[42]

But residency was in reality a local issue. The people of Plymouth, after all, lived in its individual towns. As a result, cases concerning unacceptable inhabitants and those who lived alone seldom reached the colony's courts, although there were a few from the Cape. At the March 1638/39 term of the General Court, the Grand Jury separately indicted Joseph Windsor and Anthony Besse of Sandwich for living disorderly lives alone. These two incidents may have gone to the Grand Jury because of additional complications. Windsor had

been warned about living alone over the previous six months, and
Besse had opened his quarters to a second bachelor.[43]

From the number of recorded cases, the problem of strangers
was of greater concern. The charge that the town admitted too many
unacceptable settlers had been one of the issues in the settlement of
Sandwich's land controversy in the 1630's.[44] Earlier, and more
specifically, the Court had ordered James Skiffe of Sandwich to return
Henry Ewer and his wife to their original community. Skiffe,
apparently, had brought the Ewers into Sandwich without
authorization.[45] Similarly, in March 1660/61 the Court ordered
Richard Child to stop building a cottage in Yarmouth, and instructed
Anthony Thacher and Thomas Howes to enforce the restriction.
Child refused to cease construction, but did appear at the June 1661
meeting of the General Court to pledge that Yarmouth would be free
of any charges caused by his children. The Court then allowed him to
occupy his cottage.[46] There were other instances. In 1680 the
Barnstable selectmen brought a complaint against the residency of
Ephraim and Marcy Phillips, who had moved there from Taunton
without the consent of the town.[47] The Yarmouth constable made a
similar complaint three years later regarding the settlement of one
John Abraham.[48] In the turmoil surrounding the Glorious Revolution
and the problem of incorporation into Massachusetts, Cape Cod
apparently became a center for unauthorized settlement. At its June
1690 meeting, the General Court noted that several people had settled
on Cape Cod without permission, were cutting timber illegally, and
generally living disorderly lives. It ordered the treasurer of the
colony, William Bradford, to prosecute them for trespass.[49]

Individual towns on the Cape had similar regulations about
newcomers. Although the approaches to the question were usually
different, the intent was the same. Each community undertook to
control who could or could not settle in the town. As early as 1640,
Barnstable met the problem by prohibiting any inhabitant from selling
his house without first offering it to the town. If the town did not buy
the house, it allowed itself two months to provide an acceptable
purchaser, after which the owner could sell to anyone.[50] While the
success of the measure cannot be determined, it must be assumed
Barnstable made serious efforts to prevent the last option. The other
Cape towns did not enact their restrictions as early, although there is
no indication that they did not follow Barnstable's restrictive
practices. At a 16 July 1662 town meeting, Eastham allowed those
responsible for granting land in the town to force undesirable

newcomers to leave, unless the voters in general approved of them.[51] Yarmouth made its restrictions formal in January of 1681/82, when it required the taking of the colony's oath of fidelity as a prerequisite for residency.[52] Presumably, men qualified to take the oath would make acceptable residents. The Sandwich records do not include any specific regulations on the admission of residents, but the town's efforts in that direction can be seen in its admission of particular individuals to the status of inhabitant.[53] The other Cape Cod communities similarly recorded the admission of individual residents, indicating they took seriously their power to control the makeup of their citizenry.[54]

All in all, Plymouth Colony and its individual towns demonstrated a vigilant interest in their inhabitants. Both levels of government made persistent efforts to control the privilege of residency, and continued to keep a most attentive eye on the personal lives of those who had won the prize. But it must be acknowledged there were lapses in the ideal of uniformity. There were those who settled who were not wanted. Some who were acceptable did not always behave responsibly and had to be punished. But the problems and the violations are scattered and sometimes even rare. It is less important that the violations of the colony's moral standards imply the failure of its ideals and more significant that the relative sparseness of them indicates their general acceptance.

Notes

1. *Ply. Col. Recs.,* 11:17, 96, 101, 173, 177, 197; *General Laws, 1685,* pp. 25-26. In addition to the fine of twenty shillings for the fourth violation, the Court required the individual to post bond guaranteeing his future good behavior. Ibid. For the fines against selling liquor to the Indians, see *Ply. Col. Recs.,* 11:54, 184, 218, 234, 235, 256; *General Laws, 1672,* pp. 44-45. With the consent of a Magistrate or the selectmen, it was possible to give an Indian a small dose of liquor for medicinal purposes. For a general discussion of the liquor issue in Plymouth Colony, see Ward, *Statism,* pp. 96-98.

2. *Ply. Col. Recs.,* 3:200; 4:29, 187; 5:31.

3. *Ply. Col. Recs.,* 5:59-60; 11:17, 113, 195, 218, 236, 244, 257, 258; *General Laws, 1672,* pp. 41-42; *General Laws, 1685,* pp. 34-36. The inspectors for Sandwich were James Skiffe and Edward Perry, for Yarmouth,

John Welden and Nathaniel Bassett, for Barnstable, James Hamblin, Jr., and James Cobb, and for Eastham, Jonathan Sparrow and Thomas Paine. The colony eventually passed a tax, based proportionally on population, on those who held licenses. Ibid., 11:222.

    4. *Ply. Col. Recs.*, 2:73, 105, 141; 3:22; 4:40; 5:223.

    5. *Ply. Col. Recs.*, 3:159, 161; 4:80.

    6. *Ply. Col. Recs.*, 3:28; 5:81, 246.

    7. *Ply. Col. Recs.*, 4:29; 5:43. Sturgess had not always been such a model of respectability, however. In March 1663/64, the Court had withdrawn his license because of the "abuse of liquor" at Yarmouth. Ibid., 4:54.

    8. *Ply. Col. Recs.*, 2:105; 4:23; 11:51, 131, 195-196. The 1662 measure required that two men in each town maintain an invoice of the liquor, gun powder, shot, and lead brought into the town. In Barnstable they were Nathaniel Bacon and Joseph Lothrop; in Eastham, Daniel Cole and Jonathan Sparrow; in Sandwich, Nathaniel Fish and Thomas Toby; and in Yarmouth, Anthony Thacher and Robert Dennis.

    9. *Ply. Col. Recs.*, 4:28.

    10. *Ply. Col. Recs.*, 4:52-53, 100-101, 152-153.

    11. *Ply. Col. Recs.*, 4:183. The eight men were Samuel Sturgess, Edward Sturgess, Eliza Hedge, Thomas Starr, John Crowe, Jr., Abraham Hedge, John McCoy, and Mark Ridley.

    12. Petition from the Church at Plymouth to the Governor and Assistants, [Plymouth], 7 March 1681/82, in "Hinckley Papers," pp. 59-61.

    13. *Ply. Col. Recs.*, 11:36, 53, 97, 174, 224-225; *General Laws, 1672*, p. 10. Interestingly, laws regarding the use of tobacco do not appear in the 1685 edition of the colony's laws. Perhaps the colony had lost the battle to control usage, and did not include laws it knew it could not enforce.

    14. *Ply. Col. Recs.*, 2:12.

    15. *Ply. Col. Recs.*, 4:47; 5:16.

    16. *General Laws, 1672*, p. 4; *General Laws, 1685*, p. 10. Granger was a servant in Duxbury, and convicted of multiple offenses against the bestiality law. *Ply. Col. Recs.*, 2:44. For a general discussion of sexual morality in the colony, see John Demos, *A Little Commonwealth: Family Life in Plymouth Colony* (London, c. 1970), pp. 82-99, 152-159 (Hereinafter cited as *Commonwealth*); Ward, *Statism*, pp. 94-96; and Stratton, *Plymouth Colony*, pp. 191-206. William Bradford interpreted Granger's case as symptomatic of a general moral decline, and asked a committee of clergymen to clarify just what unnatural acts were punishable by death. Each clergyman responded separately to the questions, signifying a less than unanimous

opinion. Bradford, *Plymouth Plantation*, pp. 316-317, 404-413; Langdon, *Pilgrim Colony*, pp. 64-65; and Stratton, *Plymouth Colony*, p. 158.

17. Lothrop, "Diary," pp. 35-36; *Ply. Col. Recs.*, 1:125, 137, 141; 8:176, 200. Carsley's name is crossed off on both the Constable list for 1639/40 and the 1658 Freeman list. He was excommunicated on 5 September 1641, and ordered by the Court to post bond for his appearance three months later. His 1639/40 replacement as Constable indicates his troubles started before either Lothrop or the colony recorded specific notice of them. The outcome of his trial is not noted in the records.

18. *Ply. Col. Recs.*, 2:35-36. One John Keene was required to watch the whipping because, although he had resisted the overtures of the two men convicted, he was judged not wholly blameless.

19. *Ply. Col. Recs.*, 2:137, 163.

20. *General Laws, 1672*, p. 5; *General Laws, 1685*, p. 10. The guilty party was Ambrose Fish of Sandwich, and the victim was Lydia Fish. Ambrose was the son of Nathaniel Fish, an early settler of Sandwich. Ambrose's relationship to Lydia is exceedingly unclear. She was neither a sister nor a cousin, as none of Sandwich's three original Fish brothers had a daughter named Lydia. She may have been the daughter of his father's second wife, Lydia Miller, from a previous marriage. A blood relation is unlikely, given the lack of the death penalty. *Ply. Col. Recs.*, 5:245-246; Savage, *Genealogical Dictionary*, 2:161; Lester W. Fish, *The Fish Family in England and America*, (Rutland, VT, 1948), pp. 344-349; Lydia B. Brownson, Grace W. Held, and Doris V. Norton (comps.), Genealogical Notes on Cape Cod Families, 1620-1901, Sturgis Library, Barnstable, Massachusetts, s.v. "Fish;" Stratton, *Plymouth Colony*, pp. 198-199.

21. *Ply. Col. Recs.*, 11:12, 46, 95, 172; *General Laws, 1672*, pp. 5-6; *General Laws, 1685*, p. 23. Both partners were treated as equally guilty in fornication cases.

22. *Ply. Col. Recs.*, 3:11; Lothrop, *Diary*, p. 34.

23. *Ply. Col. Recs.*, 4:77, 84, 99, 101. John Ewer had twenty shillings of his three-pound fine for fornication with Miss Turner rebated in October 1669. Whether this fine was the result of the first, second, or a possible third fornication conviction for Turner is not clear. *Ply. Col. Recs.*, 5:27. Her activities, or the reputation for them, do not seem to have had any long term detrimental impact on her. She eventually married John Jennings in Sandwich, and one of their sons was an early school teacher in the town. Lovell, *Sandwich*, p. 144.

24. *Ply. Col. Recs.*, 3:91. Presumably, that was the end of the case, as the issue did not reappear. Miss Powell's beloved may have been David O'Kelley, despite the printed record's Ogillior. If so, the Court perhaps

dropped the case because Jane Powell married David O'Kelley, and they moved to Yarmouth. See Lovell, *Sandwich*, p. 40. Local churches also took action when members were involved. The Barnstable Church excommunicated John Allen for fornication in 1674. West Parish Records, p. 11.

25. *Ply. Col. Recs.*, 3:6. The Court later reduced Launders's fine. Ibid., p. 42.

26. *Ply. Col. Recs.*, 2:37, 42, 85-86; 5:51. For other cases from Cape Cod, see ibid., 1:93-94; 2:112; 3:6, 75; 5:112.

27. *Ply. Col. Recs.*, 11:12, 95, 172; *General Laws, 1672*, p. 5; *General Laws, 1685*, pp. 22-23. For a general discussion of adultery in Plymouth Colony, see Demos, *Commonwealth*, pp. 96-97; and Ward, *Statism*, p. 96.

28. *Ply. Col. Recs.*, 2:28. The second whipping was to be in Yarmouth. A few months later, Mrs. Linceford was presented again for adultery, this time with Thomas Tupper of Sandwich. Ibid., pp. 36-37.

29. *Ply. Col. Recs.*, 5:43, 48.

30. *Ply. Col. Recs.*, 3:211, 221-223. After the divorce, Burgess married Lydia, and the couple moved to Rhode Island for a fresh start. Lovell, *Sandwich*, p. 121.

31. *Ply. Col. Recs.*, 6:190.

32. *Ply. Col. Recs.*, 11:13, 29, 52-53, 108, 190-191; *General Laws, 1672*, pp. 27-28; *General Laws, 1685*, pp. 47-48.

33. *Ply. Col. Recs.*, 2:155. Hinckley must have regarded Barnstable as enough responsibility. Two years after Hinckley's appointment, the Court appointed Anthony Thacher to the post for Yarmouth. Ibid., 3:15.

34. *Ply. Col. Recs.*, 2:112. Miss Gaunt was probably related to Peter Gaunt of Sandwich and working as a servant in Coggin's Barnstable household.

35. *Ply. Col. Recs.*, 2:136.

36. *Ply. Col. Recs.*, 3:46, 47, 52. See also Lovell, *Sandwich*, pp. 34-35. If the date of the marriage were not too early, the controversy could be tied to Perry's Quakerism. Quaker marriages consisted of the couple's mutual pledges before God and other Quakers, without an intermediary clergyman or public official. Jones, *Quakers, Colonies*, p. 147. The relationships in this situation are unclear, especially as to whether Mary was Edmund Freeman's daughter. Further it is possible Freeman's second wife was a widowed Mrs. Perry. If both of these conditions were true, then it was a case of Freeman's daughter marrying his stepson, a highly unusual circumstance. And even if Mary were not a daughter, a stepson marrying within the family would have aroused alarm. For a discussion of the

genealogical issues from this perspective, see Stratton, *Plymouth Colony*, pp. 293-294. Lovell, *Sandwich*, p. 5, asserts Freeman's second wife was named Raymen or Raymond. If true, the relationship between Mary Freeman and Edward Perry before their marriage would have been less of a problem, but the intensity of opposition to it seems less understandable.

37. West Parish Records, pp. 27-28; Jenkins, "First Parish," in Trayser, *Barnstable*, pp. 40-42.

38. For lying, see *Ply. Col. Recs.*, 11:63, 95-96, 128, 138, 173; *General Laws, 1672*, p. 9; *General Laws, 1685*, p. 25. The time in the stocks was not to exceed two hours for lying, and the fine was reduced to five shillings in 1685. For swearing, see *Ply. Col. Recs.*, 11:33-34, 95, 172-173; *General Laws, 1672*, p. 23; *General Laws, 1685*, p. 23. Three hours in the stocks was the maximum time for swearing, and like lying, the fine was reduced to five shillings in 1685, although a second offense still brought a ten shilling exactment.

39. *Ply. Col. Recs.*, 2:37; 4:89.

40. Lothrop, *Diary*, pp. 37, 38. Jackson was later readmitted to church membership and moved to Scituate.

41. Lothrop, *Diary*, pp. 37-38.

42. *Ply. Col. Recs.*, 11:26, 40, 44, 109, 111, 118, 191, 193, 204, 248; *General Laws, 1672*, pp. 29-30; *General Laws, 1685*, 66. 60-61. See also Ward, *Statism*, pp. 99-100.

43. *Ply. Col. Recs.*, 1:118.

44. *Ply. Col. Recs.*, 1:131.

45. *Ply. Col. Recs.*, 1:106.

46. *Ply. Col. Recs.*, 3:207, 212, 220.

47. *Ply. Col. Recs.*, 6:38. The Court supported the selectmen, authorizing them to return the Phillipses to Taunton.

48. *Ply. Col. Recs.*, 6:125.

49. *Ply. Col. Recs.*, 6:244. Much is missing from the records on this issue. Who the individuals were and the outcome of Bradford's actions are not included.

50. Barnstable Town Records, 1640-1753, p. 2.

51. Eastham Record of Town Meetings, 1654-1745, p. 11.

52. Yarmouth Town Records, 1677-1726, p. 20.

53. Sandwich Town Records, 1652-1692, pp. 147, 181.

54. Eastham Record of Town Meetings, 1654-1745, pp. 29, 30, 39; Barnstable Town Records, 1640-1753, passim. Barnstable is the only town to give even a hint of the acceptance procedure. At a town meeting on 26 March 1689/90, Benjamin Davis was proposed as a resident, or "townsman," and "by silence admitted thereto." Ibid., p. 151.

VIII

"to maintain their Just Rights"

IN much the same manner that Plymouth authorities expanded their regulation of the colony's religious affairs by suppressing Quakers, requiring tax support for ministers, and enforcing moral standards, they also became increasingly involved in the colony's political activities. As with religious issues, it was a move from a fairly unstructured and broadly participatory system to one marked by intensified control and growing restrictions. In the creation of their political society in the New World, the Pilgrims who had arrived off Cape Cod in the late autumn of 1620 had not planned very far ahead, and in reality could not have done so. Neither the opportunities of the frontier nor the impact of the later settlement of Massachusetts could have been foreseen, much less planned for. Other than a desire to settle in a place they could call their own, secure from outside interference, they seem to have trusted to their God, and expected the future to take care of itself.

To their credit, the Pilgrim leaders of the expedition had recognized the difficulties of their situation at the outset. Even before exploring for a permanent home, they had established Plymouth Colony's basic political outlook when they assembled all the adult males of the party to sign the Mayflower Compact. In that Compact, the colony's leaders attempted to deal with two divergent issues. On the one hand, they wanted to insure that representatives from the

Leyden congregation would hold the positions of authority and provide the colony's guidance. On the other, they recognized the need for the support of all adult males within the colony's jurisdiction if the enterprise were not to collapse from the lack of cooperation. The early leadership of Plymouth by those from Leyden, and the general support of all settlers for the colony attest to the success of the Mayflower Compact. The same principles which had guided the organization of political power in the Mayflower Compact also governed the colony throughout the period of independence. At both the colonial and local level, Plymouth expected political prerogative would be restricted to those in sympathy with its original goals. But those who governed recognized they needed the support of the governed if the colony was to succeed. To that end they encouraged at least some participation on the part of free adult males by allowing them to vote for the colony's leaders. At the local level, they virtually required involvement by a system of extensive office holding on the part of nearly all free adult males.

At the head of the list of responsible leaders, and at the top of the political pyramid, was the governor. Here, the attempt to retain political authority in the hands of trusted leaders is clearly evident. In its over seventy years of independence, the colony had only six governors, three of whom account for sixty years of tenure in the office. Two of the position's long-term holders were men from Cape Cod, Eastham's Thomas Prence and Barnstable's Thomas Hinckley.[1] Throughout most of Plymouth's history, election to the post meant permanence in it. Only during the 1630's, no doubt reflective of the readjustments being made as Plymouth shifted from being a town to a colony, were men regularly elected to one-year terms and turned out of office at the end.[2]

In the same way that regular reelection to the governorship represented dependability and consistency in political leadership, the 1633 order requiring the government of the colony and the residence of the governor to be located in the town of Plymouth were efforts to preserve the preeminence of the original settlement in the face of expansion. The constraint was a particular problem for Thomas Prence. He was living in Duxbury when elected to his second one-year term as governor, and entered into rather complicated arrangements to prevent having to move to Plymouth.[3] By the time of his 1657 election, he had moved to Eastham, and continued living there for nearly half of his subsequent sixteen-year term. By 1664 or 1665, however, the General Court had persuaded him to return to

Plymouth with the offer of a large house and farm, as well as thirty pounds, probably for moving expenses.[4] The residency requirement lapsed in the later years of the seventeenth century. Thomas Hinckley of Barnstable, elected in 1681, is mentioned too frequently in the town's local records for him to have moved to Plymouth. The colony faced problems far greater than the location of the governor's home by the 1680's, and apparently let Hinckley live where he wanted.

The same level of continuity seen in the governorship is reflected in the selection of Magistrates or Assistants. In 1636 the General Court established there would be seven Assistants chosen along with the Governor at the annual Court of Election in June. Together these eight men comprised the Court of Assistants. The Governor received a double vote, thus eliminating ties.[5] The 378 potential one-year openings were, in fact, held by thirty men. Excluding the six men who were selected to the position fewer than four times, the average length of service was slightly over sixteen years.[6] Cape Cod communities provided eight Assistants, one-third of those who filled the office for long periods of time. The one-third fraction is typical of the Cape's contribution to Plymouth Colony. The region contained approximately one-third of the colony's towns, and provided roughly the same proportion of its yearly tax receipts and its soldiers in time of war. None of the Cape's Assistants served fewer than the six years of Edmund Freeman, and for unexplained reasons, most Cape Assistantships were held in the latter years of the colony's independence. In fact, after 1686 the Governor and three Assistants were Cape residents. Given the Governor's double vote, Cape Codders controlled a majority of the Court of Assistants.[7]

As political power diffused over the colony into local communities during the 1630's and 1640's, Plymouth Colony made an effort to be more inclusive in its granting of political participation. As with the original settlement, the leaders recognized the desirability of retaining authority in the hands of those most in agreement with the colony's ideals, but also understood clearly the need for popular acceptance and support. These two countervailing concerns had led originally in Plymouth to a rather loose system of political participation. During the 1620's, when the colony was small and fairly homogeneous, a wide-spread participatory political and economic system had developed. Most adult males who were not servants apparently participated in a directly democratic town meeting which was also the colonial government. Because land was owned communally for the first seven years, there was no private ownership, but when the economic reorganization of 1627 instituted private property, most free adult males participated.[8] Further, when the Court responded to expansion by creating a representative government and permitting locally elected Deputies, it continued the same policy. By requiring Deputies to be freemen, it reserved the important colony-level decisions for the more trusted element of the colony. But by allowing all those who helped pay the expenses of the town's Deputies to vote on their selection, the Court maintained an important component of general participation. Interestingly, the Court later balanced the power of local participation by authorizing itself to reject an unacceptable local selection for Deputy.[9] Plymouth had thus created a two-tiered structure, where traditional authority was protected in the General Court, and more widespread sharing of power was allowed at the local level. Later the Court solidified the arrangement by writing some of its restrictions into law, and eventually instituting qualifications at the local level.

The political composition of the colony had begun to change in the 1630's. The influx of Massachusetts settlers and the founding of new towns in that decade resulted in a broadening diversity in the backgrounds and interests of the colony's residents. Plymouth responded initially by taking more care in deciding who should become freemen and thus be allowed to vote at the colony level. At the same Court session at which it created a representative legislature, the Court instituted its first identifiable effort to screen potential voters. Certainly, the two actions were linked. At that session, the Court started the practice of evaluating potential freemen by utilizing a deferral period between nomination at one Court session and acceptance at the next. The Court made the procedure formal in 1658 when it required a one-year waiting period before granting freemanship.[10] It is also probable the 1656 requirement that a town's existing freemen must nominate potential new ones had been practiced long before the law made it mandatory.[11]

An example of these early efforts to scrutinize potential voters can be seen in a survey of the twenty-one men nominated at the March 1638/39 General Court. By 1664, when the General Court temporarily halted the regular recording of annual proposals and admissions of freemen, nine of the group had not been accepted.[12] It is possible some of the original applicants had died or left the colony, but not all of them had. Thomas Ensign was proposed five times, in 1638/39, 1640, 1651, 1652, and 1655, without being accepted. He died in 1663 or 1664 not having won the prize.[13] There were other individuals, including well known Cape Cod figures, who were either denied freemanship or waited for many years to acquire it. William Nickerson and Thomas Hatch, both of Yarmouth, were each proposed three times. Hatch never did become a freeman, and Nickerson was not accepted until the 1650's.[14] William Merrick of Eastham was propounded twice before being selected in 1658.[15] None of these examples of postponement can be interpreted as statistical proof that Plymouth followed a policy of arbitrarily denying the franchise on a systematic basis. But at the very least, it is quite evident Plymouth was beginning to scrutinize more carefully those being granted full political rights, and not infrequently finding some candidates wanting.

In the late 1650's, the advent of Quakerism made the move towards selectivity in the awarding of freemanship increasingly imperative. As part of the attempt to suppress the heretical sect, Plymouth found it desirable to clarify and legalize its practices for selecting freemen. In addition to the one-year waiting period and nomination by fellow townsmen mentioned earlier, the colony instituted its first religious qualifications for voting. While it is unlikely anyone not in sympathy with the colony's religious ideals would have become a freeman earlier, in 1658 it was believed necessary to decree specifically that Quakers, along with liars, drunkards, and swearers, would not be allowed to vote.[16] By the time the colony published its law code of 1672, it had added a restriction limiting voting in town meetings to those who were owners of taxable property worth twenty pounds.[17]

The general development of an increasingly restrictive franchise in colonial matters was similarly played out among Cape Cod towns. Just as diversity had forced a homogeneous Plymouth to regulate colonial political participation, so also did the towns increasingly restrict nominations for freemanship. And just as Plymouth had intended to preserve its traditional leadership, so also did the colony's settlements on the Cape make efforts to retain political power for those associated with the founding and early settlement of its towns.

The practice is fully evident in a survey of Cape Cod freemen. In response to a 1643 request from the Commissioners of the United Colonies for a census of men eligible for military service, Plymouth collected the names of its male inhabitants between the ages of sixteen and sixty. For reasons that are unclear, the colony also counted its freemen the same year. A survey of those included on both lists and a look at the prospects for freemanship for men on the militia roster indicates that significantly fewer than half the militia ever became voters, and that those most likely to do so were the sons or relatives of freemen in 1643.[18] The 1643 militia list included three of the Cape towns, as the census was taken before the founding of Eastham. In those three towns there were 183 potential soldiers, of whom forty were freemen. Given that boys of sixteen were included, the figure represents a fairly high proportion of voters among the militia. But over the next twenty-seven years, as the colony tightened its voting requirements, only twenty-two militia members who were not freemen in 1643 ever achieved that status in the towns of Cape Cod. While there were deaths and emigrations which would have reduced the number of original militiamen, they were not excessive. Such reductions would not seriously alter the conclusion that when the men on the militia list are followed through adulthood, only about one in three became a freeman.[19]

Among the individual Cape towns, there were important differences as to the number and proportion of freemen within the community. Sandwich was at two extremes in 1643. It had the most militia, seventy, and the fewest freemen, twelve. In fact, Sandwich consistently registered fewer freemen than its Cape Cod neighbors throughout the seventeenth century. Unfortunately, no explanation for the small number of freemen in Sandwich is discernible. There is no obvious relationship either to the earlier land problems or to the Quaker question. In 1643 Barnstable listed sixty-one militia and twenty-two freemen, and just as consistently and unexplainably would have the highest number and proportion of freemen. At the same time, Yarmouth accounted for fifty-two soldiers and sixteen freemen. Eastham was not included on the militia roster, but was on the freeman census with twelve. There were other registers of freemen taken in the colony during the seventeenth century, and they are summarized in the following chart:

CAPE COD FREEMEN[20]

	1643	1658	1670	1675	1689
Barnstable	22	41	43	44	53
Eastham	10	21	24	34	35
Sandwich	12	8	10	11	15
Yarmouth	16	14	19	19	22
Totals	60	84	96	108	125

The awarding of freemanship certainly indicates the towns of Cape Cod made efforts to limit the number of men given the vote, and to do so in a manner which retained political dominance by the town's traditional leaders. While not in a position to pass restrictive town ordinances, as the General Court could do for the colony, the towns nonetheless exercised strong influence over freemanship. They did so primarily by limiting the honor to those who were of known quality or the descendants of early founders and settlers. The practice is evident in all the towns, whether in Sandwich with its small number of freemen, or in Barnstable with its large quantity of them. By examining the surnames of those who appear on the various town rosters of freemen, it is possible to get at least an idea of the process.

One of the more telling indications of the development was the drastic decline in the percentage of new surnames found on the freemen lists as the century progressed. While the newness of the Cape Cod towns is evident in the high percentage of new surnames in the 1658 lists, the subsequent ones of 1670, 1675, and 1689, reflect primarily the inclusion of the sons of those on the earlier 1643 and 1658 rosters. New surnames represent nearly one in three of the names on the 1658 list, but on the later rosters, the proportions drop to fewer than one in seven.[21]

Taken from the other end, the same conclusion that freemanship tended to be denied newer residents and awarded to the sons of early settlers, can be seen in the steady rise in the percentage of surnames which remain the same. In the 1643 lists there are very few surname duplications. Barnstable had one, Samuel and Thomas Hinckley. Yarmouth had two, Job and Daniel Cole who were brothers, and James and Marmaduke Matthews, who are the only clear case of unrelated duplication.[22] By 1658, the repetition of surnames began to occur. For example, in that year Eastham's twenty-one freemen represented eighteen families. In 1670 seventeen families provided twenty-four freemen, and five years later twenty families furnished thirty-three freemen, a ratio which remained essentially the same in the 1689 roster.[23] In terms of actual voters in colonial elections, the result of such a practice was that in 1675 and 1689 sixty percent of Eastham's freemen came from either six or seven families, and they are all names associated with the founding and early settlement of the town.

But a question remains about those never admitted to freemanship, and the extent to which they serve as a political under class, excluded from political participation. Their names appear less often and their very exclusion makes them more difficult to trace. When they do show up, it is infrequently, and usually in the local records. Sandwich and Barnstable, however, offer two exceptions to this paucity of evidence. Because of the furor over land distribution which occurred in Sandwich in its early years, the settlement of the dispute was written into the colonial records, as well as into those of the town. Dated 1640, it precedes the freemanship list by three years, but is one of the few such rosters available. Because it is a register of landholders, it is a better record of the adult males than the 1643 militia list, which included boys as young as sixteen.[24] The land distribution list included fifty-eight individuals, representing fifty-four families. Three years later, the town's freeman list included only twelve freemen. Forty-two families, with a total of forty-six adult males, were thus without a freeman.[25] Whether total individuals or surnames are examined, one is forced to the conclusion that even before the Quaker invasion of the 1650's affected voter qualifications, freemanship in Sandwich was dominated by an extremely small proportion of the population.

The Sandwich problem is explained to some extent by the town's century-long tradition of having a very small number of freemen. But Barnstable, which consistently had the largest number of freemen of any of the Cape Cod towns, practiced a similar restrictiveness in awarding freemanship, although it was far less sharp than in Sandwich. In April 1670, Barnstable recorded eighty-four individuals from forty-eight families on a landowner tally. Of the forty-eight surnames, twenty-one did not have a family representative on the freeman list of the same year.[26] While the proportion of freeman surnames to landholder surnames is far higher in Barnstable than in Sandwich, it is noteworthy that even in the Cape Cod town with the highest number of freemen, nearly one half of its landowners did not have someone from their family with the franchise.

But freemanship was essentially a colonial rather than a local responsibility. Its major privilege or obligation was participation in the colonial government. In the early years of the colony, it had been a direct involvement, but became indirect with the establishment in 1638 of a representative government with elected Deputies. For the rest of the century, the office of Deputy symbolized an important link between the towns and the colony in Plymouth's effort both to preserve traditionalist control of the colony and to foster popular support for it among the colonists.

Even though the requirement that Deputies must be freemen limited a town's potential pool of representatives, those actually selected were an even smaller group. Some freemen were never elected, while others were continually returned to office. From 1639, when Deputies were first elected, until the incorporation of Plymouth Colony into Massachusetts, fewer than twenty freemen from each Cape Cod town actually served a term as Deputy. And within each town's select group of twenty, half or fewer were elected to the vast majority of the terms. In Barnstable, Nathaniel Bacon served as Deputy thirteen times, Joseph Lothrop, twelve. Eastham elected Jonathan Sparrow to the post on twenty-one occasions. Thomas Tupper of Sandwich held the longevity record for Cape Cod Deputies, serving twenty-three terms as a town representative.[27] As with the governorship, continuity in office, and therefore the perpetuation of the traditional values of the colony, was the hallmark of being a Deputy to the Plymouth General Court.

In addition to its role as a legislative body, the General Court, composed of the elected town Deputies, also served an important judicial function. Ultimate judicial authority lay with the General Court, but as early as 1634, the Court of Assistants began to hear civil suits involving less that forty shillings, and soon thereafter the Assistants assumed jurisdiction in virtually all cases. Throughout the rest of the century, it was the highest judicial body of the colony in civil proceedings.[28]

The General Court made a further division of its judicial authority in 1640 when it established a separate court for the towns on the Cape. At the June 1640 court of election, the General Court appointed Thomas Dimmock of Barnstable, and John Crow of Yarmouth to serve with Edmund Freeman, an Assistant from Sandwich, as a special court to hear cases in the Cape towns which concerned sums less than twenty shillings. The General Court reappointed the three men to their posts four years later, but the records do not indicate the Cape Cod court's existence past 1646.[29] No matter how long it lasted, it would have been replaced in 1665 with the establishment of "select courts," local courts presided over by a town's selectmen.[30]

The maturity and growth of Plymouth society at the end of the century forced the colony to reshape its judicial organization in 1685. It responded to the increased complexity by creating a system of county government. True to its role as one-third of the colony, the Cape Cod settlements became one of the counties. Barnstable

County, comprised of the four major Cape Cod towns and the settlements of Sepecan (Rochester), Saconesett (Falmouth), and Manamoet (Chatham) joined Plymouth and Bristol as one of the colony's three counties.[31]

Known as a County Court, the new institution was administered by the county's Assistants, aided by county residents appointed as associates by the General Court. The County Court was to meet at least twice a year, as long as there were three or more cases to decide, and at least three judges needed to be present. As an intermediate layer of government, the County Court was both an administrative and judicial body, assuming some of the responsibilities of both town government and the General Court. From the General Court it assumed control over probate matters and the important appeals function of the Court of Assistants, as well as being the Court to which the Grand Jury returned its indictments. From the town it took over the control of roads and bridges, the maintenance of a prison, the supervision of local religious activity, and the preservation of the minister's salary. To support these responsibilities, the General Court granted county courts the right to levy taxes on county residents.[32]

While the establishment of County Courts made for certain practical conveniences in the conduct of legal affairs, the courts were not met with universal approval. Scituate and Dartmouth both criticized their taxing power, apparently unhappy with an institution which levied taxes without providing for any direct participation by the taxpayers.[33] The General Court eventually responded to the criticism by ordering associates be elected by vote of the freemen beginning in 1691. Unfortunately, the collapse of Plymouth's independence precludes any assessment of whether county courts would have been more acceptable after the change. In any case, the Cape did not join the opposition. Cape Cod towns recorded no actions concerning the new County Court other than Eastham's listing of those selected for service on its juries and the levying of a tax to pay for the town's portion of the new county prison.[34]

Those men the General Court appointed as associates of the County Court reiterate the general tendency of Plymouth authorities to turn positions of responsibility over to the more established members of the community. No doubt because the Governor and three Assistants were from the Cape, the General Court usually commissioned only two associates for Barnstable County, but assigned three each for Bristol and Plymouth. The two men consistently selected were Eastham's Jonathan Sparrow and

Sandwich's Stephen Skiffe. They had both served as selectmen and Deputies, and were the sons of prominent early settlers of their respective towns.[35]

While always a presence because of the election of Deputies and the passage and enforcement of laws, the colonial government at Plymouth actually touched the residents of the Cape with a relatively light hand. Participation in the political life of the colony was limited to those who had been selected as freemen, a privilege increasingly restricted to the more prominent families who had been involved in the early settlement of the colony and its towns. It probably could not have been otherwise. Agricultural life on the Cape was difficult at best, and only those men with an established family behind them could afford the time and expense of government service at the colony level. And it may not have mattered a great deal to those who could not directly participate whether they did or not. They could at least vote for the freemen who served as Deputies, and what the General Court decided was, for the most part, less central to the residents of the Cape than what was decided close to home. Participation in local matters meant the ability to influence those decisions which most affected one's daily life and might possibly determine even survival itself. Within that local community, participation was a far more open and democratic process than any survey of freemanship qualifications or analysis of freeman rosters would indicate.

Notes

1. Peirce, *Colonial Lists*, p. 3. John Carver, the initial governor, died the first spring and served less than one year. Edward Winslow served three non-consecutive terms between 1630 and 1645, and Josiah Winslow served a seven-year term from 1673 to 1680. If Edward Winslow and John Carver are excluded, only four governors ruled Plymouth for sixty-seven of its seventy-one years.

2. There is no serious evidence that the electorate was displeased with Bradford or the others who held one-year terms, and it may well be that they and Bradford supported the yearly changes of leadership. But it was the only time it happened, and it did so during Plymouth's decade of most rapid growth, with its associated problems. Such periods bring about uncertainties and readjustments, and result in political vacillation. See Stratton, *Plymouth Colony*, p. 151.

3. *Ply. Col. Recs.*, 1:16, 79-80. It is possible he was already in Duxbury at the time of his first election, but the residence question is not mentioned in the records.

4. *Ply. Col. Recs.*, 4:44, 108; 11:212. The Court authorized John Doane to perform marriages and administer oaths in Eastham as early as June 1663. As Governor, Prence would have performed those functions, and Doane's appointment may indicate Prence had at least decided to leave the Cape, and possibly had already done so. Ibid., 4:43. Prence engaged to purchase his Plymouth home, named "Plaindealing," but died before it was paid for. When his widow was unable to continue payments, the Court returned Prence's fifty-pound initial payment to her. The Court then tried vainly to sell the house, and finally leased it to Prence's successor, Josiah Winslow. Ibid., 4:184-185; 5:117, 124, 148-149; 7:192; 11:239.

5. *Ply. Col. Recs.*, 11:156, 158; *General Laws, 1672*, p. 15. After 1679, one of the Assistants was designated Deputy Governor. *Ply. Col. Recs.*, 6:34.

6. Peirce, *Colonial Lists*, p. 4; *Ply. Col. Recs.*, 6:185, 205, 239, 262. The 378 figure represents seven Assistants for each of the 54 years from 1636 to 1686 and 1689 to 1691. Because of the Dominion of New England, there are no records for 1687 and 1688. Pierce does not extend his list beyond 1686. The six men who served three years or less were Isaac Allerton, John Atwood, John Cushing, Samuel Fuller, Stephen Hopkins, and John Howland.

7. Peirce, *Colonial Lists*, p. 4.

8. Bradford, *Plymouth Plantation*, pp. 186-188; George D. Langdon, Jr., "The Franchise and Political Democracy in Plymouth Colony," *William and Mary Quarterly*, 3d. Ser., 20(1963):513-516 (Hereinafter cited as "Franchise and Democracy"); *Pilgrim Colony*, pp. 79-80; and Stratton, *Plymouth Colony*, pp. 141-142. On the other hand, democracy was not so rampant in Plymouth that women and children were voting, as was apparently the rumor in England. See William Bradford and Isaac Allerton's letter to the London Adventurers, Plymouth, 8 Sept. 1623, in *Amer. Hist. Rev.* 8(1902/3):299.

9. *Ply. Col. Recs.*, 11:31, 91-92. Langdon, "Franchise and Democracy," pp. 521-522; *Pilgrim Colony*, p. 86. While the attempt had been made to restrict participation at the colony level, Plymouth's inclusion of virtually all male taxpayers in the electorate was a far more generous policy than the one in Massachusetts, which allowed only freemen to vote for local representatives to the General Court. Ibid.

10. *Ply. Col. Recs.*, 1:116-117; 11:79. The 1658 law requiring a waiting period also indicated strongly that those freemen selected by the

General Court were to be in sympathy with the anti-Quaker sentiments of the colony's leaders. Because a waiting period was a policy rather than a law before 1658, some men were given freemanship upon nomination in those years. The Court admitted John Mayo, Barnstable's teaching elder and later minister at Eastham, without waiting, as it did John Crow of Yarmouth, and Thomas Tupper and Thomas Burgess of Sandwich. *Ply. Col. Recs.*, 1:140, 155. The terms freeman and freemanship were used by both Plymouth and Massachusetts to signify those with the vote. The oath for freemen, dated about 1636, is in ibid., 11:8.

11. *Ply. Col. Recs.*, 3:101; 11:65. The General Court reiterated the law in June 1674. Ibid., p. 236.

12. *Ply. Col. Recs.*, 1:116-117. This list of candidates for freemanship was the first one put into the record as proposed voters, and those on it should have had the best opportunities for inclusion among the freemen of the colony. The nominees, with their dates of admission, were: Comfort Starr (4 June 1639), George Allen and Thomas Chambers (3 September 1639), William Kemp, John Twisden, and John Williams (3 December 1639), Job Cole (3 March 1639/40), John Rogers (1 March 1641/2), Dolor Davis (2 June 1646), William Harlow and Robert Shelley (6 June 1654), and Stephen Vinall (1 June 1658). Those not mentioned in the colony's records as having been admitted to freemanship were: Thomas Bonney, Thomas Ensign, Thomas Hatch, Thomas Lapham, John Lewis, Nehemiah Smyth, George Sutton, William Wad[e], and John Winter. *Ply. Col. Recs.*, 1-4:passim. The Court reinstituted the regular recording of proposed freemen in 1680. Ibid., p. 6:42.

13. *Ply. Col. Recs.*, 1:116; 2:3, 167; 3:7, 78; 4:55.

14. For Hatch, see *Ply. Col. Recs.*, 1:108, 116; 2:17; For Nickerson, see ibid., 2:3, 17, 154; 3:79. Nickerson lost his freemanship in 1656 for selling a boat to an Indian. Ibid., 3:101.

15. *Ply. Col. Recs.*, 2:167; 3:7, 137.

16. *Ply. Col. Recs.*, 11:101, 177. The lateness of a specific religious qualification for voting is in sharp contrast to the strict stipulations of Massachusetts, which in 1631 made church membership a requirement for voting. *Mass. Col. Recs.*, 1:87. That Plymouth's religious scruples concerning the franchise were restricted to Quakers is indicated by two occurrences. In replying to the investigation by the Royal Commissioners in 1665, Plymouth pointed out that men of "different judgements" had been allowed freemanship, although the respondents protected themselves by indicating that such men must be "otherwise orthodox." And later, a 1670 list of Swansea freemen includes several communicants of the local Baptist

Church. *Ply. Col. Recs.*, 4:85-86.; Langdon, "Franchise and Democracy," p. 517 and n. 18.

17. *Ply. Col. Recs.*, 11:223; *General Laws, 1672*, p. 16. The Court probably passed the law in 1669. Langdon, "Franchise and Democracy," pp. 523-524; *Pilgrim Colony*, pp. 88-89. The Court added the property qualification in order to restrict local voting to major taxpayers. Owners of small estates, such as younger sons and newcomers, were no doubt judged to have property interests and taxes too insignificant to give them the privilege of voting. The 1685 code included two efforts to reinstate a more liberal approach to the franchise. Men "generally known and approved of by the Court" could become freemen without the twenty-pound estate qualification, and those who were neither freemen nor freeholders, but had a taxable estate of thirty pounds were allowed the franchise. *General Laws, 1685*, pp. 17-18, 59.

18. The militia roster can be found in *Ply. Col. Recs.*, 8:187-196. The freemen lists are in ibid., pp. 173-177 for 1643; pp. 197-202 for 1658; pp. 203-209 for 1689; 5:274-279 for 1670; and *Public.*, Col. Soc. Mass. 24(1923):149-155 for 1675. Many of the lists have names that have been marked as deleted or deceased. On the assumption these cancellations occurred after the rosters were compiled, the complete list has been used. There are also instances of names occurring twice, but at some point one of them is usually stipulated a "junior," and thus distinguishable from a "senior." The number of cases where either deletions or duplications are unclear is far too small to have any significant impact on the conclusions.

19. Nineteen of the twenty-two militiamen who attained freemanship by 1670 did so in the towns where they were originally listed. Only three became freemen in other Cape Cod towns: John Freeman from Sandwich in Eastham; Samuel Arnold from Sandwich in Yarmouth; and Thomas Paine from Yarmouth in Eastham. *Ply. Col. Recs.*, 8:192, 194, 200, 202.

20. The colonial totals for the five censuses were: 1643, 234; 1658, 312; 1670, 364; 1675, 400; 1689, 406. The percentages of the total provided by the towns on the Cape were: 1643, 25.6; 1658, 26.9; 1670, 26.4; 1675, 27.0; 1689, 30.8.

21. The lowest percentage of new surnames was zero for the Barnstable list in 1675, indicating the inclusion of no new family names among the nine new freemen. The highest percentage was twenty-seven for the 1689 Sandwich list, but the significance of the figure is modified by noting that there were only fifteen freemen on the complete list, only four of them new. The specific averages of new surnames for the combined Cape Cod towns was 32.5 in 1658, 10 in 1670, 8 in 1675, and 13.5 in 1689.

22. Savage, *Genealogical Dictionary*, 3:176; Swift, *Old Yarmouth*, pp. 66, 72.

23. In percentage terms, fourteen percent of the 1658 list represents duplications, twenty-nine percent of the 1670 list, and forty percent of the 1675 and 1689 lists. Some names occur as often as four times, Banges on the 1675 list, and Doane, Freemen, and Snow on the 1689 one. Other multiple surnames are Cole, Higgins, Paine, Rogers, and Snow.

24. *Ply. Col. Recs.*, 1:149-150; Sandwich Town Records, 1652-1692, pp. 9-10.

25. The Fish and Wright surnames each occurred three times, and neither of them were represented in the freeman list.

26. Barnstable Town Records, 1640-1753, pp. 119-121; *Ply. Col. Recs.*, 5:277.

27. Peirce, *Colonial Lists*, pp. 8-16. The names of those elected can also be found in the lists of colonial officials given in the records of the annual Court of Elections in June. *Ply. Col. Recs.*, 1-6:passim. In all, sixty-six men were chosen Deputies from the Cape Cod towns during the period. A slight majority of thirty-four served three terms or less. The other thirty-two each served an average of nine terms.

28. *Ply. Col. Recs.*, 1:29; *General Laws, 1672*, p. 17; *General Laws, 1685*, p. 19; Langdon, *Pilgrim Colony*, p. 201; Ward, *Statism*, p. 76. Legal and judicial history has become a distinct and sophisticated field of historical analysis, somewhat beyond the limits of this study. Most of the New England work is concerned with Massachusetts, but for Plymouth, see George L. Haskins, "The Legal Heritage of Plymouth Colony," in David H. Flaherty (ed.), *Essays in the History of Early American Law* (Chapel Hill, NC: c. 1969), pp. 121-34; and Julius Goebel, Jr., "King's Law and Local Custom in Seventeenth Century New England," also in Flaherty, (ed.), *Essays*, pp. 83-120. The Haskins article originally appeared in *University of Pennsylvania Law Review* 110(1962):847-859, and in an earlier version in *Social Education* 26(1962):7-12, 22. Goebel's essay was first published in *Columbia Law Review* 31(1931):416-448.

29. *Ply. Col. Recs.*, 1:155; 2:73. The Court granted Rehoboth a similar privilege in 1647. Ibid., p. 118. The distance from Plymouth, where Court of Assistants meetings were held, was no doubt the reason for these local courts. The special court for the Cape towns was in existence at least until 1646. References to it can be found in ibid., pp. 24, 28, 109.

30. *Ply. Col. Recs.*, 11:213; *General Laws, 1672*, pp. 18-19; *General Laws, 1685*, p. 22.

31. *General Laws, 1685*, p. 20.

32. *Ply. Col. Recs.*, 6:193-194; *General Laws, 1685*, pp. 6-7, 19-22; Langdon, *Pilgrim Colony*, pp. 204-207.

33. Langdon, *Pilgrim Colony*, pp. 205-206.

34. Eastham Record of Town Meetings, 1654-1745, pp. 35-37.

35. *Ply. Col. Recs.*, 6:235, 243, 247, 268. On 4 November 1690, the Court added William Bassett of Sandwich to the list of Barnstable County associates. Why it felt the need of a third man is unclear, but at the same meeting elaborate measures were taken to settle the colony's financial accounts, perhaps in preparation for Plymouth's incorporation into Massachusetts. Ibid., p. 254.

IX

"to call men to labor thereat"

THROUGHOUT the century the distinctions about governmental structure and responsibility made at the signing of the Mayflower Compact remained part of Plymouth's view of itself. At the colonial level, Plymouth's government attempted to preserve the original goals of the Pilgrim founders by restricting political participation to those in sympathy with them. At the local level, however, government encouraged a more general participation in order to build support for the colony from all members of society.

In large part, participation in town affairs reflected the communal nature of local government in seventeenth-century Plymouth Colony. It was a political system with neither professional administrators nor permanent employees. The business, as well as the labor, of the town were done by its residents, with minimal compensation, as part of their responsibilities toward their communities. For the same reason that the colony generally allowed all taxpayers to vote for Deputies to the General Court because they paid the expenses, town governments allowed all those obligated to work for the town to participate in the decisions which would require their service. There are no indications in the local records that any of a town's free adult males were excluded from voting in local matters. The problem, rather, was getting residents to participate in town government, not in excluding a particular group. Just as the General

Court levied fines against men who would not serve when elected to positions of leadership, towns similarly placed fines on those residents who failed to attend town meetings. Eastham assessed a two-shilling fine for non-attendance in 1659, and in 1673 awarded half of it to the Constable for his efforts in collecting it. Sandwich's penalty for non-attendance was the loss of one's vote, as well as a two-shilling, six-pence fine. Yarmouth exacted six pence from latecomers, and twelve from those who failed to attend at all.[1] Civic responsibility, much less political power, were duties apparently not always sought, nor appreciated when granted.

But participation was necessary, whether for surveying boundaries, repairing roads, collecting taxes, or serving on juries. In the end it was the holding of public office which best exemplified the type of general participation which marked local government in Plymouth Colony. A survey of town officials and the men who filled the positions indicates it was the rare individual indeed who escaped filling a public post. Nearly every adult male served in some capacity at one time or another, and many did so frequently, sometimes in multiple offices. In addition to town Deputies, who were both colonial and local officials, there were three town positions deemed significant enough to have their holders consistently listed in the colonial records and their duties and responsibilities outlined in the codified laws of the colony. Those positions were Constable, Surveyor of Highways, and Selectman. Election to one or more of them was almost as certain as the taxes levied to meet their expenses.

The Constable, elected by town voters, was the chief agent of the colonial government at the local level. Generally responsible for maintaining "the King's peace," he collected taxes, confiscated property when they were not paid, and impressed wagons and boats to deliver the goods to Boston or Plymouth. He also convened town meetings, investigated suspicious people, collected fines, and administered corporal punishment on fellow residents. It was not an enviable job by any means. It represented governmental power as it touched the citizenry in a number of restrictive ways, and appears to have been a responsibility to be avoided if possible and taken only reluctantly when one's turn came around. The four-pound fine levied against those who refused to serve if elected and the seven-year grace period allowed before another term needed to be taken attest to the position's undesirability.[2]

A survey of Cape Cod men who held the office during the approximately five decades before the loss of independence, indicate most men served their virtually obligatory term as Constable and that was all. The four Cape Cod towns elected one hundred thirty-eight men as Constables during the period, and only eighteen of them served more than one term. Just two men in Eastham served more than once, Henry Atkins and Thomas Paine. Yarmouth elected Emanuel White as the only Cape Codder to serve successive terms, although it selected three other men who served two or more times. Seven men in Barnstable repeated in the office, including Thomas Huchens, who for unfathomable reasons, was willing to take the job seven times.[3]

What amounts to virtually annual turnover in the office of Constable should come as no surprise. Constables were required to keep extensive accounts of the money they collected, and to submit them for audit at the end of their term. There were fines for the failure to do so. Aggrieved citizens sued them for abusing their powers and also for the return of property they confiscated by court order. Angry residents unable to bring a lawsuit merely threatened them, requiring Constables to bring suit themselves for protection.[4] The surprise is not that the post changed hands so frequently, but that anyone would assume it twice. Just as unsurprisingly, a good number of men refused to accept the position at all. The General Court frequently fined men for refusing to accept what may well have been the most personally onerous responsibility in the colony.[5]

The position of Surveyor of Highways was similar to that of Constable in its importance to both the town and the colony. Its chief responsibility was the maintenance of the town's roads, and necessitated determining what work needed to be done, and ordering fellow citizens to perform it.[6] While there was more duplication in the holding of the office than was true in the Constable's position, it was apparently not an office actively sought. Most of those elected Surveyors seem to have been merely fulfilling one of the obligations of residency, and in the process avoiding the fines assessed for refusal to do so. A review of those who held the office indicates that one hundred thirty-eight men functioned as highway surveyors, about one-third of them more than once. Those who repeated in the position rarely did so more than two or three times.[7]

The failure to require freemanship for those positions which were purely local in nature, like Constable and Surveyor, accomplished two goals. It spread the responsibility for the operation of government among nearly all adult males, while reserving the decision making powers to a more select, and by implication a more trustworthy, group of freemen. Indeed, to have required freemanship for public office would no doubt have brought local government to a standstill. About all that was really necessary was a willingness to do the work involved with the position, and the capabilities of every man were easily determined in the small homogeneous communities of seventeenth-century Plymouth.

The last major local office, the only one not marked by rapid turnover, was that of Selectman. It had begun as a position responsible only for the setting of property values for taxation, but evolved into one accountable for local judicial decisions. Called a Select Court, its jurisdiction included the summoning of witnesses and the trying of local cases involving claims of forty shillings or less, as well as settling disputes dealing with Indian claims for damage done to their crops by the cattle of white settlers. It had been an appointive office during the Quaker period, used primarily to enforce the laws against suspicious newcomers, but became an elective one in 1665. The 1665 law allowed the election of three or five men by local voters, but stipulated that selectmen must be freemen and approved by the General Court.[8] The requirement of freemanship and approval by the General Court indicated that only dependable men were to be trusted with judicial decisions. It also meant, given the fairly restrictive number of freemen in each town, that repetition in office was the general rule.

On Cape Cod, the choice of selectmen within each community followed an amazingly similar pattern. Over the twenty-five years in which the names of selectmen were recorded in the records, each of the four towns had a total of only twelve or thirteen freemen who filled the position.[9] In contrast to Surveyors of Highways and Constables, the same men were often reelected. But they were reelected, or more importantly not reelected, in a very interesting pattern. Half of those elected in each town served an average of three terms or less, and the other half served an average of nine or more. Men like Nathaniel Bacon and William Crocker in Barnstable or Edmund Freeman, Sr. and William Bassett in Sandwich were elected for one or two terms, usually successively, and then disappear from the ranks. At the other extreme were men like Edmund Hawes and John Miller who each served twenty years in Yarmouth, Joseph Lothrop who served twelve years in Barnstable, or Thomas Tupper and William Swift who each served twelve years in Sandwich. Apparently the electorate decided some men performed the judicial functions of selectmen credibly, and continually reelected them.

Others were found to be less well suited to the tasks and turned out of office. John Doane, Mark Snow, and Jonathan Sparrow, for instance, must have satisfied their fellow Eastham residents. The three men monopolized the office for a ten year period from 1677 to 1686. John Freeman and Joseph Rogers did not. They served only once.[10]

In addition to elected offices, there were other opportunities for local citizens to participate in the governmental life of the town. Certainly road maintenance headed the list. It was a responsibility which brought all able bodied men into government service whether surveyors or not. The General Court levied fines against both those who refused to take their turn, and those who refused to allow their ox or horse teams to be used. For equity's sake, it required no one be ordered to work on the roads a second time until everyone had done so once.[11] Other, somewhat more peripheral assignments involved a special service. One of the most common tasks was to be the executor of an estate. Less common, but equally important was service on a jury to investigate questionable deaths.[12]

Other appointments were to posts associated with an activity at the local level which the General Court desired to regulate. Some of them, like innkeeper, weightmaster, or justice of the peace, were common to all Plymouth Colony towns. Others were unique to Cape Cod and represent certain of the area's distinctive contributions to the colony. The positions of water bailiff and whale watcher were associated with the fishing and whaling industries which were such important parts of economic life on seventeenth-century Cape Cod. Excise collectors, who almost exclusively were appointed for towns on the Cape, indicate the commercial activity of the region.

In sum, the various offices to which one could be elected, made local government in the towns of Plymouth Colony a personal experience. Just as the 1643 militia lists can be used to evaluate an individual's potential for freemanship, they can also be utilized to survey eventual election to public office. In each of the towns on the Cape with such lists, at least one-half of the males included on them would eventually serve a stint as an elected official sometime in the seventeenth century.[13] Perhaps the most telling evidence of nearly universal participation in public office can be found in a comparison of the long-term residents of Sandwich and its elected officials. Every adult male resident but two who settled in Sandwich before 1640 and was living there past 1650 was elected at least once to a public office. Some men like Thomas Burgess and James Skiffe served in every single one. Even a few of those who lived there only briefly performed at least one assignment as an elected public official.[14] It was the same in Barnstable. Of landowners listed in the town records for both 1643 and 1670, only two had not been elected to one of the town's positions.[15] While it may be true that decisions of colony-wide significance were left to freemen elected to the General Court, the experiences of Cape Cod towns indicate that the day-to-day business of local communities was a responsibility shared almost universally by its residents.

Cape Codders, whether elected or appointed, and whether freemen or not, participated personally in the political life of Plymouth Colony. Just as most adult males could expect election as Constable or Surveyor of Highways, they could also anticipate a visit from the Constable to collect their taxes, both for the colony and for the town. Government in the seventeenth century may not have been especially complicated or sophisticated, and much of its work may have been done as public service without pay, but it was not free by any means. Paying taxes in Plymouth Colony was as inevitable as paying taxes has always been.

Initially, the Plymouth government assessed taxes for specific enterprises and listed the amount to be paid by individual taxpayers in the official records. In 1646 it started levying a general annual tax, and assessing the separate towns for a certain portion of it.[16] When it did so, an interesting indicator of the practical contribution made by the Cape to the support of the colony becomes clear. It was, roughly, a one-third participation. With the settlement of Eastham and its inclusion as a taxpaying community in the late 1640's, Cape Cod towns never paid less than twenty-nine percent of Plymouth Colony's taxes, and with one exception, never more than thirty-three.[17] The Cape paid its largest portion of colony taxes immediately following King Philip's War. Some western towns had been abandoned during the conflict, while the Cape had remained untouched. Its share of taxable property had therefore become greater, and it constituted a larger portion of the colony's inhabited towns.[18]

Among Cape towns, Sandwich and Barnstable consistently paid the larger portions of the taxes; Yarmouth and Eastham the lesser. In the early years, Sandwich apparently was the wealthiest of the Cape towns, paying nearly one-third of the region's taxes. By 1661 Barnstable had replaced it as the leading Cape taxpayer, and continued to do so into the late 1680's. The General Court regularly assessed Eastham, the smallest of the Cape Cod communities, the lowest amount. The town never paid more that twenty percent of the Cape towns' tax bill to the colony.[19]

The tax base of Plymouth Colony was property, including land, improvements, and livestock. Property needed to be assessed, or rated, and the Court required each town to elect three or four men to do it, thereby presenting local residents with another occasion for public service. To insure that towns could not avoid paying their assigned shares, the Court established fines for disregarding each stage of the tax collection process, whether it was the failure of the Constable to call a town meeting to elect raters, the refusal at the meeting to elect them, or the unwillingness of the elected raters to assess.[20] With such determination by the colony to insure that taxes were collected, acquiescence among the towns should be expected. Each of them regularly met to levy not only the taxes due the colony but also those due for their own activities.[21] To initiate the taxation process, property owners provided an invoice of their taxable property, and the men elected raters then apportioned each man's individual tax.[22] Taxes were paid in a combination of coin or goods, usually agricultural products. Rye, barley, wheat, corn, and peas were the usual commodities, with their per bushel values established separately by each taxing body. It was also possible to pay in installments, usually one in the fall and one in the spring.[23] Occasionally one met his tax bill by performing a service for the town, as Richard Bourne did in Sandwich. At other times a resident would pay the town's taxes to the colony and receive compensation, as when Samuel Freeman acquired a horse belonging to Eastham for paying the town's taxes.[24]

It fell to the Constable to collect the taxes, and he did so with various degrees of success. While in general the silence of the records indicates little long-term or serious public opposition to colonial or local taxes, the colony's extensive schedule of fines for noncompliance indicates that the government intended to collect the taxes which were due. But there are two examples which suggest that in extraordinary times local communities made their opposition to colonial activities known by refusing to pay their taxes.

As a result of the extremely high assessments associated with the costs of King Philip's War, some Sandwich taxpayers were in arrears. The General Court ordered the town's Constable specifically to collect delinquent taxes. The next year William Bassett and Steven Skiffe, two of Sandwich's most respected residents, were given broad powers to recover tax money being illegally retained by the Constable.[25] In the political turmoil of the Glorious Revolution, and in opposition to King William's War, Eastham, along with three towns not on the Cape, refused to pay taxes to the colony.[26] In the summer of 1690, with the pending loss of Plymouth's independence, there was a general tax revolt. Among the towns protesting their assessments and refusing to collect taxes were Yarmouth and Manomoit.[27] But these displays of disobedience were few. Except in times of crisis, the taxes of Plymouth Colony and its towns were not high, and property assessments were low. While it is unlikely that any man on Cape Cod paid his taxes with glee, he probably paid them with a resignation similar to that displayed when taking on the responsibilities of road maintenance or Surveyor of Highways. It was part of life in the colony.

In addition to voting, holding public office, and paying taxes, the citizens of Plymouth Colony also involved themselves with government through the judicial system. They could be personally involved in a case, either as a plaintiff or defendant in a civil suit, or as a defendant in a criminal proceeding. Even when not directly concerned with the outcome of the case, the colony's adult males could not escape the judicial system. At the initial investigative level, they served as Grand Juryman; during trials they served as witnesses; and in making the final decisions they served as jurymen. Like the other positions associated with the operation of government, jury duty was another civic obligation. And like those other positions, it was an obligation that was difficult, if not impossible, to avoid.

At the top of Plymouth's jury system was the Grand Jury, or Grand Inquest as the official records call it. Created to investigate violations of the colony's laws and bring indictments against those involved, it was a colony office. As with Deputies, individual towns elected Grand Jurymen to perform the colony's business. The General Court later assigned them the local tasks of policing the accuracy of weights and measures, checking the safety of ladders, and investigating those who appeared not to work. Although it was a colony office like Deputy, freemanship was not required for Grand Jurymen.[28] It offered another avenue for adult males to perform their public service, and towns elected large numbers of men to the position at one time or another. Over the seventeenth century, nearly forty men from each Cape Cod community served on the Grand Jury. Approximately two-thirds of them served only one term, and those who filled the post more than once rarely served more than three times.[29]

In addition to the Grand Jury, Plymouth Colony also insisted on the use of juries to decide the outcome of most trials. In fact, one of the colony's first recorded laws was the requirement that both civil and criminal proceedings be determined by a jury of twelve men, who were to follow English precedent as closely as possible.[30] The need of a jury for most trials obviously meant that large numbers of men would serve at one time or another on a trial jury, either for the colony, the county, or the town. Because the official colony records included the names of the jurymen, along with case summaries and decisions, it is possible to trace the patterns of trial jury participation. But neither the laws of the colony nor the records of its government offer any explanation as to how jurors in general or a particular jury were selected. In the early years, proximity to Plymouth and the meetings of the court was apparently a major qualification. By the late 1650's the Court had been forced to recognize jury duty as a burden and attempted to broaden the jury pool. To do so, it required each town to send one man to Plymouth to serve as a potential trial juror. The Court itself selected the individual, but the records are silent as to its methods.[31]

If the towns complied with the requirement, and there is no indication they did not, Cape men would have made nearly one hundred and fifty trips to Plymouth for jury duty in the three and a half decades the requirement was in effect. As only those who actually served as a juror are recorded, it is impossible to determine how many different men made the journey and were not called. All that can be said is that forty-seven men from the four towns actually served on a colony jury. If they are any indication, jurors represented the more politically prominent element of their respective towns. Whether it was the result of election by the town or selection by the Court is unclear. Nearly all of them were either freemen when they served or would eventually become so. Six men from Sandwich were the only Cape Codders throughout the period who were never freemen, and only one of them served more than two terms.[32]

Why, out of all the potential Cape Cod jurors there must have been, only some actually served is not clear, but the lack of pattern suggests it was pure chance. Some years no one from the Cape sat on a jury, at other times only one or two Cape men would serve, and occasionally there was a representative from each town. In a number of trials, the jury included two men from the same town, although how it occurred is unknown, given only one was required. Sometimes, a man would serve on more than one jury during a given

Court session, and occasionally a man who had been with him on the first was not on the second.[33] One apparently served on a particular jury if his name was drawn from the hat or bowl. As with other governmental positions in the colony, most of those who served did so only once or twice, and fulfilled their obligation. Only Samuel Rider of Yarmouth and Steven Skiffe of Sandwich seem to have made a business of jury duty. Skiffe was a member of the jury pool at least ten times between 1672 and 1685, and served on fifteen juries. Rider was a member thirteen times between 1665 and 1684, and served on fourteen juries. Their numerous appearances belie the randomness of jury selection, but perhaps the General Court preferred them for the pool and they were more apt to serve. Maybe they were just unlucky.[34]

It was no doubt in select courts at the local level that non-freemen participated as jurors. It would have been absolutely necessary in Sandwich, for the town never had more than twelve freemen until 1689. Unfortunately, none of the local records contain specific information regarding the process of jury selection. Sandwich was the only Cape Cod town even to mention any of the cases heard at the local level. Select courts and their juries probably operated like the courts at Plymouth. In some manner, local authorities no doubt selected jurors for local cases from among the town's adult tax payers to perform yet another public service.

Selection for the Grand Jury or a trial jury offered one of two ways the judicial system involved the residents of Plymouth. The other was by direct participation as either a plaintiff or defendant in a colony lawsuit. Here, like so many other aspects of Plymouth's governmental system, was another opportunity, if not for service, for concern. The courts of the colony were open to all, and they were freely used. Well over one hundred of the colony's recorded lawsuits originated from towns on the Cape, and nearly two hundred of its residents were involved in them.[35] They were civil suits, dealing with practical matters such as unpaid debts, the illegal cutting of hay and timber, or the failure to deliver goods that had been paid for. Occasionally, reputations were at stake, and men sued for defamation or slander, although the chances for winning the case and collecting damages were far less certain than for property lawsuits. Of the twenty-two suits from Cape Cod for slander or defamation, the plaintiff won only ten. The majority were either decided for the defendant or settled without assessing a verdict.[36] In property cases, however, the plaintiff nearly always won. There were nearly one hundred suits over property rights, and the jury decided for the plaintiff almost nine times out of ten.[37]

In addition to the colony court at Plymouth, local selectmen's courts also heard and decided lawsuits. Limited to suits involving forty shillings or less, they were the courts of original jurisdiction for minor disputes. For Cape towns, unfortunately, it is impossible to determine much about their operation. Just as the town records generally do not mention juries, neither do they make any consistent effort to record decisions. Certainly, the abundance of cases at the colonial level indicates Cape Codders were not shy about suing their neighbors, and it is unreasonable to expect that they would not have done so at the local level. But except for three decisions recorded in Sandwich and two appeals from select courts to the colony court at Plymouth, justice at the local level remains unknown. The small number of appeals probably represents general satisfaction with the select court system, but tells little about that system's operation.[38]

Government, then, in both its political and judicial aspects, was something Cape Codders knew well. Freemanship aside, they participated in it indirectly by voting for town Deputies to the General Court, and directly by serving either as Grand Jurymen or as trial jurors. Within the towns, it was impossible to avoid political involvement. Even for the small minority who did not fill a government position, attendance at town meetings was made virtually obligatory by assessing fines for absence. For the vast majority, they not only voted, but they also served. Without a professional bureaucracy, local offices were filled and community services performed by the town's citizens. Some men were apparently good at it, and filled every post the town had and did so repeatedly. Others were not so adept, and served less often. But whether it was the obligation to repair the roads, decide a lawsuit, collect taxes, or be a Deputy, the men of the Cape did what was required. Government and politics in seventeenth-century Plymouth was a participatory system in the best sense of the term.

Notes

1. The first two enactments of the first recorded General Court, 1 January 1632/33, placed heavy penalties on those elected to the governorship or council who would not serve. *Ply. Col. Recs.*, 1:5. Eastham Record of

Town Meetings, 1654-1745, pp. 6, 15; Sandwich Town Records, 1652-1692, p. 126; Yarmouth Town Records, 1677-1726, pp. 43-44. Some men may have stayed away because of the meeting's length. To ease the burden of attendance, Yarmouth agreed in 1677 that town meetings were not to exceed four hours except on special occasions. Ibid., p. 9.

2. *Ply. Col. Recs.*, 11:36, 64, 67, 88-89, 122, 127, 165-166, 215-216, 220, 223, 250; *General Laws, 1672*, pp. 21-25; *General Laws, 1685*, pp. 14-16.

3. Peirce, *Colonial Lists*, pp. 8-16. Those selected to be Constables for the following year were included in the list of elected officials recorded at the Court of Elections. *Ply. Col. Recs.*, 1-6:passim.

4. Sandwich Town Records, 1652-1692, pp. 11, 108, 129-130; *Ply. Col. Recs.*, 4:115; 5:85; 6:115; 7:218-219.

5. *Ply. Col. Recs.*, 3:168, 174, 191; 5:20-21, 100. See also Sandwich Town Records, 1652-1692, pp. 47, 163 for examples of local fines for not serving.

6. *General Laws, 1672*, pp. 33-34; *General Laws, 1685*, pp. 31-33.

7. Peirce, *Colonial Lists*, pp. 17-20. Yarmouth had the most repeaters, fifteen; Barnstable the least, ten.

8. *Ply. Col. Recs.*, 11:143, 213, 216- 218, 223, 227; *General Laws, 1672*, pp. 18-19; *General Laws, 1685*, p. 22. There was a twenty-shilling fine for refusal to serve if elected. See also Langdon, *Pilgrim Colony*, pp. 201-202; Stratton, *Plymouth Colony*, pp. 150-151; and Ward, *Statism*, pp. 75-76.

9. Peirce, *Colonial Lists*, pp. 9-16. Peirce's lists are not as clear for the office of selectman as they are for other positions. They should be supplemented with the tallies given in the Court of Election results. *Ply. Col. Recs.*, 4-6:passim.

10. The average length of service for the half who served briefly was 1.7 in Barnstable, 1.8 in Eastham, 2.0 in Sandwich, and 2.16 in Yarmouth. For the half who served extensively, the averages were 8.7 in Barnstable, 10.7 in Eastham, 10 in Sandwich, and 14.5 in Yarmouth. Service as a selectman was not without its perils, however. Samuel Smith's tirades against Josias Cooke's tenure as an Eastham selectman in 1670, forced Cooke to sue Smith for defamation. The jury decided the case in favor of Cooke, but without awarding him damages. Such problems may explain why he served only two terms. *Ply. Col. Recs.*, 7:159.

11. *Ply. Col. Recs.*, 11:56; *General Laws, 1672*, pp. 33-32; *General Laws, 1685*, pp. 31-33.

12. The first six volumes of the colony's records have numerous examples of both activities. See for example the appointment of Thomas

Howes and Samuel Mayo to be executors of the estate of Samuel Hallett, or the appointment of John Lothrop's widow as executrix of his estate. *Ply. Col. Recs.*, 2:156; 3:46. For examples of the work of a coroner's jury, see the report which found that a child of Nicholas Nickerson had accidentally choked to death on a piece of pumpkin shell, or the one which stated Isaac Robinson's son had drowned when he became entangled in marsh grass while trying to capture two geese. Ibid., 4:170; 5:7.

13. *Ply. Col. Recs.*, 8:192-195; Peirce, *Colonial Lists*, pp. 8-20. Thirty-three of the sixty-one men listed on the Barnstable list were elected to office; forty-four of the seventy in Sandwich, and twenty-six of the fifty-two in Yarmouth.

14. Lovell, *Sandwich*, p. 11; Peirce, *Colonial Lists*, pp. 12-14, 19. Six of twenty-eight men Lovell identifies as leaving Sandwich before 1650 were elected to public office before they left.

15. Barnstable Town Records 1640-1753, pp. 4-5; 119-121; Peirce, *Colonial Lists*, pp. 8-9, 17.

16. *Ply. Col. Recs.*, 1:9-11, 27-29, 38, 61, 75; 2:18, 109. The public charges to be raised for the colony and paid by the towns are listed with the records of Court orders until 1666, when they began to appear in the Treasurer's Accounts. Ibid., 2-4:passim; 8:117-169. Special levies for the support of King Philip's War and another one for King William's War in 1690 are in ibid., 5:207; 6:255. For a discussion of Plymouth Colony taxation in general, including tables of local assessments, see Joseph B. Felt, "Plymouth Colony Taxation and Valuation," *Collections*, American Statistical Association, 1, pt. 3(1874):277-289.

17. *Ply. Col. Recs.*, 2-4:passim; 8:117-169.

18. The General Court assessed the Cape for almost forty percent of Plymouth's taxes in 1678, but reverted to the usual levy by 1679. *Ply. Col. Recs.*, 8:149-150, 155-156.

19. *Ply. Col. Recs.*, 2:109, 119; 3:14; 4:5-6; 5:207; 8:123, 137-138, 169.

20. *Ply. Col. Recs.*, 11:42, 89, 142. The enforcement fines were established in 1643/44. In 1658 the Court stated it would appoint three of its own raters if the town did not do it. Ibid., p. 166. Ward, *Statism*, pp. 24-25. Tax assessors, or raters, do not appear in the records of the colony, nor consistently in the town records. It is thus impossible to determine patterns of selection for the position. The completeness of the fine schedule for noncompliance gives some indication that it was not a popular office.

21. Numerous examples of a town meeting voting either annual or special levies can be found in the local town records of Eastham, Sandwich,

or Yarmouth. Barnstable is the only town whose local records do not include them.

22. Sandwich Town Records, 1652-1692, pp. 40, 217; Eastham Record of Town Meetings, 1654-1745, p. 31. The resident paid a fine either for failure to submit an invoice or for omitting something from it.

23. Sandwich Town Records, 1652-1692, pp. 158, 181. *Ply. Col. Recs.*, 3:219.

24. Sandwich Town Records, 1652-1692, p. 10; Eastham Record of Town Meetings, 1654-1745, p. 12.

25. Sandwich Town Records, 1652-1692, pp. 145-146, 151.

26. *Ply. Col. Recs.*, 6:226-227.

27. *Ply. Col. Recs.*, 6:257-259, 265-267. See chapter thirteen for a fuller discussion of the 1690 tax revolt.

28. *Ply. Col. Recs.*, 11:11, 43, 90, 167-169; *General Laws, 1672*, pp. 20-21; *General Laws, 1685*, pp. 41-42. As with other colony and local offices, those who refused to serve paid a fine. *Ply. Col. Recs.*, 11:43, 120.

29. Peirce, *Colonial Lists*, pp. 17-20. Like the other major town officers, men elected to the Grand Jury are included in the annual Court of Election roster. *Ply. Col. Recs.*, 1-6:passim. The Grand Jury was an active body. In the ten-year period 1645 to 1654, for example, it made 120 "presentments," involving 143 people and thirty towns of the colony. It indicted some communities and individuals more than once. Forty-two of the "presentments" were of Cape Cod people, and five were of its towns. Ibid., 2:96, 97, 112, 135, 137-140, 147, 155, 162, 165, 170 173; 3:5, 10, 11, 17, 28, 36, 41, 47, 52, 69, 72-75.

30. *Ply. Col. Recs.*, 11:3, 12, 93, 167. The compilation of the colony's laws in 1658 indicates that at one point the Court of Assistants decided criminal cases without a jury where the fine was ten pounds or less, but the General Court repealed the law in 1661. It was probably an attempt to prevent juries from acquitting Quakers in trials concerning the Quakers' refusal to take the oath of fidelity. There was a similar law regarding civil cases of under forty shillings, and no repeal is noted. Ibid., p. 128.

31. *Ply. Col. Recs.*, 11:131.

32. *Ply. Col. Recs.*, 7:passim. Volume seven of the *Ply. Col. Recs.* is a separate collection of judicial actions, containing summaries of cases heard by the colony courts at Plymouth and including a list of the jurymen. There are some cases scattered throughout the Court Orders which comprise the first six volumes of *the Ply. Col. Recs.*, but they have not been included here. Many of them were criminal proceedings, and the names of the jurymen were not included. Non-freemen from Sandwich who served on colonial juries were: Elisha Bourne and Nathaniel Fish, one term each; John

Nye, Thomas Tobey, and Steven Wing, two terms each; and Caleb Nye, four terms. Ibid., pp. 79, 105, 108, 112, 150, 154, 233, 247-249, 259, 260, 275, 285, 291. The number of men actually serving from each town was: Barnstable, thirteen; Eastham, eleven; Sandwich, fifteen; and Yarmouth, eight.

33. For example, Richard Sparrow and Mark Snow of Eastham served on the same jury in June 1657, as did Thomas Huchens and Joseph Lothrop of Barnstable in March 1658/9, Josiah Snow and John Doane of Eastham in October 1678, and Steven Skiffe and Shuball Smith of Sandwich in July 1681. *Ply. Col. Recs.*, 7:83, 90, 214, 241. Cape Cod was well represented on the juries of the 7 July 1681 session of the Court. James Hamblin of Barnstable participated on three juries. He shared duties on one of them with Joseph Howes of Yarmouth, and on two with Jonathan Sparrow of Eastham. Ibid., pp. 241, 242, 243.

34. For Rider, see *Ply. Col. Recs.*, 7:126, 134, 143, 144, 147, 156, 163, 167, 171, 205, 220, 229, 273, 287. For Skiffe, ibid., pp. 174, 181, 189, 191, 196, 197, 205, 210, 213, 215, 219, 228, 234, 236, 241, 291.

35. As with the discussion of jurors, comments on trial participants is limited to those included in volume seven of the colony records.

36. *Ply. Col. Recs.*, 7:19, 30-31, 46, 50-51, 55, 63, 69, 89-90, 92-93, 97, 100, 107-108, 114, 118, 132, 155, 159, 173, 188. Four of the slander cases won by the plaintiff were those of George Barlow who used the technique to do battle against the Quakers he so aggressively persecuted. William Nickerson, in his ongoing attempt to protect himself from a host of enemies, both real and imagined, brought at least five such suits to the Plymouth court, and did not win a single one.

37. *Ply. Col. Recs.*, 7:passim.

38. The three suits recorded in Sandwich included one brought in 1669 by Richard Handy against William Swift and his daughter for her having caused Handy's horse to enter town land where horses were prohibited. The court awarded Handy five shillings and his costs. In 1676, Peter Gaunt sued Jonas Mornack over a debt of two pounds for five barrels of tar, and won the case. In 1680 John Fuller of Barnstable sued Edmund Freeman, Jr., for Freeman's failure to deliver a horse bought from him by Fuller. The court decided for Fuller, granting him the horse, six shillings damages, and costs of an additional sixteen shillings. Freeman believed himself wronged, and appealed to the next selectmen's court, but no record exists of any decision. Sandwich Town Records, 1652-1692, pp. 102-103, 134-1/2, 197. The two appeals from Cape Cod select courts were one brought by Jonathan Fish over the confiscation of his horse to pay a debt to Steven Wing, and another brought by Adam Wright of Plymouth after the Court had awarded John

Dunham of Barnstable the decision in a debt case between the two. *Ply. Col. Recs.*, 7:79, 216.

X

"to them we may go,
their land is empty"

TO its people, Plymouth Colony was more than a collection of
religious laws and principles or a society where political participation
expressed itself through public service. It was, fundamentally, an
agricultural colony, and its residents were farmers before they were
anything else. The early fur trade, begun with much promise,
remained important for only a few years. Similarly, the sale of goods
to new arrivals in Massachusetts during the 1630's ended abruptly
when the immigrants stopped coming after the outbreak of civil war in
England. Possessed of neither men with capital nor good and
convenient harbors, Plymouth never developed an extensive coastal or
overseas trade, and failed to meet the challenge of the Bay Colony's
commercial network. To the end, agriculture persisted as the center
of Plymouth's economic life. And a strenuous agricultural existence
it was. The soil was thin and sandy, its fertility at best only adequate.
Throughout the seventeenth century, Plymouth stood as the poorest of
the New England colonies, unscathed by the problems of reconciling
personal wealth with Puritan ideals.[1]

While Plymouth's people may not have prospered to the extent
of their northern neighbors, they were not without economic
ambition. Within the limits of their general farming, they were as

interested in economic improvement as any other New England settlers. The central object of that financial ambition was land. Without it there simply was no economic future, and colonial authorities understood the situation. In support of its people's territorial appetites, Plymouth's government granted numerous tracts, both large and small, to both individuals and groups. In all of it, Cape Cod played an important role. Some of the colony's earliest land grants were on the Cape, and by 1690 vast portions of the region had been conferred upon its four established communities, smaller villages, and individual owners.

In the awarding of all this land, the colony faced a basic problem. One or another native Indians or Indian tribes already possessed a claim to every acre of ground Plymouth intended to give its citizens. Whatever the nature of Indian ownership, Plymouth found it necessary to come to terms with the question of the Indians' prior interest in the land. The colony dealt with the issue in two ways. Foremost, like its Puritan neighbors, Plymouth developed a rationale which made English possession of greater significance. Once it had established the supremacy of English ownership, it then appeased Indian claimants by buying out their alleged subsidiary rights. In contrast to the policy of Roger Williams in Rhode Island, at no time did Plymouth assume the primacy of Indian ownership.

At its core, the colony believed English ownership of American territory to be based on the discoveries of English explorers. It then maintained that established colonies merely duplicated the right of English monarchs to distribute among their subjects what was theirs to give away. Once the colony had asserted its sovereign right to the territory, it next attempted to explain away the Indians' interest in the land. It did so by making a distinction between what John Winthrop would later label the "natural" Indian claim to the land and the "civil" English one. The Indians' "natural" title involved a communal and unorganized ownership, often of unoccupied land, where any tribal member used whatever land was needed. The English, however, viewed this native tribal system as significantly inferior to their own "civil" ownership. "Civil" possession meant the private ownership of specific acreage. It implied consistent occupation, use, and improvement of the same parcel of land over many years. In short, the Plymouth colonists believed they had brought civilization to New England, and with it a higher claim to the region's land. Indian ownership and use of the land was not seen as merely different, and possibly equal, but as obviously subordinate to the more civilized possession and exploitation of the colonists.[2]

Despite the assumption of the primacy of English ownership, Plymouth did not allow uncontrolled or private acquisition of land. The General Court closely regulated the founding of towns and the land grants which went with them. The Court established the fundamental restriction as early as 1643 when it the acquisition of Indian land without governmental sanction.[3] And as land transactions on the Cape repeatedly indicate, the Court further regulated land expansion by requiring the Indian rights to the land be purchased, a transaction often conducted by Assistants or other prominent men representing the Colony. Whether such regulations protected the Indian owners of the land is at best questionable. Governmental restrictions on land procurement did at least as much to assert the power and jurisdiction of the General Court as it did to protect the Indians' interests in the land. And the presence of Magistrates or other civic leaders at an Indian land sale similarly did as much to place the power of the settlers' government on the side of the English purchasers as it did to insure an equitable price or fair treatment for the Indian seller. For its part, the General Court seems to have rejected a request for land only infrequently, and to have moved against English acquisitions only when they were obtained in violation of the colony's laws. It rarely considered the impact on the Indian of an English request or purchase of land. Similarly, the price paid the Indian never approached the value of the land to the colonist. In the end, it was a question of power and aggressiveness. The stronger and more forceful English simply overran the original native inhabitants.

Consistent with these concepts of royal ownership, "civil" possession, and the superiority of English proprietorship, Plymouth had acquired jurisdiction over the lands of the Cape with the Warwick Patent of 1629. The patent originally granted control over land distribution to William Bradford and his "associates," most likely a reference to those Purchasers who had bought out the English investors in the economic reorganization of 1627. In actual practice during the 1630's, it was the Court of Assistants which awarded land. Among its grants during the decade were those establishing Sandwich, Barnstable, and Yarmouth. A few years after receiving the Warwick Patent, however, the freemen of the colony challenged the land granting authority of the Court of Assistants. The increased complexity of Plymouth's population, brought on by expansion, had created a demand that control over land distribution be broadened to a

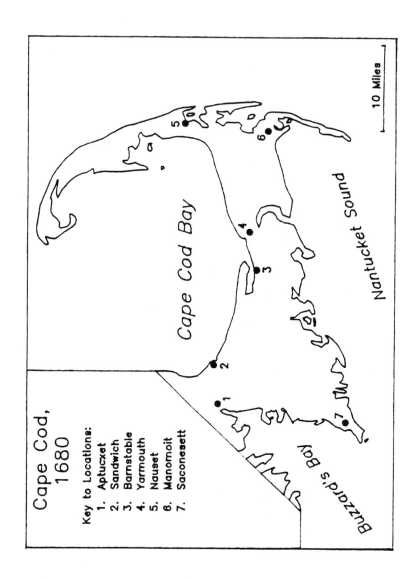

Cape Cod,
1680

Key to Locations:
1. Aptucxet
2. Sandwich
3. Barnstable
4. Yarmouth
5. Nauset
6. Manomoit
7. Saconesett

Cape Cod Bay

Nantucket Sound

Buzzard's Bay

10 Miles

larger and more representative group. After some discussion and even more delay, the Governor and Assistants finally agreed to turn the supervision of land over to the General Court, representing the interests of the freemen. In exchange, the General Court allowed Bradford and the Purchasers to reserve three large tracts for themselves.[4]

In 1640 the Purchasers selected three parcels. Two of them were on the western fringes of the colony, along Buzzard's and Narragansett Bays, and the third was on Cape Cod. The Cape section extended eastward from the Yarmouth boundary to three miles east of an Indian village at the Namskaket River and ran across the Cape from sea to sea.[5] In contrast to the two western areas, which were far from Plymouth and vulnerable to Indian hostilities, the Cape tract was both closer and safer, and therefore more desirable for immediate settlement. When the founders of Eastham selected their town's site, the Purchasers turned the outer, or eastern, portion of their tract over to the prospective settlers. Other settlements in the Purchasers' reserve would later come to include the Nickerson enclave at Manomoit, as well as the eventual villages of South Orleans, Harwich, and Brewster.[6]

Although dissatisfaction with the control of land distribution by a few prominent men had been behind the freemen's demand for change, once the General Court assumed responsibility it did not significantly alter the colony's land granting patterns. It did not have to. Secure in their control over future distributions, the freemen were not compelled to exploit a mere passing advantage. And the Court assumed control at the outbreak of civil war in England, with its severe decline in migration to New England, and the end of the region's economic boom. In fact once Bradford had turned the Warwick Patent over to the General Court, the Court returned it to him for safe keeping, and continued to distribute land on much the same principles as the Court of Assistants had previously done.

On Cape Cod, the General Court limited itself primarily to awarding land to groups of settlers from those towns already established. After the founding of Eastham in the 1640's, Plymouth no longer supported the creation of new towns on the Cape by people not already living there. Within these limits, however, the Court was extremely generous. It granted land to men from each of the Cape's four towns, and by the 1670's direct English ownership of Cape Cod acreage easily exceeded what it had been in the 1640's. Sandwich and Yarmouth had each expanded their claims into one area, while

Barnstable and Eastham had each enlarged theirs to include two sections.

Barnstable was especially desirous to expand. Located between Sandwich and Yarmouth, the town found expansion along the Cape Cod Bay shore limited, and began to look southward for more land soon after its establishment. As early as March 1641/42, the town petitioned the General Court for the opportunity to look for more land. The Court allowed it to do so, stipulating only that whatever land it chose should neither be usable as a town site itself nor belong to either of the other Cape communities. Within three months Barnstable selected an area southwest of the settlement, and the General Court appointed a committee to establish its boundaries.[7] Barnstable did not stop there. During the 1640's it purchased three more parcels of Indian land, and in 1664 added a fourth. These later territories included some lands already occupied, as well as some which extended beyond the settlement. They were apparently larger than the 1642 annexation and represent serious expansion on the part of the town. They are referred to as the town's first, second, third, and fourth purchases.

Dated 26 August 1644, Barnstable's first purchase involved land partially claimed along Cape Cod Bay, east of the Sandwich town line and extending into the middle of the Cape. It comprised most of modern West Barnstable. Barnstable purchased the territory from the Indian Serunk, and paid him in trade goods consisting of four coats and three axes.[8] Three and a half years later, Thomas Dimmock, Isaac Robinson, and Thomas Hinckley secured the town's second major piece of Indian land from the Indian Nepoyetum. It lay east of the first purchase along the bay towards Yarmouth and south into the interior. The Indian Nepoyetum received two coats, a day's plowing, and nearly one thousand feet of fence to protect his own land in exchange for what he surrendered.[9] Representatives of the colonial government had not participated in the two earlier purchases, probably because the colony's support for its acquisition had been implied in the granting of permission to settle on the Cape. But the third and fourth purchases were beyond the distributed lands of Barnstable, and when acquired saw representatives of the General Court acting as the colony's agents on behalf of the town. In May 1648, Myles Standish negotiated with Paupmumuck, Sachem of the South Sea, for a tract south of what had been bought of Serunk and east of the region held by the Mashpees. Paupmumuck reserved thirty acres for his own use and the right to hunt on the land he sold. He also received two brass kettles and the promise from the English to build half the fence necessary to enclose his thirty acres.[10] John Alden and Josiah Winslow represented the Plymouth government for the fourth and final purchase in 1664. In this last of its major acquisitions, the town obtained the land enclosed by the territory bought from Paupmumuck and Nepoyetum to the north and west, and Yarmouth and Nantucket Sound to the east and south. Ianno, the sachem, received twenty-five pounds and two pairs of pants for his land.[11] And there may have been a fifth purchase within another year or two. At its March 1664/65 meeting, the General Court noted there were Indians in the Barnstable area willing to sell land, and commissioned three men to buy it.[12]

The records of the other Cape Cod towns are not as complete regarding the purchasing of Indian lands as those of Barnstable, but there is no indication the process, or the arguments behind it, differed significantly from the Barnstable experience. Like Barnstable to its east, Sandwich was interested in expanding southward from the Cape Cod Bay shore. In 1654 the town appointed a committee of five leading townsmen to prepare a petition to the General Court requesting a grant of land at Manomet, an area at the upper end of Buzzard's Bay. The petition bore results eight years later, when the Court granted Sandwich a tract in the requested area.[13] Ten years later, in 1672, Sandwich again petitioned the Court, this time for land to expand the commons. The Court responded by allowing the town to buy what it wanted, as long as the new territory adjoined what the town already owned. In an interesting indication of the perpetuation of the Quaker controversy in Sandwich, the Court stipulated the new land was to be distributed to those most likely to support the minister.[14]

If Sandwich and Barnstable set their expansionist desires towards Nantucket Sound and Buzzard's Bay, Yarmouth and Eastham turned theirs towards the land lying between them, including the Purchasers' reserve and the region along the outer Cape. The portion of the Cape reserved to the Purchasers at the "elbow" of the Cape was called Satucket. Enough interest had been expressed in it by 1659 to require a division of jurisdiction over the territory between Yarmouth and Eastham. At its June meeting that year, the General Court ordered owners of land in the area toward Eastham to pay taxes in that town, and those with land closer to Yarmouth to pay there.[15] The next year the General Court ordered Barnstable's Bernard Lombard and Thomas Hinckley to review and report on land adjacent to the Purchasers' reservation which the Court had granted to Eastham.[16] Over the next decade a number of individuals acquired land in the area, although not all of them were residents. Among some of the earliest claimants were John Wing, Sr., who was building a house there as early as March 1658/59, and Thomas Prence who owned a mill site and other lands as early as 1661.[17] Other early land owners included John Mecoy, who became a resident, John Doane, John Bell, and Joseph Rogers. The settlement of a land dispute in the spring of 1676 between the descendants of the sachem Nepoyetum and English claimants indicated other owners of Satucket land, and a subsequent settlement of a boundary controversy among English owners disclosed others. A Yarmouth tax levy to pay for King Philip's War included seven men living in Satucket. They were Kenelm Winslow, William Griffin, Peter Worden, John Dillingham, and John, Joseph, and Anias Wing. Except for Dillingham and the three Wings, who were Quakers fleeing Sandwich, residents and owners of land in Satucket were from Yarmouth or Eastham.[18] Satucket was apparently less important for immediate habitation than as an area for speculation or future settlement. Its incorporation as the town of Harwich only after the absorption of Plymouth colony into Massachusetts reflects its slow growth as an established community.[19]

Eastham's interest in the Paomet region to its north came later and was less extensive than its movement into Satucket. The General Court assigned the territory to Eastham's jurisdiction in 1668, and some individuals claimed land there within a few years.[20] It was not until 1689, however, that nine proprietors participated in the first true division of Paomet land. In 1696 seven of them voted to prohibit the taking of firewood and timber from the area. As cited, it is not clear that the seven men who prohibited wood gathering were actually residents of the area.[21] By 1700, however, there were families living at Paomet. The proprietors voted to reserve some of their land for the support of a minister, and in 1709 the Massachusetts General Court incorporated the settlement as the town of Truro.[22]

The last of the Cape Cod areas opened up to English settlement in the seventeenth century was Saconesett, located along Nantucket Sound west of Barnstable's Indian purchases towards Buzzard's Bay. At its June 1659 meeting, the General Court permitted five Barnstable men to select land at Saconesett, and appointed Sandwich's Richard Bourne and one of the selectors, Thomas Hinckley, to negotiate with the Indians for its purchase.[23] In actions in March 1660/61 and June

1661, the Court added fourteen more men to the list of those with land interests in different areas of Saconesett.[24]

In contrast to most of the other areas of expansion on Cape Cod, the Saconesett region was quickly settled. By November 1661, Thomas Hatch and Isaac Robinson had already built homes there, and twelve individuals had received eight-acre lots. The records imply the lots were house lots, but those listed as recipients did not all take up residence in the towns.[25] Later distributions of Saconesett lands occurred in 1677 at Woods Hole, 1678 at Hog Island in the western portion of Saconesett, and in 1685 in the region's eastern section.[26]

The rapidity with which lands were divided and the number of absentee grantees indicate that speculation played an important role in the founding of the Saconesett. But the area was more than investments for Barnstable farmers, and other people joined Jonathan Hatch and Isaac Robinson at the southwestern corner of the Cape. Its proximity to Sandwich made Saconesett particularly attractive to Quakers looking for a peaceful refuge, perhaps because in 1663 the General Court placed the region under Barnstable's jurisdiction. As late as 1681, the Court ordered Saconesett men to train with Barnstable's military company.[27]

But Saconesett gradually accumulated the trappings of an independent town. In 1664/65, the Court of Assistants licensed Isaac Robinson to keep an ordinary. The community began keeping vital records at least as early as 1668. In 1672, its residents assumed control over their own local affairs, and the next year the General Court allowed the town to have a separate town clerk to record land transactions.[28] In 1675 the Court ordered Barnstable to select one of its Grand Jurymen from the village, although the order was as much Plymouth's desire to have someone in authority to oversee religious activities as it was to recognize Saconesett's growing independence.[29] In 1679 Saconesett attempted to meet the ministerial question by setting aside thirty acres of upland and a proportional amount of meadow for the support of a minister. Eight years later it added twenty more by exchange with Jonathan Dunham.[30] Satisfied that Saconesett was serious about obtaining a minister, the General Court incorporated it as a town, the first one created directly out of the expansion of Cape Codders themselves.[31]

As indicated most obviously in Manomet, Satucket, and Saconesett, most grants from the General Court to Cape Codders were made to groups rather than individuals. In this, the colony remained consistent with its earlier policies concerning the founding of towns, where the right of settlement and title to the land had been given to a specific town "committee." But there was also a new departure in these grants to those who already lived on the Cape. Settlement was not a requirement, and those with control of the land were called "proprietors," indicating they were owners, but not necessarily residents. It gave to the expansion of the 1650's and 1660's far more of a speculative nature than had been present in the period when Englishmen first opened up the Cape for settlement.

This acquisitive quality of some Cape residents is clear in the ability of some men to obtain personal grants of land outside the normal pattern of either general town distributions or colonial grants to proprietary groups. In fact, a few notable individuals even managed to acquire sizeable land holdings within the jurisdiction of established towns. Andrew Hallet, for example, had received well over two hundred acres as part of the settlement of the Yarmouth and Barnstable boundary problem in 1639.[32] The General Court awarded Myles Standish between forty and fifty acres of undistributed land in Yarmouth in 1650/51 as compensation for his efforts in settling the town's early controversies.[33] But these were somewhat unusual situations. Under Plymouth's assumptions about land ownership, each town controlled its own land, and the General Court limited itself to making grants only in the unassigned lands it claimed under the Warwick Patent. But it was quite generous with such awards, and responded favorably to a number of requests from individuals for land under its authority.

Sandwich men were the most active among Cape residents in their petitions for private land grants. In the thirty years or so from the 1650's to the 1680's, fourteen of Sandwich's better known residents received over thirty land grants from the Plymouth General Court. Unfortunately, a grant's location is not always recognizable, and its acreage is not usually indicated. But from what information is given, it appears Sandwich men received their land in either the Manomet region on Buzzard's Bay or the Mashpee district along Nantucket Sound. Indications are that grants were of good size. Of the few mentioned, none was smaller than twenty acres, and others were one hundred or more.[34]

The General Court made a far smaller number of land grants to individuals residing in the other Cape towns. Land and religious controversies had plagued Sandwich in its earlier years, and possibly the personal interest of its citizens in land beyond the town reflected both limited opportunities within Sandwich and an unwillingness of the colony to be generous to it. Outside of Sandwich, General Court grants to individuals were more limited, both in frequency and in the number of recipients. The only sizeable award was a flurry of grants from the General Court to Barnstable men in the late 1660's. Fifteen men each received a single parcel of some forty to fifty acres located along Nantucket Sound.[35]   Grants to Eastham and Yarmouth men were few in number.   Eastham's Nathaniel Sowther received unspecified acreage at Billingsgate, north of the town, as early as 1644.[36] Six other Eastham residents received grants of land near the town between 1665 and 1670.[37] The court records mention only three from Yarmouth who received similar grants.   The Court awarded Thomas Starr sixty acres near Nantucket Sound in March 1644/45, William Nickerson eighteen acres there in 1648, and in 1666 allowed Yelverton Crow to search for land which the Court promised to grant him.[38]

Not all grants to Cape Cod individuals were to Cape territory. A few enterprising Cape Codders managed to acquire land from the General Court on the western fringes of the colony. The awards all occurred in the latter years of the colony's independence, and represent a significant decline in available land on Cape Cod. Anthony Annable, John Chipman, and John Howland of Barnstable, John Wing, Sr. of Yarmouth, and Jonathan Sparrow of Eastham all received land near Taunton between 1669 and 1677.[39]   In 1673 Barnabas and Joseph Lothrop and John Thompson of Barnstable each owned land in Middleborough which was taken over by the town. As compensation for the loss, the General Court allowed the three men to select land elsewhere to replace it.[40]   After King Philip's War, Thomas Hinckley, Sr., received two hundred acres of confiscated Indian land in the Little Compton region.[41] Obviously some men on the Cape had come to recognize that economic growth in their foreseeable future lay off the Cape and in the western portions of colony.

Individual ambition and colonial control with regard to expansion met and clashed in the controversy over William Nickerson's activities at Manomoit, on the ocean side of the Cape's "elbow." On the one hand, Nickerson was like so many of his fellow Cape residents, primarily interested in the economic opportunity which Cape Cod soil offered. But Nickerson was also decidedly different from his neighbors.   He wanted to partake of that opportunity in a more unfettered environment than the colony's authorities could accept.   That Nickerson's interest in Manomoit should bring controversy is inherent in both the man himself and the land he claimed. An early resident and freeman of Yarmouth, he served in the usual town offices, including Deputy, but had been brought before the General Court in March 1641/42 for his religious dissension.[42] As the defense of his claims at Manomoit proved, he was an assertive and domineering individual. He was intent upon protecting his interests however necessary, even when his land claims conflicted with the interests of others.

Nickerson's troubles began in 1656 when the Court fined him for illegally purchasing land from the Indians and disfranchised him for selling them a boat in direct violation of a Court order to Yarmouth.[43] Before any action could be brought against him, however, Nickerson had moved to Boston so that his wife could care for her aged parents.[44] But departure from the colony did not alter his determination. From Boston, he petitioned the Court in June of the next year for the right to occupy his Cape land. Generally in support of English expansion, the Court agreed Nickerson could have at least a portion of his claim, and directed the land be examined.[45] Two years later, still in Boston, Nickerson expressed his unwillingness to accept that arrangement and again petitioned for it all. The Court responded he could have it if he would pay his fine.[46] He refused, and the matter remained unresolved.

After the deaths of his in-laws, Nickerson returned to Yarmouth, and the issue was back before the Court in 1663, no doubt because Nickerson and his family planned to take up residence in the disputed territory. In July 1663 Nickerson, six sons, and three sons-in-law petitioned to establish a settlement at Manomoit, and promised to take in as many other settlers as the land would accommodate and who would contribute to the purchase price.[47] The government gave its response in December when the Court of Assistants summoned Nickerson to attend the March 1663/64 General Court to explain his actions. When he appeared, he pleaded ignorance of the law and requested mercy. Rather than mercy, the General Court rejected his request and instead imposed a two-hundred pound fine and ordered the colony's Marshall to collect it. The ruinous nature of the penalty certainly supports the claim that Nickerson and some of his family had already settled at Manomoit by the time he attended the spring 1663/64 Court.[48]

William Nickerson's difficulties in securing his land at Manomoit were in good measure of his own making. His arrangement with the Indians in the area had been an oral agreement, and neither he nor the Indians were later able to agree on exactly what land had been bought or what price would be paid.[49] And his bargain with the Indians had been in direct violation of colonial law. Despite his claims of ignorance, it is difficult to accept that a man who had been a freeman of the colony and a Deputy to the General Court would not know of a law which dealt with such an important issue and carried such a prohibitive fine. To the authorities, Nickerson's claims were not only illegal and unclear, they were also in conflict with the Cape Cod interests of the Purchasers. In fact it was Nickerson's encroachment on the reserved rights of these original claimants which best explains the longevity and bitterness of the dispute. Because he had no deed, and in the early years had not settled, the Purchasers could not sue him in civil court for either the violation of a contract or for trespass. They were left with only political weapons, and therefore used the General Court to challenge him. For its part, the Court had simply awarded too much Indian land to too many people for too many years not to have supported Nickerson unless he had somehow infringed on the rights of influential colonists. And it must be noted, when he finally did settle with the Purchasers, the General Court quickly recognized his rights of ownership.[50]

But despite his troubles, Nickerson persevered. He believed he had acted no differently from others and was indeed carrying out the expansionist goals of the colony. With a good deal of accuracy, he interpreted the opposition to his activities not as the justified enforcement of colonial law, but harassment by those personally fearful of his challenge. Part of his determination may have been a reaction to the more aggressive policy adopted by those opposed to his efforts. At its June 1664 meeting, the General Court ordered the land Nickerson claimed sold, with Nickerson receiving whatever portion the sellers believed he deserved.[51] He countered by appealing to the Royal Commissioners, who met in Plymouth during the winter of 1664-65. Although the Commissioners thought his claims somewhat excessive, they apparently indicated to Plymouth a desire for compromise and a solution to the problem. In May 1665, the Court noted Nickerson's apology for his mistakes, and the next month remitted his fine, acknowledging collection had not been possible anyway. But while the Court had forgiven the fine, it had also perpetuated the controversy. It ordered that Nickerson be restricted to one hundred acres at Manomoit and in an effort to forestall further claims by Nickerson, granted the rest of the land to nine of the Cape's most prominent residents.[52]   Obviously, the problem was not ownership of the land, but Nickerson's ownership of it.

After 1665, the differences diffused somewhat.   By then others had established ownership, and Nickerson and his family remained as squatters.   The controversy concentrated less on Nickerson and his claims to land at Manomoit, and instead became an attack on the Plymouth government and its leaders by Nickerson, and a lawsuit against members of his family by the government.   Nickerson and two of his sons-in-law also went on the offensive, initially by writing letters attacking Thomas Hinckley, whom Nickerson probably believed was coordinating the colonial efforts against him.   They sent one letter to Barnstable and the other to Plymouth.   Hinckley apparently responded by suing Nickerson for defamation.   On 18 June 1666, Nickerson acknowledged his errors, and the following March publicly apologized to Hinckley.   Nine months later the Court fined Nickerson fifty pounds for the offense, but proposed to reduce it to twenty if Nickerson would offer a second public apology to the Court.   Having already admitted his error, and not being a wealthy man, he made the acknowledgment, although the Court found it difficult to collect even the reduced fine.[53]

The Manomoit proprietors appointed in 1665 were not idle in defense of their claims.   In October 1666 they won a trespass suit against Nickerson's three sons-in-law, although the ten shilling award for damages was more symbolic than substantial.[54]   In addition, the Court investigated Nicholas, one of Nickerson's sons, for a verbal attack on the Yarmouth minister, but released him on his promise to make a public confession at the Yarmouth meeting house.[55]   The Nickersons struck back with lawsuits of their own, and by blocking the tax-collecting work of the Yarmouth constable.[56]

Finally, Nickerson decided to take his case outside the colony, as he had previously done when he addressed the Royal Commissioners.   In an April 1666 letter, Nickerson and two of his sons-in-law appealed their case to Governor Richard Nicolls, a former Royal Commissioner and then governor of New York.   When the Plymouth General Court learned of the action, it called the three men in to defend themselves at its June 1667 meeting.   At Nickerson's request, the Court granted them a month to prepare a response.   By the time the trio appeared in Plymouth in July, the Court had learned of a second letter of Nickerson to Nicolls, written in February 1666/67.   Angry at Nickerson's behavior, the Court found the response of all three men unacceptable and bound them over to the

October Court to defend themselves. At that hearing, Nickerson
failed once again to satisfy the Court. It noted the three men deserved
to pay large fines, but that they had acknowledged some of the blame
and that Governor Nicolls had intervened on their behalf. As a result,
the Court fined Nickerson ten pounds, and his two sons-in-law five
each.[57] Given the length and seriousness of the controversy, it was
surely the fear of antagonizing a royal representative that prompted
the modest fine.

In the early 1670's, the controversy over ownership finally came
to an end. After losing a lawsuit against Mattaquason for a deed in
March 1671/72, Nickerson received one three months later. The
Indian's son, Quason, signed the deed as well, and the land acquired
was what Nickerson claimed to have bought a decade and a half
before.[58] A month after the June 1672 Indian deed, Nickerson settled
with those to whom the land had been assigned in 1665. Nickerson
paid them ninety pounds, and they abandoned their claim to
Nickerson's land.[59] With these two deeds, Nickerson received what
he had struggled so long to acquire. But he did not stop. Protected
now by the cloak of legitimacy, he continued to add to his holdings.
In three separate purchases over the subsequent decade, he
accumulated enough adjacent land to total four thousand acres.[60] It
was a princely domain, matched by few other men, on or off the
Cape. Certainly one must admire his spirit and tenacity. While he
ignored the Indians, may not always have had the law on his side, and
exasperated his fellow colonists with his judicial and political
maneuvering, one cannot help but admire the willingness of the man
to struggle on.

The settlement of the ownership problem, however, did not
bring immediate success to the small settlement. Populated only by
Nickerson and his family of adult children until the resolution of the
land title problem in the 1670's, Manomoit fell under the jurisdiction
of other Cape Cod towns, and gained independent status only after
1691. The General Court had originally placed the region under the
jurisdiction of Yarmouth in 1665, when it had negated Nickerson's
claim and given the land to others.[61] Three years later, the Court
transferred jurisdiction to Eastham, where it remained. Nickerson
appeared on Eastham's tax lists during the 1670's, and his son-in-law
Nathaniel Covell served as Deputy Constable for Manomoit as an
agent of the Eastham Constable.[62]

With the arrival of additional settlers after his acquisition of the
land title, Nickerson petitioned the General Court for Manomoit to

become a town in 1675. The Court rejected the plea, asserting Manomoit was not large enough to function independently. It left the settlement under the oversight of Eastham, but allowed it to keep its Deputy Constable and to elect a Grand Juryman.[63] Ever persistent, Nickerson tried a different approach three years later. In March 1678/79, he petitioned for independence again, this time stressing the difficulty of attending worship services in Eastham, and proposing that the community build its own meeting house and hire a minister. The Court responded more positively to this petition than to the previous one. It agreed that Manomoit could become independent if it succeeded in its proposals.[64] Unfortunately for the settlement, it failed to fulfill its promises, and at its June 1679 session the Court rejected the proposition. The Court continued Manomoit's Deputy Constable and own Grand Juryman, and added the requirement that the community raise five pounds per year for the building of either a meeting house or home for a minister.[65] The Court increased Manomoit's independence in July 1681, by permitting it to select its own Lieutenant to train its troops.[66] Finally, in February 1690/91, the General Court allowed Manomoit to become a town and to elect a Deputy for the Court. The town selected Gershom Hall, in itself an interesting comment on the Nickersons, and Hall attended his only session the following June.[67] It had been a long and strife-ridden process, but Manomoit had become a town.

By the time of the incorporation of Plymouth Colony into Massachusetts, much of Cape Cod's land had fallen under English control. While large portions of the territory were not actually being farmed, various towns and individuals had scattered and extended their claims and jurisdiction far enough that it was the English, and not the Indians, who dominated the land of the Cape. Only the far outer Cape north of Paomet and the Mashpee region along Nantucket Sound remained as large tracts of as yet unclaimed territory.

Notes

1. For a general discussion of Plymouth's economic life, see Langdon, *Pilgrim Colony*, pp. 141-151. For a more specialized analysis of farm life in the Old Colony, see Darrett B. Rutman, *Husbandmen of Plymouth: Farms and Villages in the Old Colony, 1620-1692* (Boston, 1967); and John J. Waters, "The Traditional World of the New England Peasant: A View from

Seventeenth-Century Barnstable," *New England Historic and Genealogical Register*, 130(1976):3-21. A more comprehensive description of New England agriculture can be found in Howard S. Russell, *A Long Deep Furrow: Three Centuries of Farming in New England*, abridg. Mark Lapping (Hanover, NH, 1982), especially pp. 3-54. See also William Cronon, *Changes in the Land: Indians, Colonists, and the Ecology of New England* (New York, c. 1983) for an analysis of the interaction and impact of Indian and English agricultural practices on the landscape of New England.

2. Robert Cushman, *Reasons and Considerations Touching the Lawfulness of Removing out of England*, in Young (ed.), *Chronicles*, pp. 243-245; John Winthrop, *General Considerations [for the Plantations of New England]*, in Winthrop Papers, 2:117-121; and Francis Higginson's version of the same, with altered wording in ibid., p. 120. The problem of land ownership and the morality of the settlers' arguments has been extensively debated by historians. See Gary B. Nash, *Red, White, and Black: The Peoples of Early America*, 2d. ed. (Englewood Cliffs, NJ, 1982), pp. 79-81 for a good concise discussion. For greater detail, see Chester E. Eisinger, "The Puritans' Justification for Taking the Land," *Essex Institute Historical Collections*, 84(1948):131-143; Wilcomb Washburn, "The Moral and Legal Justification for Dispossessing the Indians," in James M. Smith (ed.), *Seventeenth-Century America: Essays in Colonial History* (Chapel Hill, NC, c. 1959), pp. 15-32; Ruth Barnes Moynihan, "The Patent and the Indians: The Problem of Jurisdiction in Seventeenth-Century New England," *American Indian and Culture Research Journal*, vol. 2, no. 1, (1977):8-18; Francis Jennings, *The Invasion of America: Indians, Colonialism, and the Cant of Conquest* (New York, c. 1975), pp. 82-84 (Hereinafter cited as *Conquest*); and Alden T. Vaughan, *New England Frontier: Puritans and Indians, 1620-1675*, rev. ed. (New York, c. 1979), pp. 107-115 (Hereinafter cited as *Frontier*). See also Peter Carroll, *Puritanism and the Wilderness: The Intellectual Significance of the New England Frontier, 1629-1700* (New York, 1969).

3. *Ply. Col. Recs.*, 11:41. In 1674 the Court interpreted the restriction to include receiving Indian land by gift. Ibid., 5:151.

4. *Ply. Col. Recs.*, 1:119, 131; 2:4-5, 10-11; 11:116; Bradford, *Plymouth Plantation*, pp. 308. A copy of Bradford's surrender of the Patent can be found in ibid., pp. 428-430 and in Misc. Bound Manuscripts, Massachusetts Historical Society, Boston, MA. See also Langdon, *Pilgrim Colony*, pp. 39-43; Stratton, *Plymouth Colony*, pp. 75-76.

5. *Ply. Col. Recs.*, 2:10; William C. Smith, *A History of Chatham, Massachusetts*, 3d ed. (Chatham, MA, 1981), p. 47, n. 16 (Hereinafter cited as *Chatham*).

6. Smith, *Chatham*, pp. 47-49.

7. *Ply. Col. Recs.*, 2:36, 42. For discussions of the Barnstable land purchases, see Cobb, "Beginnings" in Trayser (ed.), *Barnstable*, pp. 29-30; and McKenney, "The Beginnings," in *Seven Villages*, pp. 13-14.

8. Barnstable Town Records, 1640-1753, p. 5.

9. Barnstable Town Records, 1640-1753, p. 6.

10. Barnstable Town Records, 1640-1753, pp. 7-8. Plymouth's acknowledgment of such purchases is shown in the inclusion of a shortened version of the agreement in its records. *Ply. Col. Recs.*, 2:130-131.

11. Barnstable Town Records, 1640-1753, pp. 2, 4, 11-12.

12. *Ply. Col. Recs.*, 4:82.

13. Sandwich Town Records, 1652-1692, p. 25; *Ply. Col. Recs.*, 4:18.

14. *Ply. Col. Recs.*, 5:94.

15. *Ply. Col. Recs.*, 3:165-166.

16. *Ply. Col. Recs.*, 3:194.

17. *Ply. Col. Recs.*, 3:156, 217; 5:239; Josiah Paine, *A History of Harwich, Barnstable County, Massachusetts, 1620-1800* (Rutland, VT, 1937), pp. 39-40 (Hereinafter cited as *Harwich*).

18. *Ply. Col. Recs.*, 4:131, 159; Paine, *Harwich*, pp. 42-46, 54-56, 61. Other identifiable owners of Satucket land included Jonathan Bangs, Thomas Clarke, Giles Hopkins, John Rogers, Paul Sears, Mark Snow, and William Twining.

19. *The Acts and Resolves, Public and Private, of the Province of the Massachusetts Bay*, 21 vols. (Boston, 1869-1922), 1:181 (Hereinafter cited as *Mass. Prov. Recs.*). When established, the town included all the land between Yarmouth on the west and Eastham on the east, extending from sea to sea.

20. *Ply. Col. Recs.*, 4:185; Shebnah Rich, *Truro--Cape Cod, or Land Marks and Sea Marks*, 2d ed. (Boston, 1884), p. 83 (Hereinafter cited as *Truro*). Thomas Paine bought land at Paomet from Thomas Prence in 1670 and from Jabez Howland in 1673.

21. Proprietors' Records cited in Rich, *Truro*, pp. 80-81. The men mentioned in the 1689 division were Jonathan Bangs, Thomas Clark, Israel Cole, Constant Freeman, Caleb Hopkins, Thomas Paine, who received a double portion, Joseph Rogers, John Snow, and William Twining. The only men listed in the 1689 division who participated in the 1696 vote were Cole, Hopkins, and Paine. The newcomers were Jonathan Paine, Stephen Snow, Ephraim Doane, and John Savage.

22. *Mass. Prov. Recs.*, 1:642. Rich, *Truro*, pp. 115-117; John B. Dyer, "Truro on Cape Cod: an Historical Address," *Cape Cod And all the Pilgrim Land*, 5(1921):7.

23. *Ply. Col. Recs.*, 3:164. The other Barnstable men allowed to look for land at Saconesett were Nathaniel Bacon, Henry Cobb, Samuel Hinckley, and John Jenkins.

24. *Ply. Col. Recs.*, 3:208, 216-217. The Barnstable men were Anthony Annabel, Peter Blossom, John Cooper, John Dunham, John Finney, Matthew Fuller, John Howland, Abraham Pierce, and Isaac Robinson. There were four men from Plymouth, Thomas Burnham, Samuel Fuller, John Morton, and William Nelson, who received a half share. Nathaniel Thomas, who may have been from Marshfield, also became an investor. Samuel Fuller is specifically mentioned in the official records as being of Plymouth, and was the uncle of Matthew and Samuel Fuller of Barnstable. Savage, *Genealogical Dictionary*, 2:215-216.

25. Falmouth Proprietors' Records, 1661-1804, pp. 1-2. Those who received land in addition to Hatch and Robinson were Anthony Annabel, Peter Blossom, John Chapman, James Cobb, Thomas Ewer, Samuel Fuller, James Hamlin, Samuel Hinckley, John Jenkins, Thomas Lothrop, William Nelson, and Nathaniel Thomas.

26. Falmouth Proprietors' Records, 1661-1804, pp. 3-4; Charles W. Jenkins, *Three Lectures on the Early History of the Town of Falmouth* (Falmouth, MA, 1889), pp. 18-20, 25-26.

27. *Ply. Col. Recs.*, 4:41; 6:67.

28. *Ply. Col. Recs.*, 4:80; 5:105, 131; Falmouth Town Meetings, Births, Marriages Deaths, 1668-1753.

29. *Ply. Col. Recs.*, 5:173.

30. Falmouth Proprietors Records, 1661-1804, pp. 8, 10. The General Court acknowledged the earlier reservation when it recorded the Sandwich--Saconesett boundary in 1681. *Ply. Col. Recs.*, 6:71-72.

31. *Ply. Col. Recs.*, 6:189. By 1694, the Massachusetts General Court had assigned the name Falmouth to Saconesett. *Mass. Prov. Recs.*, 1:178.

32. *Ply. Col. Recs.*, 1:121, 130, 135.

33. *Ply. Col. Recs.*, 2:164-165.

34. *Ply. Col. Recs.*, 3:52, 68, 84-85, 104, 167, 193-194, 217; 4:3, 4, 45, 97, 119, 128, 131, 132, 152, 161-162; 5:38, 96, 98-99, 131; 6:16, 66. The Sandwich men given land in these awards were, James Barlow, Miles Black, Richard Bourne, Thomas Burgess, Thomas Butler, Thomas Dexter, Edmund Freeman, Sr., and Jr., Robert Lawrence, William Paybody, James Skiffe, Josias Standish, Thomas Tobey, Thomas Tupper, and John Vincent. Some men, like Bourne, Butler, and Tupper received multiple grants.

35. *Ply. Col. Recs.*, 4:128, 160-161, 189; 5:37-38; 6:54-55. The Barnstable men who received grants from the General Court were Nathaniel Bacon, Daniel and James Cole, John Cooper, Edward and John Doty, John

Finney, Thomas Hinckley, Thomas Huchens, Barnabas and John Lothrop, Bernard Lumbard, Isaac Robinson, John Thompson, and Thomas Walley.

36. *Ply. Col. Recs.*, 2:76.

37. *Ply. Col. Recs.*, 4:110, 129, 131; 5:30, 39. The recipients were Josias Cooke, John Doane, Giles Hopkins, John Mayo's widow, Joseph Rogers, and Jonathan Sparrow.

38. *Ply. Col. Recs.*, 2:81-82, 129; 4:128.

39. *Ply. Col. Recs.*, 5:20, 24, 239.

40. *Ply. Col. Recs.*, 5:132-133.

41. *Ply. Col. Recs.*, 6:44.

42. *Ply. Col. Recs.*, 2:16, 36, 41, 130, 176; 3:79. For biographies and favorable assessments of Nickerson, see Smith, *Chatham*, pp. 56-59, 94-96; and James W. Hawes, "Historical Address," *Library of Cape Cod History and Genealogy*, no. 78 (1912):3-6. For a shorter sketch, see Swift, *Yarmouth*, p. 65.

43. *Ply. Col. Recs.*, 3:101. A general, and exhaustive, discussion of Nickerson's troubles with the Plymouth government is in Smith, *Chatham*, pp.55-77.

44. Smith, *Chatham*, pp. 60-61.

45. *Ply. Col. Recs.*, 3:120.

46. *Ply. Col. Recs.*, 3:165.

47. *Ply. Col. Recs.*, 4:153-154.

48. *Ply. Col. Recs.*, 4:49, 58-59; Smith, *Chatham*, pp. 64-66. Smith alleges the Marshall could not find any property of Nickerson to confiscate, which is quite possible, given his recent return from Boston.

49. *Ply. Col. Recs.*, 4:64, 162-163.

50. The warrant to the Marshall ordering him to collect Nickerson's two-hundred pound fine includes a reference to Nickerson having acted to the "prejudice of many the more ancient inhabitants and freemen" of the colony. It is the only clear reference to the Court's acknowledgment of Nickerson's challenge to the interests of the Purchasers. *Ply. Col. Recs.*, 4:59. See also Smith, *Chatham*, pp. 68-69, especially n. 38, 71-74.

51. *Ply. Col. Recs.*, 4:64.

52. *Ply. Col. Recs.*, 4:87, 96-97, 101-102; *Cal. State Papers, Col. Ser., 1661-1668*, #1103. The nine new owners came from every Cape town except Sandwich. They were Barnstable's Nathaniel Bacon, Thomas Hinckley, and William Sargeant; Eastham's John Freeman and Joseph Rogers; and Yarmouth's Thomas Folland, Edmund Hawes, Thomas Howes, Sr., and Anthony Thacher.

53. *Ply. Col. Recs.*, 4:134-135, 140. The lower fine is included in the Treasurer's accounts for March 1666/67, but Nickerson admitted in 1668

that he had not paid it. The colony's Treasurer had to sue his son-in-law for the fine. Ibid., 7:149; 8:119.

54. *Ply. Col. Recs.*, 7:132.

55. *Ply. Col. Recs.*, 4:158.

56. *Ply. Col. Recs.*, 4:183-184; 7:90, 95, 106.

57. *Cal. State Papers, Col. Ser., 1661-1668*, #1440, #1483, #1547; *Ply. Col. Recs.*, 4:134, 155-156, 157-158, 168. The Treasurer's accounts for October 1667 include all three fines. Ibid., 8:122. Richard Nicolls to Thomas Prence, Fort James, New York, 14 August 1667, Winslow Papers, Box 1, #30, Mass. Hist. Soc.

58. Ply. Col. Deeds, vol. 3, pt. 1:251. There is a copy of the deed in Misc. Bound Manuscripts, Massachusetts Historical Society, Boston, MA,

59. *Ply. Col. Recs.*, 7:171. The partners' deed to Nickerson is in Ply. Col. Deeds, vol. 3, pt. 2:252. The report of John Freeman and Jonathan Sparrow, appointed to survey Nickerson's land, contains a summary of the affair. Ibid., 6:109. See also Smith, *Chatham*, pp. 71-74, where he discusses and cites the original deeds.

60. *Ply. Col. Recs.*, 5:147, 154; Smith, *Chatham*, pp. 76-77 especially notes 58 and 59.

61. *Ply. Col. Recs.*, 4:96-97; Smith, *Chatham*, pp. 79-80. Yarmouth took its jurisdiction seriously, as indicated by Thomas Howes's complaint against the Nickersons regarding the difficulty of collecting taxes from them. Howes was Yarmouth's Constable. *Ply. Col. Recs.*, 4:183-184.

62. *Ply. Col. Recs.*, 4:185; 5:147-148; Barnstable Record of Town Meetings, 1654-1745, p. 26; Smith, *Chatham*, pp. 80-81, 83.

63. *Ply. Col. Recs.*, 5:171. In order to retain at least some Eastham influence, if not control, over the selection, those selected were to be chosen by the voters of Eastham and Manomoit together.

64. *Ply. Col. Recs.*, 6:4.

65. *Ply. Col. Recs.*, 6:14.

66. *Ply. Col. Recs.*, 6:67.

67. *Ply. Col. Recs.*, 6:256, 263. While William Nickerson, the patriarch of the clan, was in his mid eighties, it is nonetheless remarkable that Manomoit's only representative to the Plymouth General Court did not come from among Nickerson's many sons. Smith estimates the population of the town at the time of its incorporation at between 150 and 200. Smith, *Chatham*, p. 104.

XI

"in respect of the land and fish"

BECAUSE of the importance of land in Plymouth's agricultural society, problems concerning its jurisdiction and ownership were a constant issue in the affairs of the colony's towns. Boundaries for towns and individual land titles were often unclear, and a regular function of the Plymouth government was the appointment of men to determine boundary lines and settle land disputes. But however important land was to the people of seventeenth-century Cape Cod, agricultural products were not all that contributed to the economic survival of the region. The harvesting of fish and whales from the oceans surrounding the Cape provided an important secondary economic activity which also necessitated governmental intervention. Plymouth Colony not only licensed those who fished the Cape's waters, but also regulated the processing of its whales.

Initially, the General Court was silent on the establishment of boundaries for its land grants. Given what must have seemed like an unlimited supply of land and a view that regarded Indian claims as inferior, specific boundaries were not deemed necessary. The Court established boundaries for Sandwich and Yarmouth only after their founding groups had selected a site and settled the towns.[1] Richard Collicut's Barnstable grant is not included in the records, but the town's later boundary problems indicate that the situation was little different.[2] By the 1640's, however, the General Court had developed a more regular procedure. When the Court allowed Plymouth residents to move to Nauset, it included the boundaries of the grant.[3] The Court continued that practice when it later endorsed the expansion of the Cape's established towns.

But the establishment of boundaries, whether before or after settlement, did not prevent disputes over what had been done. Boundary lines delineated by natural features were often unclear, and those who surveyed them were just as imprecise in what they laid out. Controversies between towns and individuals over exactly what was owned by whom should be expected. Of the town boundaries on the Cape, the one between Barnstable and Sandwich was the most difficult to stabilize, requiring the General Court to intervene on several occasions over many years. The early 1637/38 line established just after settlement by John Alden and Myles Standish had not lasted, and in March 1651/52, the General Court commissioned Standish to return to the Cape in order to rectify the Barnstable--Sandwich boundary question.[4] Whatever Standish did on his second effort failed as well. By late 1659, a joint committee of Sandwich and Barnstable men had run a new boundary line, apparently at the expense of Barnstable. At a town meeting in January 1659/60, Sandwich stated its intention to utilize the new favorable boundary and in forceful words appointed a three-man committee to defend its position.[5] Barnstable, obviously peeved at the boundary as established, countered by creating its own committee to run a more advantageous line. To reinforce its claim, Barnstable recorded its line, and ordered the eviction of anyone found within the town who was not a recognized Barnstable resident.[6] In June the General Court tried again to settle the Barnstable--Sandwich boundary controversy. It ordered John Alden and Josiah Winslow to survey the line a fourth time.[7]

Later events reveal that Alden and Winslow were only partially successful at best. Although the towns ceased challenging each other directly, they continued the controversy by attacking the ownership of land by residents of the other town. The problem finally centered on Matthew and Samuel Fuller, Sr., of Barnstable and their ownership of land at Scorton Neck, claimed by Sandwich. On 1 July 1672, the Court appointed James Cudworth and Robert Studson to settle the quarrel between Sandwich and the Fullers regarding the boundary.[8] In rebuttal three weeks later, Sandwich reasserted its title to the land and strongly stated its willingness to defend it.[9] Over the next five years the General Court finally settled the boundary. Based primarily upon the testimony of the Indian Secunke and his two sons, the General Court determined in 1672 that the disputed territory fell under Barnstable's jurisdiction and therefore belonged to the Fullers.[10]   Sandwich kept up the dispute in 1673/74 by sending a committee to Plymouth to answer the Indians' statements, in 1674 by suing Samuel Fuller for trespass, and in 1676 by petitioning the Court for a reversal of the decision.[11]   In response to Sandwich's request, the Court agreed to discuss the issue again at its June 1677 meeting, but made it clear the Fullers and representatives of both towns were to be present.   After what the records note was an extended discussion, the Court decided not to reverse itself and allowed the earlier decision granting the land to Barnstable and the Fullers to stand.[12]

With the boundary issue out of the political and judicial arenas, events moved gradually towards a resolution. In August both towns appointed committees to draw another boundary. In 1682 they agreed to identify the boundary with markers, and in 1685 the Barnstable town records included the boundary's location.[13] After four and a half decades of wrangling, the issue finally had come to its permanent solution.

The Sandwich--Barnstable boundary disagreement similarly involved Barnstable's Thomas Dexter, Sr. At issue was a piece of meadow near, if not adjacent to, the Fullers' property at Scorton Neck and similarly claimed by Sandwich.   As early as October 1653, Dexter requested the General Court's assistance in establishing his boundaries, and the Court commissioned two men to determine their location if the parties could not agree among themselves.[14] Seemingly, they could not. Dexter was back before the General Court in 1664 and complained specifically against the town of Sandwich regarding his lands. To settle the problem, the Court appointed four men to investigate. Finally, in March 1673/74, two of them, Thomas Prence and Constant Southworth, submitted their report, which awarded the disputed territory to Barnstable and Dexter.[15]   The length of these controversies, which lasted for years, and the depth of rancor expressed, especially by the Sandwich town meeting, are a strong reminder of both the significance of land to the people of the Cape and the importance of protecting local independence.

The establishment of boundaries for the other communities on the Cape was both quicker and less controversial. In no case did serious controversy develop, and the process went more smoothly. In June 1654, the General Court recorded the boundaries of the Purchasers' reserve between Eastham and Yarmouth, and in the process established a boundary for each town.[16] Five years later the Court noted a committee report which recorded Yarmouth's western boundary with Barnstable.[17] The two towns jointly resurveyed that line in 1685 as part of the effort to insure land titles during the unsettled period of the Dominion of New England.[18] In the 1670's, a problem arose between Yarmouth and the settlers at Satucket, when the latter expanded into land claimed by Yarmouth. Yarmouth appointed a committee to identify its boundary in the disputed area in 1679, and the next year voted to defend it.[19] The General Court ordered the boundary between Sandwich and Plymouth laid out in June 1663, and appointed Thomas Hinckley, Thomas Dexter, Sr., and Constant Southworth to do it. For some reason neither town recorded the boundary, and in 1670 Sandwich asked the Court to do so. When the Court complied, it noted some of Sandwich's other boundaries as well.[20] The Court finally recorded the Sandwich--Saconesett boundary in July 1681.[21] In response to an order of the General Court, in 1683 Sandwich men joined with Plymouth and Saconesett men to identify and mark clearly Sandwich's boundary with each town.[22]

In addition to the problem of boundaries between English towns, there was also the question of boundaries between towns and Indian tribes. It was a general issue similar to the one faced more particularly by William Nickerson in Manomoit. English buyers and Indian sellers could not agree on exactly what acreage had been transferred. Barnstable's records are the most complete, but it is difficult to believe the problem was unique to that town. In May 1655 Barnstable directed its Deputies to push the General Court for a settlement of the town's Indian boundaries.[23] The Court agreed, and appointed Josiah Winslow and John Alden to the task. The two men did not move as quickly as Barnstable had hoped, and in 1657 the town appointed its own committee to determine the line. Finally the next year, Winslow and Alden submitted their report, which merely reiterated an unspecified previous agreement.[24] Winslow and Alden must not have adopted the Barnstable committee's boundary, as Barnstable was dissatisfied with their report. Alden and Winslow were back in Barnstable on the same errand in 1662. This time the town appointed four prominent citizens to negotiate with Alden and Winslow in order to insure a decision favorable to Barnstable.[25] Again, Barnstable was frustrated with the outcome, and appealed directly to the General Court. In August 1664, the Court appointed Governor Prence, John Alden, Thomas Hinckley, and Constant

Southworth to settle the Indian boundary problem in Barnstable. A body composed of the Governor and Treasurer of the colony and two Assistants, one of whom was the leading citizen of Barnstable, must have been what was needed to mediate the dispute. At least the question disappears from both the colonial and town records.[26]

The deep concern for land titles as demonstrated in the colony's consideration of boundary disagreements is further reflected in the colony's insistence on the recording of particular land grants and the boundaries of individual holdings. While these actions were often used to aid in restricting newcomers and protecting the economic interests of earlier settlers, they were also important as guarantees of property ownership. In 1645 the General Court began the process when it ordered its Assistants to acknowledge and record land holdings.[27] In recognition of the increase in land transactions which a growing colony generated, the General Court expanded the recording system nine years later. On 10 June 1654, the Court ordered each town to elect a five-man committee and empowered it to hear the land claims of its residents and register their titles in the town's official records. Any claim left unchallenged after two years was to be regarded as permanent.[28]

In recognition of the difficulty of the task, the Court had allowed the towns five years to complete the assignment. Although the records are incomplete, there is no evidence that any of the Cape Cod towns did not eventually comply. Barnstable started the process within three weeks of the Court's order. At a meeting on 26 June 1654 the town selected its five-man committee, which soon began to record the holdings of Barnstable's land owners.[29] Indeed, that ongoing tabulation continued into the 1670's, and encompasses more pages of Barnstable's local records than any other topic.[30] The first mention of Eastham's compliance was in December 1658, when the town elected its committee. Unfortunately, the town did not see fit to note the committee's work in its official records.[31] Yarmouth's concurrence with the Court's directive cannot be determined. Its records do not cover the years involved, but there is no evidence that the town did not follow the General Court's command. Surely, given its treatment of Sandwich, the General Court would have taken notice of any delinquency on Yarmouth's part.

Sandwich was the only Cape Cod town that evidenced difficulty in fulfilling the wishes of the Court. The registry of land holdings occurred in Plymouth Colony during the Quaker turmoil, and as the center of Quakerism, Sandwich had other, more important, problems.

It did, however, at least make an attempt. At a town meeting the end of October 1658, Sandwich elected the mandatory committee, including seven men rather than the required five, and voted to pay them for their efforts.[32] The committee appears to have done some of its assignment but then abandoned the project.[33] The Court of Assistants noted the failure of Sandwich to identify and record the bounds of its residents' land holdings, and at its 6 February 1665/66 meeting, fined the town for its negligence. It ordered Sandwich to appoint three or four men to take on the assignment, and agreed to remit the assessed fine if it were speedily accomplished.[34]   It apparently was. At a town meeting in March 1666/67, the town noted the specific order of the Court, elected five men to comply with it and quickly completed the identification and recording of the land holdings of Sandwich.[35] The rapidity with which Sandwich obeyed the Court's order regarding land registration certainly indicates that the previous delay had been less an unwillingness to conform to the Court's directive than a consideration of more immediate problems.

This sweeping concern of the General Court for the recording of land holdings and its frequent involvement in a variety of boundary disputes strongly attest to the overwhelming importance of land to the economy of seventeenth-century Cape Cod. For the colony, land was similar to religious belief, personal morality, and political participation. It was a fundamental part of the purposes and survival of the colony, too important to be left to local control. But it was also the case that land was not the only aspect of economic life on Cape Cod. Practically enveloped by the sea, the Cape also depended on whales and fish as important adjuncts to its economic existence. They were such an important appendage that they too fell under the supervision of the colonial government.

The demarcation and defense of favorable boundaries on Cape Cod were, therefore, more than merely issues of politics and property. They were also closely related to the fishing and whaling opportunities of the region. All the Cape towns were on the coast, and their boundaries marked not only their lands, but also their rights to fish and whales. John Smith's descriptive name for the Cape made the point, and the presence of whales and the possibilities of whaling was one of the reasons the Pilgrims had originally considered the tip of the Cape for their settlement.[36]

These early observations were certainly true. There is no doubt that whales became an important economic consideration for the towns and people of the Cape specifically, and for the colony in general. The attention paid to them by town meetings and the General Court confirms their significance. John Winthrop noted their importance in 1635 when he commented that some Massachusetts men had gone to the Cape to gather oil from beached whales.[37] More directly, in its long boundary quarrel with Barnstable, Sandwich made it quite clear that jurisdiction over beached whales was as much at issue as the possession of crop or pasture land.[38]

The whales processed on Cape Cod were Atlantic right whales, so called because they were the correct, or "right," whales for human use. They were a coastal, migratory whale, which floated when dead, and produced a good quality oil. Most of the whales utilized by seventeenth-century Cape Codders were beached whales, which had run aground by themselves. Other whales were taken directly at sea. Some were killed at sea or driven on to the shore from boats, and others were "drift" whales which had died at sea and were later hauled to shore. Over the century, the number of beached whales increased, as efforts to kill them at sea failed, and their wounded or dead carcasses later washed up on the shore.[39] However obtained, whales, and especially their oil, were an important item in the economy of Plymouth Colony. Despite whale's obvious economic significance, the historical sources are strangely silent respecting their number and processing, and it is difficult to determine how much oil a particular whale would yield. The official records are similarly of little help, referring only to whale oil owed to the colony or to those who processed it for the town. One clue comes from Edward Randolph. Writing to England in January 1687/88, he estimated Plymouth had exported two hundred tons of whale oil in the previous months, and predicted that whale oil would replace the fur trade as a staple of the colony's economy.[40] Another comes from Wait-Still Winthrop. In a letter to his brother he mentioned a report of twenty-nine whales having been killed in one day, and that on a previous visit to Plymouth he had learned of a group who had killed six whales within a few days.[41] Offsetting these rather generous estimates, is Thomas Hinckley's reference to small whales which produced between seven and twenty barrels of oil.[42]

Despite the rather obvious quantity and value of whales, in the first decade or so of settlement, the General Court chose not to regulate them. Both drift and beached whales apparently belonged to whomever claimed them. Winthrop's comment about Massachusetts men going to the Cape for whales, and the failure of Plymouth to make mention of it or protest against it, imply that such was the situation. But by the early 1650s the Plymouth government had come to recognize that the competition surrounding whales required governmental oversight. It intervened to assert ownership by Plymouth colonists and also to garner some of the profits for itself.

At its 29 June 1652 meeting, the General Court enacted its first law on whales. At its core, the law assigned beached whales and drift whales within a harbor or one mile from shore to the town where they were found. Beyond those limits, whales belonged to whomever brought them in. In addition, the Court mandated that the owners of every whale cut up were to pay one barrel of oil to the colony Treasurer. It also ordered each town to have an agent to collect the oil, and after 1656, to ship it directly to Boston.[43] The Cape's whale oil output was fairly steady throughout the century. All of the towns are mentioned in the Treasurer's accounts at one time or another as having produced whale oil. For example, the account submitted at the August 1654 General Court noted among the colony's credits a barrel of oil from Eastham.[44] The accounts for 1660 listed over eight barrels due the colony which were in the hands of Sandwich's John Ellis.[45] The next year, the towns of the colony owed for over fifteen barrels of oil.[46] Except for a brief item in 1685, whale oil dropped out of the Treasurer's accounts as a specific item in the middle of the 1660s. But it appeared in other colonial and local records often enough to signal that it remained an important commodity in the colony's economy.[47]

Under the general policy of town ownership of whales, each community assumed responsibility for those whales found within its waters or beached on its shores, and regarded them as town resources, to be used to the benefit of its residents. In January 1653/54, Sandwich ordered the proceeds of whaling to be divided equally among all its residents.[48] Eastham, on the other hand, decided on an alternating system. One-half of the town's residents received the proceeds of the first whale, and the other half the second.[49] Reflective of the competition for whales which their value created, Yarmouth prohibited non-residents from assembling within the town's borders to catch whales and fined residents for entertaining such poachers.[50] The discovery of whales came in for special consideration. Towns granted a double share of the proceeds to anyone who located a whale, and punished those who did not report finding one.[51] Eastham won a lawsuit against Ralph Smith in the spring of 1661 for his illegal appropriation of a whale, and the Court of Assistants fined him twenty shillings for lying about it.[52] In 1685

Eastham confiscated the whale blubber and bone in the possession of three men after they had cut up a whale without informing the town.[53] To reduce the inconvenience of everyone participating in cutting up those whales which were reported, Yarmouth, Eastham, and Sandwich each assigned the task to either an individual or a small committee of residents. The town compensated them either by direct payment, as in Eastham and Yarmouth, or dividing the yield, as in Sandwich.[54] It was important and profitable enough that Thomas Prence assumed responsibility of whales in Eastham. He entered into a partnership with two Boston men in 1659, and the group hired Nathaniel May of Eastham to do the processing.[55]

By the end of the 1650s, whaling on Cape Cod was so successful that the Plymouth government undertook to alter its policy on whales in order to increase its share of the oil. It adopted the principle of monopoly rights which it had used in organizing the Kennebec trade previously, and which it would later use regarding fishing privileges as well. To that end, at its June 1661 meeting, the Court asserted whales no longer belonged to the towns, but instead were to be the property of the colony. Rather than claiming a one-barrel assessment and allowing the town the bulk of the oil, the General Court proposed to take the greater part for itself and pay the towns two hogsheads of oil as payment for processing it. If the towns refused this new arrangement, the Court authorized the colony's Treasurer to turn the whales over to someone else and allow the town two hogsheads of oil in exchange for permitting the renter access to the whale and supplying firewood to boil the blubber. The Court further intended to increase its share of the colony's whale oil by stipulating it was entitled to one half of any drift whale brought in from outside the towns' one-mile limits.[56]

The towns of the Cape, to whom the proposal had been made, unanimously rejected it and protested successfully against it. Constant Southworth, Plymouth's Treasurer, made the General Court's counter-offer on 1 October 1661. Noting their objections to the earlier scheme, Southworth proposed a one-hogshead levy for one year, and the postponement of a broader settlement of the matter until the 1662 Court of Election.[57] Before that meeting however, Yarmouth came to partial terms with the Court. It was the only Cape town to do so. In a statement dated 6 March 1661/62, Yarmouth agreed to pay the colony two barrels of oil, which equalled the Court's demand of a hogshead. Yarmouth did not accede, however, to the idea of colonial ownership of whales.[58] The other Cape communities adhered to their original opposition and did not concur with Yarmouth. In the end, the Court abandoned its assertion of ownership, and reverted to its claim to one hogshead of oil from any beached or drift whale from within a town's boundaries. The colony did continue to demand a larger portion of whales from outside those limits. It claimed one-half of any such drift whale and two hogsheads oil from any similar beached whale.[59] With the hopes that some good to the colony might come out of its surrender of jurisdiction over whales, the Court suggested that some of the oil be used to support the ministry.[60]

The 1662 arrangement lasted until nearly the end of the colony's independence. Prompted by a number of lawsuits and contests over the ownership of drift whales, in 1690 the General Court instituted a series of specific actions to be followed by the claimants of whales. Central to the enforcement of these more exact requirements was the office of whale viewer. Appointed by the Court, his main responsibility was to identify and record both drift and beached whales to insure their oil became the property of those who could legitimately claim it.[61] The necessity of dealing at length with the question of whales at a time when the very existence of the colony was under question, reveals the important place whales had maintained throughout Plymouth and Cape Cod's first century.

Like whales, the fish of Cape Cod Bay and its adjacent waters had long been known and caught. The early explorers of the region had frequently commented on them, and proximity to the North American fishing grounds had been the reason for many of the early temporary settlements. Gosnold's Cape Cod label had not been done without justification. The objects of all this interest were cod and mackerel, which migrated to coastal waters in warmer weather, and sea bass, which were a shore fish by nature. Although cod were sometimes caught individually with baited hooks, most fish were taken in the seventeenth century by the use of nets or seines thrown by crews of three or four men from small boats along the shore. Once caught, the fish were dried and salted, packed in barrels, and shipped to Boston, where they became an important item among New England's exports. The Earl of Bellomont estimated in 1700 that Massachusetts shipped fifty thousand barrels of dried fish a year. The best of it eventually appeared on the tables of European Catholics, and the worst in the plates of West Indian slaves.[62]

Plymouth's initial settlers had been slow to take advantage of New England's fishing opportunities. The Pilgrims possessed neither experience as sailors or fishermen nor capital to build ships, and their failed fishing efforts at Cape Ann in 1624 did not encourage them to alter the situation. During the first decade of the colony, Englishmen with rights from the Council for New England conducted the fishing. After 1630 men from Massachusetts took it over, encouraged by such favorable legislation as exemptions from taxes and military service.[63] Despite Plymouth colonists' failure to exploit their fishing opportunities, the colony did successfully manage to retain authority over those who did. Plymouth's control over the fish in its seas is in pointed contrast to its inability to make good its claim to full mastery over the whales on its shores. Taken directly from the ocean rather than off the beaches of established towns, fish were not a jurisdictional issue between the colony and its towns, and therefore more easily managed by the General Court.

With no serious interest in the fishery in the early years, Plymouth had equated fish with wild animals and birds, and regarded them as free for the taking.[64] But as Massachusetts men took over the fishing, Plymouth came to recognize something of its untapped opportunity. In 1646 the General Court instituted a licensing system both to control and profit from the Bay Colony's use of the fishery.[65] By 1650, however, Plymouth was interested in joining the fishing business itself. Its desire to exploit its fisheries may well have been heightened by the departure of the English fishermen from Cape Cod waters due to the English Civil War and a knowledge of the encouragement of colonial fishing which would soon be given in the Navigation Act of 1651.[66] At its October 1650 meeting, the General Court ended both the licensing system and the privilege of Massachusetts men to fish at the Cape. Citing trouble with the Massachusetts fishermen, and noting that some men from Plymouth wanted to fish at the Cape, the Court replaced the former arrangement with a monopoly grant of fishing rights to some of their own. The Court granted fishing privileges to Thomas Prence, Myles Standish, and William Paddy, and allowed them to include men from Plymouth, Duxbury, and Eastham.   The next year the Court increased the prestige of the group by adding William Bradford.[67]   It was obviously a speculative business venture and designed to eliminate competition not only from Massachusetts but also from those towns in the colony which had not been settled by emigrants from the original Plymouth.

At least some of those excluded from fishing at the Cape protested the monopoly.   In 1652, the Grand Jury questioned its validity, but monopolies were an established practice and there is no evidence the Court responded in any other way than ignoring the issue.[68] Given the status of the monopoly's chief members, it would be difficult to envision any other outcome. Neither is there any evidence regarding the broader operation of the fishing monopoly. Those who held it did not pay for it, and for a number of years offshore fishing at the Cape appears only intermittently in the records of the General Court and the colony Treasurer. When references do occur, they are to restrictions on Massachusetts fishermen. In 1661, the General Court prohibited strangers or foreigners from fishing at the Cape without permission, and ordered those who had it to abide by the colony's laws. They were also to pay six pence a hundredweight for their fish.[69] A few years later, in 1668, the Court found it necessary to complain to Massachusetts about the polluting practices of its fishermen. The Court accused the Bay Colony men of cutting fish up on board their vessels and throwing the refuse into the sea, where it annoyed both the fish and the people of Plymouth.[70] These two examples indicate that Plymouth fishery holders may have rented out their monopoly, with a surcharge going to the colony. The existence of offshore fishing boats and the presence of fish waste may also reveal an inability on the part of either the monopoly or the government to enforce fishing regulations.

Whatever the operation of the Cape Cod fisheries had been under the private monopoly established in 1650, the General Court reorganized it and brought it under closer governmental supervision in the 1670s. Complaining of the refuse left by fishermen on the Cape's beaches, in 1670 the General Court levied a forty-shilling fine on the perpetrators, and created the office of water bailiff to collect it. The Court also authorized the bailiff to collect a tax of six pence a barrel on fish caught by residents of Plymouth, and triple that amount for fish taken by non-residents.[71] Two years later, it empowered the bailiff to seize the fish of those who had not paid the levy. Over the next decade, the General Court increased its restrictions on fishing at the Cape, especially for mackerel. At the same session it imposed general levies on fish, the Court attempted to preserve the mackerel supply by prohibiting commercial fishing for them before the first of July.[72] The Court later restricted the netting of mackerel from the shore to a thirty-two day period in the fall, and for a few years prohibited the practice completely.[73]

During the same period it was imposing fees and restrictions on the Cape Cod fisheries, the General Court also assumed more direct control over them. Although the General Court granted the request of some residents of Hull to fish at the Cape in 1671, by 1677 it desired that Plymouth men control the fishing at Cape Cod.[74] At its July meeting, the Court rented the business to a group of four Plymouth men for seven years. They were to pay thirty pounds per year for the privilege, and were to hire non-Plymouth men only when residents of the colony refused to participate. Massachusetts was unhappy with these new limitations. Upon complaint of one Ambrose Gale, who had long fished in Cape waters, the Massachusetts General Court sent a letter to Plymouth. In it, the Bay Colony leaders argued for the freedom of the seas, pointed out that neither of their charters permitted such restrictions, and reminded Plymouth that New England's enemies provided enough trouble without the Old Colony adding to it.[75] Despite the special protection, Cape Codders did not see the Court's move as an opportunity to be quickly taken. A year later, the Court permitted the renters to allow half those who fished the Cape to be from Massachusetts.[76] But regardless of who caught the fish, under colonial jurisdiction and a more entrepreneurial operation, the Cape Cod fishery prospered. The income from it began to appear in the records of the General Court.[77]

The major beneficiary of the General Court's assumption of direct authority over fishing was the colony's public education system. At its March 1672/73 meeting, the General Court noted that when it had previously instituted its assessments on fish caught at the Cape, it had intended the money to be used for the support of a free school in one of the towns. The Court, observing that the town of Plymouth was already supporting such a school with both public funds and private donations, granted the previous two years' fishing profits to Plymouth for its school. With the prospect that others in the colony would also donate to the school, the Court appointed Thomas Hinckley as its representative to administer the money.[78] A Deputies' poll among the freemen indicated general support for the idea, and in 1674 the Court made the practice formal by voting that future Cape Cod fishery profits be used to that end.[79] Schools other than Plymouth's eventually benefitted as well. In 1678, the General Court voted to give five pounds of the Cape Cod fishery money to the widow of Rehoboth's minister, Noah Newman, and the same amount to the town's schoolmaster.[80] In March 1681/82, the Court granted twelve pounds of the money to the Rehoboth school, eight pounds to Ichabod Wiswall's school at Duxbury, and reserved nine pounds for future use.[81]   Two years later, it divided thirty pounds among four schools and one individual.[82]

The amount of money allocated to the schools of Plymouth colony is one of the few indications of the profitability of Cape Cod fishing and of the success of the leasing arrangement adopted in 1670. Another sign of its general success is that when the seven-year lease expired in 1684, the Court continued the system.   At its June 1684 meeting, the Court appointed the colony's Treasurer and two other men to rent out the fishing at the Cape, and allowed them a month to do it.   Within the allotted time, William Clark of Plymouth had offered to pay thirty pounds for the right to fish for bass at the Cape, with the provision that the Court ban the catching of mackerel by nets.   The Court complied with his request, and ordered the Treasurer to issue him the lease.[83]   Unfortunately for Clark, John Mayo and Samuel Smith of Eastham did not observe the ban on netting.   At the instigation of Clark, the water bailiff seized several barrels of mackerel belonging to Mayo and Smith, and brought the case before the Court of Assistants at its July 1686 session.   The Court postponed the case to the October meeting.   At that meeting, Clark testified to the accuracy of the charges, and Jonathan Sparrow, as attorney for Mayo and Smith, requested a postponement to prepare a response. The Court granted Sparrow's request, but the outcome is unclear. The records of the colony do not exist for 1687.[84]   It was probably a judgment unfavorable to Clark.   At the October 1689 meeting of the General Court, Clark appeared and petitioned to be released from his fishing contract.   The Court agreed, requiring only that he pay what was due.   The Court went on to repeal the prohibition on netting mackerel, reinstituted its earlier laws regarding the Cape Cod fisheries, and turned jurisdiction of the business over to the Barnstable County Magistrates.[85]   In effect, probably little had changed.   Clark's efforts to restrict mackerel fishing had been unsuccessful, and it is doubtful that county officials made any serious alterations in the administration of the Cape's fishing.   They probably rented it out, as had previously been the case.

Akin to the open-sea fishing for cod, mackerel, and bass was the more local inland taking of alewives.   Similar to herring, they were a fish used primarily as fertilizer for crops, in the Indian manner. Caught in tidal streams by the use of weirs, alewives were left largely to local jurisdiction.   If Sandwich is typical, alewife fishing was conducted as a public service.   The town assigned one or two men the task of catching alewives, paid them for doing it, and ordered the fish distributed among the town's residents. In 1652 Sandwich commissioned Daniel Wing and Michael Blackwell to repair the weir and catch alewives for a three-year period. Nearly twenty years later, Blackwell was still taking them. In 1670 the town gave him a contract for seven years and agreed to pay him six pence per thousand fish. William Hunter replaced Blackwell in 1687, although Hunter received only four pence per thousand, and Mordecai Ellis took over the business on the same terms as Hunter in 1691.[86] The colonial government became involved in the alewife fishing only when there were disputes or when the fishing occurred outside local authority. In 1655 the General Court intervened when Sandwich challenged Thomas Burgess's catching of alewives at Manomet.[87] In March 1673/74, the Court allowed Richard Bourne to take 12,000 alewives at his land on the Cape.[88] Despite a trend towards the use of more traditional English farming techniques, involving the use of animal manure, alewife fishing apparently remained an important aspect of local economies throughout the century.

One final component of Plymouth Colony's land and economic activity relating to the Cape towns was highways and bridges. The importance of highways to the colony is reflected both in the extent of their inclusion in the compilations of Plymouth's law, and the degree to which the towns followed those laws which required them to maintain the roads. All concerned seem to have recognized the important role roads played in tying the towns together and, in turn, linking them to the colony. One of the consequences of this general acceptance of the necessity for highways is that there was little controversy, and thus little mention of them in the records. As directed by the colony's laws, the Governor, an Assistant, or later, the County Court appointed a committee of interested persons to survey the best location for a road, and the local Surveyor of Highways directed his neighbors in its construction.[89]

Only once during the seventeenth century did a serious problem with road maintenance occur on the Cape. At its June 1652 meeting, the General Court acknowledged the disrepair of the road from Sandwich southward to Barnstable, and ordered Myles Standish and Thomas Prence to investigate and see to its improvement. Later at the same meeting, the Court ordered Standish and Prence to summon a committee from all the towns on the Cape to lay out the road from Sandwich northward to Plymouth.[90] The Court pointedly intended that there be a good serviceable highway to the towns on the Cape. Its intention was not quickly fulfilled. On 3 October 1654 the Grand

Jury pointed out that the road was still not satisfactory, and held the towns through which it passed, Plymouth and Sandwich, responsible.[91]   Presumably the towns involved fulfilled their obligations, as the road to Sandwich drops from the records after the Grand Jury's action. The only other mention of Cape Cod highways in the colony's records concerns complaints from individuals concerning the impact of a specific road upon them.[92]

If the Cape towns generally conformed to the laws regarding the building and maintenance of highways, they did not do so when it came to bridges. The Eel River bridge controversy took fourteen years to settle, and even after it had supposedly ended it had a way of reappearing. The problem began in 1638 when the General Court decided to answer the need for safe, convenient crossings of the colony's rivers. At its September meeting, the General Court ordered a ferry established to traverse the North River, and bridges built over the South, Jones, and Eel Rivers. The Court viewed the ferry and bridges as colonial, rather than local, projects. It levied a special tax of twelve pence a family to pay for the North River ferry boats, and assigned individual towns the responsibility of the bridges. Scituate was to build the South River bridge, Plymouth and Duxbury the Jones River one. The Eel River bridge, south of the town of Plymouth, became the responsibility of Sandwich and Yarmouth.[93] But the Eel River was far closer to Plymouth than to Sandwich, much less Yarmouth, and neither Cape community apparently felt any need to build a bridge their residents would seldom use. They simply did not comply with the Court's order, and the Grand Jury indicted them for their failure in June 1640.[94]

Eight years later, Sandwich and Yarmouth had still not cooperated. By 1648 there were settlers at Eel River, and they had commenced the construction of the bridge themselves. Because of its expense, they requested the General Court either to make it a toll bridge or provide assistance in its costs. The Court agreed to consider the request at the next session.[95] When it made its judgment the following March, the Court noted the validity of the original 1638 order and stressed the importance of the bridge for travel to the Cape. It added Barnstable to the group, and ordered the Cape towns to pay their delinquent charges and to appear before the Court to explain themselves.[96] Their representatives must have attended the October 1649 meeting. At it, the Court ordered the Cape communities to pay the Eel River people a total of fifteen pounds, and suggested the Eel River people sue the Cape communities if they did not pay.[97] The

Cape towns still refused. In the summer of 1652, the Grand Jury indicted Sandwich and Yarmouth, while five Eel River men sued the three Cape towns for fifty pounds. The jury understandably decided in favor of the Eel River plaintiffs, and ordered the towns to pay twenty pounds damages, plus costs. The towns appealed.[98] At the appellate hearing in December, the Court of Assistants gave both parties until the General Court session in March 1652/53 to reach an agreement. If they failed to do so, then the Court would enforce the jury's decision.[99] Faced with no alternative but to pay up, the Cape towns negotiated a settlement with Eel River in which they agreed to pay ten pounds to Eel River.[100] The Court noted that the settlement had ended the controversy, and at least each party gained something. The Cape towns managed to reduce their payment, and the people at Eel River at least received some compensation.

The Eel River bridge problems taught Plymouth Colony a lesson. Deciding it was easier to do the job itself, the Court transferred the costs of bridge maintenance from the towns to the colonial government.[101] The Court briefly reverted to an assessment on towns in February 1682/83, when it ordered Sandwich, Barnstable, and Yarmouth to pay five pounds in silver to assist in repairing the Eel River bridge. The town of Plymouth was to pay the rest.[102] The small sum to pay and sharing the costs with others made it more acceptable. There is no indication of any opposition from the Cape.

In all, the Eel River bridge case is representative of an independent way of life on the Cape. Just as the people of Sandwich had made an effort to safeguard the independence of their town by protecting its Quakers, the communities of the Cape looked primarily to themselves to secure their livelihoods. Whether it was land, or whales, or taxes, William Nickerson or Sandwich, Cape Codders minded their own main chance. When their interests were at stake, or they believed themselves wronged, they attempted to protect themselves as forcefully as possible. It should not be surprising that Cape Cod people displayed the same disposition towards their Indian neighbors.

Notes

1. *Ply. Col. Recs.*, 1:57, 80, 108; 2:19. See chapter three for a full discussion of the founding of the Cape Cod towns.

2. The General Court allowed Lothrop's Scituate congregation the same privilege to search for unspecified land that it had granted the founders of Sandwich and Yarmouth. *Ply. Col. Recs.*, 11:25.

3. *Ply. Col. Recs.*, 2:81.

4. *Ply. Col. Recs.*, 1:80; 3:4.

5. Sandwich Town Records, 1652-1692, p. 54. The three men were Richard Bourne, Richard Chadwell, and John Ellis. The town added Thomas Tupper to the group a month later. Ibid., p. 55.

6. Barnstable Town Records, 1640-1753, p. 56. Those assigned to the boundary committee were Thomas Huchens, Tristram Hull, Bernard Lombard, and Thomas Lothrop. John Cooper and William Crocker joined Huchens on the eviction team.

7. *Ply. Col. Recs.*, 4:21.

8. *Ply. Col. Recs.*, 5:96.

9. Sandwich Town Records, 1652-1692, p. 112.

10. *Ply. Col. Recs.*, 5:104-105.

11. Sandwich Town Records, 1652-1692, pp. 106-107; *Ply. Col. Recs.*, 5: 221; 7:192, 194. Sandwich's lawsuit against the Fullers went to trial, but was withdrawn before the jury delivered a verdict.

12. *Ply. Col. Recs.*, 5:221, 233.

13. Sandwich Town Records, 1652-1692, pp. 178-179, 187-188; Barnstable Town Records, 1640-1753, pp. 75-76.

14. *Ply. Col. Recs.*, 3:41. Although Dexter was one of the Saugus founders and had built a mill at Sandwich, he did not settle there, but moved to Barnstable in 1646. See Lovell, *Sandwich*, p. 108.

15. *Ply. Col. Recs.*, 4:70; 6:51. John Alden and Thomas Hinckley were the other two men appointed, but who must not have served. See Lovell, *Sandwich*, p. 50, for a list of Scorton Neck landholders which does not include Dexter.

16. *Ply. Col. Recs.*, 3:53.

17. *Ply. Col. Recs.*, 3:175. The committee members were Eastham's Thomas Prence and Richard Higgins and Sandwich's Richard Chadwell and Richard Bourne. They had been selected by agreement between representatives of both Yarmouth and Barnstable. Barnstable Town Records, 1640-1753. p. 4.

18. Sandwich Town Records, 1652-1692, p. 33.

19. Yarmouth Town Records, 1677-1726, pp. 12-13.

20. *Ply. Col. Recs.*, 4:40; 5:41.
21. *Ply. Col. Recs.*, 6:71-72.
22. Sandwich Town Records, 1652-1692, p. 192.
23. Barnstable Town Records, 1640-1753, p. 6.
24. Barnstable Town Records, 1640-1753, pp. 3-4, 10-11.
25. Barnstable Town Records, 1640-1753, p. 2. The four men were Thomas Hinckley, Tristram Hull, Bernard Lombard, and Thomas Lothrop.
26. *Ply. Col. Recs.*, 4:70.
27. *Ply. Col. Recs.*, 2:93.
28. *Ply. Col. Recs.*, 11:63, 188-189. See also *General Laws, 1672*, p. 34; and *General Laws, 1685*, p. 43.
29. Barnstable Town Records, 1640-1753, pp. 15, 16. The five men appointed were Nathaniel Bacon, Abraham Blush, Henry Cobb, William Crocker, and John Phinney.
30. Barnstable Town Records, 1640-1753, *passim.* For example, an entry for 26 October 1654 lists five men and their acreages: Thomas Allen owned sixty-seven acres in nine parcels; Austin Bearce, fifty-six in five; Lemuel Shaw, thirty-five in six; George Lewis, Sr., twenty-three in four; and Isaac Wells, seventy-four in nine. Ibid., pp. 20-24.
31. Eastham Record of Town Meetings, 1654-1745, p. 4. The committee members were Josiah Cook, John Freeman, Nicholas Snow, Richard Sparrow, and Robert Waxman. The separate Proprietors' Records for Eastham do not include the early land holdings either.
32. Sandwich Town Records, 1652-1692, pp. 41-42. The town allowed five of the seven men to do the work, but none of those selected are listed. They were to receive one penny for each acre of improved, and therefore easily identified land, and four pence for each acre of land with either unknown boundaries or none at all.
33. Sandwich Proprietors Records, 1656-1680, pp. 1-3.
34. *Ply. Col. Recs.*, 4:113.
35. Sandwich Town Records, 1652-1692, p. 82; Sandwich Proprietors Records, 1656-1680, pp. 1-60. The five men were Richard Bourne, Thomas Burgess, Sr., Richard Chadwell, Edmund Freeman, and William Newland. Lovell, *Sandwich*, pp. 44-52 contains a lengthy discussion of the 1667 property survey, and locates individual holdings on a succession of maps.
36. *Mourt's Relation*, p. 30.
37. Winthrop, *Journal*, 1:148. Winthrop remarked that there were three or four whales involved, which he believed to be the number washed up on shore nearly every year.
38. Sandwich Town Records, 1652-1692, p. 55.

39. *Ply. Col. Recs.*, 11:61-62; Francis R. Hart, "The New England Whale-Fisheries," *Public.*, Col. Soc. of Mass., *Transactions*, 26(1924):65-69. See also, Alexander Starbuck, *History of the American Whale Fishery from its Earliest Inception to the Year 1876* (Waltham, MA, 1878), pp. 1-18; Frederick W. True, *The Whalebone Whales of the Western North Atlantic*, Smithsonian Contributions to Knowledge, vol. 33 (Washington, DC, 1904), pp. 19, 22-23; *See also* Edouard A. Stackpole, *The Sea-Hunters: The New England Whalemen During Two Centuries, 1635-1835* (Philadelphia, 1953), pp. 15-23.

40. Edward Randolph to Mr. Povey, Boston, 24 January 1687/88, in Thomas Hutchinson (comp.), *A Collection of Original Papers Relative to the History of the Colony of Massachusetts-bay* (Boston, 1769), p. 558 (Hereinafter cited as *Collections*). The reference may be to the liquid measure tun, and not the weight measure ton, but it is unclear. A "tun" meant a barrel containing approximately 250 gallons, and if true, in this instance would refer to a little over 50,000 gallons of whale oil shipped from Plymouth. It represents an extremely large amount of oil for a commodity which receives so little mention in the sources, but may well be accurate. In the winter of 1670, Long Islanders processed upwards of 200 tons of oil, and in 1690 Massachusetts exported 296 barrels of oil in two separate shipments. William B. Weeden, *Economic and Social History of New England, 1620-1789*, 2 vols. (Boston, c. 1890), 1:437-438.

41. Wait-Still Winthrop to Fitz-John Winthrop, Boston, 27 January 1699/1700, *Collec.*, Mass. Hist. Soc., Ser. 6, 5(1892):54-55.

42. Address and Petition from the Colony of New Plymouth to King James II, Plymouth, October 1687, in "Hinckley Papers," p. 178. The petition was a request to abolish the new laws brought on by Andros and the Dominion of New England. Its author, Thomas Hinckley, may well have purposefully underestimated the success of Cape Cod whaling in order to support his claims regarding Plymouth's poverty.

43. *Ply. Col. Recs.*, 11:61-62. See also, ibid., pp. 114-115; *General Laws, 1672*, p. 37; and *General Laws, 1685*, p. 30. Plymouth had experienced leakage in the oil barrels, and the order to have oil shipped directly to Boston was an attempt to get the oil to market as soon as possible. The owner of the whale was to bear the costs of shipment. The General Court answered the question of who owned whales washed up on the shores of the Purchasers' reserve, by ordering that they belonged to the Purchasers in the same way other whales belonged to the towns. *Ply. Col. Recs.*, 3:53.

44. *Ply. Col. Recs.*, 3:64. This barrel may have been the one the Treasurer listed as due from Eastham in his report the previous year. Ibid., p. 33.

45. *Ply. Col. Recs.*, 8:99. The Treasurer's accounts specifically include only the value of the oil, in this case a total of sixteen pounds, two shillings, and six pence. Whale oil was generally evaluated at two pounds per barrel, hence the estimate of eight barrels. See ibid., p. 94, where one barrel of oil is listed at two pounds.

46. *Ply. Col. Recs.*, 8:104.

47. *Ply. Col. Recs.*, 4:62, 99; 5:97; 8:165.

48. Sandwich Town Records, 1652-1692, p. 17. For examples of whale oil in the Sandwich town budget, see ibid., pp. 35, 56, 76, 79. By contrast, the town of Plymouth awarded one-third of its occasional whale to the finder and processor, and appropriated the other two-thirds for the town. *Ply. Town Recs.*, 1:119-120.

49. Eastham Record of Town Meetings, 1654-1745, p. 11.

50. Yarmouth town Records, 1677-1726, pp. 37-38.

51. Eastham Record of Town Meetings, 1654-1745, p. 7; Sandwich Town Records, 1652-1692, p. 17.

52. *Ply. Col. Recs.*, 3:213; 7:99.

53. Eastham Record of Town Meetings, 1654-1745, pp. 33-34.

54. Eastham Record of Town Meetings, 1654-1745, p. 7; Sandwich Town Records, 1652-1692, pp. 18-19, 47, 50, 80-81, 167, 190-191; Yarmouth town Records, 1677-1726, p. 46. Eastham's committee received two pounds for whales within the town boundaries, and three pounds for those in Paomet. Volunteers took on the task, and did it as an individual whale appeared. Ralph Smith, Jonathan Sparrow, Thomas Williams, and William Walker took the first whale. Richard Higgins agreed to provide an unnamed crew for the third. Sandwich selected a permanent group, and required it to pay a fee to the town. Richard Chadwell, Thomas Dexter, and John Ellis took on the job in 1653, and paid sixteen pounds for each whale. Ellis and James Skiffe did it in 1659. In 1683 Caleb and George Allen, Samuel Briggs, and Thomas Tupper agreed to take on the job for ten years in exchange for one-half the oil and bone. Yarmouth did not name its committee, but it paid the men forty shillings a whale in 1689. Barnstable's procedures regarding whales are not recorded, but they were probably similar to the other towns on the Cape which, as in so many other things, followed exceedingly similar programs.

55. Winslow Papers, Box 1, #10, Mass. Hist. Soc.

56. *Ply. Col. Recs.*, 11:132-133.

57. *Ply. Col. Recs.*, 4:6-7. The stipulation of a hogshead rather than a barrel levy was important. Weights and measures for the seventeenth century are difficult to determine with precision, but a hogshead held approximately twice the capacity of a barrel. A 1483 law had established a

hogshead at sixty-three gallons, and a barrel at thirty-one. The specific claim to a hogshead for the colony was an obvious attempt to increase Plymouth's share of a whale's oil. *Oxford English Dictionary*, 2d. ed., s. v. "hogshead" and "barrel."

58. *Ply. Col. Recs.*, 4:9-10.

59. *General Laws, 1672*, p. 37; *General Laws, 1685*, p. 30.

60. *Ply. Col. Recs.*, 11:135, 207-208.

61. *Ply. Col. Recs.*, 6:252-263.

62. Bernard Bailyn, *The New England Merchants in the Seventeenth Century* (Cambridge, MA, 1955), pp. 5-6, 78-82; Harold A. Innes, *The Cod Fisheries: The History of an International Economy* (New Haven, CT, 1940), 70-81, 111-119; Albert C. Jensen, *The Cod* (New York, c. 1972), pp. 86-92; Charles B. Judah, Jr. *The North American Fisheries and British Policy to 1713*, Illinois Studies in the Social Sciences, vol. 18, nos. 3-4 (Champaign, IL, 1933), pp. 60-68 (Hereinafter cited as *Fisheries*); Langdon, *Pilgrim Colony*, pp. 35-36. For the nature of the fisherman's life, see Daniel Vickers, "Work and Life on the Fishing Periphery of Essex County, Massachusetts, 1630-1675," in David D. Hall, and David Grayson Allen (eds.), *Seventeenth-Century New England* (Boston, 1984), pp. 83-117. For estimates of the amount of fish exported and the relationship between the grades of fish and their markets, see The Earl of Bellomont to the Lords of Trade, New York, 28 November 1700, in E. B. O'Callaghan (ed.), *Documents Relative to the Colonial History of the State of New York*, 15 vols. (Albany, 1853-1887), 4:790. Bellomont calculated that the better fish had brought eighteen shillings a hundredweight in 1699, but only twelve in 1700. As early as 1641, John Winthrop reckoned that New England had sent 300,000 dry fish to market. Winthrop, *Journal*, 2:42. See also *Cal. State Papers, Col. Ser., 1661-1668*, #222. For fish prices see, Daniel Vickers, "A Known and Staple Commoditie: Codfish Prices in Essex County, Massachusetts, 1640-1775," *Essex Institute Historical Collections*, 124(1988):186-203.

63. Bradford, *Plymouth Plantation*, pp. 146-147; *Mass. Col. Recs.*, 1:158, 230, 257-258, 328; George Louis Beer, *The Origins of the British Colonial System, 1578-1660* (Gloucester, MA, 1959), pp. 270-279 (Hereinafter cited as *Origins*); Judah, *Fisheries*, pp. 45-60; Raymond McFarland, *A History of the New England Fisheries* (NY, 1911), pp. 44-49.

64. *Ply. Col. Recs.*, 11:5, 114, 198.

65. *Ply. Col. Recs.*, 2:103. Plymouth required a five shilling per "share" fee, but does not define a "share."

66. Beer, *Origins*, p. 385.

67. *Ply. Col. Recs.*, 2:161-162. The only unfamiliar individual among the leaders of the fishing enterprise was William Paddy. Admitted a freeman of the colony in 1636/37, he later served numerous terms as a Deputy from Plymouth. More tellingly, he had been a one-eighth investor in a ship to be built in 1642, and in January 1641/42 the town of Plymouth had allowed him a license to build a weir for catching fish at the mouth of Plymouth harbor. He certainly had been included in the Cape Cod venture to provide the fishing expertise the other investors lacked. For Paddy, see *Ply. Col. Recs.*, 1:48, 126, 154; 2:31-32; Peirce, *Colonial Lists*, pp. 47-48, 56.

68. *Ply. Col. Recs.*, 3:10.

69. *Ply. Col. Recs.*, 11:131, 206. The colony had previously stipulated that either 120 or 132 fish equalled a hundredweight. Ibid., 27, 114, 198.

70. *Ply. Col. Recs.*, 11:220.

71. *Ply. Col. Recs.*, 11:228. Fishermen were also required to post security for the assessment before they started to fish. The Court appointed Eastham's Thomas Paine to the office of bailiff.

72. *Ply. Col. Recs.*, 11:228-229; *General Laws, 1685*, p. 31.

73. *General Laws, 1672*, pp. 38-39; *General Laws, 1685*, p. 31.

74. Petition of John Prince and Nathaniel Bosworth [of Hull] to the Government of Plymouth, Plymouth, 8 June 1671, in *Collec.* Mass. Hist. Soc., [1st Ser.], 6(1799):127-128; *Ply. Col. Recs.*, 5:63. The Court allowed the Hull petitioners to use two boats, with crews, and ordered them to make the usual payments.

75. *Mass. Col. Recs.*, 5:169-170. Plymouth's response is unrecorded.

76. *Ply. Col. Recs.*, 5:243-245. The four lessees were Edward Gray of Plymouth, Thomas Huchens of Barnstable, Thomas Paine of Eastham, and Constant Southworth of Duxbury.

77. *Ply. Col. Recs.*, 6:19, 31, 56.

78. *Ply. Col. Recs.*, 5:107-108. The sum appropriated to meet the charges of the school totaled thirty-three pounds. Ibid., 11:233. See also *Ply. Town Recs.*, 1:115. For a review of education in Plymouth colony, see "History of Free Schools in Plymouth Colony, and in the Town of Plymouth with Incidental Notes," *Collec.*, Mass. Hist. Soc., 2nd Ser., 4(1816; repr. 1846):79-96

79. *Ply. Col. Recs,*. 11:237.

80. *Ply. Col. Recs.*, 5:259-260; Richard L. Bowen, *Early Rehoboth*, 4 vols. (Rehoboth, MA, 1945-1950), 1:35 (Hereinafter cited as *Rehoboth*). Newman may have been serving, at least to some extent, as a schoolmaster in addition to his work as minister.

81. *Ply. Col. Recs.*, 5:81. The Court also gave a Mr. Thomas twenty shillings for his "paines," but neither he nor his efforts are described. Thirty

pounds was the usual fee. Josiah Winslow to [Sir Henry] Coventry, Marshfield, 1 May 1680, *Cal. State Papers, Col. Ser., 1677-1680*, #1349.

82. *Ply. Col. Recs.*, 6:102-103. Barnstable received twelve pounds, Duxbury eight, Rehoboth five, Taunton three, and a Mr. Daniel Smith, probably a schoolmaster, two.

83. *Ply. Col. Recs.*, 6:139, 140-141. William Bradford, the colony's Treasurer, John Thompson of Barnstable, and Joseph Warren of Plymouth were the committee to lease the fishing. In the official records, Clark's offer is dated 4 July, and the banning of mackerel netting is dated 1 July. It is clear from the recording of Clark's proposal that the Court banned the netting of mackerel as a result of his request. There may be an error in the dating of the proposal or in its transcription.

84. *Ply. Col. Recs.*, 6:198, 203.

85. *Ply. Col. Recs.*, 6:218-219.

86. Sandwich Town Records, 1652-1692, pp. 13, 85, 225, 241. For the use of fish as fertilizer, see Bradford, *Plymouth Plantation*, p. 85; Langdon, *Pilgrim Colony*, p. 149; Darrett, B. Rutman, *Husbandmen of Plymouth: Farms and Villages in the Old Colony, 1620-1692* (Boston, 1967), pp. 9, 10.

87. *Ply. Col. Recs.*, 3:76. The Court sided with Burgess, allowing him to take 10,000 fish twice a year.

88. *Ply. Col. Recs.*, 5:140.

89. *Ply. Col. Recs.*, 11:11, 44-45, 56, 112, 194, 219, 221; *General Laws, 1672*, pp. 33-34; *General Laws, 1685*, pp. 31-33.

90. *Ply. Col. Recs.*, 3:13, 15. On 24 February 1652/53, thirteen committeemen took their oaths before Thomas Prence. Barnstable provided three, John Finney, Jonathan Hatch, and Thomas Hinckley; Eastham two, Edward Bangs and Joseph Rogers; Sandwich six, William Bassett, Thomas Dexter, Henry Dillingham, John Ellis, James Skiffe, and John Wing; and Yarmouth two, William Hedge and Anthony Thacher. Ibid., 3:61.

91. *Ply. Col. Recs.*, 3:69.

92. For examples, see *Ply. Col. Recs.*, 3:108; 4:46, 48, 183; 5:116.

93. *Ply. Col. Recs.*, 11:28.

94. *Ply. Col. Recs.*, 1:156.

95. *Ply. Col. Recs.*, 2:127.

96. *Ply. Col. Recs.*, 2:136-137.

97. *Ply. Col. Recs.*, 2:147.

98. *Ply. Col. Recs.*, 3:10; 7:59-60.

99. *Ply. Col. Recs.*, 3:20-21. In one of the few instances of local action regarding the controversy, Sandwich elected Thomas Dexter, Sr., as

its representative to the negotiations. Sandwich Town Records, 1652-1692, p. 2.

100. *Ply. Col. Recs.*, 3:22.

101. *Ply. Col. Recs.*, 3:193; 4:108-109, 159; 5:124, 172.

102. *Ply. Col. Recs.*, 6:100. The Eel River bridge was part of a general upgrading of the colony's bridges, much like the original 1638 construction order. The Court made it very clear, that once these projects were completed, no town would be ordered to pay for any bridge beyond its boundaries.

XII

"Serviceable by their Labour . . .and . . .Friendly to the *English*

THE Englishmen who migrated to Plymouth Colony and the Cape in the seventeenth century faced numerous challenges and opportunities, most of which related to their own world of settlement. Of foremost consideration were the practical problems of creating communities, and establishing political, economic, and religious institutions.   In contrast to these immediate and ever-present concerns, the people of Plymouth Colony seemed seldom to notice that they shared their land with the region's original native settlers. The plague which had destroyed the Patuxet tribe at Plymouth in 1617, similar rampages of disease among the Indians in the early years of English settlement, and the willingness of Massasoit to leave the Pilgrims alone contributed to a sense of contentment and complacency among the English colonists respecting their Indian neighbors. Other than land purchases and an occasional native crime, the Indians rarely encroached upon the lives of the English during the first half century of settlement.

One of the few exceptions to this general state of affairs was English missionary work among the Indians, but even this important activity was not a truly colonial enterprise. Entered into only in the 1640's, and then almost reluctantly, it was an activity carried on by individuals, without the support of congregation, town, or colony. And Plymouth Colony was not unique. Its prevailing lack of official enthusiasm for missionary work was typical of its New England neighbors. The responsibility lay with both Indians and colonists. Puritanism was not inherently a proselytizing faith, and the Indians were more satisfied with their own way of life than the English would ever understand. For true success, the English needed to have been both more vigorous and perceptive in their missionary activity, and, more importantly, to have found more receptive subjects.

Certainly, one of the more significant explanations for Plymouth's lack of missionary zeal was the effort required in the establishment and expansion of the colony. Food and shelter were more crucial than Indian conversion in the 1620's and 1630's. Beyond the practical concerns of survival, however, were problems ingrained in Puritanism itself. It was a demanding and exclusive religion, requiring educated and literate followers who understood a sophisticated theology. Its exactions were difficult enough for Englishmen. They undoubtedly could be no easier for Indians. Similarly, the centrality of the independent congregation made it impossible for a formal church hierarchy to send a group of unattached clergymen into the wilderness to preach to the Indians. Puritan clergymen were, rather, servants of their congregations. Parishioners employed ministers to attend to the congregation, and not to convert Indians. That so many of Plymouth Colony's ministers understood the situation and concurred with its principles should not be surprising.[1]

If the nature of Puritanism and the lack of local support for missionaries made proselytizing demanding, the opposition of Indian spiritual and political leaders to its practice simply increased the difficulty. Sachems and shamans had too much to lose in the way of tribute and power if they or their Indian subjects converted to Christianity. They were, therefore, those most vehement in the Indian opposition to English missionary exercises. Massasoit attempted to tie future land sales to a prohibition on English proselytizing, his son, King Philip, treated John Eliot with contempt, and Josiah of Mattakesset refused to listen to the preachings of Plymouth's John Cotton for fear of rejection by his Indian subjects.[2]

The opposition of Indian leaders represents in a specific way the fundamental question concerning English missionary enterprises. For the English, conversion was not the mere application of a veneer of Christianity to an essentially Indian cultural core. It meant, instead, the transformation of the Indian into an Englishman. As expressed in the seventeenth century, at stake was the civilizing of the Indian, which meant his conversion not just to a religion, but to a way of life and thinking. As the English viewed it, in order for the Indian to become a Christian, he must first abandon being an Indian, settle in permanent villages, adopt English social and economic patterns, and finally convert. Obviously based on the assumption of the superiority of English society, it was a policy which led to the English failure to understand that the Indian perceived his way of life and his religious rituals as at least as good as the Englishman's, and for his own purposes, even better.[3]

With a combination of Indians who remained loyal to their traditional life, ministers who recognized the primacy of their congregations, and colonial governments seemingly unwilling to take the initiative, it is little wonder that missionary work in the New England colonies got off to a slow beginning. In the end, Indian missionary activity came, rather, to be supported by contributions from England and performed by individual clergymen working on their own. It was not until the 1640's, and in direct response to those critics of New England who had chastised its people for their missionary failures, that the business began. Edward Winslow, acting as an agent for Massachusetts, arranged the publication of a series of pamphlets defending New England, and lobbied extensively for the creation of an English missionary society. He attained success in 1649 with Parliament's creation of "The President and Society for propagation of the Gospel in New-England," commonly referred to as The Society. At the Restoration, it was reorganized as "The Company for Propagation of the Gospell in New England, and the parts adjacent in America." It is generally known simply as The New England Company. Both groups collected money in English parishes and distributed it in New England, utilizing the Commissioners of the United Colonies as their agents. The chief recipient of New England Company funds was John Eliot of Massachusetts, although the Mayhews on Nantucket and Richard Bourne of Sandwich also received support.[4]

The first serious Cape Cod missionary was not Bourne, however, but his minister, William Leveridge. Leveridge had turned to missionary work when the religious contention in early Sandwich overwhelmed him, and the loss of his parishioners' support discouraged him. He began by learning the Indian language, and must have had some success, stating he was learning it more quickly

than he had Greek, Latin, and Hebrew in his earlier years.[5] The
Commissioners of the United Colonies recognized his efforts in 1651.
They mentioned him as one of three men studying the Indian language
and in general preparing himself for missionary work. In May of
1653 the Commissioners voted to compensate him six pounds, three
for his own use and three to buy tools for the Indians.[6]

The Indians gave Leveridge's efforts a mixed response. He
acknowledged there were many Indians who rejected his message, but
he took pride in those few who did not. In 1651 he estimated that
twenty Indians attended his services and asserted they desired
conversion. They apparently lived together about seven miles from
Sandwich, possibly in the Mashpee region which would later become
so identified with Richard Bourne. They traveled to Sandwich for
church services, and listened to Leveridge's sermons in a specially
built wigwam near the town. True to English assumptions, Indians in
the process of becoming Christians were not to live near or worship
with those English who already were. In the end, it was his successes
with individual Indians which most encouraged Leveridge. In an
interesting observation on his fellow Englishmen, he noted
particularly that the Indians were able to look beyond the specific
failings of a few Englishmen to see the validity of Christianity, and
wished more Englishmen could be as tolerant of the Indians. But
Leveridge's troubles among his English parishioners finally
outweighed his accomplishments with his Indians, and he left
Sandwich for Long Island in 1654.[7] The United Colonies'
Commissioners recognized his contribution even after he had left New
England. They granted him five pounds for his previous service on
the Cape, and in 1657 offered him twenty pounds towards employing
an interpreter, so that he might learn the Indian language on Long
Island.[8]

One of Leveridge's supporters in Sandwich, Richard Bourne,
replaced him as missionary, probably at Leveridge's encouragement.
Bourne's background is unclear, but he apparently had migrated to
Sandwich from Plymouth or Duxbury in 1637 as part of the group
originally associated with Leveridge. In Plymouth he had held
numerous local offices, and the colony listed him as a freeman in
March 1636/37. He continued to be a public leader in Sandwich. In
1639 the town elected him a Deputy to the colony's first General
Court, the beginning of six consecutive terms.[9] When or how he
became interested in Indian missionary work is unknown. He was not
an ordained clergyman, and he does not appear to have been one

whose involvement with religion was active or extensive. His interest in Sandwich's early controversy was primarily in its land aspects, and his name is absent from those concerned with the Quaker question. It is probable Bourne assisted Leveridge in his work among the Indians, and then replaced him when he left for Long Island. What is more certain is that, like many other Cape Codders, Bourne was an active acquirer of land, and had been from his days in Plymouth. On 2 January 1636/37 the General Court confirmed a Court of Assistants grant of seven acres in Plymouth to Bourne, and two months later awarded him haying rights on land formerly worked by John Reynor, the minister.[10] He was similarly active in Sandwich. He was one of the "townsmen" representatives on the 1640 committee which divided up Sandwich's land, and received seven acres. It was one of the larger grants made to those associated with Leveridge's Plymouth group.[11] He acquired a forty-acre parcel from the town in 1660, and in the property survey of the 1660's is listed as the owner of six lots.[12] He also bought land from fellow residents, and at the end of his life transferred it to one of his sons.[13]

Bourne was also a significant recipient of land from the General Court. In November 1640 the Court included him in a multi-party land arrangement, and continued to make both individual and group grants to Bourne for many years. In 1654 he was one of five Sandwich freemen who petitioned for land at Mashpee Pond, in the heart of his Indian mission territory. He received land at Manomet the next year, and four years later two more grants, one of them at Mashpee. During the 1660's, the Court awarded Bourne four more parcels of land, one of them at Mashpee, and continued to grant him land throughout the 1670's. He also served frequently as a witness when Indians made deeds of sale.[14] At his death in 1682, his land holdings were valued at three hundred pounds.[15]

While it must be acknowledged Bourne acquired land outside of Mashpee and that it would be incorrect to argue Bourne worked among the Indians solely to gain their land, it is equally evident that the scene of his missionary activity and many of his land grants overlapped. It was, at the least, a fortunate combination of altruism and practicality, with successes at both levels. On the practical side, Bourne was a prosperous landowner. On the altruistic side, he was Plymouth's most successful missionary, eventually establishing the first formally gathered Indian congregation in the colony.

With Leveridge's departure for Long Island in the mid 1650's, Bourne assumed full responsibility for the clergyman's missionary work almost immediately and remained active in it for the rest of his life.   In its accounts for 1657, the Commissioners of the United Colonies mentioned him as one of a number of men active as Indian missionaries, and included him in a group of five who were to share 150 pounds in compensation.[16]   The following year the Commissioners awarded him fifteen pounds in salary, and continued to grant him money until at least 1672, when his yearly remuneration reached thirty-five pounds.   Something of the Commissioners' estimation of Bourne's increasing value as a missionary may be gleaned from the manner in which they regularly raised his salary.[17]

Bourne's heightened worth as viewed by the Commissioners was a reflection of his role in the expansion of Leveridge's original flock of some twenty Indians into the Cape's only full-fledged Indian congregation.   Part of that process involved the creation of a separate Indian community organized in the English manner.   Bourne assisted in the process, if he did not actually instigate it, when he petitioned the Plymouth government on behalf of the Indians in late 1664.   At a February 1664/65 meeting, the Court of Assistants responded favorably to Bourne's request by appointing six Indians as a committee to manage the community and ordering them to select one of their number as Constable.   The Court noted that the Indians were to govern with the help and advice of Bourne, and stipulated that the power of the village's Indian leaders was not to infringe on the authority of local sachems.[18]   Within two years, local Indian leaders transferred title to the land to those Indians living under Bourne's supervision.[19]

While Bourne was busy organizing his Indian followers into a separate village, he was also involved in forming them into a congregation.   In the summer of 1666, he held a meeting at the town attended by John Eliot, Governor Prence, and a number of Assistants and clergymen from the colony.   At this assemblage, the Indians made testimonials of their Christian knowledge and beliefs, all of which significantly impressed the English.   But those in attendance were not willing to allow the Indians to form their own congregation at that point.   Rather, they ordered that the Indians' statements be written down and circulated among the churches of the colony for approval.[20]   Despite the concept of the independence of the local congregation, an Indian church fellowship apparently required acceptance by its English associates.

The churches of the colony must have been satisfied with the statements from Bourne's converts.   On 17 August 1670 Bourne held an organizational meeting at Mashpee to form an Indian congregation. Some five hundred people attended, both Indians and English. Josiah Winslow and six Assistants represented the colony, and seven congregations sent their teaching elders and a "messenger." The town of Plymouth was especially well represented. It sent John Cotton, its newly ordained pastor; Thomas Cushman, its ruling elder; and Nathaniel Morton, Secretary of the colony. In a repeat of the 1666 assembly, the Indians offered their confessions of faith. This time the English accepted them, allowed the Indians to enter into a covenant of church brotherhood, and recognized them as a congregation. John Eliot, also in attendance, joined with John Cotton in ordaining Richard Bourne as the church's minister. In addition, the congregation selected a Deacon and a Ruling Elder from among its members, and the ministers baptized the children.[21]

Certainly Bourne must have looked upon his work over the preceding fifteen years with satisfaction. Those Indians under his charge had not only established their own community, but had joined into a gathered Christian congregation as well. When, in 1674, Bourne reported to Daniel Gookin of Massachusetts regarding Indian missionary work on the Cape, he counted ninety who were baptized, and twenty-seven who were in full communion. Unfortunately, Bourne did not give the total population, but there were somewhat over 200 adults in 1693.[22] Part, if not most, of Bourne's success lay with his willingness to allow the Indians to live on tribal lands and to incorporate Christianity into a traditional Indian way of life. In this he was more like the Mayhews on Nantucket than John Eliot in Massachusetts who required a virtually complete cultural transformation of his Indians.[23]

How long Bourne remained active as a minister among the Indians after the organization of the Mashpee congregation is difficult to determine. With the establishment of a gathered Indian church on lands belonging to its members, there was little left for Bourne to accomplish. He seems to have taken on the position of elder statesman, generally respected for his past contributions, but not consistently involved with the daily workings of the community. The way in which he discussed the Indian villages in his 1674 report indicates that the congregation included Indians from probably four settlements in the Mashpee region. Bourne noted members of the congregation were under the charge of four Indians, and that he utilized four others as assistants. Perhaps Bourne's major role was to deal with particular crises, as when he attended a dying Christian Indian to reinforce the native's faith.[24]

Some of Bourne's diminished involvement was no doubt the result of advancing age. He was over sixty when he reported to Gookin regarding the Mashpee congregation, and he died in 1682, probably in the summer. The inventory of his estate is dated 18 September 1682, and on the last day of October that year, the General Court granted executor powers to two of Bourne's sons, Shearjashub and Elisha.[25] Three years later, Governor Thomas Hinckley and Secretary Nathaniel Clarke signed documents which confirmed the Indians' title to their land in the Mashpee region, as well as Shearjashub's title to that of his father in the area.[26] As Shearjashub Bourne succeeded to the Mashpee lands of his father, the Indian preacher Simon Popmonet, succeeded to the pastoral responsibilities, although by 1693, Rowland Cotton, pastor at Sandwich, had assumed religious oversight of the Mashpee congregation.[27]

While Bourne's report to Gookin in 1674 included only one fully gathered Indian congregation, his own, he did mention eight other clusters of Christian Indians spread out over the colony in twenty-three villages. Most of them were on the Cape. Bourne identified seven groups of Indian settlements dispersed among seventeen villages on Cape Cod. Of the 497 Christian Indians he counted, more than ninety percent of them lived in those Cape villages.[28] It is impossible to learn anything about most of those villages or their residents. None were organized into congregations, and whatever English leadership they had did not receive the kind of official recognition given to Bourne by either the government in Plymouth or the Commissioners of the United Colonies. The only exceptions to this paucity of information are the Tuppers in the Herring Pond region north of Sandwich, and Samuel Treat at Eastham.

Thomas Tupper was one of the original Saugus grantees to Sandwich, and served the town most importantly as both a Deputy and Selectman in a long and distinguished career on the Cape. He died at Sandwich in 1676 at the age of ninety-eight.[29] He had entered missionary work in the 1650s, and due to his advanced age probably shared the responsibility with his son, Thomas, Jr.[30] There may have been a rivalry for Indian support between the Tuppers and Bourne. In his 1674 report, Bourne failed to mention either the Tuppers' missionary activities or their Indians. The omission could not have been for a lack of success, however. In 1676 the town of Sandwich allowed a group of Christian Indians, who must have been under the Tuppers, to build a meeting house.[31] And chroniclers of Cape Cod Indians other than Bourne mentioned a sizeable Indian population under the charge of Thomas Tupper, Jr. In a 1685 report for the New England Company, Thomas Hinckley stated there were 110 Indian youths and adults under the care of the younger Tupper and an Indian teacher named Charles.[32] Matthew Mayhew estimated there were 180 Indians under Tupper's care in the early 1690's, and a 1693 report asserted there were 226.[33]

If Bourne and the Tuppers supervised the Indians of the upper Cape, the Reverend Samuel Treat took charge of those at its lower end. The son of Robert Treat, a governor of Connecticut, Samuel Treat had graduated from Harvard in 1669 and assumed the pastorate at Eastham in 1673.[34] Treat set about learning the Indian language soon after his arrival in Eastham, and came eventually to preach to the Indians in it. In a report to Increase Mather in 1693, Treat noted there were 505 adult Indians in Eastham and that he did not know of any who purposefully rejected Christianity. He mentioned that his charges not only attended regular services but also kept the colony's special days of fast and thanksgiving. They did so, however, in their own communities separate from English settlers. Treat's Indians lived in four villages, each with its own schoolmaster and religious teacher. The schoolmaster taught reading and writing in the Indian language, and the teacher preached to the Indians from sermons prepared by Treat, with whom they met regularly for instruction. In addition, there were six Indian justices of the peace, responsible for the civil and legal aspects of the villages. Treat had great praise for the Indians he supervised, and maintained many of them desired baptism and the formation of a congregation. He concluded his report with a statement as applicable towards the Indians of Eastham as it was towards all of the Indians of the Cape. They were serviceable and friendly to the English, and most importantly had supported the English during King Philip's War.[35]

John Freeman of Eastham had had a somewhat less glowing account of Treat's Indians eight years previously in a report to Thomas Hinckley. Freeman mentioned only that most Indians followed Christian practices, and stated there were 379 Indians on the outer Cape, 264 at Eastham and 115 at Monomy. Freeman also criticized English missionaries as overpaid for their efforts, while Indian teachers were underpaid for theirs.[36] Thomas Hinckley used Freeman's information early the next month in compiling a report of

Indian villages in the colony which he submitted to the New England Company. In all, Hinckley asserted there were 1439 Indians above the age of twelve in the colony.[37]

Despite the segregation of Christian Indians, with its inherent inequality, and the more general function of English missionaries as agents of a cultural eradication which their critics have roundly condemned, Cape Indians may not have viewed it all as unacceptable. When New England went up in flames in the Indian war of 1675, the Indians on the Cape did not participate.

Indeed, the behavior of Cape Cod Indians is indicative of the manner in which King Philip's War failed to affect the region in any direct military manner. The Cape was the largest settled area in New England not to be raided by the Indians, and of the six Plymouth towns left alone by Philip and his allies, four of them were the Cape settlements. Certainly, its relatively isolated geographic position accounted for some of its wartime security. As opposed to the outlying settlements of the upper Connecticut River Valley or the communities close to King Philip's native soil, Cape Cod was more difficult to attack. Some of the security came also from the continued friendliness of the Cape's Indians, a factor resulting from both English missionary work and the Indians' failure to sympathize with King Philip's cause. Finally, the issues which brought on the war were more immediate to King Philip's domain in the western regions of Plymouth Colony than on the Cape. With the establishment of Swansea in 1667, Plymouth's settlers were living within King Philip's traditional homeland. They brought the Indian into direct contact with the ever-increasing proximity of English agricultural settlement, with its permanent farms and the constant foraging of English pigs and cattle among Indian crops. And with English farms came English religion, English justice, economic dependence, and a general sapping of the Indians' customary independence.

Philip greeted Plymouth's encroachments with less acceptance than had his father Massasoit, and Plymouth responded to his unhappiness with suspicion. In 1667 and again in 1671, the General Court ordered Philip to answer the Court's charges regarding his behavior. At Taunton in 1671, Plymouth forced the Indian chief to sign a treaty with the colony which required his complete acceptance of Plymouth's authority, and an uneasy peace between colonists and Indians ensued. It collapsed in January 1674/75 with the murder of John Sassamon, a Christian Indian and former aide and secretary to King Philip, who was returning to his home in Middleborough after informing Governor Winslow of a pending Indian attack on Plymouth Colony. When an Indian claiming to be a witness to Sassamon's murder stepped forward to accuse three of King Philip's Indian associates of the crime, Plymouth knew it had a case. In June 1675, the colony accepted the validity of the accuser's evidence, brought the three to trial, and executed them all. Before the month ended, King Philip and his Wampanoags had attacked Swansea, and the war which bears his name began.[38]

Governor Winslow responded to the attack on Swansea by requesting aid from Massachusetts and sending soldiers to defend the town. Among those included in the forces, headed by James Cudworth, were twenty-nine militia men from Yarmouth under the command of John Gorham, a contingent from Barnstable under Matthew Fuller, and at least a few men from Eastham. These men were no doubt part of the combined Massachusetts and Plymouth force which failed to capture Philip in its assault on Mount Hope at the end of June. Cudworth established a garrison at Mount Hope, and then ordered both Gorham's and Fuller's units into the field against the Indians, with orders either to negotiate or fight, depending on the situation. Fuller's men stayed out only one night, and had two men wounded in a brief skirmish. A small group led by his assistant, Benjamin Church, remained in the field somewhat longer. For their part, Gorham and his men persevered on the trail for a number of weeks, moving well up into Massachusetts.[39] Others from the Cape returned to defend Taunton. The Indians killed two of them, John Knowles and Samuel Atkins of Eastham, probably while the two were on a patrol.[40]

These expeditions were unproductive, however. King Philip and his followers had slipped out of the English noose and taken the war to central Massachusetts and further west into the Connecticut River Valley. For its part, Plymouth maintained its guard and at the fall meeting of the General Court updated its military structure in preparation for future combat. It reappointed James Cudworth as commanding officer of Plymouth's militia units, and designated a number of other men for important military posts. In a realistic expectation of what lay ahead, it also selected a special committee to keep an account of the colony's costs for the war. Men from the Cape were well represented among the selections. John Gorham of Yarmouth was to command the second company of men, while Cudworth commanded the first. Gorham's Lieutenant was Jonathan Sparrow of Eastham. The Court made Matthew Fuller of Barnstable

Surgeon General and his fellow townsman Thomas Huchens Commissary General. It appointed John Freeman of Sandwich and Joseph Lothrop of Barnstable to the auditing committee. In addition, the Court issued a call-up of 182 men from among the colony's local militia units. Twenty-five of the men were to replace the guard at the Mount Hope garrison and 157 were to serve when needed. As would be expected from their role in colonial taxation, the towns of the Cape provided approximately one-third of the soldiers, fifty-five of the 157 and ten of the twenty-five for garrison duty.[41]

It was these men who went into battle when the Commissioners of the United Colonies decided in November to take action against the Narragansetts, southern New England's largest and most powerful tribe. As the war had progressed, the Commissioners became convinced that the Narragansetts had violated their original pledge of neutrality, and responded by voting to send one thousand soldiers against the Indians.[42] Under the overall command of Governor Winslow of Plymouth, the combined forces rendezvoused in Rhode Island, whose governor had agreed to cooperate with the mission, and then moved against the Indians on 19 December. The English soldiers twice broke through an unfinished portion of the Indians' palisaded fort, and finally set fire to the settlement, killing an untold number of Narragansett elderly and children. Despite the slaughter of innocent Indians, the enterprise had been a military success for the English. By late afternoon The Great Swamp Fight was over, and the Narragansetts were no longer serious potential participants in King Philip's War.

The effort had had its costs, however. Of the one thousand or so New England troops, 207 were casualties, twenty-seven of them from Plymouth. Included among the casualties was John Gorham of Barnstable, who fell ill in the cold wet December weather and died a few weeks later. His was the only death among Cape Cod participants, although his fellow Captain, William Bradford, received a near fatal eye wound. Nathaniel Hall of Yarmouth and John Barker of Barnstable were also wounded, but the names of the other Cape Cod casualties are not recorded.[43]

But the defeat of the Narragansetts did not represent the conquest of King Philip and his allies. The war continued. Within a few days of the devastation of the Narragansetts, the Commissioners of the United Colonies attempted to shore up New England's forces and keep a fresh force in the field. They ordered the sick and wounded sent home, the healthy garrisoned close to the enemy, and directed the member colonies to raise another one thousand soldiers. Plymouth's share was 122, of whom forty-three were to come from the Cape.[44] The troops eventually marched into central and western Massachusetts, but there is no indication any of the soldiers actually saw action against the Indians.

With the advent of spring, parties of Indian raiders returned to Plymouth Colony, and in one of their more daring attacks, destroyed the Eel River settlement just south of Plymouth. To counter such boldness, the colony's Council of War sent a small force under Michael Peirce of Scituate into the field. His contingent had a strong Cape Cod flavor. The Lieutenant was Samuel Fuller of Barnstable, men from Cape Cod were a major portion of the force, and for the first time friendly Cape Indians aided the English.[45] When Peirce marched out against the Indians on 25 March 1676, nearly half his approximately sixty English soldiers and all his twenty Indians were from the Cape. It was the last march for nearly all of them. After spending the night in Rehoboth, Peirce's company headed toward the Pawtucket River. Pursuing a small band of Indians, the men instead found themselves drawn into an enormous ambush. When their courageous defense finally failed, nearly all the English and half the Indians lay dead. Twenty of the slain were from Cape Cod.[46] Of all the various uncertainties and crises of King Philip's War as experienced by the English, certainly none affected the towns of the Cape more harshly than the ambush of Peirce's small force. With so many dead, it would have been impossible for anyone on the Cape not to have known personally someone who had died in the Indian wars.

Peirce's smaller force and his use of friendly Indians represented an important shift in military strategy for the colony. Indians had not been utilized in the earlier campaigns, and Plymouth had expressed open fear of their potential participation as enemies. Despite the Indians' previous pledge of loyalty and promises to aid the English in the war, on 6 December 1675 the Court prohibited Cape Cod Indians from coming into the colony beyond Sandwich.[47] But the Indian raids of the spring had alarmed the colony greatly, and necessitated a different approach to the war. In an attempt to counter these new Indian raids, the Council of War had consulted Benjamin Church about Plymouth's military tactics, and it was probably he who recommended the changes.[48]

Other developments reinforced the despair which must have accompanied the news of Peirce's massacre. The Indians continued to attack outlying villages like Rehoboth, and aid from Massachusetts did not transpire. On 29 March 1676 the Council of War stepped up its military vigilance. It issued a call for its largest army yet, four hundred, including one hundred friendly Indians. One hundred and two of the Englishmen and probably most of the Indians were to come from the Cape towns. To replace such a tremendous loss of adult males in the various towns, the Council ordered those boys under the age of sixteen who were able to stand watch to do so.[49] Commanded to muster in Plymouth on 11 April, the army never materialized. Scituate, shattered by the loss of fifteen men in the Peirce defeat, and Sandwich, with its strong Quaker heritage, sent few, if any, troops. While other towns did better, the soldiers who appeared were so disorganized and inadequate that the assemblage finally broke up in confusion. The only men to march out at all were some from the Cape who went to Middleborough and then returned home, seemingly without having seen any Indians.[50]

As the Council of War had attempted to increase the colony's military activity at its March 1676 meeting, it had also tried to deal with an increased unwillingness to serve in defense of the colony. The Council devoted a good deal of its meeting to assessing fines for delinquent soldiers and the towns which failed to send them. The Council found Sandwich short five soldiers for the December 1675 muster, and levied fines against twenty-one men, at least three of them from the Cape, Sandwich's Ezra Bourne and John Smith, and Barnstable's John Fuller.[51] Recognizing the severity of the problem the towns attempted to respond. Sandwich appointed its former Quaker chaser, George Barlow, along with William Smith, Sr., as its agents to collect the fines.[52] In Barnstable the Reverend Walley called for a day of humiliation to pray for God's protection, but many stayed away from the church service, and a few people even publicly opposed it.[53]

Losing public support and unable to gather an effective colonial fighting force, Plymouth abandoned offensive action, adopted a defensive policy, and left local communities to fend for themselves. The Council of War ordered that local watches be strictly maintained, and representatives from the Cape towns met in Barnstable in April 1676 to deal with the matter. They agreed to strengthen the watch line across the Cape near Sandwich, and at the instigation of Sandwich, agreed to pay men to maintain it.[54] The representatives also agreed that Cape towns should extend refuge to the people of Bridgewater, Taunton, and Rehoboth, an offer the outlying towns politely refused.[55]

Public antagonism, Peirce's defeat, and the inability to raise an army in the early spring of 1676/77 had been the low point of the war for the English. But by early summer the conflict began to turn in their favor. With warmer weather in June, the General Court decided the colony should take the initiative, and issued what would be its last military call-up. It ordered that 150 English soldiers and fifty Indians be prepared to march to the western portion of the colony on 21 June 1676.[56] While the main army ranged across the western regions of the colony, Benjamin Church took a small force of English and Indians trained in guerilla warfare toward the southwestern part. In August, Church caught up with Philip at Mount Hope, where the war had begun. Although his ambush failed to defeat King Philip's forces, one of Church's Indian allies fatally shot the chief. Church had the slain leader quartered and left the battle site in possession of his head. Within two weeks, Church had captured the rest of Philip's forces, and the war in Plymouth Colony came to an end.

Certainly no one who had lived through it would ever forget King Philip's War. Fought on New England soil, the war had a far more immediate effect on the region than any subsequent conflict. Although troop lists and population figures for the war period are sparse at best, the Yarmouth records give some indication of the extent to which people on the Cape experienced the war. The town recorded both the names of men called to military service during the war, and those of taxpayers later assessed to pay for it. Of the sixty-four family names on the tax list, slightly more than half, thirty-four, had provided at least one person for active duty against the Indians. The general lack of duplication of names on the militia lists also suggests that responsibility for military service was spread out among all those able to serve, and that a large percentage of Yarmouth males actually did so.[57] What was true of Yarmouth was almost certainly true of the other towns on the Cape.

As is unfortunately the case in war, some soldiers return crippled or maimed, and others do not return at all. While specific numbers are impossible to determine, at least twenty-six Cape Codders were casualties of King Philip's War. Only five of them, Samuel Linnell of Barnstable, William Perry of Sandwich, and Nathaniel Hall, John Matthews, and John Paysley of Yarmouth survived. While Cape Cod's casualties were certainly significant and should not be disregarded, the Cape's entire losses were only equal to those of Scituate, the colony's largest town.[58] With a colonial death rate which may have been as high as eight percent of those who served,

and local losses on the Cape of five or six men from each town, King
Philip's War was a personal experience for every Cape Cod family.[59]

Despite the disruption of daily living, the anxiety for the future,
and the familiarity with death which King Philip's War brought to the
people of Cape Cod, at least they were spared the property destruction
which marked so much of the rest of the colony and New England as
well. But even though Cape Cod's towns were still intact when the
war was over, the conflict had presented a variety of practical
problems which needed to be solved. At the head of those issues was
the question of discharging the colony's war debt. Never a wealthy
colony, Plymouth found its participation in King Philip's War costly
and not easily repaid. At the September 1678 meeting of the
Commissioners of the United Colonies, Plymouth submitted an
accounting of its charges for the war. The colony's total was 11,743
pounds. Of that, the colony government had spent 3000, and the
individual towns the remainder.[60]

But no matter who spent the money, it was the people of
Plymouth Colony who paid the bills through an astronomical increase
in taxes. In the five years before the outbreak of the war, Plymouth's
annual assessment against its towns ranged from 188 to 296 pounds.[61]
During the war, the colony levied a special tax of 1000 pounds on 10
March 1675/76, and a small one of 164 pounds to support the troops
called up in June 1676. The next month, the colony stated its
individual towns had already spent nearly 4100 pounds in prosecuting
the war.[62] Translated into local taxes, Barnstable, the largest of the
Cape towns, had its assessment raised from under twenty-four pounds
in the years before the war to ninety-nine for the March 1675/76 tax,
and 351 for the 1676 one. The Cape's smallest town, Eastham, had a
comparable experience. From paying less than seventeen pounds
before the war, it saw its assessments rise to sixty-six and 236
pounds.

Such taxes seem confiscatory almost to the point of bankruptcy,
but there appears to have been little opposition to their collection.
The people understood that survival was at stake, and that payments
were a small price to pay for it.   Only Sandwich recorded serious
difficulty in collecting taxes during the war period. In December
1676, the town attempted to make those residents in arrears pay first,
and the town noted a general delinquency problem in 1678 and
1679.[63] Eastham, not a town which included an abundance of tax
information in its records, did, however, make note of a majority of
the taxes which comprised its five-hundred-pound war expense claim.

At a town meeting in March 1675/76, it voted three separate taxes totalling just under 160 pounds. One of sixty-six pounds was for the general prosecution of the war, one of four pounds was to purchase ammunition for the town, and one of nearly eighty-nine pounds was to pay and equip those called up for the December 1675 Swamp Fight against the Narragansetts. In July of 1676 the town voted a tax of eighty-five pounds, and two months later one of 125.[64] Sandwich made note of special taxes levied during the war period, but did not include what portion of its nearly 1100-pound expenditure was to be raised.[65]

What these taxes meant to individuals is reflected in Yarmouth's "Great Rate," levied in the spring of 1676. The town raised 297 pounds from ninety-nine people, including six women and an absentee landlord.[66] Only sixteen individuals paid less than one pound, and twenty-five paid four or more. The highest assessments were to John Severance, who paid over sixteen pounds, and Andrew Hallett, who paid over thirteen. With a common cow worth a little over two pounds, and corn at two and a half shillings a bushel, the personal financial burdens of King Philip's War made the conflict all the more devastating. And yet, the charges and the debts were paid, and the records do not reflect serious opposition to the costs, much less a refusal to pay.[67]

The colony's war expenses were paid, in large part, without any assistance from England or any direct financial reparations from the defeated Indians. From the colonists' view, however, the defeat itself and the confiscation of Indian land was compensation enough. While the other New England colonies disputed the ownership of the Narragansett country, Plymouth successfully made good its claim to Philip's homeland, Mount Hope. The colony put the 7000-acre parcel on the market with an asking price of 3000 pounds, but found no purchasers. Eventually, four Massachusetts investors bought the property for 1100 pounds, and later settled it as the town of Bristol.[68] Plymouth, in turn, used the Mount Hope money to reimburse its towns for their war expenses. At its September 1680 meeting, the Court made what was apparently its first installment when it distributed 300 pounds among the towns.[69] Sandwich received twenty-eight pounds, and allocated it proportionally among those who had originally paid the taxes.[70] The following summer, Barnstable used its share of the money to pay the carpenters building the new meeting house.[71] The Court made a second disbursement in 1683 and a third in 1684. Sandwich used part of the third payment to settle a debt with a resident and to pay the Indians bounties for wolves. Eastham apportioned its share among the taxpayers.[72] The money was not always easy to get. Yarmouth found it necessary to commission town agents to demand the colony treasurer pay the town the money due from the war.[73]

In addition to the Mount Hope money, Plymouth also received a donation of slightly over 124 pounds from a group of charitable Irishmen. In contrast to the Mount Hope proceeds, which were distributed in proportion to taxes paid, the Irish donation was given out relative to losses incurred in the war. Swansea, Dartmouth, and Rehoboth received sixty percent of the money, while towns on the Cape shared three.[74]

The taxpayers of the colony and its towns had dug deep into their pockets and paid the war's charges quickly. Colonial and local tax assessments indicate that Plymouth had paid its basic war expenses by 1678. But there were some aspects of the conflict that remained a colony responsibility. One of the most important was the question of veterans' benefits, especially for those wounded in battle. Veterans applied for relief on an individual basis, and the General Court made its decision case by case. Those veterans from the Cape who applied were not shy about asking. The Court awarded John Paysley of Yarmouth three pounds in 1680, with the provision he not bother the Court about it any more.[75] William Perry received a grant of ten pounds in 1679, and when awarded five pounds in 1686 promised he would not ask for more money unless the return of his lameness was severe.[76] Nathaniel Hall of Yarmouth was the Cape's most persistent veteran, and the one who received the most interesting compensation. In addition to the five pounds in money and ten pounds in goods awarded him in 1681, Hall also received the privilege of operating a tavern in Yarmouth. In order to protect his interests, the Court also allowed Hall the right to investigate those selling liquor at retail illegally and to keep the fines imposed on them.[77] If Hall had previously received any sympathy at all because of his wounds, he surely lost it with the Court's open invitation to meddle. In addition to his collection of fines, Hall also received money grants from the Court. It awarded him five pounds in 1683, and made it an annual payment in 1684. Upon his petition in 1685, the Court granted him another thirty pounds and raised his annual payment to six pounds. Hall appeared at the Court and accepted this latest arrangement as full satisfaction for his wounds.[78] The nature of Hall's wounds is never discussed, and one is left wondering whether his success in receiving compensation for them was the result of their severity or Hall's persistence in requesting aid.

A related problem was support for the widows and orphans of those men killed during the war. John Knowles of Eastham left a wife and children when he was killed in the early months of the war. Noting the low condition of his family, the Court granted his widow ten pounds from the profits of the Cape Cod fisheries.[79] The Court similarly ordered John Gorham's land near Swansea confirmed to his heirs after his death.[80] A more complicated situation arose over the care of Sarah Nessfield of Manomoit, left an orphan when her father was killed in the ambush of Peirce's force.   Tristram and Anne Hedges took the child in, and in October 1680 requested assistance in caring for her.   Asserting that individual towns were generally responsible for their own poor, the Court nonetheless took notice of the smallness of Manomoit, and agreed to pay two of the five pounds it awarded the Hedgeses.   Someone in Manomoit apparently was dissatisfied with the arrangement, but it is impossible to tell whether it was Hedges or the community.   Five months after ordering the payment, the General Court directed Manomoit to find a home for Sarah, and absolved the town from its three-pound payment to the Hedgeses.[81]

Despite the speed with which Plymouth settled its financial war debts, other costs were less easily handled.   The property loss is incalculable. With three towns abandoned, five damaged, three of them seriously, and only six unscathed, losses from the destruction of homes, outbuildings, crops, and animals were certainly extensive. Unfortunately, they can only be guessed at, as records do not exist. Of similar unmeasurable significance was the shaken faith of the colony in its essential virtue. Many agreed with Barnstable's minister when he pointed out that the Indian uprising of King Philip represented God's wrath.[82] While the conflict had inevitably been won by the colonists, the ambush of Captain Peirce, the difficulties of the Swamp Fight, and the imminent fear of Indian attack were a constant reminder of how close the colony had come to extinction. To the anxieties about the past would soon be added apprehension about the future, as England took an increasing interest in her New England colonies.

Notes

1. Vaughan, *Frontier*, pp. 233-240, 303-308; William Kellaway, *The New England Company, 1649-1776: Missionary Society to the American Indian* (London, 1961), pp. 4-8 (Hereinafter cited as *New England Company*). While missionary work may have been outside the practical constraints of being a Puritan minister, it was still part of the broader religious quality infusing all aspects of the colony. See David C. Stineback, "The Status of Puritan--Indian Scholarship," *New England Quarterly*, 51(1978):80-90.

2. Langdon, *Pilgrim Colony*, p. 158; David Bushnell, "The Treatment of the Indians in Plymouth Colony," *New England Quarterly*, 26(1953):207 (Hereinafter cited as "Indians in Plymouth"). See also Vaughan, *Frontier*, pp. 233-240, 303-308. For an explanation of why Indians rejected Christianity, see James P. Ronda, "'We Are Well As We Are': An Indian Critique of Seventeenth-Century Christian Missions," *William and Mary Quarterly*, 3rd Ser., 34(1977):66-82.

3. Virtually all recent writers on the Indian missionary movement agree that Puritan missionaries were the leaders in the attempt to subvert Indian culture and alter it to conform to English standards. They also generally agree that the move to destroy Indian independence was successful. Disagreement comes as to whether missionaries intended to do so. Taking a more benign view, and stressing the sincerity of the missionaries is Vaughan, *Frontier*, pp. 234-308; and more specifically relative to Plymouth, Bushnell, "Indians in Plymouth," pp. 193-218. Other historians see a basically racist policy on the part of the English, and condemn missionaries as its attack force. This view is expressed most polemically by Francis Jennings in "Goals and Functions of Puritan Missionaries to the Indians," *Ethnohistory*, 18(1971):197-212 and its revision in his *Invasion of America*, pp. 228-253. The point is made less stridently in James Axtell, *The Invasion Within: The Contest of Cultures in Colonial North America* (New York, 1985), esp. pp. 131-178. Gary B. Nash comments on the political subjection of the Indian, which was part of the civilizing process, in "Notes on the History of Seventeenth-Century Missionization in Colonial America," *American Indian Culture and Research Journal*, 2(1978):3-8. A short discussion of the issue as experienced by Eliot's Indians is in Neal Salisbury, "Red Puritans: The 'Praying Indians' of Massachusetts Bay and John Eliot," *William and Mary Quarterly*, 3rd Ser., 31(1974):27-54.

4. The standard history is Kellaway, *New England Company*. For the seventeenth century, see especially pp. 1-121. See also Frederick L. Weis, "The New England Company of 1649 and its Missionary Enterprises," *Public.*, Col. Soc. of Mass., *Transactions*, 38(1948):134-218 (Hereinafter cited as *New England Company*). Weis includes a survey of Christian Indian settlements, as well as bibliographic information about missionary writings, and lists of company officers and missionaries. See also George P. Winship, *The New England Company of 1649 and John Eliot, Public.* of the Prince Society, vol. 36, (Boston, 1920), pp. v-lxvi. Most of Winship's volume is devoted to an edition of the record book of the Company for the period 1655/56 to 1685/86. Each of these works is essentially favorable to the Company. For a contrary view, especially of John Eliot's role in the enterprise, see Jennings, *Invasion of America*, pp. 228-253. The various works Winslow published in England are collected as the "Eliot Tracts," in *Collec.*, Mass. Hist. Soc., 3rd. Ser., 4(1834):1-287. See also Vaughan, *Frontier*, pp. 270-276.

5. William Leveridge to John Wilson, Sandwich, 22 September 1651, in Henry Whitfield (comp.), "Strength out of Weakness," *Collec.*, Mass. Hist. Soc., 3rd Ser., 4(1834):180-181 (Hereinafter cited as Leveridge to Wilson). Although he does not mention it, Leveridge may have been spurred to missionary work by the appearance in 1647 of John Wilson, John Eliot, and Thomas Shephard to investigate the Yarmouth church controversy. Never modest about his accomplishments, Eliot later claimed that Leveridge entered the field at his behest. John Eliot, *A Brief Narrative of the Progress of the Gospel amongst the Indians in New England* (London, 1671; repr. Boston, n.d.), p. 20. (Hereinafter cited as *Brief Narrative*). While on the Cape, Eliot preached to the Indians through an interpreter. Thomas Shephard, "Clear Sunshine of the Gospel," *Collec.*, Mass. Hist. Soc., 3rd. Ser., 4(1834):42-44.

6. Commissioners of the United Colonies to the Corporation, New Haven, 10 September 1651; same to John Eliot, [New Haven], 12 September 1651, *Ply. Col. Recs.*, 9:196, 204; 10:34. Volumes nine and ten of *Ply. Col. Recs.* are the official records of the Commissioners of the United Colonies.

7. Leveridge to Wilson, in Whitfield (comp.), "Strength out of Weakness," pp. 181-183. Whitfield also included a testimonial in support of Leveridge's missionary work written by Anthony Besse, dated the same day as Leveridge's letter, and probably written at Leveridge's request. Ibid., p. 184.

8. *Ply. Col. Recs.*, 10:141, 196; Commissioners of the United Colonies to William Leveridge, New Haven, September 1655, Ibid., p. 183. Two years later, in an obvious attempt to make New England missionary

efforts seem more extensive than they actually were, the Commissioners mentioned Leveridge as one being encouraged to pursue missionary work. Commissioners of the United Colonies to the Corporation, Boston, 19 September 1657, ibid., p. 188.

9. *Ply. Col. Recs.*, 1:53, 58, 87, 88, 126, 141, 155; 2:16, 40, 68, 85, 95. Lovell, *Sandwich*, p. 11. For biographies of Bourne, some of which discuss the uncertain details of his pre-Sandwich life, see Lydia B. (Phinney) Brownson and Maclean W. McLean, "The Rev. Richard Bourne of Sandwich, Mass. (c. 1610-1682)," *New England Hist. and Geneal. Register* 118(1964):83-899 (Hereinafter cited as *Bourne*); Mary Farwell Ayer, *Richard Bourne, Missionary to the Mashpee Indians* (Boston, 1908) (Hereinafter cited as *Bourne*); and Stratton, *Plymouth Colony*, pp. 248-249. For a brief discussion of Bourne's missionary work by one of his successors, see Gideon Hawley, "Biographical and Topographical Anecdotes Respecting Sandwich and Marshpee, Jan. 1794," *Collec.*, Mass. Hist. Soc., [1st Ser.], 3(1794):188-193.

10. *Ply. Col. Recs.*, 1:47, 49, 55-57.

11. *Ply. Col. Recs.*, 1:149-150. See chapter four for details of the problem.

12. Sandwich Town Records, 1652-1692, p. 66; Sandwich Proprietors Records, 1656-1680, pp. 62-65.

13. Josiah Standish, Deed to Richard and Job Bourne, "Standish Collection," Pilgrim Society Archives, Pilgrim Hall, Plymouth, Massachusetts; Richard Bourne, Deed to Elisha Bourne, Pilgrim Society Archives, ibid.

14. *Ply. Col. Recs.*, 1:165; 3:68, 85, 193-194, 201, 208, 216-217; 4:3, 4, 161, 174; 5:95, 99, 131; 12:238-242.

15. Plymouth County Probate Records, County Commissioners' Office, Plymouth, Massachusetts, #544. The colony's probate records have been transcribed and collated. They are organized by "Document Set" numbers, one number for each estate. See also Brownson, *Bourne*, p. 88. In terms of the number of land transactions, Bourne's holdings were not particularly plentiful. In an index of Plymouth land records, Bourne is listed with eleven actions, eight of them acquisitions. The entries for Edward Gray, a Plymouth merchant, list twenty-three purchases and twenty-seven sales. George Bonham, who lived at Eel River, had seven purchases and thirteen sales. Mabel W. Mayer (comp.), Index to Plymouth Colony Land Records, typescript, Plymouth County Commissioners' Office, Plymouth, Massachusetts, pp. 6-7, 25-26.

16. *Ply. Col. Recs.*, 10:189. See also Lovell, *Sandwich*, pp. 56-69 for a discussion of Bourne's activities, both as landowner and missionary, in the Mashpee district.

17. *Ply. Col. Recs.*, 10:205, 219, 246, 262, 277, 296, 317, 330-331, 356. In contrast, John Eliot received the same salary, fifty pounds, throughout the period.

18. *Ply. Col. Recs.*, 4:80.

19. *Ply. Col. Recs.*, 6:159-160. Deed of land at Mashpee, 11 December 1665, Misc. Bound Manuscripts, Massachusetts Historical Society, Boston, Massachusetts; same, 20 November 1666, Mass. Archives, 33:149-150. See also a 1684 confirmation of these deeds, ibid., pp. 246-247. The deed is reprinted in Francis G. Hutchins, *Mashpee: The Story of Cape Cod's Indian Town* (West Franklin, NH, 1979), pp. 47-48. A portion of it is in Lovell, *Sandwich*, p. 65.

20. Cotton Mather, *Magnalia Christi Americana*, ed. Samuel G. Drake, 2 vols. (Hartford, CT, 1853), 1:567n.

21. Richard Bourne to Daniel Gookin, Sandwich, 1 September 1[67]4, in Daniel Gookin, *Historical Collections of the Indians in New England*, in *Collec.*, Mass. Hist. Soc., [1st ser.], 1(1792):198-199 (Hereinafter cited as *Historical Collections*); Eliot, *Brief Narrative*, pp. 19-20; *Ply. Church Recs.*, 1:146. The news was important enough that John Hull of Massachusetts mentioned it in his "Diary." Ed. S. F. Haven, *Transac.*, Amer. Antiq. Soc., 3(1857):230.

22. Bourne to Gookin in Gookin, *Historical Collections*, p. 198; Weis, *New England Company*, pp. 172-174; Rowland Cotton to Increase Mather, Sandwich, 27 June 1693, in Matthew Mayhew, *A Brief Narrative of the Success which the Gospel hath had, among the Indians of Martha's Vineyard* (Boston, 1694), p. 52 (Hereinafter cited as *Brief Narrative*).

23. Vaughan, *Frontier*, pp. 242-244, 299-300. Even Jennings offers begrudging respect for Bourne's success, noting he had more converts than Eliot and that Cape Cod Indians stayed out of King Philip's War except to help the English. Jennings, *Invasion of America*, p. 252. For a discussion of the Nantucket missionary experience, see Ronda, "Generation of Faith: The Christian Indians of Martha's Vineyard," *William and Mary Quarterly*, 3rd Ser., 38(1981):369-394; and William S. Simmons, "Conversion From Indian to Puritan," *New England Quarterly*, 52(1979):197-218.

24. Bourne to Gookin in Gookin, *Historical Collections*, pp. 198-199.

25. Plymouth County Probate Records, #544; *Ply. Col. Recs.*, 6:97; Brownson, *Bourne*, p. 88.

26. *Ply. Col. Recs.*, 6:159-160.

27. Mayhew, *Brief Narrative*, p. 52; Gookin, *Historical Collections*, p. 201, n. See also Lovell, *Sandwich*, p. 176; and Ayer, *Bourne*, p. 6.

28. Bourne to Gookin in Gookin, *Historical Collections*, pp. 196-198. Bourne, using the towns and settlements as they existed in 1674, listed two villages at the tip of the Cape, two in Eastham, one in Chatham, three in Yarmouth, five in Mashpee, including the gathered congregation, three in Sandwich, and one in Falmouth. Bourne used the Indian names of the villages, and footnotes to his listing give the 1792 locations of the villages. Nathaniel Freeman of Sandwich identified the Indian sites in a letter to the Historical Society, Sandwich, 23 September 1792, ibid., pp. 230-232. The location of the villages is confirmed in John R. Swanton, *Indian Tribes of North America*, Smithsonian Institution, Bureau of American Ethnology, Bulletin, No. 145 (Washington DC, 1952), p. 21. Weis, in Appendix I of his *New England Company*, also lists the villages, but according to the modern towns of the Cape. He assigns one each in Barnstable, Dennis, Sandwich, Truro, and Wellfleet; two in Orleans; three each in Falmouth and Mashpee; and four in Bourne. Although quite specific in estimating the Indian population, Bourne was unclear as to whom, exactly, he counted. The context of his listing, which includes "men and women" and "young men and maids," and references to the number of Indians who could read and write, indicates he counted only adults, or at least omitted young children.

29. *Ply. Col. Recs.*, 1:55, 57; 2:72, 117, 123, 154, 168; 3:8, 32, 49, 63, 99, 115, 135, 166, 187, 214;4:37, 148, 149, 182; Lovell, *Sandwich*, p. 68; Weis, *New England Company*, pp. 148-149.

30. Lovell, *Sandwich*, p. 68 argues that the elder Tupper did not participate in missionary work because of his age, but that may well have not been the case. He served on a coroner's jury with his son in 1664/65, and the town elected him a selectman as late as 1669. In March of 1641/42, at the age of 64, the colony's Grand Jury had indicted him for having made sexual advances toward the willing wife of Francis Linceford of Yarmouth. Obviously, Thomas Tupper was a vigorous and virile elderly gentleman, certainly capable of a little missionary work among the Indians in the 1650's and 1660's. *Ply. Col. Recs.*, 2:36; 4:85, 149. Tupper, Jr. may have come to missionary work by marriage. His wife was the daughter of Nantucket's Thomas Mayhew. Sandwich Proprietors Records, 1656-1680, pp. 123-124.

31. Sandwich Town Records, 1652-1692, p. 116.

32. Thomas Hinckley to William Stoughton and Joseph Dudley, Barnstable, 2 April 1685, in "Hinckley Papers," p. 133.

33. Mayhew, *Brief Narrative*, p. 53; An Account of Mr Tuppers Congregation of Indians, 1693, "Indians," Pilgrim Society Archives, Pilgrim Hall, Plymouth, Massachusetts. See also Weis, *New England Company*, pp.

148-149, 154-156. The variation in population figures is probably the result of inconsistency in age limits and the number of villages included.

34. Eastham Record of Town Meetings, 1654-1745, pp. 17-19. See Sprague, *Trinitarian Congregational*, pp. 183-186 for a brief biography. Two eulogistic summaries of Treat's life are Pratt, *Eastham*, pp. 36-38; and Lucy E. Treat, "The 'Good White Father' of the Nauset Indians," *Americana*, 27(1933):41-44. See also Sibley, *Harvard Graduates*, 2:304-307.

35. Samuel Treat to Increase Mather, Eastham, 23 August 1693, in Mayhew, *Brief Narrative*, pp. 46-49.

36. John Freeman to Thomas Hinckley, Eastham, 20 March 1684/85, in "Hinckley Papers," p. 131-132.

37. Thomas Hinckley to William Stoughton and Joseph Dudley, Barnstable, 2 April 1685, in "Hinckley Papers," pp. 132-134. For observations in 1698, see Grindal Rawson and Samuel Danforth, "Account of an Indian Visit, A. D. 1698," in *Collec.*, Mass. Hist. Soc., [1st Ser.], 10(1809):133.

38. The standard modern history of King Philip's War is Douglas E. Leach, *Flintlock and Tomahawk: New England in King Philip's War* (New York, 1958) (Hereinafter cited as *Flintlock and Tomahawk*). See especially pp. 14-35 for a discussion of the background of the conflict. I have relied on Leach for the general chronology of the war and on Langdon, *Pilgrim Colony*, pp. pp. 152-163 for those aspects of it directly associated with Plymouth Colony. See also Stratton, *Plymouth Colony*, pp. 107-122. A recent general history, popular in tone, is Russell Bourne, *The Red King's Rebellion: Racial Politics in New England, 1675-1676* (New York, 1990). For a view of the causes of the war which sees them as a prelude to the "Second Puritan Conquest," see Jennings, *Invasion of America*, pp. 290-297, and as a counter to Jennings, Philip Ranlet, "Another Look at the Causes of King Philip's War," *New England Quarterly*, 61(1988):79-100. For a contemporary account which sympathizes with the Indian side of the issue, see John Easton, *A Relacion of the Indyan Warre, 1675*, in Charles H. Lincoln (ed.), *Narratives of the Indian Wars, 1675-1699* (New York, 1913), pp. 7-17 (Hereinafter cited as *Narratives*). The death of John Sassamon, the truthfulness of the Indian witness, the guilt of the defendants, the fairness of the trial, and the responsibility of King Philip have all been topics of historical speculation for years. It is highly doubtful the truth will ever be known. See James P. and Jeanne Ronda, "The Death of John Sassamon: An Exploration in Writing New England Indian History," *American Indian Quarterly*, 1(1974):91-102 for a discussion of the many ambiguities surrounding both the episode and its subsequent historical investigation. The

official record of the trial, the brevity of which itself presents questions, is in *Ply. Col. Recs.*, 5:167-168.

39. William Hubbard, *A Narrative of the Troubles with the Indians in New England*, ed. Samuel G. Drake, 2 vols. (Roxbury, MA, 1865; repr. New York, 1971), 1:79-80 (Hereinafter cited as *Narrative*). Hubbard originally published his history in Boston in 1677. Benjamin and Thomas Church, *Entertaining Passages Relating to Philip's War Which Began in the Month of June, 1675*, ed. Henry Martyn Dexter (Boston, 1865), p. 40 and n. (Hereinafter cited as *Entertaining Passages*). Benjamin Church's son, Thomas, actually wrote the history, but his father verified the narrative before its original publication in 1716. For those who prefer a modern edition of Church's history, see Alan and Mary Simpson (eds.), *Diary of King Philip's War, 1675-1676* (Chester, CT, c. 1975). The third major contemporary account of King Philip's War is Increase Mather, *A Brief History of the War with the Indians in New-England*, ed. Samuel G. Drake (Boston, 1862) (Hereinafter cited as Brief History). Mather originally published his work in 1676 as a competitor to Hubbard's history. His discussion of Gorham and Fuller after the attack on Mount Hope, pp. 59-61, follows Hubbard. See also a letter of John Gorham, Mendum [Mendon], 1 October 1675,. It is reprinted in Swift, *Old Yarmouth*, pp. 105-106. See Douglas Edward Leach, "The Military System of Plymouth Colony," *New England Quarterly*, 24(1951):351-354 for a description of how armies were created by requisitioning a portion of each town's militia company.

40. John Freeman to Josiah Winslow, Taunton, 3 [July] 1675, in *Collec.*, Mass. Hist. Soc., [1st Ser.], 6(1799):91. Freeman was Eastham's local military leader, and may have had part of the town's militia under him at Taunton. The colony later indicted three Indians for the murder of Knowles and Atkins, as well as a third soldier, John Tisdall. The jury found one of the Indians innocent of the charges, but was suspicious of the other two. Unable to find any of them guilty, the jury recommended banishment for all three. *Ply. Col. Recs.*, 5:224.

41. *Ply. Col. Recs.*, 5:175-176. For the towns on the Cape, the call-ups were: Barnstable, 16 for general duty and 2 for the garrison; Eastham, 8 and 2; Sandwich, 16 and 3; Yarmouth, 15 and 2. For two examples of guarded watchfulness on the Cape, see a reference to the punishment of Joseph Burgess of Sandwich for his assault on the town guard, and the assignment of special protection for Thomas Hinckley's home. Ibid., 5:181.

42. *Ply. Col. Recs.*, 10:357, 365, 458.

43. N[athaniel] S[altonstall], *A Continuation of the State of New-England, 1676*, in Lincoln, *Narratives*, p. 60. Saltonstall lists twenty Plymouth soldiers wounded, and five lost in the woods, in addition to the two

Captains. They buried Gorham in Swansea on 5 February 1675/76. *Ply.*
Col. Recs., 8:61.   On Bradford's wound, see John Cotton to Increase
Mather, Plymouth, 3 January 1675/76, in *Mather Papers*, p. 228. Saltonstall
divided the Massachusetts casualties into thirty slain and seventy-nine
wounded, a ratio which gives a figure close to the eighty dead usually
attributed to the battle. See Leach, *Flintlock and Tomahawk*, p. 132. Lovell,
Sandwich, p. 73 asserts there were about forty casualties from among the
Plymouth forces.   See also Hubbard, *Narrative*, 1:155-156 and n.; and
Mather, *Brief History*, p. 110. Swift, *Old Yarmouth*, p. 107 mentions Hall's
wound, and maintains no Cape Codders lost their lives in the Great Swamp
Fight. See also Swift, *Right Arm*, p. 111.

44. *Ply. Col. Recs.*, 5:184-185.   The Council of War assigned
Barnstable 13 soldiers, Eastham 9, Sandwich 11, and Yarmouth 10.

45. *Ply. Col. Recs.*, 5:187.

46. Noah Newman to John Cotton, Rehoboth, 27 March 1676 in
Bowen, *Early Rehoboth*, 3:14-15.   The Cape Cod dead were: from
Barnstable, Samuel Boreman, Samuel Childs, Eleazer Clapp, Samuel Fuller,
Samuel Lennet, and John Lewis; from Eastham, John M[ayo?], Joseph
Nessfield, John Walker, and Nathaniel Williams; from Sandwich, David
Besse, Caleb Blake, Job Gibbs, Benjamin Nye, and Stephen Wing; and from
Yarmouth, Henry Gage, John Gage, William Gage, Henry Gold, and John
Matthews.   An endorsement by John Cotton indicates Clapp and Matthews
were later found alive.   Newman listed fifty-two English killed, while
Mather, in his *Brief History*, pp. 127-128 and n. claimed forty-nine English
and eight Indian deaths.   In an appeal to Massachusetts for aid, Governor
Winslow apparently lumped the English and their Indian allies together and
estimated nearly 100 troops under Peirce, of whom only seven survived.
Josiah Winslow to John Leverett, Marshfield, 27 March 1676, Mass.
Archives, 68:177.   See also Hubbard, *Narrative*, 1:173-175; and John
Leverett to Josiah Winslow, Boston, 26 March 1676, in *Collec.*, Mass. Hist.
Soc., [1st Ser.], 6(1799):89.   Philip Walker, a resident of Rehoboth and
possibly a cousin of Eastham's slain John Walker, commemorated Peirce's
defeat in a poem, "Captan Perse & his coragios Company."   Edited with a
literary orientation by Diane Bornstein, it can be found in *Proceed.*, Amer.
Antiq. Soc., New Sers., 83(1973):67-102.   It is presented from a military
perspective in Bowen, *Early Rehoboth*, 3:34-50.

47. *Ply. Col. Recs.*, 5:70-71, 177-178, 183.   This policy was entirely
consistent with an earlier decision by the Council of War to sell into slavery
fifty-seven Indians who had come into Sandwich to surrender. Ibid., p. 174.

48. Church, *Entertaining Passages*, pp. 66-68.

252 Cape Cod and Plymouth Colony

Cape Cod and Plymouth Colony

49. *Ply. Col. Recs.*, 5:193. The number of men to be provided by the Cape towns was Barnstable, 30; Eastham, 18; Sandwich, 28; and Yarmouth, 26.

50. *Ply. Col. Recs.*, 5:193-194.

51. *Ply. Col. Recs.*, 5:189-191.

52. Sandwich Town Records, 1652-1692,pp. 117-118, 119-120.

53. Thomas Walley to John Cotton, [Barnstable,] 26 June 1676, in Whitehill (ed.), "Walley Letters," pp, 255-256.

54. *Ply. Col. Recs.*, 5:185-187; Sandwich Town Records, 1652-1692, pp. 127-128. The costs of the watch were an issue of some debate the following winter, and Eastham appointed two men to negotiate a settlement with Sandwich for part of its costs. Eastham Record of Town Meetings, 1654-1745, pp. 22, 25.

55. *Ply. Col. Recs.*, 5:194; Sandwich Town Records, 1652-1692, p. 123; Thomas Cooper and others to Thomas Hinckley, Rehoboth, 14 April 1676; Richard Williams and others to Thomas Hinckley, Taunton, 15 April 1676; and James Keith to Thomas Hinckley, Bridgewater, 17 April 1676, all in "Hinckley Papers," pp. 2-8.

56. *Ply. Col. Recs.*, 5:197. The individual town assignments were: Barnstable, 15; Eastham, 10; Sandwich, 15; and Yarmouth, 13.

57. Yarmouth Town Records, 2:[3-4]. This volume is both undated and unpaged. The soldier lists are on pages three and four when the volume is turned over and begun from the back. The rosters are reprinted in Swift, *Old Yarmouth*, pp. 108-111.

58. Robert S. Wakefield, "Plymouth Casualties in King Philip's War," *The American Genealogist*, 60(1984):236-242. Wakefield counted 110 casualties, but certainly missed several. For instance, he does not include either Paysley or Perry. *Ply. Col. Recs.*, 6:18, 52.

59. Langdon, *Pilgrim Colony*, pp. 181-182.

60. *Ply. Col. Recs.*, 10:392. The account of costs from the towns ranged from Middleborough's low of 100 pounds to Scituate's high of 1200. The individual claims of the Cape Cod towns in the colony's account were Barnstable, ł 800.17.09; Eastham, ł 500; Sandwich, ł 1099.08.04; and Yarmouth, ł 497.12.08. The Cape's nearly ł 3000 represents nearly one-quarter of the colony's total costs, and over one-third of the individual town expenses.

61. *Ply. Col. Recs.*, 8:134-135, 137-138, 141-142, 144.

62. *Ply. Col. Recs.*, 5:191-192, 197, 207; "Account of Disbursements of the Several Towns" in "Hinckley Papers," p. 10. A similar increase in expenses can be seen in the accounts of the colony treasurer, Constant Southworth. His accounts for the colony before 1674 and after 1678 show

expenditures between 300 and 500 pounds. In 1676, they were 1082, and in 1677, 815. *Ply. Col. Recs.*, 8:132, 136, 139, 141, 145, 146, 148, 154.

63. Sandwich Town Records, 1652-1692, pp. 131-132, 145-146, 148-149.

64. Eastham Record of Town Meetings, 1654-1745, p. 21.

65. Sandwich Town Records, 1652-1692, pp. 121, 124, 125, 134.

66. Yarmouth Town Records, 2:[6-7]. See footnote 57 for an explanation of the lack of dating and paging. The tax list is published in Freeman, *Cape Cod*, 2:194-195; and Swift, *Old Yarmouth*, pp. 112-114.

67. See Langdon, *Pilgrim Colony*, pp. 182-184; and Leach, *Flintlock and Tomahawk*, pp. 109-111, for discussions of how the colonies financed the war.

68. King Charles II to Gov. Josiah Winslow and the General Court of New Plymouth, Whitehall, 12 January 1679/80, in "Hinckley Papers," pp. 31-33; *Ply. Col. Recs.*, 6:36-37, 77; Plymouth Colony Deeds, vol. 5, pt. 1:1-3. See also *Cal. State Papers, Col. Ser., 1677-1680*, # 1042, #1082; Leach, *Flintlock and Tomahawk*, p. 248. The colony had previously sold Showamutt, a large tract southwest of Taunton, to a group of twenty-nine investors for 800 pounds. *Ply. Col. Recs.*, 5:191; 8:148; [Agreement], 10 May 1677, Misc. Bound Manuscripts, Massachusetts Historical Society, Boston, Massachusetts.

69. *Ply. Col. Recs.*, 6:50.

70. Sandwich Town Records, 1652-1692, p. 159.

71. Barnstable Town Records, 1640-1753, p. 118.

72. Sandwich Town Records, 1652-1692, pp. 205, 209; Eastham Record of Town Meetings, 1654-1745, pp. 32.

73. Yarmouth Town Records, 1677-1726, p. 26. Mount Hope money appeared in the Treasurer's accounts for 1685, the only time it did. *Ply. Col. Recs.*, 8:165.

74. *Ply. Col. Recs.*, 5:222-223. Barnstable received three pounds, Yarmouth and Eastham ten shillings each, and Sandwich nothing. Nathaniel Mather, brother of Increase and minister of a Dublin church, was the man behind the donation. Nathaniel Mather *et al.*, [Directions regarding relief aid], Dublin, 7 August 1676, MS 2287, Rare Books and Manuscripts, Boston Public Library, Boston, Massachusetts; Sibley, *Harvard Graduates*, 1:157-161.

75. *Ply. Col. Recs.*, 6:52.

76. *Ply. Col. Recs.*, 6:18, 188. The Court retained Perry's award of five pounds in 1686 as payment for a fine of Henry Perry.

77. *Ply. Col. Recs.*, 6:65, 130.

78. *Ply. Col. Recs.*, 6:112, 130-131, 169.

79. *Ply. Col. Recs.*, 5:177.

80. *Ply. Col. Recs.*, 5:241.

81. *Ply. Col. Recs.*, 6:54, 56.

82. Thomas Walley to John Cotton, [Barnstable], 16 February 1675/76, in "Walley Letters" pp. 252-253; same to same, Barnstable, 25 July and 2 August 1675, Cotton Papers, pt. 6, #25, #26, Boston Public Library.

XIII

"The afflicted state of the countrey"

KING Philip's War had thrust Plymouth into England's broad imperial sphere in a way the colony had not previously experienced it. Founded without a charter and remaining relatively small and unpretentious in the shadow of Massachusetts Bay, Plymouth had not claimed much of the mother country's official attention in the 1620's and 1630's, and it received even less during the tumultuous years of the Civil War. But policy changes in England after 1650 began a series of events which gradually, but inevitably, brought Plymouth into England's expanding imperial system. As a result, the colony's concerns shifted more and more outside itself, and developments on the Cape became less central.

Increasingly in the latter half of the seventeenth century, England thought of her colonies as commercial allies in a European struggle for wealth and power. As she passed legislation to regulate the trade of her colonies, England also stepped up her interest in their internal affairs. Immediately after the restoration of the monarchy in 1660, much of her concern lay with the allegiance of those colonies during the previous Commonwealth and Protectorate period. Because of past suspicions and the presumed affinity of New England Puritanism for Cromwellian government, much of England's attention focused on the northern colonies. What began in 1664 as an investigation of the region's past loyalties, became an involvement which would lead eventually to the reorganization of New England, the loss of Plymouth's independence, and ultimately to the colony's incorporation into Massachusetts.[1]

The process had begun with the Restoration. Plymouth had acknowledged the Stuart return to the throne rather quickly with a petition to the new king, Charles II. Passed at its election meeting in June 1661, the colony's petition established themes Plymouth would repeat for three decades. It appealed for confirmation of Plymouth's traditional religious and civil liberties as they had been established in earlier monarchies, and supported its request by recounting Plymouth's role in expanding the English empire.[2] Nothing came of the effort. England made no specific response to the petition, and the colony's half-hearted effort may well have been a lost opportunity for Plymouth. Connecticut and Rhode Island had each sent a prominent colonist as a representative to England at the time, and their agents returned with colonial charters. Had Plymouth done the same, the next thirty years of the colony might have been far different.

But no response from England was better than a negative one, and if the records of the Cape Cod towns are any indication, the people of the colony were not concerned about the King's failure to confirm their traditional liberties. It was better to exercise them without royal sanction than have them taken away by royal decree. But English neglect came to an end in 1664. Having secured his rule at home, Charles II began extending his control to the colonies, and was especially anxious to assert his jurisdiction over Massachusetts. On 23 April 1664, the King sent four commissioners to New England to settle a variety of intercolonial disputes and to attempt the capture of New Netherland. More importantly for Plymouth, the King empowered the group to investigate the state of affairs in New England, concentrating its efforts on Massachusetts. In a specific directive to Plymouth, the King informed the colony that the Commissioners would settle the colony's boundary and jurisdictional controversy with Rhode Island.[3]

The Commissioners encountered a chilly reception in Boston, and decided to visit the smaller colonies first. They were no doubt in search of general support for use either in their negotiations with Massachusetts or in their attempts to isolate the Bay Colony, should bargaining fail. In response to the pending visit, all the colony's freemen met at Plymouth on 8 June 1664 to prepare for the arrival of the King's agents. They agreed to petition the King for a confirmation of their patent, asserted the colony's jurisdiction over the disputed territory, and agreed to tax themselves to entertain the Commissioners in an appropriate manner.[4]   The opportunity to demonstrate their hospitality came at the end of February 1664/65. The Commissioners called for a formal session with the General Court to be held on 20 February, and held a more open general meeting to hear petitions and statements from interested parties.   William Nickerson of Monomy was the only private individual whose appearance has been recorded.   He sought the Commissioners' assistance in his ongoing land controversy on the Cape, and while the Commissioners were sympathetic to his concern, regarded the four-mile-square parcel as an unreasonable request.   They ultimately turned the issue back to the Plymouth General Court for settlement.[5]

Nickerson may have lost some support from the Commissioners because of their generally favorable impression of Plymouth Colony. Their recommendations to the General Court while visiting the colony could easily be accommodated, and the Commissioners later noted they had been well received in Plymouth and had heard few complaints.[6]   Plymouth's impression on them was evidently good enough that the Commissioners were willing to support the colony's request for a charter.   Recognizing Plymouth's poverty, the Commissioners offered to secure the colony a charter in exchange for allowing the King to select the colony's governor from among three of their own nominations. After postponing discussion on the matter, the General Court finally declined the offer.[7]

The mutual goodwill between the colony and the commissioners was such that the General Court agreed it would trust the Commissioners to represent the colony in any English discussion of the Plymouth--Rhode Island boundary settlement.[8]   Whether Plymouth once again missed an opportunity to lobby the mother country for its own charter will never be known.   In the end, however, Plymouth believed that it had survived the Restoration and its Royal Commissioners intact and relatively unscathed.   Although its security within the empire had not been improved, neither had it been lessened.   On 22 October 1668 the General Court voted to make 25 November a day of thanksgiving for the continuation of Plymouth's civil and religious liberties.[9]

Having weathered the storms of the Restoration, Plymouth Colony and its people returned to their traditional pattern of noninvolvement in England's imperial design.   But the failure to pursue a royal charter more energetically in the 1660's stood the colony ill in the aftermath of King Philip's War.   When Plymouth attempted to gain Mount Hope, it faced not only the charge of having caused the war in the first place, but of not having a charter to support its claim to the territory once it was over. Governor Winslow understood the limitations, but forged ahead anyway. He wrote to the King on 26 June 1677, claiming that the colony had merely been protecting the King's interest in a war which it had not provoked, and accompanied his letter with some Indian souvenirs taken from King Philip. Two weeks later, Nathaniel Morton forwarded a narrative of the war in which he defended Plymouth's actions and reiterated the colony's claim to the Mount Hope lands.[10] Neither Winslow's nor Morton's efforts ever reached the King, and the colony waited in vain for a reply. When two years later the colony learned its previous efforts had never been delivered, it sent a second petition, along with copies of the earlier ones. The King's agent responded by informing the colony that their second letters had been sent to a committee, and closed with a request that Plymouth give a civil reception to the King's agent in New England, Edward Randolph, about to embark on his second tour of duty in New England.[11]

The King need not have worried. Randolph had visited Plymouth on his first journey through New England, and been favorably impressed with Governor Winslow. He believed Winslow to be a man loyal to the crown, and one less than sympathetic to the independent stance of Massachusetts. Randolph even reported that Winslow supported the installation of a Governor General for New England and the submission of Plymouth to him. It was a statement agents of Massachusetts later claimed Winslow had denied ever making.[12]

Randolph's return to New England in late 1679 brought encouraging news about Mount Hope, and a letter from Charles II followed in January. The King sent word that upon the recommendation of the Lords of Trade, he was granting Plymouth the Mount Hope territory it sought, and was also willing to consider granting the colony a royal charter. Having won in its struggle for Mount Hope, the colony was thus encouraged to revive its expectations for a royal charter.[13] It was an effort which turned out to be more difficult and costly than the colony realized, and one in which the towns of the Cape were more involved than in the earlier questions of the Restoration and the Royal Commissioners or the acquisition of Mount Hope. But despite the King's offer, it was a quest doomed from the start. Both Stuart kings were actually more interested in extending their authority over the colonies by limiting charters, not granting them, and the English bureaucracy hoped to centralize control of the colonies, not disburse it.[14]   When the campaign for a charter encountered the realities of the Dominion of New England and became embroiled in the uncertainties of the Glorious Revolution, it was simply too much. The colony fell apart, finally landing in the lap of Massachusetts.

England's problem with a charter for Plymouth was that the government possessed neither a copy of the earlier patent nor maps of the area to work from. And Plymouth seemed unwilling to provide them. In his response regarding the lost souvenirs and letters, Winslow had declined to send a copy of the colony's patent because the action had not been authorized by the General Court. But he optimistically expected the Court to appoint an agent soon who would deliver them personally. That opportunity occurred at the Court of Election in June 1680. At the meeting, the General Court heard the King's letter regarding Mount Hope and the charter suggestion read to it, and responded by unanimously voting to send one or two agents to England to press for a royal charter.[15]   But by September, the enthusiasm for the colony's own representative to England had waned. Instead, the colony merely forwarded a petition to the King requesting a charter similar to Connecticut's. Asserting it had no one good enough to send to England as its agent, Plymouth instead commissioned Governor Thomas Culpepper of Virginia, who was returning to England, to present the petition for the colony.[16] Whether by failing to send an agent Plymouth had missed its third opportunity to secure a royal charter will remain a mystery, but the colony certainly had not helped its cause.

Finally, sometime in 1681, Plymouth decided to dispatch a representative to carry on the effort with more gusto than a non-resident, and more presence than no one at all. The colony selected for the post James Cudworth, one of its most distinguished elder statesmen. Unfortunately, like so much of the colony's efforts, Cudworth's mission came to nothing. He had nearly died of a serious illness two years before, and was over seventy when he accepted the responsibility. Cudworth's health and the strains of the voyage were too much for the elderly gentleman. He died soon after his arrival in England, and never presented the colony's position or supporting papers to anyone. With no one to speak directly and specifically for the colony, Plymouth reverted to its usual practice of pleading its case by petition and letter.[17]

Plymouth's prospects in England, left unattended by the death of Cudworth, were further weakened by an increased English emphasis on subduing Massachusetts before dealing with other New England colonies and issues.[18] Plymouth recognized the importance of the problems for the colony presented by the death of Cudworth and the growth of English concern, but was unable to solve them. At a specially called session on 6 February 1682/83, the General Court decided that the colony must send its own agent to England, and agreed that the Reverend Ichabod Wiswall of Duxbury should be appointed. To negotiate with Wiswall about the mission and assist him in preparing for it, the Court appointed a three-man committee, including Barnstable's Barnabas Lothrop.[19] The Court immediately wrote the Duxbury church requesting it permit Wiswall to serve as agent and sent two men to await the reply. The congregation met on the fourteenth of the month, and voted solidly against permitting Wiswall to leave, despite the lobbying of the Court's agents, and Wiswall's willingness to serve and his promise to return to Duxbury when the mission was completed.[20] Wiswall would eventually go to England as the colony's agent, but not until there had been changes in England's monarch, political climate, and imperial organization. Defeated in its plan to send an agent, the General Court forwarded another address and supplemental papers to the King. Governor Thomas Hinckley, who had become governor at the death of Winslow in 1680, also wrote to plead the colony's case.[21]

By the time Plymouth's latest petition arrived in England, decisions had been reached in the mother country that would make a charter for the colony forever unattainable. From the start, Edward Randolph and the English bureaucracy behind him had been primarily interested in curtailing the independence of Massachusetts, and as that effort rapidly concluded, English interest in Plymouth just as quickly disappeared. When the Bay Colony refused to cooperate with English demands or accept any revision of its original charter, England responded with a series of legal maneuvers which resulted finally in the revocation of the charter and the dissolution of the Massachusetts government in the fall of 1684.[22]

The Lords of Trade began immediately to develop a plan for a replacement government for Massachusetts, but the death of Charles II delayed its implementation.[23] At the suggestion of Edward Randolph, England established a temporary government to rule the colony. Consisting of a President and appointed council, its jurisdiction included the Narragansett Country, New Hampshire, and

Maine. Although Plymouth was not part of this arrangement and continued to exist as a self-governing colony, the colonial consolidation under the new Massachusetts government presented an uncertain future for the colony of the Pilgrims.[24] The incorporation of formerly independent areas into Massachusetts severely weakened Plymouth's prospects for a royal charter. Instead, the colony faced the possibility of inclusion in another jurisdiction. The provisional government of Massachusetts also introduced religious liberty and abolished the Bay Colony's legislative assembly, actions which similarly could not have offered much encouragement that Plymouth would retain its traditional ways. Despite these ill winds of change, Plymouth had routinely acknowledged the accession of James II and sent off letters to the Privy Council and the Lords of Trade and Plantations, as well as a petition to the king. All of these documents reiterated Plymouth's standard request, the retention of the colony's prevailing rights and privileges.[25]

Plymouth's efforts were so much chaff in the wind. The colony's worst fears came to be realized, and then some, with the arrival of Sir Edmund Andros at Boston on 20 December 1686. Protected by two companies of royal soldiers, he came as the English-appointed Governor of the Dominion of New England, a jurisdiction which now included Plymouth.[26] On the day of his arrival, Andros set about establishing his government, ordering all the colonies under his authority to submit to his rule, and directing them to send representatives to his council. Five of the twenty-five appointed members of that council from the colonies were from Plymouth, with two of them, Thomas Hinckley and Barnabas Lothrop, from Barnstable.[27]

Representation on the Dominion's Council did little to protect Plymouth from the authoritarian rule of Andros. The Governor had been given the power to rule New England, and he intended to do so in a manner consistent with the wishes of his sovereign and the demands of his administrative superiors. In the process of fulfilling his mission, Andros antagonized every interest group that could conceivably have supported him, and angered so much of the New England population generally, that his subjects ousted him as soon as the opportunity presented itself. Of particular concern for Council members from Plymouth was the problem of distance. The Council met in Boston, and the journey there was difficult enough from Plymouth, to say nothing of the trek for Hinckley and Lothrop from Barnstable. Expenses were not paid, and the cost of attending sessions which lasted as long as two weeks merely added to the burden. While all five Plymouth members appeared for the first full meeting of the Council, only Thomas Hinckley consistently attended subsequent gatherings of the entire Council. After June 1687, the work of the Council came more and more to be done by a small group. Among Plymouth's representatives, only Nathaniel Clark, a supporter of Andros and the Dominion, attended with any regularity. Expenditures of time and money, coupled with intensifying public hostility to the Andros regime, kept the rest of Plymouth's members away.[28]

Inclusion in the Dominion had meant the end of a separate government for Plymouth, and the General Court had ceased meeting in June 1686.[29] Instead of legislation passed by town Deputies in the General Court at Plymouth, laws came from Andros, who received instructions from the king and acceptance from his Council. In the nearly two and a half years Andros ruled Plymouth, from his arrival in December 1686 until his overthrow in the spring of 1689, he instigated policies and promulgated laws that challenged the very core of what Plymouth had been from the days of the *Mayflower* landing. From taxes to probate, and from land titles to religion, Andros changed the course of people's lives in a way almost no one liked and nearly everyone came to oppose.[30] Indeed, the rapidity with which complaints arose and their very volume emphasizes Plymouth's opposition to Andros and the Dominion of New England. The colony's first salvo, Thomas Hinckley's petition to Sir Edmund Andros requesting freedom of religion and the retention of Cape Cod fishing rights was dated 2 February 1686/87, just forty-four days after Andros had landed in Boston, and thirty-five days after the first Council meeting.[31]

As Andros's rule progressed, his tax policies became a central issue. Within weeks of his arrival, Andros had established both a poll tax and a personal property tax for the Dominion, each of which was a new form of levy for the residents of Plymouth. Both Governor Hinckley and other colony residents complained about these innovative assessments. They pointed out that the assessment value assigned to property far exceeded its actual market value and that the levies were of Massachusetts origin, previously unknown in Plymouth. The Governor, strongly supported by the Barnstable County Grand Jury, similarly advanced the broader constitutional view that taxes imposed without the consent of the people's elected representatives were not valid.[32]

Of related financial importance for the towns of the Cape was Andros's assumption of the ownership of drift whales. Traditionally the property of the town where they beached, whales became crown property under the Dominion of New England. Cape Codders and others protested, in an attempt to regain this small supplement to local revenues, but without avail.[33] Andros and his Council similarly appropriated the granting of fishing rights in Cape Cod waters. The fees had previously gone to support education in the colony, and the problem was acute enough that Governor Hinckley made a special appeal for the return of their control to the colony.[34] Thus, in both the levying and collecting of Dominion taxes in Plymouth, Andros overturned the colony's established system, and especially so on the Cape.

The cessation of Plymouth as a colony meant the concentration of judicial proceedings in Boston, just as it had tax collection. Much of the problem was distance. Hinckley estimated the cost of probating wills in Boston to be ten times what it would have been in the county where the deceased had lived. He and others were similarly critical of the requirement that civil cases of small value, especially those involving minor trespass suits, must be heard in Boston as well. As with probate, they believed the cases could have been equally as well handled in the originating county.[35] And once in Boston, the litigants and petitioners paid huge fees to the Dominion's court officials. Hinckley likened to extortion the thirty-five shilling fee to settle a fifty-two pound estate, and a forty shilling charge to issue letters of estate administration to a widow.[36]

In addition to overturning the tax and judicial institutions of Plymouth, Andros and his Council also attacked the land owning pattern of the colony. Empowered to introduce a quitrent system into the Dominion, Andros began cautiously by establishing a rent of two shillings and six pence for each new grant of one hundred acres. He intended to expand the quitrent arrangement to owners of property already held by calling for them to confirm their land on the same terms.[37] For decades, the residents of Plymouth had been accustomed to owning land by grant from either the town or the General Court under authority of the Warwick Patent of 1629. Over half a century later, they were not about to accept either Andros's assertion of crown ownership of undistributed land or his imposition of quitrents on what they already possessed.

Cape Codders were among the most vocal in the opposition to the new land policies. In its "Proposal" regarding the Dominion, the

Barnstable Grand Jury joined with the colony in an attack on the Dominion's land policies. Both groups requested that men be allowed to enjoy what they already possessed without disturbance, and not be required to pay fees for confirmations or annual quitrents.[38] Individuals also responded to the new land policies. Thomas Tupper of Sandwich complained that Andros's control over land distribution violated the wishes of the town's original grantees regarding the division of reserved common land.[39]

Closely related to the question of land grants was the issue of land records. With the center of power in Boston, the Andros government decreed that the official records of Plymouth be forwarded there, and Plymouth officials opposed the directive. In his list of complaints about the Dominion to Blathwayt, Governor Hinckley argued that government records should be where they could be consulted by those who needed them, without the expense of traveling to Boston.[40]

And finally, as though assaults on the legislative, judicial, economic, and political systems of Plymouth were not enough, the Dominion of New England introduced liberty of conscience, which for Plymouth meant the abolition of a tax-supported Congregational ministry and the inauguration of Anglicanism. It was an issue of great concern in Plymouth. At an early Council meeting, both Hinckley and Walley had strongly attacked a proposal which suggested voluntarism in the payment of ministers.[41] In general, Plymouth Colony and its leaders argued for the colony's local self determination. Hinckley wrote Blathwayt that a town should be allowed to select its own minister, as long as he was a law abiding citizen. The colony's "Address" supported the same position.[42]

In the same way that the authorities had destroyed colonial power by consolidating it in Boston, Andros and the Dominion of New England intended to nullify local self-determination and silence opposition, by restricting town meetings to an annual election of public officials. Some towns on Cape Cod expressed their opposition to this attempt to abolish local government not by public protest, but by ignoring the limitation when necessary. Eastham was the only town to comply completely. It held its last regular meeting on 29 July 1686, and there are no records of another one until after the eviction of Andros.[43] Yarmouth found it necessary to conduct a major business meeting, on 12 May 1687, but restricted its other meetings to elections until August 1689.[44] Sandwich, having done battle with the colony government over the Quakers a quarter century before, was similarly willing to defy the Dominion. It reduced the frequency of its meetings between October 1686 and August 1689, but held three meetings to conduct business not sanctioned by Andros. In April 1687 the town authorized William Hunter to catch and distribute alewives, in June it appointed Shuball Smith as military clerk, and in November it settled its accounts with him for his work as town Constable. The town also held two votes concerning the division of common land during the period.[45] Barnstable and Falmouth seem to have conducted business as usual. Barnstable devoted a great deal of time to issues concerning the construction of a mill, as well as making a number of land grants and accepting a report from its Surveyor of Highways.[46] Falmouth settlers defied both the ban on meetings and the quitrent program when they distributed and recorded land grants and voted to utilize forty acres of town land to encourage a minister to settle among them.[47] While Cape Cod towns restricted their public activity somewhat during the Dominion of New England, they transacted purely local business when it was necessary. They did not, however, take any broader action which would directly challenge the authority of Andros and his administration. On colonial issues, they seemed satisfied to let their former Governor and current Council member, Thomas Hinckley of Barnstable, speak for them, with the assistance of a petition from the county's Grand Jurymen.

The Cape towns may have kept diplomatically silent and prayed for relief during the Andros years, but they were not silent when the opportunity came to expel the hated regime and replace it with the former government. The end of the Dominion of New England began in old England with the departure of James II for France and the arrival of the Dutch prince William of Orange, husband of James II's Protestant daughter Mary.[48] Word of these momentous changes reached Boston in early April, and despite Andros's efforts to conceal the information, it soon became well known. Before the month was over, the people of Boston had arrested and imprisoned Andros, and forced his military units to surrender. Having overthrown the despised administration without learning whether William's revolution had been successful, Massachusetts revived its pre-Dominion government and awaited English developments.[49]

A number of people quickly informed Thomas Hinckley of Boston's ouster of Andros.[50] Following an unofficial meeting in May, the General Court reassembled formally in June, conducted elections, and resumed governing the colony under the former patent.

The government's continuity with the past was indicated on the Cape by the reelection of most of the same men as Deputies.[51] With a reference to the illegal and arbitrary power of Andros, the General Court declared its loyalty to William and Mary and instructed Governor Hinckley to petition the new monarches for a resumption of the colony's civil and religious liberties. Hinckley sent his petition, probably written by the Reverend Samuel Lee of Bristol, to Sir Henry Ashurst for submission to the King and Queen. Ashurst, active in the New England Company and a friend of Puritan colonists, would become an important representative of Plymouth in the last years of the colony.[52]

Unfortunately for the colony and its residents, the revival of Plymouth's former government did not bring with it the restoration of peace and prosperity. What Plymouth needed by 1689 was not just a return to its earlier government, but also a period of benign neglect in which it could recover from the human and financial costs of King Philip's War and the turmoil and anxieties of the Andros regime. Left alone, Plymouth might have pulled itself back together and survived as the small unpretentious colony it had become. But the calm never came. Embroiled in a frontier war in Maine, abandoned by friends and enemies alike in England, and overburdened by the costs of dealing with those problems, Plymouth colony began to collapse almost into chaos. When the fog finally cleared, the colony of William Bradford and the other *Mayflower* passengers was gone, now a part of Massachusetts.

The frontier war against the French had started in Maine in the summer of 1688. With the overthrow of Andros and its accompanying uncertainties, the conflict had gone badly for the English, and had spread west into New York and south to within forty miles of Boston.[53] In the summer of 1689, the Massachusetts General Court assumed leadership of the war effort in New England, and requested the aid of its neighbors.[54] On 14 August Plymouth's General Court met to discuss the issue. The Court agreed, rather warily, to aid the Bay Colony, and appointed Governor Hinckley and John Walley to ascertain that the war was necessary and to insure Plymouth's financial contribution would not be excessive. To forestall a military draft, the Court ordered local militia officers to encourage volunteers for the army. To prevent additional taxes, it ordered Deputies and Selectmen to encourage loans to the government to pay for the expedition. As guidelines for this voluntary force, the court set goals of fifty-six men and sixty-seven pounds, ten shillings.

Indicative of the growth of the colony to the west since King Philip's War, the Cape's share of both totals was noticeably below its former one-third contribution.[55]

Plymouth's participation in the expedition to Maine was one of the colony's two forays into combat during the frontier war. At the request of Massachusetts, Benjamin Church was the force's leader, and he took his small army against the French at Casco Bay in the fall of 1689. Included in it were men from Sandwich and Yarmouth, and probably from Eastham and Barnstable as well. Captain William Bassett of Sandwich is the only Cape Codder whose name is recorded.[56] There is even less certainty about the details of Plymouth's participation in Sir William Phips's ill-fated attack on Quebec in 1690. In June, the General Court authorized the service of 150 Englishmen and fifty Indians for an assault on Canada, and in December levied a tax of 1350 pounds to pay for "the late expeditions to Canada and eastward."[57] The colony raised money and troops, but the details of both are scant.

Plymouth's participation may have been slight because the colony came more and more to view its role in the war as defensive. In April the Council of War had required local watches established, an inventory of armaments taken, and ordered neighboring towns to come to the aid of a community under attack.[58] That same month Governor Hinckley begged off from involvement in assisting New York, citing the French threat by sea to the towns of the Cape.[59]

It is far more likely, however, that Plymouth withdrew from the frontier war because of its own overwhelming problems. The Dominion of New England had left the colony without the firm leadership of the General Court, and despite the ease with which the former government had been reestablished, there were those who had hoped otherwise. Some towns had proposed expanding the franchise, and another had requested the abolition of county government.[60] More importantly, popular support for the war against the French had not been strong and there was opposition to the reinstatement of pre-Dominion militia officers. The situation was so bad in Taunton, the Court finally accepted the existence of two competing companies, each with its own captain, and separate training day.[61] Other individuals simply refused to serve, despite the four-pound fine for doing so. Among those brought before the Council of War for their reluctance to participate was Joseph Halley, Jr. of Sandwich. Young Halley had been ill when the troops had left Sandwich, and the Council reduced his four-pound fine to two.[62]

As if recalcitrant soldiers and squabbles over officer elections were not enough, Plymouth also faced significant trouble in collecting its taxes in the years following the collapse of the Dominion. Opposition to Andros's arbitrary taxation schemes had bred an antagonism toward taxes in general, and the same kind of opposition that rejected former officers also rejected former taxation policies. That the taxes being raised required part payment in coin, and appeared to be leading to a return to the confiscatory situation following King Philip's War, only made the problem worse.

In the last eighteen months of the colony's independence, the General Court enacted six tax levies totalling nearly 3800 pounds. Nearly all of the money was for the war against the French.[63] Severe drought, experience with tax resistance, a new independence and unruliness within the towns, anxieties about the future, and the sheer burden of the taxes themselves combined to create widespread opposition to their collection. Communities on the Cape were not immune to the fever. Eastham was one of four towns singled out by the General Court for its failure to pay its share of the October 1689 tax for the campaign at Casco. The Court allowed all the towns an additional three weeks to pay, and imposed a twenty-five pound fine if they did not. Eastham must have paid, for when the Court acknowledged the payment of taxes in arrears in June 1690, Eastham, along with Yarmouth and Monomy, were listed as having paid.[64] The two 1350-pound taxes in November and December of 1690 were the ones which naturally created the most opposition. At its 11 February 1690/91 session, the General Court admitted there was legitimate opposition from those who claimed that many Deputies had not been able to participate in the voting. The Court noted those men were then in attendance, and promptly reenacted both levies. At the same session, the Court also remitted ten pounds of Sandwich's tax and five of Monomy's. Both communities had complained to the Court about their assessments.[65] Despite efforts to make towns pay their taxes, the situation deteriorated. In June 1691, the Court admitted that Constables were not able to collect taxes. It offered the Constables a two-month extension on collection and authorized imprisonment for anyone who did not pay. In an acknowledgment of the difficulty of local tax collecting, the Court instructed newly-elected Constables to maintain peace and prevent riots and tumults when seizing property for tax purposes.[66]

The tax revolt of 1690 was played out against a backdrop of ever increasing uncertainty. While James II had officially allowed

Plymouth to reestablish its former government, he had not done so with permanence in mind. The overthrow of Andros and the Dominion had required the mother country to reevaluate its policies towards New England, and such an activity could not avoid a consideration of the future of a charterless Plymouth. As the whole affair eventually worked out, the slide towards Plymouth's loss of independence had probably begun when Increase Mather slipped out of Boston and sailed to England to present Massachusetts's case against Sir Edmund Andros to King Charles II.[67]

The accession of William and Mary and the removal of the Andros administration in New England had made Mather's goal unnecessary. His endeavors shifted from lobbying against the Dominion and its Governor to an attempt to restore the original charter. When he could not do that, he battled to protect the established traditions of Massachusetts as best he could. Along the way, Mather made some effort to assist Plymouth in its final attempt at a charter, although Plymouth's apparent lack of interest and Mather's primary concern for Massachusetts made the effort fruitless. He encouraged Governor Hinckley to raise money for the support of the charter effort, and commented that it could be sent too late, but never too soon. Pleading the costs of the French war and the colony's tax problems, Hinckley responded some months later that Plymouth did not have money for a general oiling of the ways, but might find some if a patent was truly possible.[68]

Meanwhile, with the Dominion behind it, Massachusetts had sent two of its assembly's strongest supporters of the old charter, Elisha Cooke and Thomas Oakes, to assist Mather. Duxbury's Ichabod Wiswall, a friend of Cooke, accompanied them.[69] It is unlikely he went as an official agent of Plymouth, although the General Court may have considered sending him in 1685, and his subsequent actions indicate that he acted in what he believed to be the best interests of the colony.[70] Hinckley wrote his letter to Mather about money from Boston in early February 1689/90, close to the time Wiswall, Cooke, and Oakes would have sailed. In the political climate of the times it is inconceivable that Hinckley would not have discussed with Wiswall how the minister could best serve the colony during his time in England.

Wiswall certainly had his work ahead of him. During the summer of 1690, the English government gave up considering a charter for Plymouth, and instead joined the colony to New York. Mather protested, and had jurisdiction transferred over to

Massachusetts. Wiswall, in turn, objected to annexation by the Bay, and had the provision cancelled. Before Plymouth's place in New England could be settled, Parliament dissolved and the proposed charter disappeared with it.[71] Wiswall reported on the failed annexation efforts in an October 1690 letter to Governor Hinckley, in which he especially reminded the Governor to remember 10 Ecclesiastes 19--"Money answereth all things."[72] John Cotton of Plymouth even suggested the Governor go himself to England.[73]

Hinckley rejected Mather's proposal, and he might as well have rejected Wiswall's appeal for money. Faced with the general tax and military problems and a near rebellion in Bristol County, the Governor and the General Court adopted the only sensible tactic. Rather than a colony tax, the Court turned the matter over to the towns. Each town was to hold a meeting, have the issue explained, and decide whether and how much it would be willing to contribute toward the expected costs of 500 pounds.[74] Cape towns were a major portion of those towns which agreed to contribute. At a town meeting two weeks after the General Court's appeal, Barnstable voted to sell sections of the town's common land to raise forty or fifty pounds, and appointed a committee to supervise the sale. Two weeks after that, the town confirmed its action and voted to gamble thirty pounds for the venture if it was likely to succeed.[75] Meeting on 23 February 1690/91, Eastham's voters agreed unanimously that the colony should obtain a patent, and probably less than unanimously that a tax should be levied to help pay for it. John Freeman advanced thirty-six pounds for the cause, and the town mortgaged two islands in Cape Cod Bay to secure the loan. In April it levied a tax to pay the mortgage.[76] Yarmouth similarly voted in support of a separate patent, and like Barnstable voted to sell a portion of its land to raise the money.[77] If Sandwich joined its sister towns on the Cape in supporting the Court's appeal, it is not recorded.

It would have made little difference if she had done so. The colony fell far short of its goal, and returned what money it had collected to the towns which had given it. In similar letters to Wiswall and Mather, Thomas Hinckley acknowledged that without money, Plymouth was not likely to get a charter and that annexation would follow. He hoped, at least, it would be to Massachusetts.[78] He was correct in both his prediction and his hope. English officials had been discussing various drafts of a charter for Massachusetts since late 1690. When it finally passed the Great Seal on 7 October 1691, its jurisdiction included Plymouth Colony. In such a manner, therefore, the colony of William Brewster, John Carver, William Bradford, Edward Winslow, and the other *Mayflower* Pilgrims slipped quietly into history.

The failure of Plymouth to preserve its independence in the three decades following the Restoration was probably inevitable. The obstacles to success were just too numerous. At the imperial level, it simply made good sense to join Plymouth to Massachusetts. As England entered its century-long struggle with France, it would be easier to administer fewer and larger colonies when it came time to send troops to the frontier. Plymouth's continued autonomy within the empire had been hindered most by the lack of a charter and the independence, protection, and authority a charter presented. Like New Haven and Connecticut nearly thirty years before, Plymouth's larger, chartered neighbor swallowed it up.

Within the colony itself, the lack of a charter had meant that the Plymouth General Court ruled by persuasion and consensus in which nearly all free males participated at the local level. When that consensus disappeared in the late 1680's, the colonial government found it increasingly difficult to govern. It did not help that the colony was poor. Plymouth had never been really prosperous, and the expense of King Philip's War had left its residents weakened financially, suspicious of taxes generally, and less ready to support colony projects wholeheartedly. In short, the colonists were not willing to make the sacrifices necessary to pay what was needed to secure a charter.

And finally, a lack of strong political leadership certainly contributed to the demise of the colony's independence. Governor Hinckley did not arouse strong positive statements from those political figures who came in contact with him. One English official in the colonies thought him "weak" and "unfit," and there are hints of dissatisfaction with Hinckley's leadership in the letters of Cotton and Increase Mather and Ichabod Wiswall.[79] Hinckley's lack of assertiveness, on the other hand, may simply have been a reflection of the general lack of determination displayed by the colony's failure to have an effective agent after the Restoration. The Governor may have understood the situation clearly, and like Increase Mather for Massachusetts, did the best he could for his colony with what money and support was available.

As to the colonists themselves, the passing of Plymouth independence seemed to have little impact. The economic base of the Old Colony, as Plymouth would come to be called, changed not at all, and the political leadership only slightly. The new Massachusetts charter had given four of the twenty-seven seats on the Governor's Council to the former Plymouth Colony, and Wiswall and Mather recommended appointing men who had served in the same capacity under Andros: Thomas Hinckley, William Bradford, John Walley, and Barnabas Lothrop.[80]

In Plymouth, the General Court held its last recorded meeting on 7 July 1691, and by the following summer Cape Cod towns were electing representatives to the Provincial legislature of Massachusetts. Eastham sent Jonathan Sparrow and Jonathan Bangs. Sparrow had been a Deputy to the final Plymouth General Court and a former town selectman; Bangs was a former selectman and Deputy. Reflective of the military nature of the New Massachusetts governor, Sir William Phips, both Sparrow and Bangs were officers in Eastham's militia.[81] Yarmouth selected John Thacher and Jeremiah Howes. Thacher had been elected an Assistant at the 1691 General Court and was a local militia officer. Howes had been a recent Deputy and selectman.[82] Deputies from the other two Cape Cod communities are not recorded, but it is unlikely they broke the political practices and election traditions which had developed in the colony over the decades. In sum, the election of former political leaders to office in the Provincial government of Massachusetts reflected the basic continuity of life on Cape Cod. Given the troubles and uncertainties of the 1670's and 1680's, the incorporation of Plymouth into Massachusetts may well have restored a sense of calmness and sureness to the people of Cape Cod. Past questions about the future had been answered, and wrapped in what may have been viewed as the protective blanket of Massachusetts, Cape Codders returned to the basic responsibilities of family and farm.

Notes

1. For general discussions of Plymouth's relations with England in the years after 1660, see Langdon, *Pilgrim Colony*, pp. 188-200; and Stratton, *Plymouth Colony*, pp. 123-124. See also Michael Garibaldi Hall, *Edward Randolph and the American Colonies, 1676-1703* (Chapel Hill, NC, c. 1960), pp. 1-20 (Hereinafter cited as *Randolph*). For general discussions of English colonial policy in the years following the Restoration, see Jack M. Sosin, *English America and the Restoration Monarchy of Charles II:*

Transatlantic Politics, Commerce, and Kinship (Lincoln, NE, c. 1980), pp. 98-124, 253-272 (Hereinafter cited as *Restoration*); Richard R. Johnson, *Adjustment to Empire: The New England Colonies, 1675-1715* ([New Brunswick, NJ], 1981), pp. 3-36 (Hereinafter cited as *Adjustment*); David S. Lovejoy, *The Glorious Revolution in America* (New York, c. 1972), pp. 122-142 (Hereinafter cited as *Glorious Revolution*); and W. A. Speck, "The International and Imperial Context," in Jack P. Greene and J. R. Pole (eds.), *Colonial British America: Essays in the New History of the Early Modern Era* (Baltimore, MD, c. 1984), pp. 384-393.

   2. *Cal. State Papers, Col. Ser., 1661-1668*, #102.

   3. *Cal. State Papers, Col. Ser., 1661-1668*, #713, #722. The four Commissioners were Sir Robert Carr, Sir George Cartwright, Richard Nicolls, and Samuel Maverick. Carr, Cartwright, and Nicolls were all military men, indicating the importance of capturing New Netherland among their responsibilities. Maverick was no friend of New England, having run afoul of the Massachusetts authorities for his role in the Child affair nearly twenty years before. Winthrop, *Journal*, 2:316; Lovejoy, *Glorious Revolution*, pp. 127-128; Sosin, *Restoration*, p. 108. See Plymouth's address to Charles II and other letters regarding the Rhode Island boundary dispute, in Winslow Papers, Box 1, #22, #23, #26, #28, Mass. Hist Soc.

   4. *Ply. Col. Recs.*, 4:62-63. The General Court responded to the tax authorization by levying a sixty pound assessment, forty-five of it for the Commissioners' entertainment. The charges for the Cape towns were: Barnstable, ⅟ 5, 11s.; Eastham, ⅟ 4, 1s.; Sandwich and Yarmouth, ⅟ 5, 1s. each. Three and one-half months later, the Court voted another 100 pounds for the purpose, with Barnstable assessed ⅟ 9, 5s.; Eastham ⅟ 6, 15s.; and Sandwich and Yarmouth ⅟ 8, 8s. 8d. each. Ibid., pp. 71-72.

   5. Robert Carr, George Cartwright, and Samuel Maverick to Thomas Prence, Boston, 7 February 1664/65, in Winslow Papers, Box 1, #18, Mass. Hist. Soc.; Report of the Royal Commissioners, in Hutchinson (comp.), *Collection*, pp. 416-417. See also *Cal. State Papers, Col. Ser., 1661-1668*, #933, #1440, #1483, #1547; *Ply. Col. Recs.*, 4:101-102. See chapter ten for a discussion of Nickerson's land problems on the Cape.

   6. *Ply. Col. Recs.*, 4:85-87; *Cal. State Papers, Col. Ser., 1661-1668*, #956, #1000.

   7. *Cal. State Papers, Col. Ser., 1661-1668*, #1103; *Ply. Col. Recs.*, 4:92.

   8. *Ply. Col. Recs.*, 4:92.

   9. *Ply. Col. Recs.*, 5:7-8.

10. *Cal. State Papers, Col. Ser., 1677-1680*, #314, #333. The text of Winslow's original letter and his later explanation of its loss are in *Proceed., Mass. Hist. Soc.*, 7(1864):481-484.

11. *Cal. State Papers, Col. Ser., 1677-1680*, #1042. #1131; *Ply. Col. Recs.*, 6:20-21.

12. *Cal. State Papers, Col. Ser., 1675-1676*, #953, #1037; ibid., *1677-1680*, #740; Edward Randolph to Charles II, [Boston], 20 September 1676 in Robert N. Toppan (ed.), *Edward Randolph, Public.* of the Prince Society, 7 vols. (Boston, 1898-1909), 2:222-223; 3:17-18 (Hereinafter cited as *Randolph*).

13. *Cal. State Papers, Col. Ser., 1677-1680*, #1206, #1256. The full text of the King's letter is in "Hinckley Papers," pp. 31-33. See also William Blathwayt to Thomas Hinckley, London, 29 February 1679/80, in ibid., pp. 33-34; and Governor Winslow's letter of thanks to the King, Marshfield, 3 July 1680, in ibid., pp. 40-41.

14. For a discussion of the royal attitude regarding colonial charters in the later Stuart period, see Philip S. Haffenden, "The Crown and the Colonial Charters, 1675-1688," *William and Mary Quarterly*, 3rd. Ser., 15(1958):297-311, 452-466.

15. *Ply. Col. Recs.*, 6:36-37. Winslow conveyed that decision to the King a month later. "Hinckley Papers," pp. 40-41; *Cal. State Papers, Col. Ser., 1677-1680* #1421.

16. "Hinckley Papers," pp. 48-52 has the full text of the petition. See also *Cal. State Papers, Col. Ser., 1677-1680*, #1507. Culpepper appeared before the Lords of Trade and Plantations in April of 1681, and the Lords considered the petition the following October. Ibid., #82, #269.

17. John Cotton to Increase Mather, Plymouth, 12 March 1678/79, in *Mather Papers*, pp. 250-251; *Cal. State Papers, Col. Ser., 1681-1685*, #1389; Thomas Hinckley to William Blathwayt, Boston, 26 May 1682, in "Hinckley Papers," pp. 65-67; same to same, Barnstable, 8 November 1682, in ibid., pp. 74-81.

18. William Blathwayt to Thomas Hinckley, Whitehall, 27 September 1683, in "Hinckley Papers," pp. 91-92; Edward Randolph to Thomas Hinckley, Boston, 29 October 1683, in ibid., pp. 93-94; same to same, Boston, 24 November 1683, in ibid., pp. 96-97; Thomas Hinckley to William Blathwayt, Barnstable, 22 November 1683, in ibid., pp. 94-96.

19. *Ply. Col. Recs.*, 6:99-100.

20. Plymouth General Court to Duxbury Church, Plymouth, 8 February 1682/83, in "Hinckley Papers," pp. 84-85; Report of Samuel Arnold and Ephraim Morton [Duxbury?, ca. 14 February 1682/83], in ibid., pp. 85-87. Duxbury's reluctance to allow Wiswall to serve as the colony's

agent may have been based on his short tenure in the town. His ordination had occurred only a little over two years before. John Alden and Josiah Standish for the Duxbury Church to John Cotton and the Church at Plymouth, Duxbury, 9 November 1682, Cotton Papers, pt. 8, #25, Boston Public Library.

21. Address of Plymouth Colony to King Charles II, [Plymouth, November 1683], in "Hinckley Papers," pp. 98-102; Edward Randolph to Thomas Hinckley, Whitehall, 4 March 1683/84, in ibid., p. 122; Thomas Hinckley to William Blathwayt, Plymouth, 16 March 1683/84, in ibid., pp. 123-126; *Cal. State Papers, Col. Ser., 1681-1685*, #1389.

22. Langdon, *Pilgrim Colony*, pp. 211-213. For discussions of the annulment of the Massachusetts charter and the creation of the Dominion of New England, see Viola F. Barnes, *The Dominion of New England: A Study in British Colonial Policy* (New Haven, c. 1923; repr. New York, 1960), pp. 5-70 (Hereinafter cited as *Dominion*); Hall, *Randolph*, pp. 53-107; Johnson, *Adjustment*, pp. 36-70. Lovejoy, *Glorious Revolution*, pp. 143-159. All of these studies stress the centrality of Massachusetts, and treat Plymouth only peripherally.

23. *Cal. State Papers, Col. Ser., 1681-1685*, #1928, #1941, #1953. Most of their proposals were later incorporated into both Dudley's and Andros's commissions.

24. *Cal. State Papers, Col Ser., 1685-1688*, #319, #328; Commission of Joseph Dudley as President of the Council for New England, [8 October 1685], in *Public.*, Col. Soc. Mass., 2(1913): 37-43; Barnes, *Dominion*, pp. 47-49.

25. *Ply. Col. Recs.*, 6:160; *Cal. State Papers, Col. Ser., 1685-1688*, # 147, #219; Thomas Hinckley to Lords of the Privy Council, Plymouth, 24 April 1685, and Petition of the General Court to King James II, Plymouth, 4 June 1685, both in "Hinckley Papers," pp. 135-138

26. Commission of Sir Edmund Andros as Governor of the Territory and Dominion of New England, 3 June 1686, in *Public.*, Col. Soc. Mass., 2(1913):44-56.

27. Mass. Archives, 126:186, 209. See Randolph's written order to Council members to attend the 30 December 1686 meeting in Toppan, *Randolph*, 4:133; Robert N. Toppan (ed.), "Andros Records," *Proceed.*, Amer. Antiq. Soc., 13(1899-1900):240 (Hereinafter cited as "Andros Records"). These "records" are minutes of Council meetings. Barnes, *Dominion*, p. 73. The other Plymouth councilors were Nathaniel Clark and William Bradford from Plymouth, and John Walley from Bristol. All five had served on Randolph's temporary council prior to the arrival of Andros. Mass. Archives, 126:77-78. Representation from the components of the

Dominion, in addition to the five from Plymouth, were Massachusetts, 7; New Hampshire, 1; Maine, 2; Narragansett Country, 1; Rhode Island, 7; Connecticut, 2. After New York and the Jerseys were added, there were 8 members from New York and none from the Jerseys. Barnes claims six members for Plymouth, but cites no source, and a review of the attendance records of Council meetings lists only the five names given here. See Toppan, "Andros Records," pp. 240-268, 463-499. All of Plymouth's Council members except Clark had previously been recommended for government service by Edward Randolph. Memorial of Mr. Randolph, in Toppan, *Randolph*, 4:46; *Cal. State Papers, Col. Ser., 1685-1688*, #350, #1702.

28. Toppan, "Andros Records," pp. 240-268, 463-499. After June 1687, Hinckley attended 3 meetings, Lothrop 4, Walley, 4, and Bradford, 1. Rarely were there two members from Plymouth in attendance at a meeting, and usually none. Few of those meetings had 8 or more members present. See also Edward Randolph to John Povey, Boston, 21 May 1687, where he admits to the length and expense of the meetings and the prospect that the conditions will reduce attendance in the future. Toppan, *Randolph*, 4:163. For Clark's sympathy for the Dominion, see the Declaration of Sundry Inhabitants of Plymouth Against Nathaniel Clark, April 22, 1689, in "Hinckley Papers," p. 197; and the postscript of Samuel Prince to Thomas Hinckley, Boston, 22 April 1689, in ibid., p. 196. Prince was Hinckley's son-in-law.

29. *Ply. Col. Recs.*, 6:204.

30. The fullest discussion of Andros's rule is in Barnes, *Dominion*, pp. 71-230, where she gives a chapter to each of the major issues. See also Lovejoy, *Glorious Revolution*, pp. 179-195. For a discussion of the Dominion in Plymouth, see Langdon, *Pilgrim Colony*, pp. 214-221.

31. "Hinckley Papers," pp. 149-150.

32. Thomas Hinckley to William Blathwayt, Boston, 28 June 1687, in "Hinckley Papers," pp. 154-156; [Thomas Hinckley], "Plea," [June 1687], in ibid., pp. 162-166; Barnstable County Grand Jury, "Proposal for an Address to the King," [1687], in ibid., p. 168; "Address and Petition of New Plymouth to King James II," [Plymouth?, 1687], in ibid., pp. 173-174. As an example of the tax assessment--market value discrepancy, Hinckley mentioned horses which could be bought for one pound being assessed for five. The Governor's "Plea" appears to be a lawyer's argument defending some group or person being tried for refusal to pay Dominion taxes. Ibid., p. 162, note.

33. "Address and Petition," in "Hinckley Papers," pp. 178-179; Hinckley's petition to Sir Edmund Andros, in ibid., pp. 149-150. For an

example of the impact of the Dominion of New England ownership of whales on an individual Cape Codder, see the petition of Eastham's Elisha Paine, 30 March 1688/89, Mass. Archives, 128:134-135.

34. Thomas Hinckley for Plymouth Colony to Sir Edmund Andros and his Council, [Barnstable?], February 1686/87, in "Hinckley Papers," pp. 149-150.

35. Hinckley to Blathwayt, in "Hinckley Papers," pp. 156-159; Barnstable County Grand Jury, "Proposal," in ibid., p. 168; "Address and Petition," in ibid., pp. 176-177.

36. Hinckley to Blathwayt, in "Hinckley Papers," pp. 156-157.

37. Barnes, *Dominion*, pp. 174-178.

38. Barnstable County Grand Jury, "Proposal," in "Hinckley Papers," p. 168; "Address and Petition," in ibid., pp. 177, 179.

39. Mass. Archives, 126:321-325; Sandwich Town Records, 1652-1692, p. 228.

40. Hinckley to Blathwayt, in "Hinckley Papers," pp. 157-158; "Address and Petition," in ibid., p. 177.

41. Toppan, "Andros Records," pp. 257-258. The mention of the debate is one of the few times the "Records" include any suggestion of a controversial issue being discussed. The Governor must have disapproved, either of the topic or the acrimony. After listening for awhile, he postponed debate. In a letter to Hinckley, 22 June 1686, Randolph argued it was as justified for Andros to demand Plymouth support an Anglican clergyman as it was for Plymouth to demand Quakers support a Congregational one. Toppan, *Randolph*, 4:87.

42. Hinckley to Blathwayt, in "Hinckley Papers," pp. 159-161; "Address and Petition," in ibid., p. 179-181.

43. Eastham Record of Town Meetings, 1654-1745, pp. 36-37.

44. Yarmouth Town Records, 1677-1726, pp. 37-44.

45. Sandwich Town Records, 1652-1692, pp. 191, 223, 225-228.. Sandwich also held election meetings on 13 and 28 May 1688, and a proprietors' meeting in March 1688/89.

46. Barnstable Town Records, 1640-1753, pp. 127-143.

47. Falmouth Proprietors Records, 1661-1804, pp. 9-13.

48. For discussions of the Glorious Revolution in England, written from the perspective of the New England colonies, see Lovejoy, *Glorious Revolution*, pp. 220-234; and Barnes, *Dominion*, pp. 231-238.

49. For a description of the Boston rebellion by a Plymouth observer, see Samuel Prince to Thomas Hinckley, Boston, 22 April, 1689, in "Hinckley Papers," pp. 192-196. Nathaniel Byfield of Bristol also wrote a report, although he was not an eyewitness, *An Account of the Late Revolution*

in New England, in Charles M. Andrews, (ed.), *Narratives of the Insurrections, 1675-1690* (New York, 1915; repr., 1967), pp. 170-175 (Hereinafter cited as *Insurrections*). Prince's report is also in ibid., pp. 185-190. See also Johnson, *Adjustment*, pp. 88-91; Lovejoy, *Glorious Revolution*, pp. 239-245; Barnes, *Dominion*, pp. 238-246.

50. In addition to the letter of his son-in-law, Hinckley also received a letter from Thomas Danforth, a steadfast Massachusetts opponent of Andros and the Dominion, Boston, 20 April 1689, in "Hinckley Papers," pp. 191-192; a joint report by Plymouth's William Bradford and Nathaniel Thomas, Plymouth, 20 April 1689, in ibid., pp. 190-191; and an official account from Isaac Addington, clerk of the interim Council of Massachusetts, Boston, 30 April, 1689, in ibid., pp. 197-199.

51. *Ply. Col. Recs.*, 6:205-207. Exercising caution, Barnstable's Barnabas Lothrop refused to accept his election as an Assistant, although he had taken his place by the October 1689 meeting. Ibid., pp. 205, 217. Langdon, *Pilgrim Colony*, p. 224. Sandwich reelected Thomas Tupper and Steven Skiffe as its Deputies and Eastham did the same for Jonathan Sparrow and Mark Snow. Yarmouth reelected Jeremiah Hawes, but replaced Silas Sears with John Miller. Barnstable reelected Shuball Dimmock, but substituted John Gorham for Joseph Lothrop. *Ply. Col. Recs.*, 6:185-186, 205-206.

52. *Ply. Col,. Recs.*, 6:208-209; *Cal. State Paper, Col. Ser., 1689-1692*, #183; Thomas Hinckley to Sir Henry Ashurst, Plymouth, 6 June 1689, in "Hinckley Papers," pp, 201-202. Ashurst presented Plymouth's petition sometime before the middle of August. Sir Henry Ashurst to Thomas Hinckley, 13 August 1689, in ibid., p. 206.

53. Langdon, *Pilgrim Colony*, pp. 224-232 discusses Plymouth's role in what colonists called King William's War. For broader views of the struggle, see Douglas Edward Leach, *The Northern Colonial Frontier, 1607-1763* (New York, c. 1966), pp. 109-115; and Johnson, *Adjustment*, pp. 121-129.

54. Simon Bradstreet for the Massachusetts General Court to Thomas Hinckley and the Plymouth Council, Boston, 17 July 1689, in "Hinckley Papers," pp. 203-204. Bradstreet's second letter to Hinckley, written sixteen days later shows some impatience with Plymouth's failure to respond quickly. Ibid., pp. 204-205.

55. *Ply. Col. Recs.*, 6:212-216. The Cape's share of the financial support was ₤19, 10s., and local assessments were: Barnstable and Sandwich ₤5 each, Eastham and Yarmouth ₤4 each, Saconesett ₤1, and Monomy 10s. Its share of the soldiers was sixteen, with Barnstable and Eastham providing four each, Sandwich and Yarmouth three each, and Monomy and Saconesett

one each. The Court also ordered each town to provide equipment for its soldiers.

56. William Bassett to Thomas Hinckley, Casco, [23] September 1689, in "Hinckley Papers," pp. 214-216. See also a second-hand report from Hinckley's son-in-law. Samuel Prince to Thomas Hinckley, Sandwich, 27 September 1689, in ibid., pp. 216-217; and two letters of Benjamin Church to Thomas Hinckley and John Walley, Falmouth, [Maine], 18 October and 31 October 1689, in ibid., pp. 220-223. The colony later awarded Bassett £ 3 for his efforts. *Ply. Col. Recs.*, 6:229.

57. Benjamin Church, *The History of Philip's War . . . also, of the French and Indian Wars at the Eastward*, ed. Samuel G. Drake, 2d ed. (Boston, 1829), pp. 180-182. *Ply. Col. Recs.*, 6:248-251; 254-255. At least some Indians participated in the campaign, as upon their petition, the General Court allowed them equal shares in the plunder. *Ply. Col. Recs.*, 6:261-262. The December tax of £ 1350 was the second one of that amount in two months, the November levy being only partially devoted to the Canadian campaign. Ibid., p. 253. Each county paid almost an equal one-third of the November tax. Barnstable County's assessment was £ 452 [1]4s. 9d., divided among the towns thusly: Barnstable, £ 112 10s.; Eastham, £ 93 19s. 6d.; Monomy, £ 18 18s 9d.; Rochester, £ 13 15s.; Saconesett, £ 15 3s. 9d.; Sandwich, £ 93 15s; Yarmouth, £ 104 2s. 9d.

58. *Ply. Col. Recs.*, 6:237.

59. Thomas Hinckley to Jacob Leisler, Barnstable, 17 April 1690, in "Hinckley Papers," pp. 242-244. The Governor sent a similar letter to Governor Simon Bradstreet of Massachusetts two days later. In ibid., pp. 244-246.

60. Langdon, *Pilgrim Colony*, p. 224.

61. *Ply. Col. Recs.*, 6:224-225, 231, 237; John Walley to Thomas Hinckley, n.p., [13 August 1689], in "Hinckley Papers," pp. 208-209; same to same, Bristol, 16 April 1690, in ibid., pp. 239-242; Walter Dean and Others to Thomas Hinckley, Taunton, 7 April 1690, in ibid., 234-238.

62. *Ply. Col. Recs.*, 6:233, 238-239.

63. *Ply. Col. Recs.*, 6:215, 220-221, 233, 251, 253, 254-255, 260. £ 200 was costs for the charter efforts in England, £ 50 was an excise on inns and innkeepers, and a portion of the 5 June 1690 levy was for "debts." For a discussion of the tax problem in Plymouth in the 1690's, see Richard LeBaron Bowen, "The 1690 Tax Revolt of Plymouth Colony," *New Eng. Hist. and Geneal. Reg.*, 112(1958):3-14. I believe Bowen has overestimated the amount of taxes levied, but not the depth of feeling among Plymouth residents against them.

280 *Cape Cod and Plymouth Colony*

64. *Ply. Col. Recs.*, 6:226-227, 246. John Walley made note of the tax resistance in a postscript of a letter from Benjamin Church to Thomas Hinckley, Boston, 4 November 1689, in "Hinckley Papers," p. 223; and Hinckley alluded to the problem in a letter to Increase Mather, 4 February 1689/90 in ibid., pp. 227-229. Nickerson's settlement at Manomoit came also to be referred to as Monomy in the colonial records during the 1680's.

65. *Ply. Col. Recs.*, 6:257, 258-259. The official records contain an inserted list of men admitted to freemanship at a Barnstable County Court on 24 June 1690, but it is clear the actions taken were in February 1690/91.

66. *Ply. Col. Recs.*, 6:265-266. At the same session, the Court noted four Bristol County towns, where the tax hostility had been most vocal, had even refused to send delegates to the Court. Ibid., pp. 263, 265.

67. For a detailed analysis of Increase Mather's activities in England from 1688 to 1691, see Michael G. Hall, *The Last American Puritan: The Life of Increase Mather, 1639-1723* (Middletown, CT, 1988), pp. 212-254 (Hereinafter cited as *Mather*). For a somewhat shorter survey, see Johnson, *Adjustment*, pp. 204-239. Lovejoy, *Glorious Revolution*, pp. 348-350; and Langdon, *Pilgrim Colony*, pp. 235-240, cover the issue with a Plymouth perspective.

68. Increase Mather to Thomas Hinckley, Deal, Kent, 12 September 1689, in "Hinckley Papers," pp. 209-211; Thomas Hinckley to Increase Mather, Boston, 4 February 1689/90, in ibid., pp. 227-229.

69. Langdon, *Pilgrim Colony*, pp. 237-238; Hall, *Mather*, p. 232; Johnson, *Adjustment*, p. 180.

70. Wiswall had raised a number of questions about the financial aspects of being an agent to England in a letter to Hinckley written 6 November 1685, in "Hinckley Papers," pp. 145-146. Wiswall's Duxbury congregation made a formal protest to Massachusetts regarding their minister's journey to England, indicating its members, at least, believed Wiswall had some official role for Massachusetts. Duxbury Congregation to the Governor and Council of Massachusetts, Duxbury, 1 March 1689/90, Mass. Archives, 11:51.

71. Cotton Mather to Thomas Hinckley, Boston, 26 February 1690/91, in "Hinckley Papers," pp. 248-249; Increase Mather to same, London, 24 May 1690, in ibid., pp. 254-255; Ichabod Wiswall to same, London, 17 October 1690, in ibid., pp. 276-278; Increase Mather, "A Brief Account Concerning Several of the Agents of New-England, Their Negotiation at the Court of England," in Andrews (ed.), *Insurrections*, pp. 269-297. The date given for Cotton Mather's letter in "Hinckley Papers" is 26 April 1690, where the "ii" [2] is a misprint for "11" [11] and has sometimes been read as

April 1690, rather than the February 1690/91 it should be. See Johnson, *Adjustment*, p. 180, n. 106.

72. "Hinckley Papers," p. 277, and note.

73. John Cotton to Thomas Hinckley, Plymouth, 6 February 1690/91, in "Hinckley Papers," pp. 278-280..

74. *Ply. Col. Recs.*, 6:259. The date should be 11 February 1690/91 for the reasons given in note 65 above.

75. Barnstable Town Records, 1640-1753, p. 156.

76. Eastham Record of Town Meetings, 1654-1745, pp. 39-42.

77. Yarmouth Town Records, 1677-1726, pp. 52-53.

78. Thomas Hinckley to Increase Mather, Barnstable, 16 October 1691, in "Hinckley Papers," pp. 287-292; same to Ichabod Wiswall, Barnstable, 17 October 1691, in ibid., pp. 292-297. Edward Randolph had made such a proposal over ten years before. Edward Randolph to Josiah Winslow, Boston, 24 February 1679/80, in Winslow Papers, Box 1, #113, Mass. Hist. Soc.

79. *Cal. State Papers, Col. Ser., 1681-1685*, #1024.

80. *Cal. State Papers, Col. Ser., 1689-1692*, #1772.

81. Eastham Town Meetings, pp. 43-44; *Ply. Col. Recs.*, 6:10, 106, 207, 262.

82. Yarmouth Town Records, 1677-1726, pp. 62-63; *Ply. Col. Recs.*, 6:205, 241, 262.

BIBLIOGRAPHICAL ESSAY

THE material used to produce the preceding narrative can be divided into three general categories: those works which are chronologically limited to seventeenth-century Plymouth Colony; those which are geographically oriented towards Cape Cod; and those more general works which in some way deal with the issues of early New England history relevant to Plymouth Colony. The following essay will discuss those works in the first two categories which are basic to a general understanding of Cape Cod in the seventeenth century. The third category, important for its coverage of the historiographical aspects of broader New England issues occurring in Plymouth Colony, have been discussed in introductory documentation to the relevant chapters. They are far less central to an overall view of Cape Cod, and those readers seeking a place to begin their quest for more information about them are referred to the notes which accompany each chapter.

Among those personal narratives which deal with seventeenth-century Plymouth Colony, none is more important than William Bradford's *Of Plymouth Plantation*. Of the various editions of Bradford's famous history, Samuel Eliot Morison's (New York, 1959) is the one most generally available and easily the most readable. The more scholarly edition by Worthington C. Ford (2 vols.; Boston, 1912) is truer to Bradford's original and includes extensive annotation and commentary, almost to the point of providing a descant to the original. For those with a research interest in Plymouth history, it is the one to consult. Although more limited in its scope, *A Journal of the Pilgrims at Plymouth: Mourt's Relation*, edited by Dwight B.

Heath (New York, c. 1963) should also be consulted. The book was originally published in London in 1622 with a preface signed by one G. Mourt, of whom nothing of certainty has ever been discovered. It has been referred to as *Mourt's Relation* since Thomas Prince did so in 1736. One of the first, and therefore more generally available sources for Plymouth history, *Mourt's Relation* has been edited and republished a number of times for nearly two centuries. Of those easily obtainable, the one in Alexander Young (ed.), *Chronicles of the Pilgrim Fathers of the Colony of Plymouth, from 1602 to 1625* (Boston, 1841) is heavily annotated. A more recent annotated edition is by Jordan D. Fiore (ed.), *Mourt's Relation: A Journal of the Pilgrims of Plymouth* (Plymouth, MA, 1985). In whatever edition, the book is a delightful and even humorous account of the early activities of the Pilgrims, and is more complete than Bradford's history on those events it chronicles. Edward Winslow's *Good Newes from New England: Or a true Relation of things very remarkable at the Plantation of PLIMOUTH in New England* continues *Mourt's Relation*. Edited by George E. Bowman, it was published serially in volumes 25 (1923) and 26 (1924) of *The Mayflower Descendant*. It is also included in Young's *Chronicles*, but has not received the attention from modern editors that it richly deserves.

The most important supplement to these personal accounts of Plymouth Colony, is the *Records of the Colony of New Plymouth in New England*. Edited by Nathaniel B. Shurtleff and David Pulsifer in twelve volumes (Boston, 1855-1861; reprinted, New York, 1968), these official documents contain records of the General Court and the Court of Assistants, as well as the accounts of the colony treasurer, vital statistics, freemen and militia lists, judicial decisions, the laws of the colony, and deeds. Volumes ten and eleven are the records of the Commissioners of the United Colonies. The colony's official records provide information about all aspects of the public affairs of Plymouth, and are simply indispensable for any historical understanding of the colony.

Of similar central importance for a study of seventeenth-century Plymouth are two surveys of the colony's history by modern historians. George D. Langdon, Jr.'s *Pilgrim Colony: A History of New Plymouth, 1620-1621* (New Haven, 1966) treats the colony largely from a political view, and does so in an analytically balanced and comprehensive manner. It is the book where one should start. Covering similar ground, but with a genealogical approach which attempts to emphasize the people of Plymouth, is Eugene Aubrey

Stratton, *Plymouth Colony: Its History & People, 1620-1691* (Salt Lake City, c. 1986). Stratton divides his presentation into three parts, seven chronological narratives, seven topical essays, and nearly 150 pages of biographical sketches. A third significant work is Harry M. Ward, *Statism in Plymouth Colony* (Port Washington, NY, c. 1973). With a narrower focus than either Langdon or Stratton, Ward discusses the involvement of government in the life of Plymouth Colony and offers a number of thoughtful suggestions. All three of these works are primarily useful for providing the broader colonial perspective against which Cape Cod developments occurred.

Only one compilation of personal papers covers those wider general events on the Cape. It is the collected papers of Thomas Hinckley, a resident of Barnstable and Plymouth's last governor. The originals are held by the Rare Book and Manuscript Division of the Boston Public Library, but the Massachusetts Historical Society published them in number 4 of its *Collections* series, volume 5(1861):1-308. Comprised primarily of letters, it is an important collection of material not only of Cape Cod issues, but also on the troubles in Plymouth Colony under the Dominion of New England and during the turmoil surrounding Plymouth's incorporation into Massachusetts.

Because of the historical emphasis on Plymouth, as both town and colony, Cape Cod events are best covered at the local level, in both town records and local histories. But three works, all from the nineteenth century, attempt to override the essential local orientation of Cape Cod history in the past century. Earliest among them is Frederick Freeman's *History of Cape Cod: The Annals of Barnstable County and of Its Several Towns, Including the District of Mashpee* (2 vols.; Boston, 1860). Volume one consists of a history of the Cape, with many excerpts from source material and annotated explanations of information known only by nineteenth-century residents of the Cape. The local flavor of Cape Cod history is reflected in volume two, which consists of similar material organized by town. Somewhat different in its approach is Simeon Deyo's edited work, *History of Barnstable County, Massachusetts* (New York, 1890). In addition to a number of chronological and topical essays, Deyo also maintains a local orientation with a separate chapter on each of the individual Cape Cod towns. The only one of these three nineteenth-century works which attempts to give an integrated narrative history of the Cape is Charles F. Swift, *Cape Cod: The Right Arm of Massachusetts, An Historical Narrative* (Yarmouth, 1897). Because of its effort to evaluate and analyze, Swift's work is easily the most valuable of the three for any modern study of the Cape. But all of them are pivotal to a study of the Cape, and are decidedly more important than their lack of frequency in the documentation would indicate.

These general studies of Cape Cod appear only occasionally because it is in the town records and local histories that the history of the Cape Cod is largely told. For Barnstable, those records are the Barnstable Town Records, 1640-1753. As with all the extant local records of the Cape Cod towns, the problems of reading those records in the original, presented by their fragile condition and the difficulties of distance, have been solved by the microfilming activities of the Church of Jesus Christ of Latter Day Saints. In the early 1970s, the church microfilmed not only the original records, but also the nineteenth-century transcriptions made by town clerks, and both versions of the records for each town are readily available to anyone who requests them through the local Church's Family History Library. Combined with the colony's records, these registers of local actions form the basis of any study of Cape Cod in the seventeenth century.

Barnstable's early religious history is covered by three important items. Of particular significance is the *Diary* of John Lothrop, Barnstable's first minister. It is particularly important for its coverage of the Scituate background and subsequent founding of Barnstable. In 1769 Ezra Stiles discovered Lothrop's autograph record of his seventeenth-century pastorate in both Scituate and Barnstable and copied it. The original was then in the hands of Elijah Lothrop of Gilead, Connecticut, and has since become lost; Stiles's copy is all that remains. It is part of the Stiles Papers, held by the Beinecke Rare Book and Manuscript Library at Yale University, and has been used with their permission. Amos Otis edited a major portion of the *Diary* in the nineteenth century, omitting the last few pages as well as a rather graphic description of William Carsley's excommunication for homosexuality in 1641. Otis's version of the *Diary*, along with some similar material from the time of the Reverend John Russell in the 1680's is published as "Scituate and Barnstable Church Records," *New Eng. Hist. & Geneal. Reg.* 9(1855):279-287, 10(1856):37-43, 345-351. A photocopy of the Stiles transcription is at the Sturgis Library, Barnstable, Massachusetts. A small but significant collection of letters by Lothrop's successor, Thomas Walley, is edited by Walter M. Whitehill, and published in the *Proceedings* of the American

Antiquarian Society, 58(1948):247-262. The church history of the town is rounded out by the Records of the West Parish of Barnstable, Massachusetts, 1668-1807. Photostat copies are available at the Massachusetts Historical Society and a small number of major historical research libraries. West Parish was the successor to the original Barnstable congregation when the town divided in 1717.

Barnstable has also had its fair share of historians, three of whose books are good places to begin. The introductory essays in Donald G. Trayser (ed.), *Barnstable: Three Centuries of a Cape Cod Town* (Hyannis, 1939) are helpful, as is O. Herbert McKenny's essay "The Beginnings" in the town's Revolutionary Bicentennial volume *Seven Villages of Barnstable* (Barnstable, 1976). For those interested in Barnstable genealogy, the place to start is Amos Otis, *Genealogical Notes of Barnstable Families*, 2 vols. (Barnstable, 1888, 1890; repr. Baltimore, 1991).

Eastham has two sets of relevant local records. Of primary significance is its Record of Town Meetings, 1654-1745, which records the political aspects of the settlement. The town's Record of Land and Meadow Grants, 1654-1743, has some usable material from the seventeenth century, although it is primarily a record of the eighteenth-century proprietors. There is nothing comparable to the writings of Walley and Lothrop for the religious history of the town. The only town history dates from the pre-Civil War era. It is Enoch Pratt, *A Comprehensive History Ecclesiastical and Civil of Eastham, Wellfleet and Orleans . . .*(Yarmouth, 1844). Rather antiquarian and genealogical in its outlook, it does contain biographical information on Eastham's early settlers and excerpts from the original records. It should be supplemented with Josiah Paine, "Eastham and Orleans Historical Papers," in *Library of Cape Cod History and Genealogy*, no. 55 (1914), and Donald G. Trayser, Alice A. Lowe, and Henry Beston, *Eastham, Massachusetts, 1651-1691* (Eastham, 1951).

Sandwich's early records are its Town Records, 1651-1692, which are quite complete, and a set of Proprietors Records, 1657-1691, which is somewhat less useful. There are two histories of the town, a rather popular account by Harriot Buxton Barbour, *Sandwich, The Town that Glass Built* (Boston, 1948), and a more comprehensive one by R. A. Lovell, Jr., *Sandwich: A Cape Cod Town* (Sandwich, 1984). There is little of the town's history and few of its people that Lovell does not include.

Yarmouth's local records are available only for the period after 1677, as Record of Town Meetings, 1677-1726. For the period they cover, they are as complete as the fuller records of the other towns. There are two surveys of the town's history. The earlier one is Charles F. Swift, *History of Old Yarmouth, Comprising the Present Towns of Yarmouth and Dennis* . . ., edited by Charles A. Holbrook (Yarmouth Port, 1975). Swift originally published his book in 1884. The more recent history is Marion Vuilleumier, *The Town of Yarmouth, Massachusetts: A History, 1639-1989* (Yarmouth, 1989).

For the towns founded by the expansion of Cape Cod in the 1650s, Saconesett (Falmouth), Manomoit (Chatham), and Truro (Paomet), there is a good less material than for the four earlier communities. For Saconesett, there are the Falmouth Proprietors Records, 1661-1804. It concentrates on land holdings, but its early pages contain some relevant material for the early years of the towns. For two brief popular accounts of the early history of the town, see Alice A. Ryder, *Lands of Sippican on Buzzard's Bay* (New Bedford, 1934), and Thoedate Geoffrey [Dorothy Godfrey Wayman], *Suckaneset: Wherein May be Read a History of Falmouth, Massachusetts (1661-1930)* (Falmouth, 1930). There are no town records before 1693 for Manomoit, but the early chapters of William C. Smith, *History of Chatham, Massachusetts*, 3rd. ed. (Chatham, 1981) offer a detailed and well documented narrative of the first years of the town. Shebna Rich, *Truro--Cape Cod: Landmarks and Seamarks* (Boston, 1884) does for Paomet what Smith does for Chatham.

If the survey of colony and town records and the perusal of colony and town histories leave the reader anxious for more, there are bibliographies of the Pilgrims, Plymouth Colony, and Cape Cod which will more than satisfy the hunger. The sources for particular topics covered in this volume is one such bibliography, and the bibliographies of the books mentioned will provide others. The reader can also consult the bibliography in George F. Willison, *Saints and Strangers* (New York, 1945), as well as Laurence R. Pizer, *Pilgrim Historians*, volume 2, number 1, of *The Pilgrim Journal*, January, 1988, and George D. Langdon, Jr., "Bibliographic Essay," in *Occasional Papers in Old Colony Studies*, number 1, July 1969. Chapter 14 of Stratton's *Plymouth Colony*, entitled "Writers and Records" is also helpful. For such a relatively small group of fairly unimportant English colonists, the settlers of Plymouth Colony have generated an almost overwhelming amount of historical information. The interested reader will spend many pleasurable and profitable hours immersed in it.

INDEX

Abraham, John, denied
  residency, p. 138
Adultery, punishment of, p. 134
Adventurers (London), efforts to
  reimburse, p. 29; and
  financial reorganization,
  pp. 32-33
Alcohol, use and regulation of,
  pp. 127-130; excise tax on,
  pp. 129-130; importation
  of, p. 130
Alden, John, land agent to
  Sandwich, p. 70; buys land
  of Indians, p. 183;
  appointed to determine
  Barnstable--Sandwich
  boundary, p. 200;
  appointed to determine
  Barnstable--Indian
  boundaries, pp. 202-203
Alewives, see Fisheries (inland)
Allen, George, land of, p. 83, n.
  11; violates religious laws,
  p. 114
Allen, Ralph, (Quaker), p. 91;
  violates religious laws, pp.
  113, 114

Allen, Robert, opposes minister,
  p. 78
Allen, William (Quaker), pp. 90,
  96; fined, p. 94
Andros, Sir Edmund, arrival in
  Boston, p. 261
Annable, Anthony, land of, p.
  187
Anne (ship), arrival of, p. 30
Aptucxet (trading fort), pp. 33-
  35; see also p. 40, n. 43
Archer, Gabriel, cited, p. 16, n.
  5
Argall, Samuel, explores Cape
  Cod Bay, p. 7
Armstrong, Gregory, and
  founding of Yarmouth, p.
  49
Aspinet, (Indian), death of, p. 29
Assistants, as distributors of land,
  p. 67; office of and tenure
  in, p. 147; see also Court
  of Assistants
Atkins, Henry, elected constable,
  p. 163
Atkins, Samuel, killed in King
  Philip's War, p. 235
Austin, Anne (Quaker), pp. 89-90

Bachelor, Stephen, and founding
    of Yarmouth, p. 49
Bacon. Nathaniel, elected
    selectman, p. 164
Bangs, Edward, and founding of
    Eastham, pp. 53, 80
Bangs, Jonathan, elected Deputy
    to Massachusetts General
    Court, p. 272
Baptism, issue in Scituate, p. 47;
    see also p. 55, n. 15
Barker, John, injured in King
    Philip's War, p. 236
Barlow, George, as Under
    Marshall in Sandwich, pp.
    98-101
Barnes, Joshua, appointed to land
    committee, p. 74; ordered
    to appear at General Court,
    p. 76
Barnstable (town), founding of,
    pp. 46-48; land granted for,
    p. 48; religious controversy
    in, pp. 71-73; ministers in,
    pp. 72-73; problems hiring
    minister in, pp. 111-112;
    efforts to create established
    church in, p. 115; and tax
    for minister's salary in, pp.
    118-119; other support for
    ministers in, p. 119; votes
    to build meeting house, p.
    120; regulation of residency
    in, p. 138; freemanship in,
    pp. 150-152; Deputies
    elected from, p. 153;
    election of local officials in,
    p. 166; and colony taxes,
    pp. 166-167; land
    purchases of, pp. 182-183;

land grants to individuals
    in, p. 187; boundary
    controversy with Sandwich,
    pp. 200-201; boundary with
    Yarmouth, p. 202;
    boundaries with Indians,
    pp. 202-203; land titles
    recorded in, p. 203;
    opposition to colony
    ownership of whales in, pp.
    207-208; highway to
    Sandwich repaired in, pp.
    214-214; militia of, in King
    Philip's War, p. 235; taxes
    for King Philip's War paid,
    pp. 240-241; allocation of
    Mount Hope money by, p.
    241; votes to support
    voluntary levy, p. 270; *see
    also* individual ministers
Barnstable County, established,
    pp. 153-154; Court at, p.
    154; prison in, p. 154;
    associates of, pp. 154-155;
    assumes control over
    fisheries, p. 212
Barnstable Harbor, Indians
    entertain Pilgrims at, pp.
    24-25
Bassett, William, elected
    selectman, p. 164; soldier
    in King Philip's War, p.
    267
Bell, John, land of, p. 184
Besse, Anthony, indicted for
    living alone, pp. 137-138
Bestiality, p. 131
Billington, John, lost on Cape
    Cod, pp. 23-25
Blackwell, Michael, supervises
    alewife fishing, p. 213

Botfish, Robert, land of, p. 83, n. 11

Boundaries, need to establish, p. 199; Indian, pp. 202-203; *see also* individual towns.

Bourne, Ezra, fined for failure to serve in King Philip's War, p. 238

Bourne, Richard, elected Deputy, p. 45; land of, p. 83, n. 11, 229; purchases Saconesett, p. 184; supervises alewife fishing, p. 213; succeeds Leveridge as missionary, p. 228; missionary work at Mashpee of, pp. 229-232; reports on Mashpee Indians, pp. 231-232

Bourne, Shearjashub, succeeds to father's Mashpee lands, p. 232

Bradford, William, explores Cape Cod, p. 11; expeditions to Cape Cod, 1622, pp. 26-27; 1623, p. 28; 1627, p. 31; purchases land for Sandwich, pp. 45-46; and Quakers, p. 105, n. 14; ultimatum about religious diversity, p. 115; assumes fishing monopoly, p. 209

Bradford, William, [Jr.], injured in King Philip's War, p. 236; appointed to Massachusetts Governor's Council, p. 272

Bray, Thomas, punished for adultery, p. 134

Brereton, John, cited, p. 16, n. 5

Bridges, regulation of, p. 214; *see also* Eel River bridge

Burgess, Thomas, Jr., punished for adultery, p. 134; elected to political office, p. 165

Canacum (Indian), death of, p. 29

Cape Cod, explored by Pilgrims, pp. 9-13; early expeditions to, 1621, pp. 23-25; 1622, pp. 26-28; 1623, p. 28; 1630/31, p. 32; characteristics of its early settlers, p. 51; motivation for settlement of, p. 66; towns of, oppose established church, pp. 115-118; use and regulation of tobacco on, pp. 127-130; violations of sexual regulations on, pp. 131-136; Assistants elected from, p. 147; special court at, p. 153; and local taxes, p. 166; Indian settlements on and numbers of, pp. 232-234; opposition to King Philip's War from, p. 238; elects to assume responsibility for own defense, p. 238; towns of offer sanctuary to the displaced, pp. 238-239

Cape Cod Bay, arrival of *Mayflower*, p. 1; exploration by St. Brendan and the Irish, p. 2; by Vikings, p. 2; by Bartholomew Gosnold, pp. 2-3; by Martin Pring, pp. 3-4; by Samuel de Champlain, pp. 4-6; by

George Waymouth, pp. 7-
8; by Henry Hudson, p. 8;
by Samuel Argall, p. 7; by
Edward Harlow, p. 7; by
John Smith, p. 7; by
Thomas Dermer, p. 8
Carman, John, land of, p. 83, n.
11
Carsley, John, punished for
premarital sex, p. 134
Carsley, William, punished for
homosexuality, p. 131
Casco Bay, attacked, p. 267
Chadwell, Richard, land of, p.
83, n. 11
Champlain, Samuel de, explores
Cape Cod Bay and
Nantucket Sound, pp. 4-6
Charles II, intervenes in Quaker
disturbance, p. 101;
Plymouth recognizes, p.
256; death of, p. 260
Chase, William, opposes
Marmaduke Mathews, pp.
75-76; violates religious
laws, p. 114
Chatham, see Manomoit
Chatham Harbor, expedition to,
p. 24
Chipman, John, land of, p. 187
Christoferson, Wenlock
(Quaker), visits Plymouth,
pp. 93-94
Church, Benjamin, leads attack
on Mount Hope, p. 239; in
King William's War, p. 267
Clark, William, assumes fishing
monopoly, p. 212
Clergy, see Ministers
Cod, see Fisheries (ocean)

Collicut, Richard, and founding
of Barnstable, p. 46; see
also p. 54, n. 13
Commissioners of the United
Colonies, as agents of New
England Company, pp.
227-229; vote compensation
for Richard Bourne, p. 230
Constable, responsibilities of, pp.
162-163
Cook, Josiah, and founding of
Eastham, pp. 53, 80;
elected Deputy, p. 53
Cooke, Elisha, Massachusetts
agent to England, p. 269
Copeland, John (Quaker), visits
Plymouth, p. 92
Corn Hill, Pilgrims at, pp. 9, 11
Cotton, Rowland (minster),
assumes supervision of
Mashpee congregation, p.
232
Court of Assistants, functions of,
p. 153; and land
distribution, p. 179
Courts, participation in colonial,
p. 170; in local, p. 173; see
also Trial Juries
Crocker, Francis, marriage of, p.
135
Crocker, William elected
selectman, p. 164
Crosby, Thomas (minister), p.
111
Crowe, John, and founding of
Yarmouth, p. 50; appointed
to land committee, p. 74;
land of, p. 79
Cudworth, James, disfranchised
for aiding Quakers, p. 95;
appointed to determine

Barnstable--Sandwich
boundary, p. 200; officer in
King Philip's War, p. 234;
agent for Plymouth, p. 259
Culpepper, Thomas, agent for
Plymouth, p. 259
Cummaquid, *see* Barnstable
Harbor

Darby, John, land of, p. 79
Davis, Nicholas and wife,
punished for premarital sex,
pp. 133-134
Dennis, Robert, ordered to
appear at General Court, p.
76; land of, p. 79;
appointed to land
distribution committee, p.
79
Deputies, need for, pp. 44, 45;
election of, pp. 148, 152-
153; to Massachusetts
General Court, p. 272
Dermer, Thomas, explores Cape
Cod Bay, p. 8
Dexter, Thomas, land of, p. 83,
n. 11; and Barnstable--
Sandwich boundary, p.
201; appointed to determine
Sandwich--Plymouth
boundary, p. 202
Dillingham, Edward, land of, p.
83, n. 11
Dillingham, John, land of, p. 184
Dimmock, Thomas, and founding
of Barnstable, pp. 46-48;
elected Deputy, p. 48;
supports Lothrop, p. 83, n.
16; buys land of Indians, p.
182

Doane, John, and founding of
Eastham, pp. 53, 80;
elected selectman, p. 165;
land of, p. 184
Dominion of New England, pp.
261-265; failure of
Plymouth representatives to
attend council of, pp. 261-
262; tax policies and
opposition to, p. 262;
assertion of whale
ownership and opposition
to, p. 263; assumption of
judicial authority and
opposition to, p. 263;
imposition of quitrents and
opposition to, pp. 263-264;
land records to be kept in
Boston and opposition to,
p. 264; introduction of
religious freedom and
opposition to, p. 264;
restriction of local
government and opposition
to, p. 264-266
Dunham, Thomas, marriage of,
p. 135
Duxbury, opposes Ichabod
Wiswall as agent, p. 260
Dyer, Mary (Quaker), visits
Plymouth, p. 93

Eastham, founding of, pp. 51-
53; taxed by colony, p. 53;
Plymouth background of, p.
80; and tax for minister's
salary in, p. 118; other
support for ministers in, p.
119; votes to build meeting
house, p. 120; regulation of
residency in, p. 138;

freemanship in, pp. 150-
152; Deputies elected from,
p. 153; town meeting
participation in, p. 162; and
colony taxes, pp. 166-167;
shares in Satucket land, p.
183; land grants to
individuals in, p. 187;
assumes jurisdiction over
Manomoit, p. 189;
boundary with Yarmouth,
p. 202; land titles recorded
in, p. 203; regulations
about hunting of whales in,
pp. 206-207; whale oil
from, to colony, p. 206;
opposition to colony
ownership of whales in, pp.
207-208; militia of in King
Philip's War, p. 235; taxes
for King Philip's War paid,
pp. 240-241; allocation of
Mount Hope money, p.
242; opposition to taxes in,
pp. 168, 268; votes to
support voluntary levy, p.
270; representatives in
Massachusetts General
Court, p. 272; for Indians,
see Samuel Treat
Edge, Mr., land of, p. 83, n. 11;
see also Hedge
Education, supported by
fisheries, pp. 211-212
Eel River, controversy over
bridge, pp. 214-215;
settlement at destroyed in
King Philip's War, p. 237
Eliot, John (minister), visits
Yarmouth, p. 78

Elizabeth Islands, settlement at by
Bartholomew Gosnold, p. 3
Ellis, John, punished for
premarital sex, p. 134
Ellis, Mordecai, supervises
alewife fishing, p. 213
Ensign, Thomas, denied
freemanship, p. 148
Ewer, Henry, denied residency,
p. 138
Expansion, early motives for, pp.
43-44

Falmouth, see Saconesett
Feake, Henry, land of, p. 83, n.
11
Ferries, regulation of, p. 214
First Encounter (with Indians), p.
13
Fish, Ambrose, punished for
rape, p. 132
Fish, importance of, pp. 208-209;
see also Fisheries
Fisher, Mary (Quaker), pp. 89-90
Fisheries (inland), regulation of,
pp. 212-213
Fisheries (ocean), regulation of,
pp. 209-211; monopoly of,
pp. 209-210; and education,
pp. 211-212
Fitzrandall, Nathaniel, opposes
established church, p. 116
Fornication, pp. 132-133
Fortune (ship), arrival of, p. 25
Freeman, Edmund, and founding
of Sandwich, pp. 44-45;
purchases land for
Sandwich, pp. 45-46;
political career of, p. 55, n.
5; land of, p. 83, n. 11;
elected selectman, p. 164

Freeman, Edmund, Jr., aids
Quakers, p. 95
Freeman, John, elected
selectman, p. 165; reports
on Indians, pp. 233-234;
appointed auditor in King
Philip's War, p. 236
Freeman, Mary, marriage of, p.
135
Freemanship, qualifications for,
pp. 148-152; impact of
Quakerism on, p. 149;
admission to, pp. 148-152,
157, n. 12, 158, n. 19;
denial of, p. 157, n. 12;
local restrictions on, p. 149
Fuller, John, fined for failure to
serve in King Philip's War,
p. 238
Fuller, Matthew, opposes
established church, p. 115;
and Barnstable--Sandwich
boundary, pp. 200-201;
officer in King Philip's
War, p. 235
Fuller, Samuel, Sr., and
Barnstable--Sandwich
boundary, pp. 200-201;
officer in King Philip's
War, p. 237

Garrett, Richard, stranded on
Cape Cod, p. 32
Gaunt, Lydia, punished for
adultery, p. 134
Gaunt, Mary, marriage of, p. 135
Gaunt, Peter (Quaker), pp. 91,
96, 99; violates religious
laws, p. 114
General Court, grants land to
Barnstable, p. 48;

intervenes in Sandwich land
controversy, pp. 67-71;
orders apprehension of
Joseph Hull, p. 72;
intervenes in Barnstable
religious controversy, pp.
72-73; intervenes in
Yarmouth dispute, pp. 73-
80; restricts speculators, p.
74; appoints George Barlow
as Under Marshall, p. 98;
functions of, p. 153;
assumes control over land
distribution, pp. 179-181;
distributes land to groups,
pp. 181-186; to individuals,
pp. 186-187; awards
Nickerson's Manomoit
lands to others, p. 189-190;
intervenes in recording of
Sandwich land titles, p.
204; regulates whale
hunting, pp. 206-208;
asserts town ownership of
whales, p. 207; regulates
fisheries, pp. 209-211;
prepares for King Philip's
War, p. 235; petitions
Charles II, pp. 259, 260;
commissions Thomas
Culpepper agent, p. 259;
commissions James
Cudworth agent, p. 259;
commissions Ichabod
Wiswall agent, p. 260;
petitions James II, p. 261;
ends meetings, 1686, p.
262; opposes religious
freedom, p. 264;
recognizes William and
Mary, p. 266; requests

voluntary levy, p. 270; see
    also Assistants, Deputies
Glorious Revolution, in Boston,
    p. 265; in Plymouth, pp.
    265-266
Glover, John, divorce of, p. 134
Gorham, John, officer in King
    Philip's War, p. 235; killed,
    p. 236
Gosnold, Bartholomew, early
    life, p. 2; explores Cape
    Cod Bay and Nantucket
    Sound, pp. 2-3
Government, local, participation
    in, see individual towns
Governor, office and residency
    of, pp. 146-147; see also
    individual governors
Grand Jury, responsibilities and
    membership of, p. 168
Granger, Thomas, executed for
    bestiality, p. 131
Gray, John, indicted for
    swearing, p. 137; violates
    religious laws, p. 114
Great Swamp Fight, p. 236
Griffin, William, land of, p. 184

Hall, Gerhsom, elected Deputy,
    p. 192
Hall, Nathaniel, injured in King
    Philip's War, p. 236;
    receives veterans' benefits,
    p. 242
Hallett, Andrew, land of, pp. 73-
    74, 186
Halley, Joseph, Jr., fined for
    failure to serve in King
    Philip's War, p. 267
Halloway, Joseph, land of, p. 83,
    n. 11

Hammon, Mary, punished for
    lesbianism, p. 132
Harlow, Edward, explores Cape
    Cod Bay, p. 7
Harper, Robert, violates religious
    laws, p. 114
Hatch, Thomas, denied
    freemanship, p. 149
Hawes, Edmund, land of, p. 79;
    elected selectman, p. 164
Hedge, William, violates
    religious laws, p. 114
Herring Pond, missionary work
    at, pp. 232-233
Higgins, Richard, and founding
    of Eastham, pp. 53, 80;
    elected Deputy, p. 53
Highways, maintenance of, p.
    165; importance of, p. 213;
    repair of Plymouth--
    Barnstable, pp. 213-214
Hinckley, John and Bethia,
    marriage of, pp. 135-136
Hinckley, Thomas, as governor,
    p. 146; residency problem
    of, p. 147; buys land of
    Indians, p. 182; purchases
    Saconesett, p. 184; land of,
    p. 187; appointed to
    determine Sandwich--
    Plymouth boundary, p.
    202; appointed to determine
    Barnstable--Indian
    boundaries, pp. 202-203;
    on whale oil, p. 205;
    administers fisheries money
    for education, p. 211;
    reports on Indians, pp. 233-
    234; petitions Charles II, p.
    260; petitions Sir Edmund
    Andros, p. 262; opposes

religious freedom, p. 264; petitions William and Mary, p. 266; and incorporation of Plymouth into Massachusetts, p. 271; appointed to Massachusetts Governor's Council, p. 272

Hog Island, land distributed at, p. 185

Holder, Christopher (Quaker), visits Plymouth, p. 92

Homosexuality, pp. 131-132

Hopkins, Stephen, and founding of Yarmouth, p. 49

Howes, Jeremiah, elected Deputy to Massachusetts General Court, p. 272

Howes, Thomas, and founding of Yarmouth, p. 50; appointed to land committee, p. 74; ordered to appear at General Court, p. 76; land of, p. 79

Howland, John, land of, p. 187

Huchens, Thomas, elected constable, p. 163; officer in King Philip's War, p. 236

Hudson, Henry, explores Cape Cod Bay, p. 7

Hull, Joseph, and founding of Barnstable, pp. 46-48; elected Deputy, p. 48; minister in Barnstable and Yarmouth, pp. 72-73; *see also* p. 56, n. 19

Hunter, William, supervises alewife fishing, p. 213

Ianno (Indian), sells land to Barnstable, p. 183

Indian Missions, colonial ideas about, pp. 225-226; Indian opposition to, pp-. 226-227; at Mashpee, pp. 229-232; at Herring Pond, pp. 232-233; at Eastham, p. 233

Indian trade, controlled by Undertakers, p. 33

Indians, trade with Bartholomew Gosnold, p. 3; with Martin Pring, p. 4; attack Samuel de Champlain, p. 5; captured by Thomas Hunt, p. 7 grave site of, p. 12; entertain Pilgrims at Barnstable Harbor, pp. 24-26; land ownership of, p. 178; boundaries with Barnstable, p. 202; settlements of, on Cape Cod, p. 232; population of on Cape Cod, pp. 230-234; participate as allies in King Philip's War, p. 237; *see also* Indian Missions, King Philip's War, and individual tribes and individual Indians

Ireland, donation of, to Plymouth Colony after King Philip's War, p. 242

Iyanough (Indian), aids Pilgrims, pp. 24-25; death of, p. 29

Jackson, Samuel, excommunicated for lying, p. 137

James II, recognition of, p. 261

Jenkins, John (Quaker), p. 99

Jones, Mary, punished for adultery, p. 134

Jones, Teague, violates religious
  laws, p. 114
Judicial System, *see* Courts
Juet, Robert, cited, p. 18, n. 29
Juries, *see* Trial Juries and Grand
  Juries

King Philip's War, pp. 234-243;
  causes of, p. 234; casualties
  in, pp. 235, 236, 238, 239;
  militia call-ups, pp. 236,
  237, 238, 239; failure of
  call-up, p. 238; attack on
  Narragansetts, p. 236;
  Indians participate as allies,
  p. 237; cost and financing
  of, pp. 240-242; and tax
  collection problems, p. 167;
  veterans' benefits, pp. 242-
  243; widows' and orphans'
  benefits, p. 243
King William's War, and tax
  collection problems, p. 167;
  Plymouth support for, pp.
  266-267; attacks on Casco
  Bay and Quebec, p. 267
King's Missive (concerning
  Quakers), p. 101
Kirby, Richard (Quaker), p. 96;
  violates religious laws, p.
  113
Kirby, Sarah (Quaker), whipped,
  p. 96
Knott, Martha, marriage of, p.
  135
Knowles, John, killed in King
  Philip's War, p. 235;
  widow of, receives benefits,
  p. 243

Land, distribution of, pp. 66-67;
  English and Indian
  ownership compared, p.
  178; recording of titles, p.
  203
Landers, Jane (Quaker),
  whipped, p. 96
Launders, Thomas, and wife
  punished for premarital sex,
  p. 133
Leddra, William (Quaker), visits
  Plymouth, p. 93
Lesbianism, p. 132
Leveridge, William (minister),
  joins Edmund Freeman at
  Sandwich, p. 45; petitions
  General Court about land,
  pp. 67-69; submits land
  petition, p. 67; appointed to
  admit new settlers in
  Sandwich, p. 70; land of, p.
  83, n. 11; as minister, p.
  110; Indian missionary
  work of, pp. 227-228;
  Indian response to, p. 228;
  compensation for, p. 228
Linceford, Anne, punished for
  adultery, p. 134
Linnett, David, punished for
  fornication, p. 133
Little James (ship), arrival of, p.
  30; *see also* p. 38, n. 30
Living alone, regulation of, pp.
  137-138
Lothrop, Barnabas, land of, p.
  187; to aid Ichabod Wiswall
  as agent, p. 260
Lothrop, John (minister), and
  founding of Barnstable, pp.
  46-48; negotiates with
  Plymouth leaders, p. 48; as

minister, pp. 72-73; *see also* p. 55, n. 16

Lothrop, John, [Jr.], appointed to Massachusetts Governor's Council, p. 272

Lothrop, Joseph, elected selectman, p. 164; land of, p. 187; appointed auditor in King Philip's War, p. 236

Lumpkin, William, violates religious laws, p. 113

Lying and swearing, punishment of, pp. 136-137

Mackerel, *see* Fisheries (ocean)

Manomet, expedition to, p. 28; purchased by Sandwich, p. 183; alewife fishing at, p. 213

Manomoit, nonpayment of taxes by, p. 168; land problem at, pp. 187-191; assigned to Eastham, p. 191; becomes town, pp. 191-192; *see also* William Nickerson

Marchant, Abisha, punished for adultery, p. 134

Marriage, regulation of, pp. 134-135

Mashpee, Richard Bourne's land at, p. 229; his missionary work at, pp. 229-232; Indian town created at, pp. 230-231

Massachusetts (colony), and founding of Sandwich, p. 44; of Barnstable, p. 46; of Yarmouth, pp. 49-50; and Quakers, p. 90

Massachusetts (Indians), trading expedition to, p. 27; complain against Wessagusett, p. 27

Massasoit, (Indian), cured by Edward Winslow, p. 28

Mather, Increase, agent to England and proposal to incorporate Plymouth into Massachusetts, pp. 269-270

Mathews, Marmaduke (minister), problems of ministry in Yarmouth, pp. 73-77, 110

Mathews, Samuel, violates religious laws, p. 114

Mattachiest, expedition to, p. 28

Mayflower (ship), arrival at Cape Cod, p. 1; to Plymouth Harbor, pp. 13-14

Mayflower Compact, pp. 8-9

Mayhew, Matthew, reports on Indians, p. 233

Mayo, John (minister), teaching elder in Barnstable, p. 72; as minister in, p. 111

Mayo, John, [Jr.], violates fishing monopoly, p. 212

Mecoy, John, land of, p. 184

Merrick, William, admitted freeman, p. 149

Miller, John (minister), in Yarmouth, pp. 77-78, 110; land of, p. 79

Miller, John, [Jr.], elected selectman, p. 164

Ministers, problems hiring, pp. 110-112; *see also* individual towns and individual ministers

Missionaries, *see* Indian Missionaries

Mitchell, Edward, punished for homosexuality, p. 132

Monomy [Manomoit], opposition
    to taxes in, p. 268
Morton, Nathaniel, history of
    King Philip's War, p. 258
Mount Hope, attacked, pp. 235,
    239; confiscated and sold,
    pp. 240-241; Plymouth's
    attempt to acquire, p. 258;
    proceeds of its sale
    distributed, pp. 241-142

Nantucket Sound, Samuel de
    Champlain at, p. 6
Narragansetts (Indians), trading
    expedition to, p. 30;
    attacked in King Philip's
    War, p. 236
Nauset, Samuel de Champlain at,
    pp. 5, 6; expeditions to,
    1621, pp. 23-25; 1622, pp.
    26-27; as settlement site, p.
    52; land grants for, pp. 52-
    53; *see also* Eastham
Nausets (Indians), attack
    Pilgrims, p. 13; return John
    Billington, p. 24; trade with
    Pilgrims, p. 26
Nepoyetum (Indian), sells land to
    Barnstable, p. 182
Nessfield, Sarah, receives
    orphan's benefits, p. 243
New England, interim
    government for, pp. 260-
    261
New England Company, created,
    p. 227; *see also* Indian
    Missions
New Netherland, early contact
    with, pp. 34-35
Newland, Mrs. (Quaker), p. 96

Newland, William (Quaker), pp.
    96, 99; fined, pp. 94-95
Nickerson, William, ordered to
    appear at General Court, p.
    76; appointed to land
    distribution committee, p.
    79; land of, p. 79; admitted
    freeman, p. 149; land
    problem at Manomoit, pp.
    187-191; appeals to Royal
    Commissioners, p. 189;
    appeals to Governor
    Richard Nicolls, pp. 190-
    191
Nickerson, Nicholas, violates
    religious laws, pp. 113, 114
Norman, Sarah, punished for
    lesbianism, p. 132
Norton, Humphrey (Quaker),
    visits Plymouth, pp. 92-93

Oakes, Thomas, Massachusetts
    agent to England, p. 269
Old Comer, *see* Purchasers

Paddy, William, assumes fishing
    monopoly, p. 209
Paine, Thomas, elected
    constable, p. 163
Palmer, William, appointed to
    land committee, p. 74
Pamet River, Martin Pring's fort
    at, p. 4; discovered by
    Pilgrims, p. 11
Paomet, settlement of, p. 184;
    landowners of, p. 194, n.
    21
Patents, *see* individual patents
Paupmumuck (Indian), sells land
    to Barnstable, pp. 182-183

Payne, Thomas, elected Deputy, p. 50; land of, p. 79

Paysley, John, receives veterans' benefits, p. 242

Pearson, Peter (Quaker), visits Plymouth, p. 93

Peirce Patent, 1621, p. 25

Peirce, Michael, massacre of his forces, p. 237

Perry, Edward, marriage of, p. 135

Perry, William, receives veterans' benefits, p. 242

Phillips, Ephraim and Marcy, denied residency, p. 138

Pilgrims, decision to settle at Plymouth, pp. 1, 13-14; explore Cape Cod, pp. 9-13; political ideas of, pp. 145-146; *see also* Plymouth (colony)

Plymouth (colony), early conditions in, pp. 25, 26; aids *Sparrowhawk*, pp. 31-32; financial reorganization of, pp. 32-33; land distribution in, pp. 66-67; opposition to Quakers, pp. 89-94; punishes Quakers, pp. 93-97; special problems with female Quakers, p. 96; laws to protect religion in, pp. 113-114; efforts to create established church in, pp. 115-121; and tax for minister's salary, p. 118; regulation of tobacco and alcohol, pp. 127-128; political participation in, pp. 147-148; county government established in, pp. 153-154; taxation policies of, pp. 166-167; tax assessors and assessments for, p. 167; regulation of land distribution in, p. 179; and Restoration, pp. 255-257; petitions Charles II, p. 256; prepares for Royal Commissioners, pp. 256-257; fails to receive charter, pp. 256, 257, 259-259, 261, 269; requests Mount Hope, p. 260; opposes Dominion of New England, pp. 262-265; political deterioration of, pp. 267-269; incorporated into Massachusetts, p. 270; *see also* Dominion of New England, General Court

Plymouth (town), decision to settle at, pp. 13-14; entertains Wessagusett settlers pp. 25-26; entertains *Sparrowhawk* passengers pp. 31-32; and founding of Eastham, pp. 51-53; boundary with Sandwich, p. 202; highway to Sandwich repaired, pp. 213-214

Plymouth Harbor, entered by Samuel de Champlain, p. 5; by Pilgrims, p. 13

Popmonet (Indian), succeeds Richard Bourne as Mashpee minister, p. 232

Potter, Mr., land of, p. 83, n. 11

Powell, Jane, indicted for fornication, p. 133

Pratt, Joshua, land agent to
     Yarmouth, p. 73
Premarital sex, punishment of,
     pp. 133-134
Prence, Thomas, and founding of
     Eastham, pp. 53, 80; land
     agent to Sandwich, p. 69;
     as governor, p. 146;
     residency problem of, pp.
     146-147; land of, p. 184;
     appointed to determine
     Barnstable--Sandwich
     boundary, p. 201;
     appointed to determine
     Barnstable--Indian
     boundaries, pp. 202-203;
     and whales at Eastham, p.
     207; assumes fishing
     monopoly, p. 209;
     supervises repair of
     Barnstable--Plymouth
     highway, p. 213
Preston, Edward, punished for
     homosexuality, p. 132
Pring, Martin, explores Cape
     Cod Bay, pp. 3-4
Provincetown, as potential
     settlement, p. 12
Provincetown Harbor, anchorage
     of Pilgrims at, pp. 2, 9; of
     Martin Pring at, p. 4
Purchasers, p. 33; and founding
     of Eastham, p. 52; as
     distributors of land, p. 66;
     land reserved for, p. 181;
     clash with William
     Nickerson, p. 189

Quakers, arrival in New
     England, p. 89; beliefs of,
     p. 89; Plymouth attitudes
against, pp. 89, 91-92;
     itinerant, visit Plymouth,
     pp, 90-94; impact in
     Plymouth of, p. 94; as local
     issue, p. 97; fines imposed
     on, pp. 100-101; views on
     marriage of, pp. 135, 142,
     n. 36; *see also* individual
     Quakers
Quebec, attacked, p. 267

Randolph, Edward, on whale
     oil, p. 205; on Josiah
     Winslow, p. 258
Rape, p. 132
Rasieres, Isaack de, visits
     Plymouth, p. 34
Reap, William (Quaker), visits
     Plymouth, p. 93
Religion, laws to protect and their
     violations, pp. 113-114; *see
     also* Quakers
Representative government, *see*
     Deputies, General Court
Residents, admission of, pp. 70,
     75, 137-138
Restoration, in Plymouth Colony,
     pp. 255-257
Reyner, John (minister), p. 110
Rider, Samuel, jury member, p.
     170
Roads, *see* Highways
Robinson, Isaac, disfranchised
     for aiding Quakers, p. 95;
     buys land of Indians, p. 182
Rogers, Joseph, elected
     selectman, p. 165; land of,
     p. 184
Rosier, James, cited, p. 18, n. 28
Rouse, John (Quaker), visits
     Plymouth, p. 92

Royal Commissioners, intervene in Nickerson dispute, p. 189; visit Plymouth, pp. 256-257

Russell, Jonathan (minister), p. 112

Saconesett, purchase and settlement of, pp. 184-185; assigned to Barnstable, p. 184; recognized as town, p. 185; votes support for minister in, p. 185; boundary with Sandwich, p. 202

St. Brendan, explores Cape Cod Bay, p. 2

Sandwich, founding of, pp. 44-46; recognized as town, p. 45; land purchased for, pp. 45-46; ministers in, pp. 67-70; land controversy in, pp. 67-71; redistribution of land in, p. 69; land distribution committee of, pp. 70-71; itinerant Quakers in, pp. 89-94; early Quakerism, p. 91; Quakerism as town issue, p. 97; accepts Quakers, pp. 101-102; and tax for minister's salary in, p. 118; other support for ministers in, p. 119; votes to build meeting house, p. 120; town meeting participation in, p. 162; election of local officials in, pp. 165-166; and colony taxes, pp. 166-167; land purchase of, p. 183; land grants to individuals in, pp.

186, 195, n. 3; boundary controversy with Barnstable, pp. 200-201; boundaries with Plymouth, Saconesett, and Yarmouth, p. 202; difficulties of recording land titles in, pp. 203-204; regulations about hunting of whales in, pp. 206-207; whale oil from, to colony, p. 208; opposition to colony ownership of whales in, pp. 207-208; alewife fisheries in, pp. 212-213; highway to Plymouth and Barnstable repaired, pp. 213-214; Eel River bridge controversy, pp. 214-215; fined for failure to provide troops in King Philip's War, p. 238; taxes for King Philip's War paid, pp. 240-241; allocation of Mount Hope money, pp. 241-242; opposition to taxes in, pp. 167, 268; for Indians, *see* Richard Bourne, Thomas Tupper, Mashpee, and Herring Pond

Sassamon, John, murder of, p. 234; trial of his alleged murderers, p. 235

Satucket, divided between Yarmouth and Eastham, p. 183; settlement of, p. 184

Saugus, Massachusetts, residents of found Sandwich, pp. 44-45

Scituate, residents of found Barnstable, pp. 46-48; and

baptism issue in, p. 47;
land problems in p. 47
Sea Bass, *see* Fisheries (ocean)
Select Court, responsibilities of,
p. 163
Selectmen, qualifications for and
responsibilities of, p. 164;
election of, pp. 164-165
Serunk (Indian), sells land to
Barnstable, p. 182
Sexual practices, regulation of,
pp. 131-136
Shelley, Goody, excommunicated
for lying, p. 137
Shelley, Hannah, punished for
fornication, p. 133
Shephard, Thomas (minister),
visits Yarmouth, p. 78
Ships, *see* individual vessels
Shipwrecks, *see Sparrowhawk*;
Richard Garrett
Simpkins, Nicholas, appointed to
land committee, p. 74
Sippican, land granted at, to
Scituate, p. 47
Skiffe, James, elected to political
office, p. 165
Skiffe, Steven, associate of
County court, p. 155; jury
member, p. 170;
Smalley, John, and founding of
Eastham, pp. 53, 80
Smith, John (minister), p. 110
Smith, John, explores Cape Cod
Bay, pp. 7, 8
Smith, John, fined for failure to
serve in King Philip's War,
p. 238
Smith, Ralph (minister), p. 110
Smith, Ralph, fined for lying, p.
137

Smith, Samuel, violates fishing
monopoly, p. 212
Snow, Elizabeth, violates
religious laws, p. 114
Snow, Jabez, punished for
premarital sex, p. 134
Snow, Mark, elected selectman,
p. 165
Snow, Nicholas, and founding of
Eastham, pp. 53, 80
Society of Friends, *see* Quakers
Southworth, Constant, appointed
to determine Barnstable--
Sandwich boundary, p.
201; appointed to determine
Sandwich--Plymouth
boundary, p. 202;
appointed to determine
Barnstable--Indian
boundaries, pp. 202-203
Sparrow, Jonathan, associate of
County Court, p. 155;
elected selectman, p. 165;
land of, p. 187; officer in
King Philip's War, p. 235;
elected Deputy to
Massachusetts General
Court, p. 272
Sparrowhawk (ship), wrecked on
Cape Cod, p. 30; aided by
Plymouth, p. 31;
passengers of, to Plymouth,
pp. 31-32; *see also* p. 39,
n. 35
Squanto (Indian), captured by
Thomas Hunt, pp. 7-8;
remains in New England,
p. 8; to Cape Cod with
Pilgrims, pp. 24-26; death
of, p. 24

Stage Harbor (Chatham), Samuel de Champlain at, p. 6

Standish, Myles, explores Cape Cod, pp. 9-11; expedition to Nauset, p. 28; at Wessagusett, p. 28; land agent to Sandwich, p. 69; to Yarmouth, pp. 76, 78-79; buys land of Indians, p. 182; land of, p. 186; appointed to determine Barnstable--Sandwich boundary, p. 200; assumes fishing monopoly, p. 209; supervises repair of Barnstable--Plymouth highway, p. 213

Starr, Thomas, ordered to appear at General Court, p. 76; appointed to land distribution committee, p. 79

Studson, Robert, appointed to determine Barnstable--Sandwich boundary, p. 200

Sturgess, violates religious laws, p. 114

Surveyor of Highways, responsibilities of, p. 163

Sutton, William, violates religious laws, p. 113

Swan (ship), arrival and fishing expedition of, p. 26

Swansea, attacked, p. 235

Swift, William, elected selectman, p. 164

Tabor, Philip, elected Deputy, p. 50; appointed to land committee, p. 74

Taunton, Indian treaty at, p. 234

Tax revolt, 1690, p. 268

Taxation, assessors and assessment of, p. 167; opposition to, pp. 167-168; *see* Plymouth (colony) and individual towns

Thacher, Anthony, and founding of Yarmouth, p. 50; appointed to land committee, p. 74; land of, p. 79

Thacher, John, elected Deputy to Massachusetts General Court, p. 272

Thacher, Peter (minister), pp. 111-112

Thompson, John, land of, p. 187

Thornton, Thomas (minister), pp. 110-111, 114

Tilley, Hugh, and founding of Yarmouth, p. 50; ordered to appear at General Court, p. 76

Tobacco, use and regulation of, pp. 127, 130-131

Town meetings, participation in, pp. 161-162

Townsmen, *see* Residents

Treat, Samuel (minister), p. 111; missionary work at Eastham of, p. 233; reports on Indians, p. 233

Treaty, Indian, at Taunton, p. 234

Trial Juries, responsibilities and membership of, pp. 169-170

Tupper, Thomas, elected selectman, p. 164; missionary work at Herring Pond of, pp. 232-233

Tupper, Thomas, Jr., missionary
work at Herring Pond of,
pp. 232-233
Turner, Ruhamah, punished for
fornication, p. 134

Under Marshal, *see* George
Barlow
Undertakers, assume financial
responsibility for Plymouth
debts, p. 33
Upsall, Nicholas (Quaker), at
Sandwich, pp. 90-91

Vassall, William, and baptism,
p. 47
Vikings, explore Cape Cod Bay,
p. 2
Vincent, John, elected Deputy, p.
45; land agent to
Yarmouth, p. 73; land of,
p. 83, n. 11
Voting, *see* Freemanship

Walley, John, appointed to
Massachusetts Governor's
Council, p. 272
Walley, Thomas (minister), p.
110
Wampum, importance of, p. 34
Warwick Patent, 1629/30, p. 44;
distribution of land under,
pp. 66, 181
Waymouth, George, explores
Cape Cod Bay, pp. 6-7
Wellfleet Harbor, Samuel de
Champlain at, p. 5;
Pilgrims at, pp. 12-13
Wessagusett, settlers of, at
Plymouth, pp. 25-26;
fishing expedition of, to

Cape Cod, p. 26; Indian
complaints against, p. 27;
Pilgrim assault on, p. 28;
see also p. 37, n. 26
Whales, importance of, pp. 204-
205; hunting of, pp. 204-
208; ownership of, pp. 204-
208; regulations about
hunting of, pp. 206-208
Wheldon, Gabriel, and founding
of Yarmouth, p. 49
White, Emanual, opposes
minister, p. 78; elected
constable, p. 163
Wilson, John (minister), visits
Yarmouth, p. 78
Wing, Anias, land of, p, 184
Wing, Daniel, supervises alewife
fishing, p. 213
Wing, John, land of, pp. 184,
187
Wing, Joseph, land of, p. 184
Wing, Stephen (Quaker), fined,
p. 95
Winslow, Edward, cures
Massasoit, p. 28; advocates
Indians missions, p. 227
Winslow, Josiah, buys land of
Indians, p. 183; appointed
to determine Barnstable--
Sandwich boundary, p.
200; appointed to determine
Barnstable--Indian
boundaries, p. 202;
petitions Charles II, p. 258
Winslow, Kenelm, Jr., violates
religious laws, p. 114; land
of, p. 184
Winsor, Joseph, indicted for
living alone, pp. 137-138

Winthrop, Wait-Still, on whale oil, p. 205

Wiswall, Ichabod, agent for Plymouth, p. 260; representative to England, pp. 269-270

Woods Hole, land distributed at, p. 185

Worden, Peter, violates religious laws, p. 113; land of, p. 184

Yarmouth, founding of, pp. 48-50; ministers in, pp. 73-77; land and religious controversy in, pp. 73-80; land distribution committee of, pp. 74, 78; special Court of Assistants at, p. 76; Massachusetts ministers visit, p. 78; established church in, pp. 115-117; and tax for minister's salary in, p. 118; other support for ministers in, p. 119; votes to build meeting house, p. 120; regulation of residency in, p. 138; freemanship in, pp. 150-152; Deputies elected from, p. 153; town meeting participation in, p. 162; nonpayment of taxes by, p. 168; shares in Satucket land, p. 183; land grants to individuals in, p. 187; boundaries with Eastham, Barnstable, and Satucket, p. 202; land titles recorded in, p. 203; regulations about hunting of whales in, pp. 206-207;

opposition to colony ownership of whales in, pp. 207-208; and Eel River bridge controversy, pp. 214-215; militia in King Philip's War, p. 235; participation in King Philip's War, p. 239; taxes for King Philip's War paid, pp. 240-241; votes to support voluntary levy, p. 270; elects Deputes to Massachusetts General Court, p. 272